Secrets and Lies DIGITAL SECURITY IN A NETWORKED WORLD

Robert Harris

ISBN-13:
978-
1976133367

Contents

Contents

1

Introduction

During March 2000, I kept a log of security events from various sources. Here are the news highlights:

Someone broke into the business-to-business Web site for SalesGate.com and stole about 3,000 customer records, including credit card numbers and other personal information. He posted some of them on the Internet.

For years, personal information has "leaked" from Web sites (such as Intuit) to advertisers (such as DoubleClick). When visitors used various financial calculators on the Intuit site, a design glitch in the Web site's programming allowed information they entered to be sent to DoubleClick. This happened without the users' knowledge or consent, and (more surprising) without Intuit's knowledge or consent.

Convicted criminal hacker Kevin Mitnick testified before Congress. He told them that social engineering is a major security vulnerability: He can often get passwords and other secrets just by pretending to be someone else and asking.

A Gallup poll showed that a third of online consumers said that they might be less likely to make a purchase from a Web site, in light of recent computer-security events.

Personal data from customers who ordered the PlayStation 2 from the Sony Web site were accidentally leaked to some other customers. (This is actually a rampant problem on all sorts of sites. People try to check out, only to be presented with the information of another ran-dom Web customer.)

Amazon.com pays commissions to third-party Web sites for referrals. Someone found a way to subvert the program that manages this, enabling anyone to channel information to whomever. It is unclear whether Amazon considers this a problem.

The CIA director denied that the United States engages in economic espionage, but did not go on to deny the existence of the massive intelligence-gathering system called ECHELON.

Pierre-Guy Lavoie, 22, was convicted in Quebec of breaking into several Canadian and U.S. government computers. He will serve 12 months in prison.

Japan's Defense Agency delayed deployment of a new defense computer system after it discovered that the software had been developed by the members of the Aum Shinrikyo cult.

A new e-mail worm, called Pretty Park, spread across the Internet. It's a minor modification of one that appeared last year. It spreads automati-cally, by sending itself to all the addresses listed in a user's Outlook Express program.

Novell and Microsoft continued to exchange barbs about an alleged secu-rity bug with Windows 2000's Active Directory. Whether or not this is a real problem depends on what kind of security properties you expect from your directory. (I believe it's a design flaw in Windows, and not a bug.)

Two people in Sicily (Giuseppe Russo and his wife, Sandra Elazar) were arrested after stealing about 1,000 U.S. credit card numbers on the Internet and using them to purchase luxury goods and lottery tickets.

A hacker (actually a bored teenager) known as "Coolio" denied launching massive denial-of-service attacks in February 2000. He admitted to hacking into about 100 sites in the past, including cryptography company RSA Security and a site belonging to the U.S. State Department.

Attackers launched a denial-of-service attack against Microsoft's Israeli Web site.

Jonathan Bosanac, a.k.a. "The Gatsby," was sentenced to 18 months in prison for hacking into three telephone company sites.

The military of Taiwan announced that it discovered more than 7,000 attempts by Chinese hackers to enter the country's security systems. This tantalizing statistic was not elaborated on.

Here are some software vulnerabilities reported during March 2000:

A vulnerability was reported in Microsoft Internet Explorer 5.0 (in Windows 95, 98, NT 4.0, and 2000) that allows an attacker to set up a Web page giving him the ability to execute any program on a visitor's machine.

By modifying the URL, an attacker can completely bypass the authentica-tion mechanisms protecting the remote-management screens of the Axis StarPoint CD-ROM servers.

If an attacker sends the Netscape Enterprise Server 3.6 a certain type of long message, a buffer overflow crashes a particular process. The attacker can then execute arbitrary code remotely on the server.

It is possible to launch some attacks (one denial-of-service attack, and another attack against a CGI script) that Internet Security Systems's RealSecure Network Intrusion Detection software does not detect.

By sending a certain URL to a server running Allaire's ColdFusion prod-uct, an attacker can receive an error message giving information about the physical paths to various files.

Omniback is a Hewlett-Packard product that performs system backup rou-tines. An attacker can manipulate the product to cause a denial-of-ser-vice attack.

There is a vulnerability in the configuration of Dosemu, the DOS emula-tor shipped with Corel Linux 1.0, that allows users to execute commands with root privileges.

By manipulating the contents of certain variables, an attacker can exploit a vulnerability in DNSTools 1.0.8 to execute arbitrary code.

SGI has a package called InfoSearch that automatically converts text docu-mentation to HTML Web content. A bug in the CGI script allows attackers to execute commands on the server at the Web server privi-lege level.

Several vulnerabilities were discovered in the e-mail client The Bat!, allowing an attacker to steal files from users' computers.

Microsoft's Clip Art Gallery lets users download clip art files from the Web. Under certain conditions, a malformed clip art file can let arbi-trary code execute on the user's computer.

If you send a long login name and password (even an incorrect one) to BisonWare's FTP Server 3.5, it will crash.

An intruder can crash Windows 95 and 98 computers using specially coded URLs.

Here is a list of the 65 Web sites known to be defaced during the month, as listed at the attrition.org Web site. In this context, "defaced" means that someone broke into the Web site and modified the home page:

Tee Plus; Suede Records; Masan City Hall; The Gallup Organization; Wired Connection; Vanier College; Name Our Child; Mashal Books; Laboratório de Matemática Aplicada da Universidade Federal do Rio de Janeiro; Elite Calendar; Centro de Processamento de Dados do Rio de Janeiro; Parliament of India; United Network for Organ Sharing; UK Jobs; Tennessee State University; St. Louis Metropolitan Sewer District; College of the Siskiyous; Russian Scientific Center for Legal Informa-tion, Ministry of Justice; RomTec Plc; Race Lesotho; Monmouth Col-lege; University of St. Thomas Library; Int Idea Sweden; Goddard College; Association of EDI Users; Bitstop, Inc; Custom Systems; Clas-sic Amiga; 98 Skate; CU Naked; Korea National University of Educa-tion; PlayStation 2; Association for Windows NT System Professionals; K.Net Telecomunicações Ltda.; CyberCT Malaysia; Birmingham Windows NT User Group; Bloem S.A.; Aware, Inc.; Ahmedabad Telephone Online Directory, Ahmedabad Telecom District; Fly Pak-istan; Quality Business Solutions; Out; Internet Exposure; Belgium Province de Hainaut; Glen Cove School District; Germantown Acad-emy; Federatie van Wervings en Selectiebureaus; Engineering Export Promotion Council, Ministry of Commerce, India; AntiOnline's Anti-Code; Pigman; Lasani; What Online; Weston High School; Vasco Boutique; True Systems; Siemens Italy; Progress Korea; Phase Devices Ltd.; National Treasury Employees Union; National Postal Mail Handlers Union; Metricks; Massachusetts Higher Education Network; The London Institute; Fort Campbell School System; and MaxiDATA Tecnologia e Informatica Ltda.

And finally, attacks against a home computer, attached to the Internet via a cable modem, belonging to a random friend of mine:

- Twenty-six scans, looking for vulnerabilities to exploit.
- Four particularly determined attempts at breaking into the computer, includ-ing basic vulnerability scans and piles of other crafty hacker tricks.

Actually, the lists only run through March 7, 2000. I got tired of keeping records after that.

Looking over this list, what strikes me is the wide array of problems, vulnerabilities, and attacks. Some of these vulnerabilities are in supposedly secure software products; one is even in a security product. Some of them are in e-commerce systems that were probably designed with security in mind. Some of them are in new products, others are in products that have been sold for years. Sometimes the vendor doesn't even agree that there is a problem.

The first seven days of March 2000 were not exceptional. Other weeks would have similar logs; some would have much worse. In fact, data portend that things are getting worse: The number of security vul-nerabilities, breaches, and disasters is increasing over time. Even as we learn more about security—how to design cryptographic algorithms, how to build secure operating systems—we build things with less security. Why this is so, and what can be done about it, is the subject of this book.

SYSTEMS

The notion of a "system" is relatively new to science. Eastern philoso-phers have long seen the world as a single system with various compo-nents, but Westerners have segmented the world into separate things that interact in different ways.

Machines have only recently become systems. A pulley is a machine; an elevator is a complex system with many different machines. Systems interact: An elevator interacts with the building's electrical system, its fire-control system, and probably even its environmental control system. Computers interact to form networks, and networks interact to form even larger networks, and . . . you get the idea.

Admiral Grace Hopper said: "Life was simple before World War II. After that, we had systems." This is an insightful comment.

Once you start conceptualizing systems, it's possible to design and build on a more complex scale. It's the difference between a building and a skyscraper, a cannon and a Patriot missile, a landing strip and an airport. Anyone can build a traffic light, but it takes a different mindset to conceive of a citywide traffic control system.

The Internet is probably the most complex system ever developed. It contains millions of computers, connected in an inconceivably complex physical network. Each computer has hundreds of software programs run-ning on it; some of these programs interact with other programs on the computer, some of them interact with other programs on other comput-ers across the network. The system accepts user input from millions of people, sometimes all at the same time.

As the man said: "Sir, it is like a dog standing upon his hind legs, you are not surprised to see it not done well, you are surprised to see it done at all."

Systems have several interesting properties relevant to this book.

First, they are complex. Machines are simple: a hammer, a door hinge, a steak knife. Systems are much more complicated; they have com-ponents, feedback loops, mean times between failure, infrastructure. Digital systems are daedal; even a simple computer program has hundreds of thousands of lines of computer code doing all sorts of different things. A complex computer program has thousands of components, each of which has to work by itself and in interaction with all the other components. This is why object-oriented programming was developed: to deal with the complexity of digital systems.

Second, systems interact with each other, forming even larger sys-tems. This can happen on purpose—programmers use objects to deliber-ately break large systems down into smaller systems, engineers break large mechanical systems into smaller subsystems, and so on—and it can happen naturally. The invention of the automobile led to the development of the modern system of roads and highways, and this in turn interacted with other systems in our daily lives to produce the suburb. The air-traffic control system interacts with the navigation systems on aircrafts, and the weather prediction system. The human body interacts with other human bodies and with the other systems on the planet. The Internet has intertwined itself with almost every major system in our society.

Third, systems have emergent properties. In other words, they do things that are not anticipated by the users or designers. The telephone system, for example, changed the way people interact. (Alexander Graham Bell had no idea that a telephone was a personal communications device; he thought you could use it to call ahead to warn that a telegram was coming.) Automobiles changed the way people meet, date, and fall in love. Environmental-control systems in buildings have effects on people's health, which affects the health care system. Word processing systems have changed the way people write. The Internet is full of emergent properties; think about eBay, virtual sex, collaborative authoring.

And fourth, systems have bugs. A bug is a particular kind of failure. It's an emergent property of a system, one that is not desirable. It's differ-ent from a malfunction. When something malfunctions, it no longer works properly. When something has a bug, it misbehaves in a particular way, possibly unrepeatable, and possibly unexplainable. Bugs are unique to systems. Machines can break, or fail, or not work, but only a system can have a bug.

SYSTEMS AND SECURITY

These properties all have profound effects on the security of systems. Finessing the precise definition of **secure** for now, the reason that it is so hard to secure a complex system like the Internet is, basically, because it's a complex system. Systems are hard to secure, and complex systems are that much more operose.

For computerized systems, the usual coping mechanism is to ignore the system and concentrate on the individual machines . . . the technolo-gies. This is why we have lots of work on security technologies like cryp-tography, firewalls, public-key infrastructures, and tamper-resistance. These technologies are much easier to understand and to discuss, and much easier to secure. The conceit is that these technologies can mysti-cally imbue the systems with the property of `<reverence type = "hushed"> Security </reverence>`.

This doesn't work, and the results can be seen in my security log from seven days of March 2000. Most of the security events can be traced to one or more of the four system properties previously listed.

Complex. The security problem with Windows 2000's Active Directory can be directly traced to the complexity of any computer-based directory system. This is why I believe it is a design flaw; Microsoft made a design decision that facilitated usability, but hurt security.

Interactive. An interaction between the software on Intuit's Web site and the software that DoubleClick uses to display ads to Web users resulted in information leaking from one to the other.

Emergent. According to the news story, Sony programmers had no idea why credit card information leaked from one user to another. It just hap-pened.

Bug Ridden. The vulnerability in Netscape Enterprise Server 3.6 was caused by a programming bug. An attacker could exploit the bug to cause a security problem.

Many pages of this book (Part 3 in particular) are devoted to explaining in detail why security has to be thought of as a system within larger systems, but I'd like you to keep two things in mind from the beginning.

The first is the relationship between security theory and security practice. There has been a lot of work on security theory: the theory of cryptography, the theory of firewalls and intrusion detection, the theory of biometrics. Lots of systems are fielded with great theory, but fail in practice.

Yogi Berra once said, "In theory there is no difference between the-ory and practice. In practice there is."

Theory works best in ideal conditions and laboratory settings. A common joke from my college physics class was to "assume a spherical cow of uniform density." We could only make calculations on idealized systems; the real world was much too complicated for the theory. Digital system security is the same way: We can design idealized operating systems that are provably secure, but we can't actually build them to work securely in the real world. The real world involves design trade-offs, unseen variables, and imperfect implementations.

Real-world systems don't lend themselves to theoretical solutions; thinking they do is old-school reductionist. It only works if the spherical cow has the same emergent properties as the real Holstein. It often doesn't, and that's why scientists are not engineers.

The second thing to keep in mind is the relationship between prevention, detection, and reaction. Good security encompasses all three: a vault to protect the lucre, alarms to detect the burglars trying to open the vault, and police that respond to the alarms and arrest the burglars. Digital security tends to rely wholly on prevention: cryptography, firewalls, and so forth. There's generally no detection, and there's almost never any response or auditing. A prevention-only strategy only works if the prevention mechanisms are perfect; otherwise, someone will figure out how to get around them. Most of the attacks and vulnerabilities listed in this chapter were the result of bypassing the prevention mechanisms. Given this reality, detection and response are essential.

PART 1

THE LANDSCAPE

Computer security is often advertised in the abstract: "This system is secure." A product vendor might say: "This product makes your network secure." Or: "We secure e-commerce." Inevitably, these claims are naïve and simplistic. They look at the security of the product, rather than the security of the system. The first questions to ask are: "Secure from whom?" and "Secure against what?"

They're real questions. Imagine a vendor selling a secure operating system. Is it secure against a hand grenade dropped on top of the CPU? Against someone who positions a video camera directly behind the keyboard and screen? Against someone who infiltrates the company? Probably not; not because the operating system is faulty, but because someone made conscious or unconscious design decisions about what kinds of attacks the operating system was going to prevent (and could pos-sibly prevent) and what kinds of attacks it was going to ignore.

Problems arise when these decisions are made without consideration. And it's not always as palpable as the preceding example. Is a secure telephone secure against a casual listener, a well-funded eavesdropper, or a national intelligence agency? Is a secure banking system secure against consumer fraud, merchant fraud, teller fraud, or bank manager fraud? Does that other product, when used, increase or decrease the security of whatever needs to be secured? Exactly what a particular security technol-ogy does, and exactly what it does not do, is just too abstruse for many people.

Security is never black and white, and context matters more than technology. Just because a secure operating system won't protect against hand grenades doesn't mean that it is useless; it just means that we can't throw away our walls and door locks and window bars. Different security technologies have important places in an overall security solution. A system might be secure against the average criminal, or a certain type of industrial spy, or a national intelligence agency with a certain skill set. A system might be secure as long as certain mathematical advances don't occur, or for a certain period of time, or against certain types of attacks. Like any adjective, "secure" is meaningless out of context.

In this section, I attempt to provide the basis for this context. I talk about the threats against digital systems, types of attacks, and types of attackers. Then I talk about security desiderata. I do this before discussing technology because you can't intelligently examine security technologies without an awareness of the landscape. Just as you can't understand how a castle defended a region without immersing yourself in the medieval world in which it operated, you can't understand a firewall or an encrypted Internet connection outside the context of the world in which it operates. Who are the attackers? What do they want? What tools are at their disposal? Without a basic understanding of these things, you can't reasonably discuss how secure anything is.

2

Digital Threats

The world is a dangerous place. Muggers are poised to jump you if you walk down the wrong darkened alley, con artists are scheming to relieve you of your retirement fund, and co-work-ers are out to ruin your career. Organized crime syndicates are spreading corruption, drugs, and fear with the efficiency of Fortune 500 companies. There are crazed terrorists, nutty dictators, and uncontrollable remnants of former superpowers with more firepower than sense. And if you believe the newspapers at your supermarket's checkout counter, there are monsters in the wilderness, creepy hands from beyond the grave, and evil space aliens carrying Elvis's babies. Sometimes it's amazing that we've survived this long, let alone built a society stable enough to have these discussions.

The world is also a safe place. While the dangers in the industrialized world are real, they are the exceptions. This can sometimes be hard to remember in our sensationalist age—newspapers sell better with the headline "Three Shot Dead in Random Act of Violence" than "Two Hundred and Seventy Million Americans have Uneventful Day"—but it is true. Almost everyone walks the streets every day without getting mugged. Almost no one dies by random gunfire, gets swindled by flim-flam men, or returns home to crazed marauders. Most businesses are not the victims of armed robbery, rogue bank managers, or workplace violence. Less than one percent of eBay transactions—unmediated long-distance deals between strangers—result in any sort of complaint. People are, on the whole, honest; they generally adhere to an implicit social contract. The general lawfulness in our society is high; that's why it works so well.

(I realize that the previous paragraph is a gross oversimplification of a complex world. I am writing this book in the United States at the turn of the millennium. I am not writing it in Sarajevo, Hebron, or Rangoon. I have no experiences that can speak to what it is like to live in such a place. My personal expectations of safety come from living in a stable democracy. This book is about the security from the point of view of the industrialized world, not the world torn apart by war, suppressed by secret police, or controlled by criminal syndicates. This book is about the relatively minor threats in a society where the major threats have been dealt with.)

Attacks, whether criminal or not, are exceptions. They're events that take people by surprise, that are "news" in its real definition. They're disruptions in the society's social contract, and they disrupt the lives of the victims.

THE UNCHANGING NATURE OF ATTACKS

If you strip away the technological buzzwords and graphical user interfaces, cyberspace isn't all that different from its flesh-and-blood, bricks-and-mortar, atoms-not-bits, real-world counterpart. Like the physical world, people populate it. These people interact with others, form complex social and business relationships, live and die. Cyberspace has communities, large and small. Cyberspace is filled with commerce. There are agreements and contracts, disagreements and torts.

And the threats in the digital world mirror the threats in the physical world. If embezzlement is a threat, then digital embezzlement is also a threat. If physical banks are robbed, then digital banks will be robbed. Invasion of privacy is the same problem whether the invasion takes the form of a photographer with a telephoto lens or a hacker who can eavesdrop on private chat sessions. Cyberspace crime includes everything you'd expect from the physical world: theft, racketeering, vandalism, voyeurism, exploitation, extortion, con games, fraud. There is even the threat of physical harm: cyberstalking, attacks against the air traffic control system, etc. To a first approximation, online society is the same as offline society. And to the same first approximation, attacks against digital systems will be the same as attacks against their analog ana-logues.

This means we can look in the past to see what the future will hold. The attacks will look different—the burglar will manipulate digital connections and database entries instead of lockpicks and crowbars, the terrorist will target information systems instead of airplanes—but the motivation and psychology will be the same. It also means we don't need a completely different legal system to deal with the future. If the future is like the past—except with cooler special effects—then a legal system that worked in the past is likely to work in the future.

Willie Sutton robbed banks because that was where the money was. Today, the money isn't in banks; it's zipping around computer networks. Every day, the world's banks transfer billions of dollars among themselves by simply modifying numbers in computerized databases. Meanwhile, the average physical bank robbery grosses a little over fifteen hundred dollars. And cyberspace will get even more enticing; the dollar value of electronic commerce gets larger every year.

Where there's money, there are criminals. Walking into a bank or a liquor store wearing a ski mask and brandishing a .45 isn't completely passé, but it's not the preferred method of criminals drug-free enough to sit down and think about the problem. Organized crime prefers to attack large-scale systems to make a large-scale profit. Fraud against credit cards and check systems has gotten more sophisticated over the years, as defenses have gotten more sophisticated. Automatic teller machine (ATM) fraud has followed the same pattern. If we haven't seen widespread fraud against Internet payment systems yet, it's because there isn't a lot of money to be made there yet. When there is, criminals will be there trying. And if history is any guide, they will succeed.

Privacy violations are nothing new, either. An amazing array of legal paperwork is public record: real estate transactions, boat sales, civil and criminal trials and judgments, bankruptcies. Want to know who owns that boat and how much he paid for it? It's a matter of public record. Even more personal information is held in the 20,000 or so (in the United States) personal databases held by corporations: financial details, medical information, lifestyle habits.

Investigators (private and police) have long used this and other data to track down people. Even supposedly confidential data gets used in this fashion. No TV private investigator has survived half a season without a friend in the local police force willing to look up a name or a license plate or a criminal record in the police files. Police routinely use industry databases. And every few years, some bored IRS operator gets caught looking up the tax returns of famous people.

Marketers have long used whatever data they could get their hands on to target particular people and demographics. In the United States, per-sonal data do not belong to the person whom the data are about, they belong to the organization that collected it. Your financial information isn't your property, it's your bank's. Your medical information isn't yours, it's your doctor's. Doctors swear oaths to protect your privacy, but insur-ance providers and HMOs do not. Do you really want everyone to know about your heart defect or your family's history of glaucoma? How about your bout with alcoholism, or that embarrassing brush with venereal disease two decades ago?

Privacy violations can easily lead to fraud. In the novel *Paper Moon*, Joe David Brown wrote about the Depression-era trick of selling bibles and other merchandise to the relatives of the recently deceased. Other scams targeted the mothers and widows of overseas war dead—"for only pennies a day we'll care for his grave"—and people who won sweep-stakes. In many areas in the country, public utilities are installing telephone-based systems to read meters: water, electricity, and the like. It's a great idea, until some enterprising criminal uses the data to track when people go away on vacation. Or when they use alarm monitoring systems that give up-to-the-minute details on building occupancy. Wherever data can be exploited, someone will try it, computers or no computers.

Nothing in cyberspace is new. Child pornography: old hat. Money laundering: seen it. Bizarre cults offering everlasting life in exchange for your personal check: how déclassé. The underworld is no better than businesspeople at figuring out what the Net is good for; they're just repackaging their old tricks for the new medium, taking advantage of the subtle differences and exploiting the Net's reach and scalability.

THE CHANGING NATURE OF ATTACKS

The threats may be the same, but cyberspace changes everything. Although attacks in the digital world might have the same goals and share a lot of the same techniques as attacks in the physical world, they will be very different. They will be more common. They will be more wide-spread. It will be harder to track, capture, and convict the perpetrators. And their effects will be more devastating. The Internet has three new characteristics that make this true. Any one of them is bad; the three together are horrifying.

Automation

Automation is an attacker's friend. If a sagacious counterfeiter invented a method of minting perfect nickels, no one would care. The counterfeiter couldn't make enough phony nickels to make it worth the time and effort. Phone phreaks were able to make free local telephone calls from payphones pretty much at will from 1960 until the mid-1980s. Sure, the phone company was annoyed, and it made a big show about trying to catch these people—but they didn't affect its bottom line. You just can't steal enough 10-cent phone calls to affect the earnings-per-share of a multibillion-dollar company, especially when the marginal cost of goods is close to zero.

In cyberspace, things are different. Computers excel at dull, repetitive tasks. Our counterfeiter could mint a million electronic nickels while he sleeps. There's the so-called *salami attack* of stealing the fractions of pennies, one slice at a time, from everyone's interest-bearing accounts; this is a beautiful example of something that just would not have been possible without computers.

If you had a great scam to pick someone's pocket, but it only worked once every hundred thousand tries, you'd starve before you robbed anyone. In cyberspace, you can set your computer to look for the one-in-a-hundred-thousand chance. You'll probably find a couple dozen every day. If you can enlist other computers, you might get hundreds.

Fast automation makes attacks with a minimal rate of return profitable. Attacks that were just too marginal to notice in the physical world can quickly become a major threat in the digital world. Many commercial systems just don't sweat the small stuff; it's cheaper to ignore it than to fix it. They will have to think differently with digital systems.

Cyberspace also opens vast new avenues for violating someone's privacy, often simply a result of automation. Suppose you have a marketing campaign tied to rich, penguin-loving, stamp-collecting Elbonians with children. It's laborious to walk around town and find wealthy Elbonians with children, who like penguins, and are interested in stamps. On the right computer network, it's easy to correlate a marketing database of zip codes of a certain income with birth or motor vehicle records, posts to rec.collecting.stamps, and penguin-book purchases at Amazon.com. The Internet has search tools that can collect every Usenet posting a person ever made. Paper data, even if it is public, is hard to search and hard to correlate. Computerized data can be searched easily. Networked data can be searched remotely and correlated with other databases.

Under some circumstances, looking at this kind of data is illegal. People, often employees, have been prosecuted for peeking at confiden-tial police or IRS files. Under other circumstances, it's called *data mining* and is entirely legal. For example, the big credit database companies, Experian (formerly TRW), TransUnion, and Equifax, have mounds of data about nearly everyone in the United States. These data are collected, collated, and sold to anyone willing to pay for it. Credit card databases have a mind-boggling amount of information about individuals' spending habits: where they shop, where they eat, what kind of vacations they take—it's all there for the taking. DoubleClick is trying to build a database of individual Web-surfing habits. Even grocery stores are giving out fre-quent shopper cards, allowing them to collect data about the food-buying proclivities of individual shoppers. Acxiom is a company that specializes in the aggregation of public and private databases.

The news here is not that the data are out there, but how easily they can be collected, used, and abused. And it will get worse: More data are being collected. Banks, airlines, catalog companies, medical insurers are all saving personal information. Many Web sites collect and sell personal data. And why not? Data storage is cheap, and maybe it will be useful some day. These diverse data archives are moving onto the public networks. And more and more data are being combined and cross-refer-enced. Automation makes it all easy.

Action at a Distance

As technology pundits like to point out, the Internet has no borders or natural boundaries. Every two points are adjacent, whether they are across the hall or across the planet. It's just as easy to log on to a computer in Tulsa from a computer in Tunisia as it is from one in Tallahassee. Don't like the censorship laws or computer crime statutes in your country? Find a country more to your liking. Countries like Singapore have tried to limit their citizens' abilities to search the Web, but the way the Internet is built makes blocking off parts of it unfeasible. As John Gilmore opined, "The Internet treats censorship as damage and routes around it."

This means that Internet attackers don't have to be anywhere near their prey. An attacker could sit behind a computer in St. Petersburg and attack Citibank's computers in New York. This has enormous security implications. If you were building a warehouse in Buffalo, you'd only have to worry about the set of criminals who would consider driving to Buffalo and breaking into your warehouse. Since on the Internet every computer is equidistant from every other computer, you have to worry about all the criminals in the world.

The global nature of the Internet complicates criminal investigation and prosecution, too. Finding attackers adroit at concealing their whereabouts can be near impossible, and even if you do find them, what do you do then? And crime is only defined with respect to political borders. But if the Internet has no physical "area" to control, who polices it?

So far, every jurisdiction that possibly can lay a claim to the Internet has tried to. Does the data originate in Germany? Then it is subject to German law. Does it terminate in the United States? Then it had better suit the American government. Does it pass through France? If so, the French authorities want a say in *qu'il s'est passé.* In 1994, the operators of a computer bulletin board system (BBS) in Milpitas, California— where both the people and the computers resided—were tried and convicted in a Tennessee court because someone in Tennessee made a long-distance telephone call to California and downloaded dirty pictures that were found to be acceptable in California but indecent in Tennessee. The bul-letin board operators never set foot in Tennessee before the trial. In July 1997, a 33-year old woman was convicted by a Swiss court for sending pornography across the Internet—even though she had been in the United States since 1993. Does this make any sense?

In general, though, prosecuting across jurisdictions is incredibly diffi-cult. Until it's sorted out, criminals can take advantage of the confusion as a shield. In 1995, a 29-year-old hacker from St. Petersburg, Russia, made $12 million breaking into Citibank's computers. Citibank eventually dis-covered the break and recovered most of the money, but had trouble extraditing the hacker to stand trial.

This difference in laws among various states and countries can even lead to a high-tech form of jurisdiction shopping. Sometimes this can work in the favor of the prosecutor, because this is exactly what the Ten-nessee conviction of the California BBS was. Other times it can work in the favor of the criminal: Any organized crime syndicate with enough money to launch a large-scale attack against a financial system would do well to find a country with poor computer crime laws, easily bribable police officers, and no extradition treaties.

Technique Propagation

The third difference is the ease with which successful techniques can propagate through cyberspace. HBO doesn't care very much if someone can build a decoder in his basement. It requires time, skill, and some money. But what if that person published an easy way for everyone to get free satellite TV? No work. No hardware. "Just punch these seven digits into your remote control, and you never have to pay for cable TV again." That would increase the number of nonpaying customers to the millions, and could significantly affect the company's profitability.

Physical counterfeiting is a problem, but it's a manageable problem. Over two decades ago, we sold the Shah of Iran some of our old intaglio printing presses. When Ayatollah Khomeini took over, he realized that it was more profitable to mint $100 bills than Iranian rials. The FBI calls them supernotes, and they're near perfect. (This is why the United States redesigned its currency.) At the same time the FBI and the Secret Service were throwing up their hands, the Department of the Treasury did some calculating: The Iranian presses can only print so much money a minute, there are only so many minutes in a year, so there's a maximum to the amount of counterfeit money they can manufacture. Treasury decided that the amount of counterfeit currency couldn't affect the money supply, so it wasn't a serious concern to the nation's stability.

If the counterfeiting were electronic, it would be different. An electronic counterfeiter could automate the hack and publish it on some Web site somewhere. People could download this program and start undetectably counterfeiting electronic money. By morning it could be in the hands of 1,000 first-time counterfeiters; another 100,000 could have it in a week. The U.S. currency system could collapse in a week.

Instead of there being a maximum limit to the damage this attack can do, in cyberspace, damage could grow exponentially.

The Internet is also a perfect medium for propagating successful attack tools. Only the first attacker has to be skilled; everyone else can use his software. After the initial attacker posts it to an archive—conveniently located in some backward country—anyone can download and use it. And once the tool is released, it can be impossible to control.

We've seen this problem with computer viruses: Dozens of sites let you download computer viruses, computer virus construction kits, and computer virus designs. And we've seen the same problem with hacking tools: software packages that break into computers, bring down servers, bypass copy protection measures, or exploit browser bugs to steal data from users' machines. Internet worms are already making floppy-disk-borne computer viruses look like quaint amusements. It took no skill to launch the wave of distributed denial-of-service attacks against major Web sites in early 2000; all it took was downloading and running a script. And when digital commerce systems are widespread, we'll see automated attacks against them too.

Computer-based attacks mean that criminals don't need skill to succeed.

PROACTION VS. REACTION

Traditionally, commerce systems have played catch-up in response to fraud: online credit card verification in response to an increase in credit card theft, other verification measures in response to check fraud. This won't work on the Internet, because Internet time moves too quickly. Someone could figure out a successful attack against an Internet credit card system, write a program to automate it, and within 24 hours it could be in the hands of half a million people all over the world—many of them impossible to prosecute. I can see a security advisor walking into the CEO's office and saying: "We have two options. We can accept every transaction as valid, both the legitimate and fraudulent ones, or we can accept none of them." The CEO would be stuck with this Hobson's choice.

3

Attacks

I'm going to discuss three broad classes of attacks. Criminal attacks are the most obvious, and the type that I've focused on. But the others—publicity attacks and legal attacks—are probably more damaging.

CRIMINAL ATTACKS

Criminal attacks are easy to understand: "How can I acquire the maximum financial return by attacking the system?" Attackers vary, from lone criminals to sophisticated organized crime syndicates, from insiders looking to make a fast buck to foreign governments looking to wage war on a country's infrastructure.

Fraud

Fraud has been attempted against every commerce system ever invented. Unscrupulous merchants have used rigged scales to shortchange their customers; people have shaved silver and gold off the rims of coins. Everything has been counterfeited: currency, stock certificates, credit cards, checks, letters of credit, purchase orders, casino chips. Modern financial systems—checks, credit cards, and automatic teller machine networks—each rack up multi-million-dollar fraud losses per year. Electronic commerce will be no different; neither will the criminals' techniques.

Scams

According to the National Consumers League, the five most common online scams are sale of Internet services, sale of general merchandise, auctions, pyramid and multilevel marketing schemes, and business oppor-tunities. People read some enticing e-mail or visit an enticing Web site, send money off to some post office box for some reason or another, and end up either getting nothing in return or getting stuff of little or no value. Sounds just like the physical world: Lots of people get burned.

Destructive Attacks

Destructive attacks are the work of terrorists, employees bent on revenge, or hackers gone over to the dark side. Destruction is a criminal attack—it's rare that causing damage to someone else's property is legal—but there is often no profit motive. Instead, the attacker asks: "How can I cause the most damage by attacking this system?"

There are many different kinds of destructive attacks. In 1988, someone wrote a computer virus specifically targeted against computers owned by Electronic Data Systems. It didn't do too much damage (actually, it did more damage to NASA), but the idea was there. In early 2000, we watched distributed denial-of-service attacks against Yahoo!, Ama-zon.com, E*Trade, Buy.com, CNN, and eBay. A deft attacker could probably keep an ISP down for weeks. In fact, a hacker with the right combination of skills and morals could probably take down the Internet.

At the other end of the spectrum, driving a truck bomb through a company's front window works too. The United States' attacks against Iraqi communications systems in the Persian Gulf are probably the best example of this. The French terrorist group Comité Liquidant ou Détournant les Ordinateurs (Computer Liquidation and Deterrence Committee) bombed computer centers in the Toulouse region in the early 1980s. More spectacular was the burning of the Library of Alexan-dria in 47 B.C. (by Julius Caesar), in A.D. 391 (by the Christian emperor Theodosius I), and in A.D. 642 (by Omar, Caliph of Baghdad): All excellent lessons in the importance of off-site backups.

Intellectual Property Theft

Intellectual property is more than trade secrets and company databases. It's also electronic versions of books, magazines, and newspapers; digital videos, music, and still images; software; and private databases available to the public for a fee. The difficult problem here is not how to keep private data private, but how to maintain control and receive appropriate compensation for proprietary data while making it public.

Software companies want to sell their software to legitimate buyers without pirates making millions of illegal copies and selling them (or giving them away) to others. In 1997, the Business Software Alliance had a counter on its Web page that charted the industry's losses due to piracy: $482 a second, $28,900 a minute, $1.7 million an hour, $15 billion a year. These numbers were inflated, since they make the mendacious assump-tion that everyone who pirates a copy of (for example) Autodesk's 3D Studio MAX would have otherwise paid $2,995—or $3,495 if you use the retail price rather than the street price—for it. The prevalence of software piracy greatly depends on the country: It is thought that 95 percent of the software in the People's Republic of China is pirated, while only 50 percent of the software in Canada is pirated. (Vietnam wins, with 98 percent pirated software.) Software companies, rightfully so, are miffed at these losses.

Piracy happens on different scales. There are disks shared between friends, downloads from the Internet (search under *warez* to find out more about this particular activity), and large-scale counterfeiting operations (usually run in the Far East).

Piracy also happens to data. Whether it's pirated CDs of copyrighted music hawked on the backstreets of Bangkok or MP3 files of copyrighted music peddled on the Web, digital intellectual property is being stolen all the time. (And, of course, this applies to digital images, digital video, and digital text just as much.)

The common thread here is that companies want to control the dis-semination of their intellectual property. This attitude, while perfectly reasonable, is contrary to what the digital world is all about. The physics of the digital world is different: Unlike physical goods, information can be in two places at once. It can be copied infinitely. Someone can both give away a piece of information and retain it. Once it is dispersed hither and thither, it can be impossible to retrieve. If a digital copy of *The Lion King* ever gets distributed over the Internet, Disney will not be able to delete all the copies.

Unauthorized copying is not a new problem; it's as old as the recording industry. In school, I had cassette tapes of music I couldn't afford to buy; so did everyone else I knew. Taiwan and Thailand have long been a source of counterfeit CDs. The Russian Mafia has become a player in the pirated video industry, and the Chinese triads are becoming heavily involved in counterfeit software. Industry losses were estimated to be $11 billion per year, although the number is probably based on some imaginative assumptions, too.

Digital content has no magic immunity from counterfeiters. In fact, it's unique in that it can be copied perfectly. Unlike my cassette tapes, an illegal DVD of *The Lion King* or a software product isn't degraded in quality; it's another original. Counteracting that is like trying to make water not wet; it just doesn't work.

Identity Theft

Why steal from someone when you can just become that person? It's far easier, and can be much more profitable, to get a bunch of credit cards in someone else's name, run up large bills, and then disappear. It's called *identity theft,* and it's a high-growth area of crime. One Albuquerque, New Mexico, criminal ring would break into homes specifically to col-lect checkbooks, credit card statements, receipts, and other financial mail, looking for Social Security numbers, dates of birth, places of work, and account numbers.

This is scary stuff, and it happens all the time. There were thousands of cases of identity theft reported in the United States during 1999 alone. Dealing with the aftermath can be an invasive and exhaustive experience.

It's going to get worse. As more identity recognition goes electronic, identity theft becomes easier. At the same time, as more systems use electronic identity recognition, identity theft becomes more profitable and less risky. Why break into someone's house if you can collect the necessary identity information online?

And people are helpful. They give out sensitive information to any-one who asks; many print their driver's license numbers on their checks. They throw away bills, bank statements, and so forth. They're too trust-ing.

For a long time, we've gotten by with an ad hoc system of remote identity. "Mother's maiden name" never really worked as an identifica-tion system (especially now, given the extensive public databases on genealogical Web sites). Still, the fiction worked as long as criminals didn't take too much advantage of it. That's history now, and we'll never get back to that point again.

Brand Theft

Virtual identity is vital to businesses as well as individuals. It takes time and money to develop a corporate identity. This identity is more than logos and slogans and catchy jingles. It's product, bricks-and-mortar buildings, customer service representatives—things to touch, people to talk to. Brand equals reputation.

On the Internet, the barrier to entry is minimal. Anyone can have a Web site, from Citibank to Fred's Safe-Money Mattress. And everyone does. How do users know which sites are worth visiting, worth book-marking, worth establishing a relationship with? Thousands of companies sell PCs on the Web. Who is real, and who is fly-by-night?

Branding is the only answer to this question. When the Web first entered the public eye, pundits claimed that it heralded the end of the big brand. Because anyone could go on the Web and compete with the big names, brands were meaningless. The reality is exactly the opposite. Since anyone can go on the Web and compete with the big names, the only way to tell products apart is by their brands. Users look at brands, and they return to the sites they trust. A brand has real value, and it's worth stealing.

An example: A Malaysian company wanted to market condoms using the "Visa" brand. They claimed that it had nothing to do with the credit card company, but was a pun on "permit to entry." Visa was unamused, and sued. It won, and I believe this ruling has profound implications for brand ownership.

Cyberspace has many opportunities for brand theft. In 1998, someone forged a domain-name transfer request to Network Solutions and stole sex.com; the original owner is still trying to get it back. Another recent case involved a plumber who rerouted customer phone calls for another plumber to his own number. Organized crime syndicates in Las Vegas have done the same thing with escort-service phone numbers. This kind of attack is nothing new. Almon Strowger was an undertaker in Kansas City. He was convinced that telephone operators were rerouting tele-phone calls to rival businesses, so he invented the dial telephone in 1887 to bypass the operators.

Some merchants have designed their Web sites to steal traffic away from other Web sites; this is known as *page-jacking.* Also on the net are *typo pirates,* who register a domain name just a typo away from legitimate Web sites. Many porn sites do that. Big companies are not above these kinds of tactics: when MCI's 1-800-COLLECT became popular, AT&T set up a collect-calling service on 1-800-C0LLECT, with a zero instead of the letter *O,* the most common misdial. MCI stooped to the same tactic, registering 1-800-0PERATOR, with a zero instead of AT&T's *O.* Some of these tactics are illegal today; I expect more will be in the future.

Prosecution

Unfortunately, prosecution can be difficult in cyberspace. On the one hand, the crimes are the same. Theft is illegal, whether analog or digital, online or offline. So is trespassing, counterfeiting, racketeering, swindling, stalking, and a criminal-code worth of other things. The laws against these practices, complete with the criminal justice infrastructure to enforce them, are already in place. Some new laws have been passed, specifically for the digital world, but we don't know the full ramifications of those laws. The court system doesn't work on Internet time. In the United States, it can take a decade to erase a bad law, or to figure out how a law should really be applied.

Over time, the laws will better reflect the reality of the digital world. A few years ago, when a group of German hackers was caught breaking into U.S. computer systems, the German government had no criminal laws to charge them with. Today, some criminal statutes specifically make it a crime to break into remote computer systems, because the old tres-passing statues didn't deal well with trespassers sitting comfortably in their bedrooms while their computer commands "trespassed" via the tele-phone network. Likewise, statutes on stalking, invasions of privacy, copy-right, and solicitation are being modified for a world where things don't work exactly like they used to.

Eventually, people will realize that it doesn't make sense to write laws that are specific to a technology. Fraud is fraud, whether it takes place over the U.S. mail, the telephone, or the Internet. A crime is no more or less of a crime if cryptography is involved. (The New York sales clerk who, in 1999, used a Palm Pilot to copy customers' credit card numbers would be no less guilty if he used a pen and paper.) And extortion is no better or worse if carried out using computer viruses or old-fashioned compromising photos. Good laws are written to be independent of technology. In a world where technology advances much faster than congressional sessions, this is what can work today. Faster and more responsive mechanisms for legislation, prosecution, and adjudication . . . maybe someday.

PRIVACY VIOLATIONS

Privacy violations are not necessarily criminal, but they can be. (They can be a prelude to identity theft, for example.) In the United States, most privacy violations are legal. People do not own their own data. If a credit bureau or a marketing research firm collects data about you—your per-sonal habits, your buying patterns, your financial status, your physical health—it can sell it to anyone who wants it without your knowledge or consent. It's different elsewhere. Privacy laws in much of Europe (includ-ing the European Union), Taiwan, New Zealand, and Canada are more restrictive.

Other types of privacy violations are legal, too. Hiring a private investigator to collect information on a person or a company is legal, as long as the investigator doesn't use any illegal methods. All sorts of privacy violations by the police are legal with a warrant, and many are legal without. (Did you know that in the United States police don't need a warrant to demand a copy of the photographs you dropped off for developing?)

There are two types of privacy violations—targeted attacks and data harvesting—and they are fundamentally different. In a targeted attack, an attacker wants to know everything about Alice. If "Alice" is a person, it's called stalking. If "Alice" is a company, it's called industrial espionage. If "Alice" is a government, it's called national intelligence or spying. All of these will get you thrown in jail if you use some techniques, but not if you use others.

Computer security can protect Alice against a targeted attack, but only up to a point. If attackers are well enough funded, they can always get around computer security measures. They can install a bug in Alice's office, rummage through Alice's trash, or spy with a telescope. Information is information, and computer security only protects the information while it is on computers. What computer security protects against are non-invasive attacks. It forces the attacker to get close to Alice and makes privacy violations riskier, more expensive, and subject to different laws.

Data harvesting is the other type of privacy violation. This attack harnesses the power of correlation. Suppose an attacker wants a list of every widow, 70 years or older, with more than $1 million in the bank, who has given to more than eight charities in the past year, and who subscribes to an astrological magazine. Or a list of everybody in the United States who has been prescribed AZT. Or who views a particular socialist Web site. Although con artists have collected names of people who might be susceptible to particular scams for over a century, the prevalence of databases on the Internet allows them to automate and better target their searches.

Good cryptography and computer security can help protect against data-harvesting attacks (assuming it is illegal to simply buy the data from those who own the various databases) by making the collection problem intractable. Data harvesting is worthwhile only because it can be automated; it makes no sense to sort through an entire neighborhood's trashcans to cull a demographic. If all computerized data is protected, an attacker doesn't even know where to look. Even moderate levels of cryptography can protect absolutely against data harvesting.

Surveillance

One hundred years ago, everyone could have personal privacy. You and a friend could walk into an empty field, look around to see that no one else was nearby, and have a level of privacy that has forever been lost. As Whitfield Diffie has said: "No right of private conversation was enumer-ated in the Constitution. I don't suppose it occurred to anyone at the time that it could be prevented." The ability to have a private conversation, like the ability to keep your thoughts in your head and the ability to fall to the ground when pushed, was a natural consequence of how the world worked.

Technology has demolished that world view. Powerful directional microphones can pick up conversations hundreds of yards away. In the aftermath of the MRTA terrorist group's takeover of the Japanese embassy in Peru (1997), news reports described audio bugs being hidden in shirt buttons that allowed police to pinpoint everyone's location. Van Eck devices can read what's on your computer monitor from halfway down the street. (Right now this is an expensive and complicated attack, but just wait until wireless LANs become popular.) Pinhole cameras—now being sold in electronics catalogs—can hide in the smallest cracks; satellite cameras can read your license plate from orbit. And the Department of Defense is prototyping micro air vehicles, the size of small birds or butterflies, that can scout out enemy snipers, locate hostages in occupied buildings, or spy on just about anybody.

The ability to trail someone remotely has existed for a while, but it is only used in exceptional circumstances (except on TV). In 1993, Colombian drug lord Pablo Escobar was identified partly by tracking him through his cellular phone usage: a technique known as *pinpointing*. In 1996, the Russian Army killed Chechnyan leader Dzholar Dudayev with an air-to-surface missile after pinpointing his location from the transmissions of his personal satellite phone. The FBI found the truck belonging to the Oklahoma City federal building's bomber because agents collected the tapes from every surveillance camera in the city, correlated them by time (the explosion acted as a giant synch pulse), and looked for it. Invisible identification tags are printed on virtually all color xerographic output, from all of the manufacturers. (These machines also include anticounterfeiting measures, such as dumping extra cyan toner onto images when the unit detects an attempt to copy U.S. currency.) Explosives have embedded taggants.

The technology to automatically search for drug negotiations in random telephone conversations, for suspicious behavior in satellite images, or for faces on a "wanted list" of criminals in on-street cameras isn't com-monplace yet, but it's just a matter of time. Face recognition will be able to pick individual people out of a crowd. Voice recognition will be able to scan millions of telephone calls listening for a particular person; it can already scan for suspicious words or phrases and pick conversations out of a crowd. Moore's Law, which predicts the industry can double the computing power of a microchip every 18 months, affects surveillance computing just as it does everything else: The next generation will be smaller, faster, a lot cheaper, and more easily available. As soon as the recognition technologies isolate the people, the computers will be able to do the searching.

Storage is getting cheaper, too. We're only a few generations away from being able to record our entire lives—in audio and video—and save the data. It could be introduced as a preemptive defense mechanism, "in case you ever need to prove an alibi," or a public-good mechanism, because "you never know when you'll be the witness to a crime." Some-day not wearing your life recorder may be cause for suspicion.

The surveillance infrastructure is being installed in our country under the guise of "customer service." Who hasn't heard the ubiquitous message that "this conversation may be monitored or recorded for quality assur-ance purposes"? Some hotels track guest preferences in international data-bases, so that customers will feel at home even if it is their first stay in a particular city. High-end restaurants now have video cameras in the din-ing room, to study diners' eating habits and meal progress, and databases of customer preferences. Amazon.com tracks the buying behavior of dif-ferent demographic groups. Melissa virus writer David Smith was identi-fied because Microsoft Word automatically embeds identity information in all documents. Automatic toll-collection systems keep records of what cars went through different tollbooths. In 2000, some cities started mea-suring highway congestion by tracking motorists by their cell phones. There's a fine line between good customer service and stalking.

Sometimes there's no customer-service spin: Credit card companies keep detailed purchasing records so they can reduce fraud. Companies monitor employee Web site surfing to limit abuse and liability. Many air-ports record the license plates of everyone who uses the parking lot— Denver International Airport records the plates of everyone who enters airport grounds—as a security measure.

GPS, the satellite-based Global Positioning System, is a dream tech-nology for surveillance. At least two companies are marketing a smart automobile locator, based on GPS. One company is selling an automatic warehouse inventory system, using GPS and affixable transmitters on objects. The transmitters broadcast their location, and a central computer keeps track of where everything is. Spies have probably been able to use this kind of stuff for years, but it's now a consumer item so Dad knows where Junior is taking the car.

Individual privacy is being eroded from a variety of directions. Most of the time, the erosions are small, and no one kicks up a fuss. But less and less privacy is available, and most people are completely oblivious of it. Surveillance devices are getting cheaper and smaller and more ubiquitous.

It is plausible that we could soon be living in a world without expectation of privacy, anywhere or at any time.

Databases

Historically, privacy was only about surveillance. Then, in the 1960s, society reached a watershed. Computers with large databases entered business, and organizations started keeping databases on individuals. Recently, we've reached a second watershed: Networked computers are allowing disparate databases to be shared, correlated, and combined. The effects of these databases on personal privacy are still to be felt. We've managed to successfully beat back Big Brother, only to lose to a network of Little Brothers. For the first time, someone can be unsurveillably surveilled.

Recently, more and more data is being collected and saved, both because data collection is cheaper and because people leave more electronic footprints in their daily lives. More of it is being collected and cross-correlated. And more of it is available online. The upshot is that it is not difficult to collect a detailed dossier on someone.

Many of these databases are commercial: large credit databases owned by Experian, TransUnion, and Equifax; telephone databases of individual calls made; credit card databases of individual purchases. The information can be used for its original intent or sold for other purposes. Those legitimately allowed to can access it, and it is potentially available to those adroit enough to break into the computers. This can be correlated with other databases: your health information, your financial details, any lifestyle information you've made public. In 1999, there was a small press flare-up because some public television stations traded donor lists with the Democratic Party. In 2000, public furor forced DoubleClick to reverse its plans to correlate Web-surfing records with individual identities.

The Web provides even more potential for invasions of privacy. Online stores can, in theory, keep records of everything you buy. (Block-buster, for example, has a database of every video you've rented.) They can also keep records of everything you look at: every item you ask to see more information about, every topic you search for, how long you spend looking at each item . . . not just what you buy, but what you look at and don't buy.

Online law enforcement databases are a great boon to the police—it really helps to be able to automatically download a criminal record or mugshot directly to a squad car—but privacy fears remain. Police data-bases are not much more secure than any other commercial database, and the information is a lot more sensitive.

Traffic Analysis

Traffic analysis is the study of communication patterns. Not the content of the messages themselves, but characteristics about them. Who communicates with whom? When? How long are the messages? How quickly are the replies sent, and how long are they? What kinds of communications happen after a certain message is received? These are all traffic analysis questions, and their answers can reveal a lot of information.

For example, if each time Alice sends a long message to Bob, Bob sends a short reply back to Alice and a long message to five other people, this indicates a chain of command. Alice is clearly sending orders to Bob, who is relaying them to his subordinates. If Alice sends regular short messages to Bob, and suddenly sends a series of long ones, this indicates that something (what?) has changed.

Often the patterns of communication are just as important as the contents of communication. For example, the simple fact that Alice telephones a known terrorist every week is more important than the details of their conversation. The Nazis used the traffic-analysis data in itemized French phone bills to arrest friends of the arrested; they didn't really care what the conversations were about. Calls from the White House to Monica Lewinsky were embarrassing enough, even without a transcription of the conversation. In the hours preceding the U.S. bombing of Iraq in 1991, pizza deliveries to the Pentagon increased one hundredfold. Anyone paying attention certainly knew *something* was up. (Interestingly enough, the CIA had the same number of pizzas delivered as any other night.) Some studies have shown that even if you encrypt your Web traffic, traffic analysis based on the size of the encrypted Web pages is more than enough to figure out what you're browsing.

While militaries have used traffic analysis for decades, it is still a new area of study in the academic world. We don't really know how vulner-able our communications—especially our Internet communications—are to traffic analysis, and what can be done to reduce the risks. Expect this to be an important area of research in the future.

Massive Electronic Surveillance

ECHELON is a code word for an automated global interception system operated by the intelligence agencies of the United States, the United Kingdom, Canada, Australia, and New Zealand, and led by the National Security Agency (NSA). I've seen estimates that ECHELON intercepts as many as 3 billion communications everyday, including phone calls, e-mail messages, Internet downloads, satellite transmissions, and so on. The system gathers all of these transmissions indiscriminately, then sorts and distills the information through artificial intelligence programs. Some sources have claimed that ECHELON sifts through 90 percent of the Internet's traffic, although that seems doubtful.

This kind of massive surveillance effort is daunting, and provides some unique problems. Surveillance data is only useful when it is distilled to a form that people can understand and act upon. The United States intercepted a message to the Japanese ambassador in Washington, D.C., discussing the Pearl Harbor bombing, but the information only made sense in retrospect and never made it past the low-level clerks. But as dif-ficult as analysis is, even more difficult is the simple decision of what to record.

Potential ECHELON intercepts are an unending firehose of data: more than any group of human analysts can ever analyze. The intercep-tion equipment must decide, in real time, whether or not any piece of data is worth recording for later analysis. And the system cannot afford to do much "later analysis"; there's always more data being recorded. I'm sure much valuable intelligence has been recorded that a human will never scrutinize.

To build a system like this, you would have to invest in two tech-nologies: diagnostic capabilities and traffic analysis. Interception equip-ment must to be able to quickly characterize a piece of data: who the sender and receiver are, the topic of conversation, how it fits in any larger pattern of communication. (If you think this is hard for Internet e-mail, think how hard it is for voice conversations.) Much of this technology is similar to what you might find in a search engine.

Traffic analysis is even more important. Traffic patterns reveal a lot about any organization and are much easier to collect and analyze than actual communications data. They also provide additional information to a diagnostic engine. Elaborate databases of traffic patterns are undoubtedly the heart of any ECHELON-like system.

One last note: In a world where most communications are unencrypted, encrypted communications are probably routinely recorded. The mere indication that the conversers do not want to be overheard would be enough to raise an alarm.

PUBLICITY ATTACKS

The publicity attack is conceptually simple: "How can I get my name in the newspapers by attacking the system?" This type of attack is relatively new in the digital world: A few years ago, computer hacks weren't con-sidered newsworthy, and I can't think of any other technology in history that people would try to break simply to get their names in the paper. In the physical world, this attack is ancient: The man who burned down the Temple of Artemis in ancient Greece did so because he wanted his name to be remembered forever. (His name was Herostratus, by the way.) More recently, the kids who shot up Columbine High School wanted infamy.

Most attackers of this type are hackers: skilled individuals who know a lot about systems and their security. They often have access to significant resources, either as students of large universities or as employees of large companies. They usually don't have a lot of money, but sometimes have a lot of time. Furthermore, they are not likely to do anything that will put them in jail; the idea is publicity, not incarceration.

The canonical example of this is the breaking of Netscape Navigator's encryption scheme by two Berkeley graduate students in 1995. These students didn't use the weakness for ill-gotten gain; they called the *New York Times*. Netscape's reaction was something on the order of "We did some calculations, and thought it would take umpteen dollars of com-puting power; we didn't think it was worth anyone's trouble to break it." They were right; it wasn't worth anyone's trouble . . . anyone who was interested in the money. The grad students had all sorts of skills, access to all the unused computer time at their university, and no social lives.

What's important for system designers to realize is that publicity seekers don't fall into the same threat model that criminals do. Criminals will only attack a system if there's a profit to be made; publicity seekers will attack a system if there is a good chance the press will cover it. Attacks against large-scale systems and widely fielded products are best.

Sometimes these attacks are motivated by a desire to fix the problems. Many companies ignore security vulnerabilities unless they are made pub-lic. Once the researcher announces the attack, the victim company will scurry to fix the problem. In this way, attacks increase the security of systems.

Publicity attacks can be costly. Customers may desert one system in favor of another after a publicity attack, as has happened in the wake of several attacks against banking systems. And investors might desert the victim's stock. This has happened in the digital cellular industry after pub-licity attacks exposed weaknesses in various privacy and antitheft mea-sures. Citibank lost several high-profile accounts after the St. Petersburg hack. The DVD security break delayed a Sony product launch past the 1999 Christmas season. In 2000, CD Universe lost a lot of customers after a hacker stole 300,000 credit card numbers off of its Web site. Sometimes the bad press is more costly than the actual theft.

Publicity attacks have other dangers. One is that criminals will learn about these attacks and exploit them. Another is that public confidence in the systems will be eroded by the announcements. This could be a major problem in electronic commerce systems in particular. Banks like to keep successful criminal attacks against their systems quiet, so as not to alarm the public. But hackers and academics are much harder to keep quiet and are going to be all over commerce systems once they're fielded. If there are security holes anywhere, someone is going to find them and call a press conference. Maybe not the first person who finds them, but someone will. Companies need to be prepared.

Defacing someone's Web page is one form of publicity attack. It used to be big news. The 1996 hack of the Department of Justice Web site made the news. So did the 1997 hack of the AirTran site, and the 1998 hack of the *New York Times* main page.

In those days, the publicity was such that some sites didn't wait to be hacked. MGM/Universal Studios was thrilled when the Web site for its movie *Hackers* was hacked in 1995. And in 1997, Universal Pictures hacked its own Web site for *Jurassic Park: The Lost World* as a publicity stunt. (They tried to pretend it was hackers, but the parody site looked too professional, and the hacked page was uploaded to the site three days before the legitimate site came online.)

These days it happens so often that it barely rates a mention in the news. Probably every major U.S. government Web site was hacked in 1999, as were the Web sites of many local and foreign governments. I listed 65 Web site defacements in the first week of March 2000 in Chap-ter 1. Sysadmins have become inured to the problem.

Denial-of-Service Attacks

More recently, denial-of-service attacks have become the publicity attack *du jour*. This is only because of their massive press coverage, and will hopefully become old news, too. The idea is simply to stop something from working. And as anyone who has had to deal with the effects of striking workers—bus drivers, air traffic controllers, farm laborers, and so forth—can tell you, these attacks are effective.

There are other denial-of-service attacks in the physical world: boy-cotts and blockades, for example. These attacks all have analogues in cyberspace. Someone with enough phone connections can tie up all the modem connections of a local ISP. The analog cell phone networks had trouble freeing connections when a mobile user went from cell to cell; it was possible to sit on a hill with a directional antenna and, by spinning it around and around slowly, tie up all the channels in the nearby cells.

Denial-of-service attacks work because computer networks are there to communicate. Some simple attack, like saying hello, can be automated to the point where it becomes a denial-of-service attack. This is basically the SYN flood attack that brought down several ISPs in 1996.

Here's another denial-of-service attack: In the mid-1980s, Jerry Fal-well's political organization set up a toll-free number for something or other. One guy programmed his computer to repeatedly dial the number and then hang up. This did two things: It busied the phone lines so that legitimate people could not call the number, and it cost Falwell's organi-zation money every time a call was completed. Nice denial-of-service attack.

Denial-of-service attacks can be preludes to criminal attacks. Burglars approach a warehouse at 1:00 A.M. and cut the connection between the burglar alarm and the police station. The alarm rings, and the police are alerted that the connection has been broken. Burglars retreat a safe dis-tance and wait for the police to arrive. Police arrive and find nothing. (If the burglars are inventive, they cut the connection in some way that isn't obvious.) Police decide that it's a problem with the system, and the warehouse owner decides to deal with it in the morning. Police leave. Burglars reappear and steal everything.

A variant on this, which insurers have noted on several occasions, is to attack the telephone exchange that routes the alarm signals. Many alarms have a *heartbeat* back to the monitoring station, and call the police if the signal is interrupted. By attacking the exchange, every alarm is triggered and the police don't know which alarm to respond to.

Here's another example: a military base protected by a fence and motion sensors. The attackers take a rabbit and throw it over the fence; then they leave. The motion sensors go off. The guards respond, find nothing, and return to their posts. The attackers do this again, and the guards respond again. After a few nights of this, the guards turn the motion sensors off. And the attackers drive a jeep right through the fence. This kind of thing was done repeatedly against the Russian military bases in Afghanistan, and in tests against several U.S. military bases. It's surpris-ingly successful.

A similar attack was supposedly done against the Soviet embassy in Washington, D.C. The Americans fired a Canada Mint (basically, a sugar pellet) against the window. The rattle set off an alarm, but the sugar ball disintegrated and there was nothing to respond to. Then another ball. Thwap. Alarm. Nothing. Eventually the alarms were modified so that banging against the window didn't trigger them. (I don't know if any actual penetration resulted from this attack, or if it was just to nettle the Soviets.)

Closer to home, it's a common auto-theft technique to set a car alarm off at 2:00 A.M., 2:10, 2:20, 2:30 . . . until the owner turns the alarm off to appease the angry neighbors. In the morning, the car is gone.

Warfare uses denial-of-service attacks all the time. Each side tries to jam the other's radar systems and missile guidance systems, disrupt com-munications systems, and blow up bridges. One of the characteristics of denial-of-service attacks is that low-tech is often better than high-tech: Blowing up a computer center works much better than exploiting a Windows 2000 vulnerability.

Internet denial-of-service attacks are discussed in detail in Chapter 11.

LEGAL ATTACKS

In 1994, in the United Kingdom, a man found his bank account emptied. When he complained about six withdrawals he did not make, he was arrested and charged with attempted fraud. The British bank claimed that the security in the ATM system was infallible, and that the defendant was unequivocally guilty. When the defense attorney examined the evidence, he found (1) that the bank had no security management or quality assurance for its software, (2) that there was never any external security assessment, and (3) that the disputed withdrawals were never investigated. In fact, the bank's programmers claimed that since the code was written in assembly language, it couldn't possibly be the problem (because if there was a bug, it would cause a system crash). The man was convicted anyway. On appeal, the bank provided the court a huge security assess-ment by an auditing firm. When the defense demanded equal access to their systems in order to evaluate the security directly, the bank refused and the conviction was overturned.

Attacks that use the legal system are the hardest to protect against. The aim here isn't to exploit a flaw in a system. It isn't even to find a flaw in a system. The aim here is to persuade a judge and jury (who probably aren't technically savvy) that there *could* be a flaw in the system. The aim here is to discredit the system, to put enough doubt in the minds of the judge and jury that the security isn't perfect, to prove a client's innocence.

Here's a hypothetical example. In a major drug case, the police are using data from a cellular phone that pinpoints the defendant's phone at a particular time and place. The defense attorney finds some hacker expert who testifies that it is easy to falsify that kind of data, that it isn't reliable, that it could have been planted, and should not be counted as evidence. The prosecution has its own set of experts that say the opposite, and one possible outcome is that they cancel each other out and the trial goes on without the cellular-phone evidence.

The same thing can happen to audit data being used to prosecute someone who broke into a computer system, or signature data that is being used to try to enforce a contract. "I never signed that," says the defendant. "The computer told me to enter my passphrase and then push this button. That's what I did." A jury of the defendant's peers—probably just as befuddled by technology as the accused is claiming to be—is likely to sympathize.

The other side of the coin can be just as damaging. The police can use experts to convince a jury that a decrypted conversation is damning even though it is not 100 percent accurate, or that the computer intrusion detection is infallible and therefore the defendant is guilty.

When used to its fullest effect, the legal attack is potent. The attackers are likely to be extremely skilled—in high-profile cases, they can afford the best security researchers—and well-funded. They can use the discovery process to get all the details of the target system that they need. And the attack doesn't even have to work operationally; the attackers only have to find enough evidence to adduce a flaw. Think of it as a publicity attack with a bankroll and more relaxed victory conditions.

4

Adversaries

So who is threatening the digital world anyway? Hackers? Crimi-nals? Child pornographers? Governments? The adversaries are the same as they are in the physical world: common criminals looking for financial gain, industrial spies looking for a competitive advantage, hackers looking for secret knowledge, military-intelligence agencies look-ing for, well, military intelligence. People haven't changed; it's just that cyberspace is a new place to ply their trades.

We can categorize adversaries in several ways: objectives, access, re-sources, expertise, and risk.

Adversaries have varying objectives: raw damage, financial gain, information, and so on. This is important. The objectives of an industrial spy are different from the objectives of an organized-crime syndicate, and the countermeasures that stop the former might not even faze the latter. Understanding the objectives of likely attackers is the first step toward figuring out what countermeasures are going to be effective.

Adversaries have different levels of access; for example, an insider has much more access than someone outside the organization. Adversaries also have access to different levels of resources: some are well funded; others operate on a shoestring. Some have considerable technical expertise; others have none.

Different adversaries are willing to tolerate different levels of risk. Terrorists are often happy to die for their cause. Criminals are willing to risk jail time, but probably don't want to sacrifice themselves to the higher calling of bank robbery. Publicity seekers don't want to go to jail.

A wealthy adversary is the most flexible, since he can trade his resources for other things. He can gain access by paying off an insider, and expertise by buying technology or hiring experts (maybe telling them the truth, maybe hiring them under false pretenses). He can also trade money for risk by executing a more sophisticated—and therefore more expensive—attack.

The rational adversary—not all adversaries are sane, but most are rational within their frames of reference—will choose an attack that gives him a good return on investment, considering his budget constraints: expertise, access, manpower, time, and risk. Some attacks require a lot of access but not much expertise: a car bomb, for example. Some attacks require a lot of expertise but no access: breaking an encryption algorithm, for example. Each adversary is going to have a set of attacks that is affordable to him, and a set of attacks that isn't. If the adversary is paying attention, he will choose the attack that minimizes his cost and maximizes his benefits.

HACKERS

The word *hacker* has several definitions, ranging from a corporate system administrator adept enough to figure out how computers really work to an ethically inept teenage criminal who cackles like Beavis and Butthead as he trashes your network. The word has been co-opted by the media and stripped of its meaning. It used to be a compliment; then it became an insult. Lately, people seem to like "cracker" for the bad guys, and "hacker" for the good guys. I define a hacker as an individual who exper-iments with the limitations of systems for intellectual curiosity or sheer pleasure; the word describes a person with a particular set of skills and not a particular set of morals. There are good hackers and bad hackers, just as there are good plumbers and bad plumbers. (There are also good bad hackers, and bad good hackers . . . but never mind that.)

Hackers are as old as curiosity, although the term itself is modern. Galileo was a hacker. Mme. Curie was one, too. Aristotle wasn't. (Aristo-tle had some theoretical proof that women had fewer teeth than men. A hacker would have simply counted his wife's teeth. A *good* hacker would have counted his wife's teeth without her knowing about it, while she was asleep. A good *bad* hacker might remove some of them, just to prove a point.)

When I was in college, I knew a group similar to hackers: the key freaks. They wanted access, and their goal was to have a key to every lock on campus. They would study lockpicking and learn new techniques, trade maps of the steam tunnels and where they led, and exchange copies of keys with each other. A locked door was a challenge, a personal affront to their ability. These people weren't out to do damage—stealing stuff wasn't their objective—although they certainly could have. Their hobby was the power to go anywhere they wanted to.

Remember the phone phreaks of yesteryear, the ones who could whistle into payphones and make free phone calls. Sure, they stole phone service. But it wasn't like they needed to make eight-hour calls to Manila or McMurdo. And their real work was secret knowledge: The phone network was a vast maze of information. They wanted to know the system better than the designers, and they wanted the ability to modify it to their will. Understanding how the phone system worked—that was the true prize. Other early hackers were ham-radio hobbyists and model-train enthusiasts.

Richard Feynman was a hacker; read any of his books.

Computer hackers follow these evolutionary lines. Or, they are the same genus operating on a new system. Computers, and networks in particular, are the new landscape to be explored. Networks provide the ultimate maze of steam tunnels, where a new hacking technique becomes a key that can open computer after computer. And inside is knowledge, understanding. Access. How things work. Why things work. It's all out there, waiting to be discovered.

Today's computer hackers are stereotypically young (twenty-some-thing and younger), male, and socially on the fringe. They have their own counterculture: hacker names or handles, lingo, rules. And like any sub-culture, only a small percentage of hackers are actually smart. The real hackers have an understanding of technology at a basic level, and are driven by a desire to understand. The rest are talentless poseurs and hang-ers-on, either completely inept or basic criminals. Sometimes they're called *lamers* or *script kiddies*.

Hackers can have considerable expertise, often greater than that of the system's original designers. I've heard lots of security lectures, and the most savvy speakers are the hackers. For them, it's a passion. Hackers look at a system from the outside as an attacker, not from the inside as a designer. They look at the system as an organism, as a coherent whole. And they often understand the attacks better than the people who designed the systems. The real hackers, that is.

Hackers generally have a lot of time, but few financial resources. (Put one of them to work at a big company, and that will change.) Some of them are risk averse and tread gingerly around the edges of the law, but others have no fear of prosecution and engage in illegal activities with no consideration of the risk involved.

There are hacker newsgroups, hacker Web sites and hacker conven-tions. Hackers often trade attacks and automated attacking tools among themselves. There are different hacker groups (or gangs, if you are less kind), but there is no hierarchy. You can't galvanize the hacker commu-nity against a particular target; hackers go after what they can. Often they'll hack something because it's widely deployed, interesting, or because the target "deserves" it.

Unfortunately, much of what hackers do is illegal. I'm not talking about the few who work in research environments, who evaluate the security of systems in laboratory settings, and who publish analyses of products and systems. I'm talking about the hackers who break into other people's networks, deface Web pages, crash computers, spread viruses, and write automatic programs that let other people do these things. These people are criminals, and society needs to treat them as such.

I don't buy the defense that a hacker just broke in a system to look around, and didn't do any damage. Some systems are frangible, and sim-ply looking around can inadvertently cause damage. And once an unau-thorized person has been inside a system, you can't trust its integrity. You don't know that the intruder didn't touch anything.

Imagine that you come home to find a note on your refrigerator door saying: "Hi. I noticed that you had a lousy front door lock, so I broke in. I didn't touch anything. You really should get a better security system." How would you feel?

The problem starts with the hackers who write hacking tools. These are programs—sometimes called *exploits*—that automate the process of breaking into systems. An example is the Trin00 distributed denial-of-ser-vice tool. Thousands of servers have been brought down because of this attack, and it's caused legitimate companies millions of dollars in time and effort to recover from. It's one thing to research the vulnerability of the

Internet against this type of attack, and to write a research paper about defending against it. It's another thing entirely to write a program that automates the attack.

The Trin00 exploit serves no conceivable purpose other than to attack systems. Gun owners can argue self-defense, but Internet servers don't break into anyone's house at night. It's actually much worse, because once an exploit is written and made available, any wannabe hacker can download it and attack computers on the Internet. He doesn't even have to know how it works. (See why they're called "script kiddies"?) Trin00 attacks were popular in early 2000 because the exploit was available. If it weren't—even if a research paper were available—none of the script kiddies would be able to exploit the vulnerability.

Certainly the lamers that use Trin00 to attack systems are criminals. I believe the person who wrote the exploit is, too. A fine line exists between writing code to demonstrate research and publishing attack tools; between hacking for good and hacking as a criminal activity. I will get back to this in Chapter 22.

Most organizations are wary about hiring hackers, and rightfully so. There are exceptions—the NSA offering scholarships to hackers willing to work at Fort Meade, Israeli intelligence hiring Jewish hackers from the United States, Washington offering security fellowships—and some hack-ers have gone on to form upstanding and professional security companies. Recently, a handful of consulting companies have sprung up to whitewash hackers and present them in a more respectable light. And sometimes this works, but for many people it can be hard to tell the ethical hackers from the criminals.

LONE CRIMINALS

In April 1993, a small group of criminals wheeled a Fujitsu model 7020 automated teller machine into the Buckland Hills Mall in Hartford, Connecticut, and turned it on. The machine was specially programmed to accept ATM cards from customers, record their account numbers and PINs, and then tell the unfortunate consumers that no transactions were possible. A few days later, the gang encoded the stolen account numbers and PINs onto counterfeit ATM cards, and started withdrawing cash from ATMs in midtown Manhattan. They were eventually caught when the bank correlated the use of the counterfeit ATM cards with routine surveillance films.

It was a shrewd attack, and much higher tech than most banking crimes. One innovative criminal in New Jersey attached a fake night deposit box to a bank wall, and took it away early in the morning. It's worse elsewhere. A few years ago, an ATM was stolen in South Africa . . . from inside police headquarters in broad daylight.

Lone criminals cause the bulk of computer-related crimes. Sometimes they are insiders who notice a flaw in a system and decide to exploit it; other times they work outside the system. They usually don't have much money, access, or expertise, and they often get caught because of stupid mistakes. Someone might be smart enough to install a fake ATM and col-lect account numbers and PINs, but if he brags about his cleverness in a bar and gets himself arrested before cleaning out all the accounts . . . well, it's hard to have any sympathy for him. Look at the two public Internet attacks of early 2000. Someone manages to gain access to over ten thousand credit card numbers, with names and addresses. The best crime he can think of to do: extortion. Someone else manages to control a large number of distributed computers, ready to do his bidding. The best crime he can think of: irritate major Web sites.

Lone criminals will target commerce systems because that's where the money is. Their techniques may lack elegance, but they will steal money, and they will cost even more money to catch and prosecute. And there will be a lot of them.

MALICIOUS INSIDERS

A malicious insider is a dangerous and insidious adversary. He's already inside the system he wants to attack, so he can ignore any perimeter defenses around the system. He probably has a high level of access, and could be considered trusted by the system he is attacking. Remember the Russian spy Aldrich Ames? He was in a perfect position within the CIA to sell the names of U.S. operatives living in Eastern Europe to the KGB; he was trusted with their names. Think about a programmer writing malicious code into the payroll database program to give himself a raise every six months. Or the bank vault guard purposely missetting the time lock to give his burglar friends easy access. Insiders can be impossible to

stop because they're the exact same people you're forced to trust. Here's
a canonical insider attack. In 1978, Stanley Mark Rifkin was a
consultant at a major bank. He used his insider knowledge of (and access
to) the money transfer system to move several million dollars into a
Swiss account, and then to convert that money into diamonds. He also
pro-grammed the computer system to automatically erase the backup
tapes that contained evidence of his crime. (He would have gotten away
with it, except that he bragged to his lawyer, who turned him in.)

Insiders don't always attack a system; sometimes they subvert a
system for their own ends. In 1991, employees at Charles Schwab in
San Fran-cisco used the company's e-mail system to buy and sell
cocaine. A con-victed child rapist working in a Boston-area hospital
stole a co-worker's password, paged through confidential patient
records, and made obscene phone calls.

Insiders are not necessarily employees. They can be consultants and
contractors. During the Y2K scare, many companies hired programmers
from China and India to update old software. Rampant xenophobia aside,
any of those programmers could have attacked the systems as an insider.

Most computer security measures—firewalls, intrusion detection systems, and so on—try to deal with the external attacker, but are pretty
much powerless against insiders. Insiders might be less likely to attack a
system than outsiders are, but systems are far more vulnerable to them.

An insider knows how the systems work and where the weak
points are. He knows the organizational structure, and how any
investigation against his actions would be conducted. He may already
be trusted by the system he is going to attack. An insider can use the
system's own resources against itself. In extreme cases the insider
might have considerable exper-tise, especially if he was involved in
the design of the systems he is now attacking.

Revenge, financial gain, institutional change, or even publicity can
motivate insiders. They generally also fit into another of the categories: a
hacker, a lone criminal, or a national intelligence agent. Malicious insiders can have a risk tolerance ranging from low to high, depending on
whether they are motivated by a "higher purpose" or simple greed.

Of course, insider attacks aren't new, and the problem is bigger than
cyberspace. If the e-mail system hadn't been there, the Schwab employ-

ees might have used the telephone system, or fax machines, or maybe even paper mail.

INDUSTRIAL ESPIONAGE

Business is war. Well, it's kind of like war, but it has referees. The refer-ees establish the rules—what is legal and what isn't—and do their best to enforce them. Sometimes, if a business has enough money and clout, it can petition to the referees and get the rules changed. Usually, it just plays within them.

The line where investigative techniques stop being legal and start being illegal is where competitive intelligence stops and industrial espi-onage starts. The line moves from jurisdiction to jurisdiction, but there are gross generalities. Breaking into a competitor's office and stealing files is always illegal (even for Richard Nixon); looking them up in a news article database is always legal. Bribing their senior engineers is illegal; hir-ing them is legal. Hiring them and having them bring a copy of the com-petitor's source code is illegal. Pretending to want to hire their senior engineers so that you can interview them . . . that's legal, pretty sleazy, and really clever.

Industrial espionage attacks have precise motivations: to gain an advantage over the competition by stealing competitors' trade secrets. In one public example, Borland accused Symantec of stealing trade secrets via a departing executive. In another case, Cadence Design Systems filed suit against competitor Avant! for, among other things, stealing source code. In 1999, online bookseller Alibris pled guilty to eavesdropping on Amazon.com corporate e-mail. Companies from China, France, Russia, Israel, the United States, and elsewhere have stolen technology secrets from foreign competitors.

Industrial espionage can be well-funded; an amoral but rational com-pany will devote enough resources toward industrial espionage to achieve an acceptable return on investment. Even if stealing a rival's technology costs you half a million dollars, it could be one-tenth the cost of develop-ing the technology yourself. (Ever wonder why the Russian Space Shuttle looks a whole lot like the U.S. Space Shuttle?) This kind of adversary has a medium risk tolerance because a company's reputation (an intangible but valuable item) will be damaged considerably if it is caught spying on the competition—but desperate times can bring desperate mea-sures.

PRESS

Think of the press as a subspecies of industrial spy, but with different motivations. The press isn't interested in a competitive advantage over its targets; it is interested in a "newsworthy" story. This would be the Wash-ington *City Pages* publishing the video rental records of Judge Bork (which led to the Video Privacy Protection Act of 1988), the British tabloids publishing private phone conversations between Prince Charles and Camilla Parker Bowles, or a newspaper doing an exposé on this company or that government agency.

It can be worth a lot of newspaper sales to get pictures of a presiden-tial candidate like Gary Hart with a not-his-wife on his lap. Even margin-ally compromising photographs of Princess Di were worth over half a million dollars. Some reporters have said that they would not think twice about publishing national security secrets; they believe the public's right to know comes first.

In many countries, the free press is viewed as a criminal. In such countries, the press is usually not well funded, and generally more the victim of attack than the attacker. Journalists have gone to jail, been tortured, and have even been killed for daring to speak against the ruling government. This is not what I mean by the press as an attacker.

In industrial countries with reasonable freedoms, the press can bring considerable resources to bear on attacking a particular system or target. They can be well funded; they can hire experts and gain access. And if they believe their motivations are true, they can tolerate risk. (Certainly the reporters who broke the Watergate story fall into this category.) Reporters in the United States and other countries have gone to jail to protect what they believe is right. Some have even died for it.

ORGANIZED CRIME

Organized crime is a lot more than Italian Mafia families and Francis Ford Coppola movies. It's a global business. Russian crime syndicates operate both in Russia and in the United States. Asian crime syndicates operate both at home and abroad. Colombian drug cartels are also international. Nigerian and other West African syndicates have captured 70 percent of the Chicago heroin market. Polish gangsters run an elaborate car theft operation, stealing cars in the United States and shipping them back to Poland. Of course, there are turf battles between rival gangs, but there is a lot of international cooperation, too.

Organized crime's core competencies haven't changed much this century: drugs, prostitution, loan sharking, extortion, fraud, and gambling. And they use technology in two ways. First, it's a new venue for crime. They use hacking tools to break into bank computers and steal money; they steal cell phone IDs and resell them; they engage in com-puter fraud. Identity theft is a growth area; Chinese gangs are industry leaders here. Certainly electronic theft is more profitable: One big Chicago bank lost $60,000 in 1996 to bank robbers, and $60 million to check-related fraud.

The mob also uses computers to assist its core businesses. Illegal gam-bling is easier to run: Cell phones allow bookies to operate from any-where, and hair-trigger computers can erase all evidence within seconds of a raid. And money laundering is increasingly a business of computers and electronic funds transfers: moving money from one account to another to a third, changing ownership of accounts, disguising the money's origins, moving it through countries that keep less detailed records.

In terms of risk, organized crime is what you get when you combine lone criminals with a lot of money and organization. These guys know that you have to spend money to make money, and are willing to invest in profitable attacks against a financial system. They have minimal exper-tise, but can purchase it. They have minimal access, but they can purchase it. They often have a higher risk tolerance than lone criminals; the peck-ing order of the crime syndicate often forces those in the lower ranks to take greater risks, and the protection afforded by the syndicate makes the risks more tolerable.

POLICE

You can think of the police as kind of like a national intelligence organi-zation, except that they are less well funded, less technically savvy, and focused on crimefighting. Understand, though, that depending on how benevolent the country is and whether or not they hold occasional democratic elections, "crimefighting" could cover a whole lot of things not normally associated with law enforcement. Maybe they're more like the press, but with better funding and a readership that only cares about true crime stories. Or maybe you can think of them as organized crime's industrial competitor.

In any case, police have a reasonable amount of funding and exper-tise. They're pretty risk averse—no cop wants to die for his beliefs—but since they have the laws on their side, things that are risks to some groups can be less risky to the police. (Having a warrant issued, for example, turns eavesdropping from a risky attack to a valid evidence-gathering tool.) Their primary goal is information gathering, with information that stands up in court being more useful than information that doesn't.

But police aren't above breaking the law. The fundamental assump-tion is that we trust the individual or some government to respect our privacy and to only use their powers wisely. While this is true most of the time, abuses are regular and can be pretty devastating. A spate of illegal FBI wiretaps in Florida and a subsequent cover-up got some press in 1992; the 150 or so illegal wiretaps by the Los Angeles Police Department have gotten more. (Drugs were involved, of course; more than one per-son has pointed out that the war on drugs seems to be the root password to the U.S. Constitution.) J. Edgar Hoover regularly used illegal wiretaps to keep tabs on his enemies. And 25 years ago a sitting president used illegal wiretaps in an attempt to stay in power.

Things seem to have improved since the days of Hoover and Nixon, and I have many reasons to hope we won't be back there again. But the risk remains. Technology moves slowly, but intentions change quickly. Even if we are sure today that the police will follow all privacy legislation, eavesdrop only when necessary, obtain all necessary warrants, follow proper minimization procedures, and generally behave like upstanding public servants, we don't know about tomorrow. The same kind of reac-tive crisis thinking that led us to persecute suspected Communists during the McCarthy era could again sweep across the country. Census data is, by law, not supposed to be used for any other purpose. Even so, it was used during World War II to round up Japanese Americans and put them in concentration camps. The eerily named "Mississippi Sovereignty Commission" spied on thousands of civil rights activists in the 1960s. The

FBI used illegal wiretaps to spy on Martin Luther King, Jr. A national public-key infrastructure could be a precursor to national registration of cryptography. Once the technology is in place, there will always be the temptation to use it. And it is poor civic hygiene to install technologies that could someday facilitate a police state.

TERRORISTS

This category is a catchall for a broad range of ideological groups and indi-viduals, both domestic and international. There's no attempt to make moral judgments here: One person's terrorist is another person's freedom fighter. Terrorist groups are usually motivated by geopolitics or (even worse) ethnoreligion—Hezbollah, Red Brigade, Shining Path, Tamil Tigers, IRA, ETA, FLNC, PKK, UCK—but can also be motivated by moral and ethical beliefs, such as those of Earth First and radical antiabortion groups.

These groups are generally more concerned with causing harm than gathering information, so their techniques run more along the lines of denial of service and outright destruction. While their long-term goals are usually something vaguely reasonable, like the reunification of Gond-wanaland or the return of all cows to the wild, their near-term goals are things like revenge, chaos, and blood-soaked publicity. Bombings are a favorite; kidnappings also work well. It makes a big international splash when a DC-10 falls out of the sky or an abortion clinic is blown to bits, but eventually these guys will figure out that a lot more damage is done when O'Hare air traffic control starts vectoring planes into each other. Or that if they can hack the airline reservation system to find out which 747 is taking the congressional delegation to the south of France this summer, their bombing will be all that much more effective.

There are actually very few terrorists. Their attacks are acts of war more than anything else, and probably should be in the "infowarrior" cat-egory. And since terrorists generally consider themselves to be personally in a state of war, they have a very high risk-tolerance.

Unless they have a rich idealist funding their actions, most terrorists operate on a shoestring budget. Most of them are unskilled: "You there. Carry this bag. Walk into the middle of that busy market. Push this but-ton. See you in the glorious afterlife." There are exceptions (some of the organizations in the first paragraph are well-organized, well-trained, and well-supported—it is believed that the counterfeit TV descramblers sold in Ireland helped finance the IRA, for example), but the majority of groups don't have good organization or access. And they tend to make stupid mistakes.

NATIONAL INTELLIGENCE ORGANIZATIONS

These are the big boys. The CIA, NSA, DIA, and NRO in the United States (there are others), the KGB (now FAPSI for counter-intelligence and FSB for foreign intelligence) and GRU (military intelligence) in Rus-sia, MI5 (counter-intelligence), MI6 (like the CIA), and GCHQ (like the NSA) in the United Kingdom, DGSE in France, BND in Germany, Ministry of National Security in China (also called the "Technical Department"), Mossad in Israel, CSE in Canada. For most of the other adversaries, this is all a game: break into a Web site, gain some competitive intelligence, steal some money, cause a little mayhem, whatever. For these guys, it's very real.

A major national intelligence organization is the most formidable adversary around. It is extremely well funded, since it is usually considered a branch of the military. (Although the exact number is a secret, the press reports that "congressional sources" put the combined budgets of the CIA, Defense Intelligence Agency, NSA, the National Reconnaissance Office, and other federal intelligence agencies as $33.5 billion in 1997.) It is a dedicated and capable adversary, with the funding to buy a whole lot of research, equipment, expertise, and plain old skilled manpower.

On the other hand, a major national intelligence organization is usually highly risk averse. National intelligence organizations don't like to see their names on the front page of the *New York Times*, and generally don't engage in risky activities. (Exceptions, of course, exist; they're the ones you read about on the front page of the *New York Times*.) Exposed oper-ations cause several problems. One, they expose the data. National intel-ligence is based on gathering information that the country should not know. It's eavesdropping on a negotiating position, sneaking a peek at a new weapons system, knowing more than the adversary does. If the adversary learns what the intelligence organization knows, some of the benefit of that knowledge is lost.

Two, and probably more important, botched operations expose techniques, capabilities, and sources. For many years the NSA eavesdropped on Soviet car phones as the Politburo drove around Moscow. Someone leaked information about Khrushchev's health in the newspapers, and suddenly the car phones were encrypted. The newspapers didn't say anything about car phones, but the KGB wasn't stupid. The leak here wasn't that we knew about Khrushchev's health, but that we were listening to their communications. The same thing happened after some terrorists bombed a Berlin disco in 1986. Reagan announced that we had proof of Libya's involvement, compromising the fact that we were able to eavesdrop on their embassy traffic to and from Tripoli. During World War II, the Allies couldn't use much of the intelligence gleaned from decrypting German Enigma traffic out of fear that the Germans would change their codes.

Intelligence objectives include everything you'd normally think about—military information, weapons designs, diplomatic information— and a lot of things you wouldn't. The telephone system is probably a gold mine of intelligence information; so is the Internet. Several national intel-ligence organizations are actively engaged in industrial espionage (the FBI estimates "up to 20" are targeting U.S. companies) and passing the infor-mation gained to rival companies in their own countries. China is the world's worst offender, France and Japan are also bad, and there are others.

The United States is not above this. A 1999 EU report gives several examples, including the following:

- In 1994, the Brazilian government awarded a $1.4 billion contract to Raytheon Corporation, rather than two French companies. Raytheon supposedly altered its bid when it learned of details of the French proposals.
- In 1994, McDonnell Douglas Corporation won a Saudi Arabia contract over Airbus Industrie, supposedly based on inside information passed from U.S. intelligence.

Former CIA director R. James Woosley has admitted using ECHELON information about foreign companies using bribes to win foreign contracts to help "level the playing field," passing the information to U.S. companies and pressuring the foreign governments to stop the bribes. None of this is proven, though. Certainly any company that loses a bid is going to look for reasons why it wasn't its fault, and none of the "victims" have said anything in public. Still, the possibilities are disturbing.

And this kind of stuff is even worse in cyberspace. ECHELON is not the only program that targets the Internet. Singapore and China eavesdrop on Internet traffic in their countries (China uses its national firewall, the Great Wall). Internet service providers across Russia are helping the main KGB successor agencies to read private e-mails and other Internet traffic, as part of an internal espionage program called SORM-2.

National intelligence organizations are not above using hacker tools, or even hackers, to do their work. The Israeli and Japanese governments both have programs to bring hackers into their country, feed them pizza and Jolt Cola, and have them do intelligence work. Other governments go onto the Net and taunt hackers, trying to get them to work for free. "If you're so good you'll have the password to this government com-puter"—that sort of thing works well if directed against a talented teenager with no self-esteem. *The Cuckoo's Egg* by Clifford Stoll is about the exploits of three hackers who worked for the KGB in exchange for cash and cocaine.

The techniques of national security agencies are varied and, with the full weight of a nation behind them, can be very effective. British communications security companies have been long rumored to build exploitable features into their encryption products, at the request of British intelligence. In 1997, CIA director George Tenet mentioned (in passing, without details) using hacker tools and techniques to disrupt international money transfers and other financial activities of Arab businessmen who support terrorists. The possibilities are endless.

INFOWARRIORS

Yes, it's a buzzword. But it's also real. An infowarrior is a military adversary who tries to undermine his target's ability to wage war by attacking the information or network infrastructure. Specific attacks range from subtly modifying systems so that they don't work (or don't work correctly) to blowing up the systems completely. The attacks could be covert, in which case they might resemble terrorist attacks (although a good infowarrior cares less about publicity than results). If executed via the Internet, the attacks could originate from foreign soil, making detec-tion and retaliation much more difficult.

This adversary has all the resources of a national intelligence organi-zation, but differs in two important areas. One, he focuses almost exclu-sively on the short-term goal of affecting his target's ability to wage war. And two, he is willing to tolerate risks that would be intolerable to long-term intelligence interests. His objectives are military advantage and, more generally, chaos. Some of the particular targets that might interest an infowarrior include military command and control facilities, telecommunications, logistics and supply facilities and infrastructure (think "commercial information systems"), and transportation lines (think "commercial aviation"). These kinds of targets are called *critical infrastruc-ture*.

In 1999, NATO targeted Belgrade's electric plants; this had profound effects on its computing resources. In retaliation, Serbian hackers attacked hundreds of U.S. and NATO computer sites. Chinese hackers crashed computers in the Department of the Interior, the Department of Energy, and the U.S. embassy in Beijing in retaliation for our accidental bombing of their embassy in Belgrade. China and Taiwan engaged in a little cyber-war through most of 1999, attacking each other's computers over the Internet (although this was probably not government coordinated on either side).

In the past, military and civilian systems were separate and distinct: different hardware, different communications protocols, different every-thing. Over the past decade, this has shifted; advances in technology are coming too fast for the military's traditional multiyear procurement cycle. More and more, commercial computer systems are being used for military applications. This means that all of the vulnerabilities and attacks that work against commercial computers may work against militaries. And both sides of a conflict may be using the same equipment and protocols: TCP/IP, Windows operating systems, GPS satellite receivers. The U.S. Air Force's Strategic Air Command (SAC) recently switched to Windows NT on its external networks.

Militaries have waged war on infrastructure ever since they started waging war. Medieval knights killed serfs, Napoleonic armies burned crops, Allied bombers targeted German factories during World War II. (Ball bearing factories were a favorite.) Today, information is infra-structure. During Desert Storm, the Americans systematically destroyed

Iraq's command and control infrastructure. Communications systems were jammed; individual communications cables were bombing targets. Without command and control, the ground troops were all but useless. The media hype surrounding infowar is embarrassing, but the militaries of the world are taking this seriously. Here is a quote from the Chinese Army newspaper, *Jiefangjun Bao,* a summary of speeches delivered in May 1996:

> After the Gulf War, when everyone was looking forward to eternal peace, a new military revolution emerged. This revolution is essentially a transformation from the mechanized warfare of the industrial age to the information warfare of the information age. Information warfare is a war of decisions and control, a war of knowledge, and a war of intellect. The aim of information warfare will be gradually changed from "preserving oneself and wiping out the enemy" to "preserving oneself and controlling the opponent." Information warfare includes electronic warfare, tactical deception, strategic deterrence, propaganda warfare, psychological warfare, network warfare, and structural sabotage. Under today's technological conditions, the "all conquering stratagems" of Sun Tzu more than two millennia ago—"vanquishing the enemy without fighting" and subduing the enemy by "soft strike" or "soft destruc-tion"—could finally be truly realized.

War isn't necessarily a major conflict like World War II or the oft-feared United States versus USSR, Armageddon. More likely, it is a "low-intensity conflict": Desert Storm, the Argentine invasion of the Falklands, civil war in Rwanda. In *The Transformation of War*, Martin van Creveld points out that so-called low-intensity conflicts have been the dominant form of warfare since World War II, killing over 20 million people worldwide. This shift is a result of two main trends. One, it is easier for smaller groups to lay their hands on weapons of mass destruction: chemical weapons, biological weapons, long-range missiles, and so forth. Two, more nonnation states are capable of waging war. In fact, the distinction between nation and nonnation states is blurring. Organized crime groups are merging with government at various levels in countries such as Mexico, Colombia, and Russia. Infowarriors don't all work for major industrial nations. Increasingly, they work for minor political powers.

5

Security Needs

W hat kinds of security do we need, anyway? Before examin-ing (and often dismissing) specific countermeasures against the threats we've already talked about, let's stop and talk about needs. In today's computerized, international, interconnected, interdependent world, what kind of security should we expect?

PRIVACY

People have a complicated relationship with privacy. When asked to pay for it, they often don't want to. Businesses also have a complicated relationship with privacy. They want it—they know the importance of not having their dirty laundry spread all over the newspapers—and are even willing to pay for it: with locks, alarms, firewalls, and corporate security policies. But when push comes to shove and work needs to get done, security is the first thing that gets thrown out the window. Governments are comfortable with privacy: They know the importance of not having their military secrets in the hands of their enemies. They know they need it, and know that they are going to have to pay dearly for it. And they accept the burden that privacy puts on them. Governments often get the details wrong, but they grok the general idea.

Almost no one realizes exactly how important privacy is in his or her life. The Supreme Court has insinuated that it is a right guaranteed by the Constitution. Democracy is built upon the notion of privacy; you can't

59

have a secret ballot without it. Businesses can't function without some notion of privacy; multiple individuals within a company need to know proprietary information that people outside the company don't. People want to be secure in their conversations, their papers, and their homes.

In the United States, individuals don't own the data about themselves. Customer lists belong to the businesses that collect them. Personal data-bases belong to the database owner. Only in rare instances do individuals have any rights or protections about the data that are collected about them.

Most countries have laws protecting individual privacy. The EU, for example, has the Data Protection Act of 1998. Organizations that collect personal data must register with the government, and take precautions against misuse of that data. They are also prohibited from the collection, use, and dissemination of personal information without the consent of the person. Organizations also have the duty to tell individuals about the reason for the information collection, to provide access and correct inaccurate information, and to keep that information secure from access by unauthorized parties. Individuals have a right to see their own personal data that has been collected and have inaccuracies corrected. Individuals also have the right to know what their data is being collected for, and to be sure that their data isn't being sold for other purposes. They also have the right to "opt out" of any data collection that doesn't appeal to them. Data collectors have the responsibility to protect individual data to a reasonably high degree, and to not share the data with anyone who does not adhere to these rules.

That last clause has caused a contretemps between the EU and the United States, since the United States does not enforce any controls on personal data and allows companies to buy and sell it at will. At this writing, the United States and the EU have tentatively agreed on safe-harbor provisions for American companies that meet "adequate" levels of privacy by July 2001. Some members of Congress have tried several times to pass pro-privacy legislation (although nothing as encompassing as what the EU does), but have been blocked through industry pressure. The lobbying group NetCoalition.com, which includes AOL, Amazon.com, Yahoo!, eBay, and DoubleClick, believes in self-regulation, which is the equiva-lent of no privacy protection. Unfortunately, much of the industry feels that privacy is bad for business; invading personal privacy is sometimes the only way some companies see to make money.

On to business privacy. Businesses don't generally need long-term privacy. (Trade secrets—the formula for Coke, for example—are the exceptions.) Customer databases might need to remain confidential for a few years. Product development data, only a few years—and for computer-related businesses, a lot less than that. Information about general financial health, business negotiations, and tactical maneuvers: weeks to months. Marketing and product plans, strategies, long-range negotia-tions: months to years. Detailed financial information might need to be secure for a few years, but probably not more. Even corporate five-year plans are obsolete after nine months. We live in a world where informa-tion diffuses rapidly. Last week's business secrets have been supplanted by this week's new business secrets. And this week's business secrets are next week's *Wall Street Journal* headlines.

Governments need short-term privacy as well. Often the interests of one country run counter to the interests of another country, and govern-ments need to keep certain pieces of information secret from that other country. Unfortunately, countries are a lot bigger than companies. It's impossible to tell everyone in the United States a secret without it leaking to the government of China. Therefore, if the United States wants to keep a secret from the Chinese, it has to keep it a secret from almost all Americans as well.

These secrets are usually military in nature: strategy and tactics, weapons capabilities, designs and procurements, troop strengths and movements, research and development. Military secrets often broaden into state secrets: negotiating positions on treaties and the like. And they often overlap into corporate secrets: military contracts, bargaining posi-tions, import and export dealings, and so forth.

The exceptions to this short-term privacy need are embarrassments: personal, political, or business. Union Carbide would have been happier if information about Bhopal stayed secret for longer than it did. Govern-ments don't want their political embarrassments leaking into the press. (Think Watergate. Think Iran-Contra. Think almost any political scandal uncovered by the media.) People don't want their personal pasts made public. (Think Bill Clinton. Think Bob Livingston, the Congressman and Speaker of the House nominee who resigned in 1999, after a 20-year-old affair was made public. Think Arthur Ashe, whose AIDS condition was discovered by the press.) In about two decades, we're going to have elections where candidates are going to have to try to explain e-mail that they wrote when they were adolescents.

The few instances of very long privacy requirements I know of are government related. U.S. census data—the raw data, not the compilations—must remain secret for 72 years. The CIA mandates that the identities of spies remain secret until the spy is dead and all the spy's children are dead. Canadian census data remains secret forever.

MULTILEVEL SECURITY

Militaries have a lot of information that needs to be kept secret, but some pieces of information are more secret than others. The locations of Navy ships might be of moderate interest to the enemy, but the launch codes for the missiles on those ships are much more important. The number of bedrolls in the supply chain is of marginal interest; the number of rifles is of greater interest.

To deal with this kind of thing, militaries have invented multiple levels of security classifications. In the U.S. military, data is either Unclassified, Confidential, Secret, or Top Secret. Rules govern what kind of data falls into what classification, and different classifications have different rules for storage, dissemination, and so forth. For example, different strength safes are required for different classifications of data. Top Secret data might only be stored in certain guarded, windowless, rooms without photocopiers, and might need to be signed out.

People working with this data need security clearances commensurate with the highest classification of information they are working with. Someone with a Secret clearance, for example, can see information that is Unclassified, Confidential, and Secret. Someone with a Confidential clearance can only see Unclassified and Confidential data. (Of course, clearance is not a guarantee of trustworthiness. The CIA's head Russian counterintelligence officer, Aldrich Ames, had a Top Secret security clearance; he also was a Russian spy.)

Data at the Top Secret level or above is sometimes divided by topic, or compartment. The designation "TS/SCI," for "Top Secret/Special Compartmented Intelligence," indicates these documents. Each compartment has a codeword. TALENT and KEYHOLE, for example, are the keywords associated with the KH-11 spy satellites. SILVER, RUFF, TEAPOT, UMBRA, and ZARF are others. (UMBRA applies to communications intelligence, and RUFF applies to imagery intelligence.)

Compartments are topical access barriers; someone who has a Top Secret clearance with an additional KEYHOLE clearance (sometimes called a "ticket") is not authorized to see Top Secret COBRA data.

These compartments are a formal codification of the notion of "need to know." Just because someone has a certain level of clearance doesn't mean he automatically gets to see every piece of data at that clearance level. He only gets to see the data that he needs to know to do his job. And there are other designations that modify classifications: NOFORN is "No Foreign Nationals," WNINTEL is "Warning Notice, Intelligence Sources and Methods," LIMDIS is "Limited Dissemination."

Other countries have similar rules. The United Kingdom has one additional classification level, Restricted, which falls between Unclassified and Confidential. The United States has something similar called FOUO—For Official Use Only—which means "Unclassified, but don't tell anyone anyway."

Two points are salient here. One, this kind of thing is much easier to implement on paper than on computer. Chapter 8 talks about some of the multilevel security systems that have been built and used, but none of them have ever worked on a large scale. And two, this kind of thing is largely irrelevant outside a military setting. Corporate secrets just don't work this way; neither do individuals' secrets. Security in the real world doesn't fit into little hierarchical boxes.

ANONYMITY

Do we need anonymity? Is it a good thing? The whole concept of anonymity on the Internet has been hotly debated, with people weighing in on both sides of the issue.

Anyone who works on the receiving end of a crisis telephone line— suicide, rape, whatever—knows the power of anonymity. Thousands of people on the Internet discuss their personal lives in newsgroups for abuse survivors, AIDS sufferers, and so on, that are only willing to do so through anonymous remailers. This is social anonymity, and it is vital for the health of the world, because it allows people to talk about things they are unwilling to sign their name to. For example, some people posting to alt.religion.scientology do so anonymously, and would not do so otherwise.

Political anonymity is important, too. There is not, and should not be, any requirement that all political speech be signed. Just as someone can do a mass political mailing with no return address, they can do the same over the Internet. This matters more in certain parts of the world: In 1999, online anonymity allowed Kosovars, Serbs, and others caught up in the Balkan war to send news about the conflict to the rest of the world without taking the life-threatening risk of revealing their identities.

On the other hand, people are using the anonymity of the Internet to send threatening e-mail, publish hate speech and other obloquies, disperse computer viruses and worms, and otherwise roil the good citizens of cyberspace.

There are two different types of anonymity. The first is complete anonymity: a letter without a return address, a message in a bottle, a phone call in a world without Caller ID or phone tracing. The person initiating the communication is completely anonymous: No one can figure out who it is, and more importantly, if the person initiates another communication, the recipient doesn't know it came from the same person.

The second type of anonymity is more properly called *pseudonymity.* Think of a Swiss bank account (although the Swiss actually stopped doing this in 1990), a Post Office box rented with cash under an assumed name (although this is no longer possible in the United States without a fake ID), an Alcoholics Anonymous meeting where you're just known as "Bob." It's anonymous in that no one knows who you are, but it is pos-sible to link different communications from the same pseudonym. This is exactly what a Swiss bank needs: It doesn't care who you are, only that you're the same person that deposited the money last week. A merchant doesn't need to know your name, but it does need to know that you legitimately bought the merchandise you are now trying to return.

Both types of anonymity are hard in cyberspace, because so much of the infrastructure is identifying. The new Intel Pentium III–class microprocessors have unique serial numbers that can be tracked, as do Ethernet network cards. Microsoft Office documents automatically con-tain information identifying the author. Cookies track people on the Web; even anonymous e-mail addresses can theoretically be linked back to the real person by tracking IP addresses. And many flaws have been found in the various products that promise anonymous browsing. Superficial anonymity is easy, but true anonymity is probably not possible on today's Internet.

Commercial Anonymity

The notion of pseudonymity brings us nicely to anonymity in financial transactions. What about it? A small group is a vocal proponent of financial anonymity. It's no one's business—not the government's, not the merchants', not the marketers'—what people buy, whether it be X-rated videos or surprise birthday presents. Unfortunately, there is also a large group of nonvocal proponents of financial anonymity: drug dealers and other maleficent elements. Can these two sides reconcile?

Obviously they can, because cash exists. The real question is whether we will ever get an electronic version of cash. I don't believe we will, except for low-value transactions.

Anonymity is more expensive because extra risks are associated with an anonymous system. (Government regulations also affect things.) Banks aren't stupid; they prefer a less risky system. And choosing an anonymous system is more expensive than a system based on accounts and relationships. Banks could build the extra costs into the system, but customers aren't willing to pay for it. If you are a merchant, try this experiment. Put a sign up in your store with the words "5 percent discount if you give us your name and address and let us track your buying habits." See how many customers prefer anonymity. People talk as if they don't want megadatabases tracking their every spending move, but they are willing to get a frequent-flyer affinity card and give all that data away for one thousandth of a free flight to Hawaii. If McDonald's offered three free Big Macs for a DNA sample, there would be lines around the block.

On the other hand, put up a sign saying "5 percent discount if you give us the name and address of your child's daycare center" and you're likely to get a different reaction. There are some things most people want to keep private, and there are people who want to keep most things private. There will always be the Swiss-bank style anonymous payment systems for the rich, who are willing to pay a premium for their privacy. But the average consumer isn't one of those people. Average consumers will have personal exceptions, but in general they don't care about anonymity. Banks have no reason to give it to them, especially while the government is pressuring them not to.

Medical Anonymity

And then there are medical databases. On the one hand, medical data are only useful if shared. Doctors need to know the medical history of their patients, and aggregate medical data is useful for all sorts of research. On the other hand, medical information is about as personal as it gets: genetic predisposition to disease, abortions and reproductive health, emotional health and psychiatric care, drug abuse, sexual behav-iors, sexually transmitted diseases, HIV status, physical abuse. People have a right to keep their medical information private. People have been harassed, threatened, and fired after personal medical information was made public.

And it's not hard to get this information. Nicole Brown Simpson's medical records were leaked to the press within a week after her 1994 murder. In 1995, the *Sunday Times* of London reported that the going price for anyone's medical record in England was £200. And these cases are from wealthy countries; just imagine what kinds of abuses are possible in countries like India or Mexico, where a $10 bill can tempt even the most virtuous civil servant.

Computerized patient data is bad for privacy. But it's good for just about everything else, so it's inevitable. HIPAA (the Health Insurance Portability and Accessibility Act) now has standards for computerized medical records. It makes it easier to provide information when and where it is needed, for a population that is less likely to have a family doc-tor and more likely to move around the country, visiting different doctors and hospitals when necessary. Specialists can easily call up vital data. Insur-ance companies like it because it allows more automation, greater stan-dardization, and cheaper processing: If all the data are electronic, then it will be cheaper to process claims. And researchers like it because it allows them to make better use of the available data: For the first time they can look at everything, in standard form.

This is a big deal, probably as important as the financial and credit databases mentioned previously. We as a society are going to have to balance the need for access (which is much more evident for medical information than financial information) with the need for privacy. Computerization is coming to the medical profession, like it or not. We need to make sure it's done correctly.

PRIVACY AND THE GOVERNMENT

The government, and the FBI in particular, likes to paint privacy (and the systems that achieve it) as a flagitious tool of the Four Horsemen of the Information Apocalypse: terrorists, drug dealers, money launderers, and child pornographers. In 1994, the FBI pushed the Digital Telephony Bill through Congress, which tried to force telephone companies to install equipment in their switches to make it easier to wiretap people. In the aftermath of the World Trade Center bombing, they pushed the Omnibus Counterterrorism Bill, which gave them the power to do rov-ing wiretaps and the President the power to unilaterally and secretly clas-sify political groups as terrorist organizations. Thankfully, it didn't pass. After TWA Flight 800 fell out of the sky in 1996 because of a fuel-tank explosion, the FBI played on rumors that it was a missile attack and passed another series of measures that further eroded privacy. They're continu-ing to lobby for giving the government access to all cryptographic keys that protect privacy, or weakening the security so that it doesn't matter.

For the past few decades, computer privacy in the United States has been limited by what are called *export laws*. Export laws limit what kind of encryption U.S. companies can export. Since most software products are global, this effectively limited the strength of the cryptography in mass products like Internet browsers and operating systems.

Since 1993, the U.S. government has been advocating something called key escrow, which I discuss in detail in Chapter 16. This is the sys-tem that gives the police access to your encryption keys.

The debate is ongoing. The FBI has been pushing for stronger anti-privacy measures: the right to eavesdrop on broad swaths of the telephone network, the right to install listening devices on people's computers— without warrants wherever possible. At the time of writing (early 2000), we have new export rules for mass-market software, a variety of encryp-tion liberalization bills are in Congress, and several court cases about export controls are working their way to the Supreme Court. Changes happen all the time; anything I say here could be obsolete by the time this book is published.

Also interesting (and timeless) are the philosophical issues. First, is the government correct when it implies that the social ills of privacy out-weigh the social goods? I argued in the previous section that the benefits of anonymity outweigh the problems. It is the same with privacy. It has many positive uses, and the positive uses are much more common than the negative ones.

Second, can a government take a technology that clearly does an enormous amount of social good and, because they perceive that it hin-ders law enforcement in some way, limit its use? The FBI shibboleth is that encryption is a great hindrance to criminal investigations, and that they are only asking for the same eavesdropping capabilities they had ten years ago. However, they offer no evidence, and the historic record con-vincingly shows that wiretaps are not cost-effective crimefighting techniques. Widespread cryptography may be a step back for law enforce-ment's desires, but it may not be a step back in convicting criminals.

I don't know the answers. A balance exists between privacy and safety. Laws about search and seizure and due process hinder law enforce-ment, and probably result in some criminals going free. On the other hand, they protect citizens against abuse by the police. We as a society need to decide what particular balance is right for us, and then create laws that enforce that balance. Warrants are a good example of this balance; they give police the right to invade privacy, but add some judicial over-sight. I don't necessarily object to invasions of privacy in order to aid law enforcement, but I vociferously object to the FBI trying to ram them through without public debate or even public awareness.

In any case, the future does not look good. Privacy is the first thing jettisoned in a crisis, and already the FBI is trying to manufacture crises in an attempt to seize more powers to invade privacy. A war, a terrorist attack, a police action . . . would cause a sea change in the debate. And even now, in an environment that is most conducive to a reasoned debate on privacy, we're losing more and more of our privacy.

AUTHENTICATION

Privacy and anonymity might be important for our social and business well-being, but authentication is essential for survival. Authentication is about the continuity of relationships, knowing who to trust and who not to trust, making sense of a complex world. Even nonhumans need authentication: smells, sounds, touch. Arguably, life itself is an authenti-cating molecular pit of enzymes, antibodies, and so on.

People authenticate themselves zillions of times a day. When you log on to a computer system, you authenticate yourself to the computer. In 1997, the Social Security Administration tried to put people's data up on the Web; they shut down after complaints that Social Security number and mother's maiden name weren't good enough authentication means, that people would be able to see other people's data. The computer also needs to authenticate itself to you; otherwise, how to do you know it's your computer and not some impostor's?

Consider the average man on the street going to buy a bratwurst. He examines storefront after storefront, looking for one that sells bratwurst. Or maybe he already knows his favorite bratwurst store, and just goes there. In any case, when he gets to the store he authenticates that it is the correct store. The authentication is sensory: He sees bratwurst on the menu, he smells it in the air, the store looks like the store did the last time he was there.

Our man talks to the deli man and asks for a bratwurst. To some degree, both authenticate each other. The deli man wants to know if the customer is likely to pay. If the customer is dressed in rags, the deli man might ask him to leave (or at least to pay beforehand). If the customer is wearing a balaclava and brandishing an AK-47, the deli man might simply run away.

The customer, too, is authenticating the deli man. Is he a real deli man? Will he deliver me my bratwurst, or will he just give me a pile of sawdust on my bun? What about the restaurant? There's probably some kind of certificate of cleanliness, signed by the local health inspector, on the wall somewhere if the customer cares to check. More often, the customer trusts his instincts. We've all walked out of restaurants because we didn't like the "feel" of the place.

The deli man hands over the bratwurst, and the customer hands over a $5 bill. More authentication. Is this bill authentic? Is this bratwurst-looking thing food? We're so good at visual (and olfactory) authentication that we don't think about it, but we do it all the time. The customer gets his change, checks to make sure it is legal tender, and puts it in his pocket.

If the customer paid using a credit card, there would be lot of behind-the-scenes authentication. The deli man would swipe the card through a

VeriFone reader, which would dial into a central server and make sure the account was valid and had enough credit for the purchase. The deli man would be expected to examine the card to make sure it isn't a forgery, and check the signature against the one on the back of the card. (Most merchants don't bother, especially for low-value transactions.)

If the customer paid by check, there would be another authentication dance. The deli man would look at the check, and possibly ask the customer for some identification. Then he might write the customer's driver's license number and phone number on the back of the check, or maybe the customer's credit card number. None of this will actually help the deli man collect on a bad check, but it does help him track the customer down in the event of a problem.

Attacking authentication can be very profitable. In 1988, Thompson Sanders was convicted of defrauding the Chicago Board of Trade. He synthesized a nonexistent trader, complete with wig, beard, and fake credentials. This fake trader would place large risky orders, then claim those that were profitable and walk away from those that were not. The brokers on the other side of the losing transactions, unable to prove who they made the trade with, would be responsible for the losses.

Back to the deli. Another customer walks in. She and the deli man are old friends. They recognize each other—authenticating each other by face. This is a robust authentication system; people recognize each other even though she has a new hairstyle and he is wearing a new toupee and glasses. Superheroes realize this, and wear masks to hide their secret iden-tity. That works better in comic books than in real life, because face-to-face authentication isn't only face recognition (otherwise the blind would never recognize anyone). People remember each other's voice, build, mannerisms, and so forth. If the deli man called his friend on the phone, they could authenticate each other without any visual cues at all. Commissioner Gordon ought to figure out that Bruce Wayne is really Batman, simply because they talk on the phone so often.

In any case, our bratwurst-filled customer finishes eating. He says goodbye to the deli man, sure in the knowledge that he is saying good-bye to the same deli man who served him his bratwurst. He leaves through the same door that he came in by, and goes home.

Easy enough, because everyone involved was there . . . in the deli. Plato (and Hume) distrusted writing because you couldn't know what was true if the person wasn't right there in front of you. What would he say about the World Wide Web: no handwriting, no voice, no face . . . nothing but bits.

The same customer who bought the bratwurst is now surfing the Net, and he wants to buy something a little less perishable: a painting of a bratwurst, for example. He fires up his trusty search engine and finds a few Web sites that sell bratwurst paintings. They all take credit cards over the Internet, or let him mail a check in. They all promise delivery in three to four days. Now what?

How does the poor customer know whether to trust them? It takes some doing to put up a storefront; on the Web, anyone can do it in a few hours. Which of these merchants are honest, and which are scams? The URL might be that of a trusted name in the bratwurst-painting business, but who's to say that the URL is owned by that same trusted name? Northwest Airlines has a Web site where you can purchase tickets: www.nwa.com. Until recently, a travel agent had the Web site www.northwest-airlines.com. How many people bought from the latter, thinking they were buying from the former? (Many companies do not own their namesake domain name.) Some companies embed their competitors' names in their Web site (usually hidden) in an effort to trick search engines to point to them instead of their competitors. Internic.net, which is where you go to register domain names, is not the same as Internic.com. The latter started out as a spoof, morphed into Internic Software, and now registers domain names as well. They probably get a considerable business from the confused. And there's an even more sinister thought: Who's to say that some illicit hacker hasn't convinced the browser to display one URL while pointing to another?

The customer finds a Web site that looks reasonable and chooses a bratwurst painting. He then has to pay the merchant. If he's buying anything of value, we are going to need some serious authentication here. (If he's spending 25 cents for a virtual newspaper, it's a little easier to let this slide.) Is this digital cash valid? Is this credit card valid, and is the customer authorized to use it? Is the customer authorized to write a digi-tal check? Some face-to-face merchants ask to see a driver's license before accepting a check; what can a digital merchant examine before accepting a digital check?

This is the most important security problem to solve: authentication across digital networks. And there are going to be as many different solutions as there are different requirements. Some solutions are going to have to be robust, protecting values in the millions of dollars. Some won't have to be strong: authentication for a merchant's discount card, for example. Some solutions are going to be anonymous—cash, or a card that lets you in to a particular area of the Net without necessarily revealing your name—while others will need strong audit trails. Most will have to be international: a Net-based passport, commerce systems used for interna-tional commerce (which is all of them, these days), digital signatures on international contracts and agreements.

Often computer authentication is invisible to the user. When you use your cell phone (or your pay-TV system), it authenticates itself to the net-work so the network knows who to bill. Military aircraft have IFF (iden-tification friend or foe) systems to authenticate themselves to allied aircraft and antiaircraft batteries. Burglar alarms include authentication, to detect someone splicing a rogue alarm (that will never go off) into the circuit. Tachographs, used in trucks throughout Europe to enforce driving rules, such as mandatory rest periods, use authentication techniques to prevent fraud. Prepaid electricity meters in the United Kingdom are another example.

When thinking about authentication, keep in mind these two differ-ent types. They might feel the same, but the techniques used are very dif-ferent. The first one is session authentication: a conversation, either face to face, over the telephone, or via an IRC (Internet Relay Chat) link. Sessions can also be a single shopping expedition at an online store. What is authenticated here is the continuity of the particular conversation: Is the person who said this the same person who said the previous thing? (That's easy to do on the phone or face to face—the person sounds or looks the same, so it's probably the same person. On the Net, it's a lot harder.)

The other is transaction authentication: a credit card purchase, a piece of currency. The authentication here is whether or not the transaction is valid: whether the parties should accept the transaction or call the cops. The issues surrounding this kind of authentication are the same whether the transaction is done over the Net, over the telephone, or face to face.

Think of a merchant checking a $100 bill to make sure it's not counter-feit, or comparing the signature on a credit card with the signature on the sales slip.

INTEGRITY

Sometimes when we think of authentication, we really mean integrity. The two concepts are distinct but sometimes confused. Authentication has to do with the origin of the data: who signed the license to practice medicine, who issued the currency, who authorized this purchase order for 200 pounds of fertilizer and five gallons of diesel fuel? Integrity has to do with the validity of data. Are these the correct payroll numbers? Has this environmental test data been tampered with since I last looked at it? Integrity isn't concerned with the origin of the data—who created it, when, or how—but whether it has been modified since its creation.

Integrity is not the same as accuracy. Accuracy has to do with a datum's correspondence to the flesh-and-blood world; integrity is about a datum's relation to itself over time. They are often closely related.

In any society where computerized data are going to be used to make decisions, the integrity of the data is important. Sometimes it is important on an aggregate scale: if that faulty statistic about children below the poverty line is accepted as fact, it could change the amount of federal aid spent. Someone who fiddles with the closing prices for a handful of NAS-DAQ stocks could make a killing on the resultant confusion. Sometimes it is important to an individual: You can really mess up someone's day tampering with his DMV records and marking his license as suspended. (This was accidentally done in 1985 in Anchorage, Alaska, to 400 people, at least one of whom had to spend the night in jail. Think of the fun someone could have doing it on purpose.)

There have been several integrity incidents regarding stocks. In 1997, a company called Swisher that makes toilet bowl deodorizers got a big boost to its stock prices because the news services kept mixing up its stock symbol with that of *another* company called Swisher, which makes cigars. Swisher(1) was a much smaller company than Swisher(2), so when you plugged in the mistaken earnings figures, it looked like an incredibly undervalued stock. Some guys on the Motley Fool Web site figured out what had happened and sold Swisher(1)'s stock short, figuring it would come back down when investors realized their mistake.

In 1999, an employee of PairGain Technologies posted fake takeover announcements designed to look like they came from the Bloomberg news service, running the stock up 30 percent before the hoax was exposed.

These attacks are not about authentication—it doesn't matter who collected the census data, who compiled the closing stock prices, or who input the motor vehicle records—they're about integrity. There are many other databases where integrity is important: telephone books, medical records, financial records, and so on.

If there's a mystery writer in the audience, I always thought that a cool way to murder someone would be to modify the drug dosage data-base
in a hospital. If the physician isn't paying close enough attention—he's tired, the drug is an obscure one, some MacGuffin is distracting him— he might just prescribe what the computer tells him to. This might be far-fetched today—there's still a lot of reliance on hard-copy documentation like the *Physician's Desk Reference* and *AHFS Drug Information*—but it won't be soon. Millions of people are getting medical information online. For example, drugemporium.com queries another site, drkoop.com, to search for any harmful drug interactions among the products in your order (which can include prescription drugs). Users are admonished not to rely on this information alone, but most of them probably will anyway. Someone playing with the integrity of that data can cause a lot of harm.

And even if no malice is involved, any online system that deals with prescriptions and treatments had better implement integrity checking against random errors: No one wants a misplaced byte to result in an acci-dental hospital death, neither the patient nor the software company who is going to have to deal with the lawsuits.

In the physical world, people use the physical instantiation of an object as proof of integrity. We trust the phone book, the *Physician's Desk Reference*, and the *U.S. Statistical Abstracts* because they are bound books that look real. If they are fake, someone is spending a lot of money mak-ing them look real. If you pull a Dickens novel off the shelf and start read-ing it, you don't think twice about whether it is real or not. The same with a clipping from *Business Week*; it's just a piece of paper, but it looks and feels like a page from the magazine. If you get a photocopy of the clipping, then it just looks like a page from the magazine. If someone retypes the article (or downloads it from LEXIS-NEXIS) and e-mails it to you . . . then who knows.

On August 1, 1997, I received an e-mail from a friend; in it was a copy of Kurt Vonnegut's 1997 MIT commencement address. At least, I assumed it was Vonnegut's 1997 MIT commencement address. My friend mailed it to me in good faith. But it wasn't Kurt Vonnegut's 1997 MIT commencement address. Vonnegut didn't deliver the 1997 commence-ment address at MIT. He never wrote the speech, or delivered it any-where. The words were written by Mary Schmich, and published in her June 1, 1997, *Chicago Tribune* column.

Contrast that with another piece of alleged Vonnegut writing I received, about 15 years previous. This was before the World Wide Web, before I even had an e-mail address (but not before the Internet). This was an essay entitled "A Dream of the Future (Not Excluding Lobsters)"; a friend sent a photocopy in the mail. The copy was clearly from a publica-tion. Yes, it could have been faked, but it would have been a lot of work. This was before the era of desktop publishing, and making something look like it was photocopied out of *Esquire* magazine was difficult and expensive. Today it's hard to tell the difference between the real thing and a canard.

I've been e-mailed articles from magazines and newspapers many times. What kind of assurance do I have that those articles are really from the newspapers and magazines they are claimed to be from? How do I know that they haven't been subtly modified, a word here and a sentence there? What if I make this book available online, and some hacker comes in and changes my words? Maybe you're reading this book online; did you ever stop to think that these might not be my actual words, that you're trusting the server you downloaded the book from? Is there a mechanism that you can use to verify that these are my words? If enough years go by, more people will have read the altered version of the book than my original words. Will anyone ever notice? How long before the modified version becomes the "real" version? When will Vonnegut's denial be forgotten and his commencement address become history?

The temptation to falsify, or modify, data remains. A rune-covered stone discovered in Minnesota supposedly described a visit by the Vikings in 1362; never mind that it contained a word only found in modern

Swedish. Paul Schliemann (Heinrich Schliemann's grandson) claimed to have discovered the secret of Atlantis in the ancient Mayan Troano Codex, which he read in the British Museum. Never mind that no one could read Mayan, and that the Codex was stored in Madrid. Bismarck's rewrite of the 1870 Ems telegram effectively started the Franco-Prussian War. In 1996, when David Selbourne tried to pass off his translation of a thirteenth-century Italian traveler's visit to China (beating Marco Polo by three years); he used the "owner of the manuscript allowed him to translate it only if he swore himself to secrecy" trick to avoid having to produce a suitable forgery.

The problem is that the digital world makes this kind of thing easier, because it is so easy to produce a forgery and so hard to verify the accu-racy of anything. In May 1997, a 13-year-old Brooklynite won a national spelling bee. When the *New York Post* published the Associated Press photo of her jumping for joy, it erased the name of her sponsoring news-paper, the *New York Daily News*, from a sign around her neck. Video, too: When CBS covered the 2000 New Year celebration, they digitally superimposed their own logo over the 30-by-40-foot NBC logo in Times Square. And fake essays and speeches, like the Vonnegut speech, are posted on the Internet all the time.

Images can have powerful effects on people. They can change minds and move foreign policy. Desert Storm pictures of trapped Iraqis being shot up by Coalition airpower played a large part in the quick cease-fire: Americans didn't like seeing the lopsided carnage. And remember Soma-lia? All it took was a 30-second video clip of a dead Marine being dragged through the streets of Mogadishu to undermine the American will to fight. Information is power. And next time, the video clip could be a fake.

It sounds spooky, but unless we pay attention to this problem we will lose the ability to tell the real thing from a fake. Throughout human history, we've used context to verify integrity; the electronic world has no context. In the movie *The Sting,* Newman and Redford hired a cast of dozens and built an entire fake horseracing-betting parlor in order to con one person. A more recent movie, *The Spanish Prisoner,* had a similar big con. Cons this involved were popular around the time of the Depression; for all I know it's still done today. The mark is taken because he can't imagine that what he's seeing—the rooms, the people, the noise, the action—is really only a performance enacted solely for his benefit.

On the Net, this is easy to do. In a world without physical cues, people need some new way to verify the integrity of what they see.

AUDIT

Double-entry bookkeeping was codified by 1497 by Luca Pacioli of Borgo San Sepolcro, although the concept is as much as 200 years older. The basic idea is that every transaction will affect two or more accounts. One account is debited by an amount exactly equal to what the other is credited. Thus, all transactions are always transfers between two accounts, and since they always appear with a plus sign in one account and a minus sign in the other, the total over all accounts will always be zero.

This system had two main purposes. The two books would be kept by two different clerks, reducing the possibility of fraud. But more impor-tantly, the two books would be routinely balanced against each other (businesses would balance their books every month; banks, every day). This balancing process was an audit: If one clerk tried to commit fraud— or simply made a mistake—it would be caught in the balancing process, because someone other than the clerk would be checking the work. Additionally, there would be outside audits, where accountants would come in and check the books over again . . . just to make sure.

Audit is vital wherever security is taken seriously. Double-entry bookkeeping is just the beginning; banks have complex and comprehensive audit requirements. So do prisons, nuclear missile silos, and grocery stores. A prison might keep a record of everyone who goes in and out the doors, and balance the record regularly to make sure that no one unexpectedly left (or unexpectedly stayed). A missile silo might go even further and audit every box and package that enters and leaves, comparing ship-ping and receiving records with another record of what was expected. A grocery store keeps a register tape of all transactions that happen at the register, and compares how much money the register thinks is in the drawer with what is actually in the drawer.

These are not preventive security measures (although they may dissuade attacks); audit is designed to aid forensics. Audit is there so that you can detect a successful attack, figure out what happened after the fact, and then prove it in court. A system's particular needs for audit depend on the application and its value. You don't need much of an audit trail for a stored-value card system for photocopy machines at a university; you need a much stronger audit trail if the cards are going to be used to make high-value purchases that can be converted back to cash.

Auditing can be difficult on computers. Register tapes make good audit records because the clerk cannot change them: Transactions are printed sequentially on a single sheet of paper, and it is impossible to add or delete a transaction without raising some suspicion. (Well, there are some attacks: blocking the writing, simulating running out of ink, disabling the writing for a single transaction, forging an entire tape, and so forth.) On the other hand, computer files can easily be erased or modified; this makes the job of verifying audit records more difficult. And most sys-tem designers don't think about audit when building their systems. Recall the built-in audit property of double-entry bookkeeping. That auditabil-ity fails when both books are stored on the same computer system, with the same person having access to both. But this is exactly how all computer bookkeeping programs work.

ELECTRONIC CURRENCY

Back in the old days (1995 or so), everyone thought that we would have to develop new forms of money to deal with electronic commerce. Many companies died, trying to redefine money. Some companies tried to create an electronic equivalent of cash; others tried to create electronic equivalents of checks and credit cards. One of the last vestiges of this, the joint Visa/MasterCard SET protocol, is designed to use existing credit cards together with an Internet-specific system to make credit cards safe for e-commerce.

It turns out that it doesn't matter. Credit cards are fine for the Inter-net, and most everyone uses them with alacrity to buy books, clothing, pay-per-porn, and everything else. Still, security breaches like the series of credit card number thefts in 2000 make you wonder. Is there ever going to be an Internet-specific form of payment?

This is more of a regulatory question than a security question. The security needs for electronic commerce can be cobbled together from the previous sections: authentication, privacy, integrity, nonrepudiation, audit. The requirements are pretty simple: We need the ability to transfer monetary value over computer networks. Looking closer, there are several ways to achieve this. We can take any of the existing commerce metaphors—cash, checks, debit cards, credit cards, letters of credit—and move them to cyberspace. Different metaphors have different rules and requirements.

Some requirements depend on who has what liability. Merchants and credit card companies hold most of the liabilities for stolen credit cards and fraudulent credit card transactions, so electronic versions of those systems are generally designed to make their lives easier, and not the consumers'.

Different physical implementations also have different requirements. Is this an online system or an offline system? Things are simpler if you can assume an online connection with a bank (such as ATMs require). If you're building a commerce system for use in parts of the world where telephone lines are scarce (like parts of Africa), you can't make that assumption. Does the system have to work in a software environment, or can we assume a secure-hardware token like a smart card? And does this system have to be anonymous, like cash, or include identities, like credit cards? Finally, what government regulations does this system have to meet? This depends not only on the metaphor chosen, but also the regulations of the particular government or governments who have jurisdiction over the system.

We're already seeing some of this. We're not seeing digital cash, but we're seeing alternative "points" systems that are the same thing as currency. Flooz.com created a specialized currency for gift giving. Flooz can be given away as gift certificates, which makes them usable as money. Beenz.com does something similar; beenz are not real currency, but they can be used and traded as such. Other companies are following suit.

I expect this to become a big deal, and potentially dangerous, because these pseudocurrencies don't have the same regulatory rules as real money.

PROACTIVE SOLUTIONS

Traditionally, fraud prevention has been reactive. Criminals find a flaw in a commerce system and exploit it. They keep going while the system's designers figure out how to fix the flaw, or at least minimize the risk. The criminals learn that their attack doesn't work, and then go on to some other attack. And the process continues.

You can see this in credit cards. Originally, card verification was offline. Merchants were given books of bad credit card numbers every week, and they had to manually check the number against the book. Now, card verification is done online, in real time. People were stealing new cards out of mailboxes, so the credit card companies started requiring you to call in to activate your card. Now, the card and the activation notice are mailed from different points. Companies also have artificial intelligence programs checking for irregular spending patterns. ("Good morning, sir, sorry to bother you. You've been a good customer for years. We'd like to confirm that you suddenly moved to Hong Kong and spent your entire credit limit on Krugerands.")

When ATMs were first introduced by Citicorp in 1971, you would put your card into a slot and type in your PIN. The machine would ver-ify your PIN, spit the card back out at you, and then you could finish your transaction. Enterprising New York criminals would dress up in suits and wait near these machines. After a customer's PIN was verified, she would be approached by a suited criminal and be told that this machine was bro-ken, or being tested, or just out of money, and wouldn't she please use the machine over there. People in suits can be trusted, after all. After the cus-tomer left, the suit would finish the first transaction and pocket the cash.

The work-around was to hold the card until the end of the transac-tion, but that required rebuilding the hardware. The banks needed a solu-tion fast, and they figured out a fix that could be quickly installed at the ATMs: They had the nearby machines communicate with each other. As they installed the fix throughout the branches, they could watch the crim-inals migrate across the city looking for machines where the attack still worked. They then retrofitted the ATMs to hold the card until the end of the transaction. The long-term solution was to modify the back-end net-work to make sure that only one transaction per card is active at any time. This has been done, so now it doesn't matter if the card is held by the machine anymore. Now many ATMs have you swipe your card instead of inserting it, but back then there was considerable fraud while the problem was being fixed.

This notion of fixing a security flaw after it becomes a problem won't work on the Internet. Attacks can be automated, and they can propagate to unskilled attackers quickly and easily. A similar attack on whatever turns out to be the Internet equivalent of an ATM could demolish the banking system. It's not enough to react to fraud after it's been demonstrated to work; we have to be proactive and deal with fraud before it happens.

PART 2

TECHNOLOGIES

Security is layered like an onion. On the outside are the users: How they use the system, who they trust, what they do when the system fails. Inside that are the security relationships between the user and the system, and between different systems. Further inside is the software, those bug-rid-dled pieces of code that are expected to enforce whatever security rules we have. That software works on networks and computers. Looking further in toward the theoretical are the idealized protocols that the computers run. And in the center (sometimes) is the cryptography: the mathematical equations that enforce security.

Security is a process, not a product. As a process, it has many components. And like any process, some of these components are sturdier, more reliable, more oiled, more secure. Moreover, the components have to fit together. The better they fit together, the better the process works. Often it's the interfaces between components that are the least secure.

Security is also like a chain. It is composed of many links, and each one of them is essential to the strength of the chain. And like a chain, security is only as strong as the weakest link. In this part, we look at the different security technologies that make up a chain, looking from the inside of the onion to the outside.

And we try not to mix metaphors quite so badly anymore.

6

Cryptography

Cryptography is pretty amazing. On one level, it's a bunch of complicated mathematics. It's cryptographers designing ever more complicated mathematical transformations and cryptanalysts countering with ever more ingenious ways of breaking the mathe-matics. It also has a long and proud history: confidants, lovers, secret societies, and governments have been using cryptography to protect their secrets for millennia.

On another level, cryptography is a core technology of cyberspace. It lets us take all of the business and social constructs we're used to in the physical world, and move them to cyberspace. It's the technology that lets us build security into cyberspace, to deal with the attacks and attackers dis-cussed in Part 1. Without cryptography, e-commerce could never enter the mainstream. Cryptography is not a panacea—you need a lot more than cryptography to have security—but it is essential.

In order to understand security in cyberspace, you need to understand cryptography. You don't have to understand the math, but you have to understand its ramifications. You need to know what cryptography can do, and more importantly, what cryptography cannot do. You need to know how to think about cryptography in the context of computer and network security. These two chapters won't turn you into a cryptographer, only an intelligent consumer of cryptography.

To the consumer, cryptography is a shadowy protective entity—something like Batman—kind of menacing but on the side of justice, and endowed with mystic powers. If the consumer is paying attention, cryptography is a boatload of acronyms that accomplish various security tasks. IPsec, for example, secures IP traffic across the Internet. It secures virtual private networks (VPNs). Secure Sockets Layer (SSL) secures WWW connections. Pretty Good Privacy (PGP) and S/MIME secure e-mail; they prevent others from reading e-mail that isn't addressed to them, and from forging e-mail to look like it came from someone else. SET secures Internet credit card transactions. These are all protocols. There are proto-cols for digital content protection (music, movies, etc.), cell phone authentication (to stop fraud), electronic commerce, and just about every-thing else. To build these protocols, cryptographers use different algo-rithms: encryption algorithms, digital signature algorithms, and so forth.

SYMMETRIC ENCRYPTION

Historically, cryptography has been used for one thing: to keep secrets. Written language itself has been used as a form of cryptography—in ancient China only the upper classes were allowed to learn to read and write—but the first documented use of cryptography was around 1900 B.C. in Egypt: A scribe used nonstandard hieroglyphs in an inscription. There were other examples: a Mesopotamian tablet from 1500 B.C. con-taining an enciphered formula for making pottery glazes, the Hebrew ATBASH cipher from 500–600 B.C., the Greek skytale from 486 B.C., and Julius Caesar's simple substitution cipher from 50–60 B.C. The Kama Sutra of Vatsyayana even lists secret writing as the 44th, and secret talking as the 45th, of 64 arts (yogas) men and women should know and practice.

The main idea behind cryptography is that a group of people can use private knowledge to keep written messages secret from everyone else. There is a message, sometimes called the plaintext, that someone wants to keep secure. Maybe the someone (we'll call her Alice) wants to send it to someone else (we'll call him Bob); maybe she wants to be able to read it herself at some later date. What she doesn't want is for anyone other than (possibly) Bob to be able to read the message.

So Alice encrypts the message. She invents some transformation, called an algorithm, of the plaintext message into a ciphertext message. This ciphertext message is gibberish, so that an eavesdropper (we'll call her Eve) who gets her hands on this ciphertext cannot figure out the plaintext, and therefore cannot figure out what the message means. Bob knows how to reverse the transformation—how to turn the ciphertext message back into plaintext.

This works, more or less. Alice can use an algorithm of her own devising to keep her pottery glazes secret. Alice and Bob can agree on an algorithm to share their thoughts on the Kama Sutra. And an entire class of Chinese nobles (even though none of them is called Bob) can use their written language to keep state secrets safe from the peasants.

But there are complications. First, the algorithm has to be good. Eve isn't going to look at the ciphertext message, shrug her shoulders, and wander off. She's going to try to figure out what the plaintext is. If she's the World War II British government, she is going to hire the best mathematicians, linguists, and chess players in the country, stick them and 10,000 others in a secret compound at Bletchley Park, and invent the computer—just so she can break the algorithm and recover the plaintexts. Even today, the National Security Agency (NSA) is the single largest consumer of computer hardware and the single largest employer of math-ematicians in the world. Alice had better be a pretty smart cryptographer if she is going to outsmart these sorts of Eves. I'll talk more about this later.

Second, it's hard to bring people in and out of the fold. To exchange secret messages with Chinese noblemen, you had to learn how to become literate. This took time. If you later fell out of favor with the government, there was no way for them to prevent you from reading all the messages. You knew how the encryption worked, and they had to kill you if they didn't want you reading their messages. (During World War II, the American military used the Navajo language as a code. These Navajo code talkers kept their language secret from the Japanese in World War II, but the whole system would have collapsed if a single Navajo switched allegiances.)

These two problems, left unsolved, would make cryptography almost useless today. You're one of the whatever-million people on the Internet, and you want to communicate securely with 100 of your closest friends. You don't want to share a common secret language with the 100 people; you want 100 separate secure algorithms. (You need security pairwise.) And so do all the other whatever-million Internet users. This means that you have to invent 100 different encryption algorithms, exchange one with each of your close friends, program them all into your computers yourself (you wouldn't trust anyone else to do it), and hope you're smarter than everyone who might try to break your algorithm.

Not bloody likely.

Such is the beauty of a *key*. Your front door lock is mass-produced by some faceless company that hasn't the faintest idea how valuable your vintage PEZ collection is, but you don't have to trust them. They don't say: "Remember, anyone else who has the same brand lock can open the lock." You have a key. The pin settings inside your lock, which match your key, make your lock different from all the other locks in the neigh-borhood, even though they might be exactly the same make and model number. (Actually, the example is simplistic. You do have to trust them to install the lock correctly, and not to pocket an extra copy of the key. But never mind that.)

This is the same security model that Leon Battista Alberti, the famous Italian Renaissance architect, brought to cryptography in 1466 when he invented the cryptographic key. Everyone can have the same brand lock, but everyone has a different key. The design of the lock is public—lock-smiths have books with detailed diagrams, and most of the good designs are described in public patents—but the key is secret. You have a key, so you can get in your front door. If you give a key to your friend, he can get in your front door. Someone without a key cannot. (The locksmiths are the cryptanalysts; we'll get to them later.)

Applying this model to cryptography solves both of the preceding problems. Algorithms, like locks, can be standardized. The Data Encryp-tion Standard (also called DES) has been a standard cryptographic algo-rithm, worldwide, since 1977. It's been used in thousands of different products for all sorts of applications. The innermost workings of DES have been public from day one; they were published even before it was adopted as a standard. The public nature of the algorithm doesn't affect security, because each different group of users chooses its own secret key. Alice and Bob share the same key, so they can communicate. Eve doesn't know the key, so she can't read their communications—even though she has a copy of the exact same encryption software that Alice and Bob have.

Keys solve the problem of people moving in and out of a private group. If Alice and Bob share a key, and they want to let Kim Philby join their conversations, they just give him a copy of the key. If they later learn that Philby is passing secrets to the Soviet Union, they can simply agree on a new key and not tell Philby. From that moment forward, he is cut out of the system and can no longer read newly encrypted messages. (Of course, he can still read the old ones.)

This is the way conventional cryptography works today. The algorithms are designed for computers instead of pencil and paper—they operate on binary bits instead of alphabetic characters, they're designed with the efficiencies of microprocessors and integrated circuits in mind— but the philosophy is the same. The algorithm is public, and the commu-nicating parties agree on a shared secret key to use with the algorithm.

These algorithms are called *symmetric* because the sender and receiver must share the same key. The key is a string of random bits of some length: in the year 2000, 128 bits is a good key length. Different symmet-ric algorithms have different key lengths.

Symmetric algorithms can be found in encryption systems all over the computerized world. Common algorithms are DES and triple-DES, RC4 and RC5, IDEA, and Blowfish. AES is the Advanced Encryption Standard; it will soon be the U.S. government standard encryption algo-rithm. These algorithms secure private e-mail, personal computer files, electronic banking transactions, and nuclear launch codes. They protect privacy.

But they're not perfect.

The problem is distributing the keys. For this system to work, Alice and Bob need to agree on a secret key before exchanging any secret messages. If Alice and Bob are smart, they are going to change their key routinely: daily, perhaps. They need to agree on these daily keys in some secure manner, since anyone who eavesdrops on the key can eavesdrop on all communications encrypted with that key. And assuming you want pairwise security, the number of keys needed grows with the square of the number of users: Two users need just one key, but a ten-user network needs 45 keys to allow every pair of users to communicate securely. And a 100-user network needs 4,950 different keys. In the 1980s, U.S. Navy ships would often sail with a forklift-full of NSA-distributed keys—each printed on paper tape or punch cards or whatever—enough for all of their communications circuits for the entire length of their missions.

And it isn't enough to disseminate these keys securely: They have to be stored securely, used securely, and then destroyed securely. Alice and Bob need to keep their keys secret until they need to talk with one another and they need to make sure that no one gets their keys, either before they use them, while they are using them, or after they have used them.

This means that destruction is critical. Alice and Bob can't just toss their key in the Dumpster in the back and hope no one finds it. Eaves-droppers are not above storing encrypted communications that they can't read, hoping that they will find the key at some later date. The NSA's decryption of the Russian VENONA traffic (look up the story; it's cool beans) was possible only because the Soviets reused keys that should have been thrown away, and because the NSA stored the Soviet encrypted messages for over a decade.

There are many historical examples of poor key management break-ing otherwise strong encryption. John Walker was in the U.S. Navy, but he had a second career photocopying U.S. Navy key material before it was used and then mailing it to the Russians—and he was a security officer entrusted with keeping the keys secure. The Japanese death cult Aum Shinrikyo encrypted their computer records, but they were careless enough to leave a copy of the key on a floppy disk for the police to find. And this was in 1995; you'd think death cults would have learned a thing or two by then.

TYPES OF CRYPTOGRAPHIC ATTACKS

What does it mean to break an algorithm? Obviously, it means that some-one can read the message without the key. But it's more complicated than that.

If an attacker can take a ciphertext message and recover the plaintext, this is called a *ciphertext-only attack*. This almost never occurs anymore; modern algorithms are just too good to fall to this kind of attack.

A *known-plaintext attack* is more likely: The analyst has a copy of the plaintext and the ciphertext, and can then recover the key. This might sound useless, but it in fact can be very useful. If other texts are encrypted with the same key, the attacker can take the key and read more plaintext encrypted with it. For example, almost all computer files have known headers. All Microsoft Word files, for example, start with the same hundreds of bytes. (These are not the characters you see; these bytes are internal to the program and are not displayed on the screen.) If an analyst can use that known plaintext to recover the key, then she can read the entire Word file. Known-plaintext attacks were used to great effect against the German Enigma. Analysts would have a single known plain-text: Sometimes it was the daily weather report; for a while, one German outpost in Norway would dutifully send the same message every day: "Nothing to report." (Probable known plaintexts are also called *cribs*.) They would use that to break the day's key, and then use the key to read the rest of the day's encrypted messages.

Even more powerful is a *chosen-plaintext attack*. Here the analyst gets to choose the message that will be encrypted. Then she gets the encrypted message and recovers the key. This kind of attack worked against the German codes: Allies would deliberately introduce certain messages into the system in order to learn the ciphertext, or create events in cities with obscure names that are particularly useful cribs. It also works well against some smart card systems, where the attacker can feed arbitrary messages onto the card. It works in a lot of instances.

The one thing that is constant in all of these attacks is that the analyst knows the details of the algorithm. (The only modern exception I know of is the Japanese PURPLE code.) This is not just an academic shortcut; this is good design. If an algorithm is used in products, it will be reverse engineered. Once-secret algorithms that have been reverse engineered include RC4, all the digital cellular encryption algorithms, the DVD and DIVX video-encryption algorithms, and the Firewire encryption algorithm. Even algorithms buried deep in military hardware will be captured and reverse engineered: the Enigma during World War II, and just about every NATO and Warsaw Pact algorithm during the Cold War. (We don't know those, but the respective militaries do.) It is good design to assume the enemy knows the details of your algorithm, because eventually they will. Auguste Kerckhoffs first stated this thesis in 1883: There is no secrecy in the algorithm, it's all in the key.

RECOGNIZING PLAINTEXT

One question that often comes up about attacks is: How does the cryptanalyst recognize plaintext? The answer is simple: Because it looks like plaintext. It's an English-language message, or a data file from a com-puter application, a JPEG movie, or a database in a reasonable format. When you look at a decrypted file, it looks like something understand-able. When you look at a ciphertext file, or a file decrypted with the wrong key, it looks like gibberish. A person, or a computer, can see the difference.

In the 1940s, Claude Shannon invented a concept called the unicity distance. Among other things, the unicity distance measures the amount of ciphertext required such that there is only one reasonable plaintext. This number depends both on the characteristics of the plaintext and the key length of the encryption algorithm.

For example, the RC4 algorithm encrypts data in bytes. Imagine a single ASCII letter as the plaintext. There are 26 possible plaintexts out of 256 possible decryptions. Any random key, when used to decrypt the ciphertext, has a 26/256 chance of producing a valid plaintext. The analyst has no way to tell the wrong plaintext from the correct plaintext.

Now imagine a 1K e-mail message. The analyst tries random keys, and eventually a plaintext emerges that looks like an e-mail message: words, phrases, sentences, grammar. The odds are infinitesimal that this is not the correct plaintext.

For a standard English message, the unicity distance is $K/6.8$ charac-ters, where K is the key length in bits. (The 6.8 is a measure of the natural redundancy of English. For other plaintexts, it will be more or less, but not that much more or less.) For DES-encrypted ASCII, the unicity dis-tance is 8.2 bytes. For 128-bit ciphers, it is about 19 bytes. This means that for English messages longer than 19 bytes, a decryption that looks like English is most likely the correct plaintext. It's about the same for spread-sheet files, word processor files, and database files. (Actually, it can be a lot less because the file formats have standardized beginnings.) Compressed files might have unicity distance two or three times as large (but again, standardized beginnings can reduce it considerably).

The moral here is that it is easy to recognize plaintext, and it doesn't take much data to do so.

MESSAGE AUTHENTICATION CODES

Message authentication codes, or MACs, are the next primitive we'll talk about. They don't protect privacy; they ensure authentication and integrity. They ensure that the message came from the person from whom it purports to have come from (authentication), and that the message was not altered in transit (integrity).

You can think of a MAC as a tamperproof coating on a message. Anyone can read the message; the coating doesn't provide privacy. But someone who knows the MAC key can verify that the message has not been altered. More specifically, a MAC is a number that is appended to a digital message.

MACs use a shared secret key, just like symmetric encryption algo-rithms. First, Alice shares a key with Bob. Then, when she wants to send a message to Bob, she computes the MAC of the message (using the secret key) and appends it to the message. Every message has a unique MAC for each possible key.

When Bob receives the message, he computes its MAC (again, using the same shared secret key) and compares it with the MAC he received from Alice. If they match, then he knows two things: The message really does come from Alice (or someone who knows the secret of the shared key), because only that key could be used to compute the MAC; and that the message is complete and unaltered, because the MAC could only be computed from the entire and exact message. If Eve (remember our eavesdropper?) was listening in on the communications, she could read the message. However, if she tried to modify either the message or the MAC, then Bob's calculated MAC would not equal the MAC he received. Eve would have to modify the message and then modify the MAC to be correct for the new message, but she can't do that because she doesn't know the key. Banks have used this simple authentication system for decades.

Alice can use this same trick to authenticate information stored in a database. When she adds the information to the database, she calculates the MAC and stores it with the information. When she retrieves the information, she again calculates the MAC and compares it with the MAC stored in the database. If they match, she knows that no one has modified the information.

MACs are used on the Internet all the time. They're used in the IPsec protocol, for example, to ensure that IP packets have not been modified between when they are sent and when they reach their final destination. They're used in all sorts of interbank transfer protocols to authenticate messages. Most MACs are constructed using symmetric algorithms or one-way hash functions. CBC-MAC, for example, uses a symmetric algorithm. HMAC and NMAC use hash functions.

ONE-WAY HASH FUNCTIONS

One-way hash functions are like digital fingerprints: small pieces of data that can serve to identify much larger digital objects. They are public functions; no secret keys are involved.

They are called one-way because of their mathematical nature. Any-one can compute the one-way hash of anything (a text representation of this book, for example). However, given the hash of this book, it is com-putationally unfeasible to create another book that hashes to the same value or to derive the book's original text.

Hash functions can also provide a measure of authentication and integrity. If you were to download this book over the Internet, you would have no way of knowing if these are my words or if some other party changed them. However, if I handed you the hash value of this book (typically just a 20-byte code), you could hash the book and com-pare the result with the hash I gave you. If they match, it's my book, unal-tered.

Hash functions have an enormous range of applications in cryptogra-phy and computer security. Almost every Internet protocol uses them to process keys, chain a sequence of events together, or authenticate events. They are essential for digital signature algorithms (more about that later). They are probably the single most useful tool in a cryptographer's tool-box.

A bunch of one-way hash functions are in use today. SHA-1 is the U.S. government's standard hash function. The acronym stands for Secure Hash Algorithm, and is specified in the Secure Hash Standard (SHS). RIPEMD-160 is a European algorithm. MD4 is obsolete (although you still see it used occasionally), and MD5 is showing some cracks and is not used for anything new.

PUBLIC-KEY ENCRYPTION

Remember the key-distribution problem I talked about with symmetric encryption? How do two people make sure that they have the same key, so they can use a symmetric encryption algorithm or a MAC function? *Public-key cryptography* (a.k.a. *asymmetric encryption*) solves this. It allows you to send secret messages to people you haven't met yet, and with whom you haven't agreed on a secret key. It allows two people to engage in a publicly visible data exchange and, at the end of that exchange, compute a shared secret that someone listening in on the discussion can't learn. In real-world terms, it allows you and a friend to shout numbers at each other across a crowded coffeehouse filled with mathematicians so that when you are done, both you and your friend know the same random number, and everyone else in the coffeehouse is completely clueless.

If this sounds ridiculous, it should. It sounds impossible. If you were to survey the world's cryptographers in 1975, they would all have told you it was impossible. So you can imagine the surprise in 1976, when Whitfield Diffie and Martin Hellman explained how to do it. Or the sur-prise in the British intelligence community when James Ellis, Clifford Cocks, and M.J. Williamson figured out the same thing a few years before.

The basic idea is to use a mathematical function that is easy to compute in one direction and hard to compute in the other. Integer factorization is one. Given two prime numbers, it's easy to multiply them together to find the product. But given a single product, it can be impracticable to factor the number and recover the two factors. This is the kind of math that can be used to create public-key cryptography; it involves modular arithmetic, exponentiation, and large prime numbers thousands of bits long, but you can elide the details. Today, there are a good half-dozen algorithms, with names like RSA, ElGamal, and elliptic curves. (Algorithms based on something called the knapsack problem were another early contender, but over the course of about 20 years they were broken every which way.) The mathematicals are different for each algorithm, but conceptually they are all the same.

Instead of a single key that Alice and Bob share, there are two keys: one for encryption and the other for decryption. The keys are different, and it is not possible to compute one key from the other. That is, if you have the encryption key, you can't figure out what the decryption key is.

Now, here's the cool part. Bob can create a pair of these keys. He can take the encryption key and publish it. He can send it to his friends, post it on his Web site, publish it in a phone book, whatever. Alice can find this key. She can take it and encrypt a message to Bob. Then, she can send the message to him. Bob can use his decryption key (which he astutely did not post on his Web site) to decrypt and read Alice's message. Notice that Alice did not have to meet Bob in some dark alley and agree on a shared secret. Bob doesn't even have to know Alice. Actually, Alice doesn't even have to know Bob. If Alice can find Bob's public key, she can send him a secret message that can't be read by anyone but Bob. This happens to PGP users all the time; one of their keys is uploaded to a server somewhere, and then a perfect stranger sends them an encrypted message. Even if you understand the mathematics, it can be startling.

The particulars are a whole lot more subtle. For example, I left out how Bob creates his public and private keys, and how Bob keeps his private key secret. (He can't remember it; it's over a thousand random digits long.) And I skipped over the incredibly complicated problem of how Alice knows that she has Bob's key and not some old key or, worse yet, some impostor's key. We'll get back to this later.

For now, I just want to point out that no one uses public key encryp-tion to encrypt messages. All operational systems use a hybrid approach that uses both kinds of cryptography. The reason is performance. What Alice really does, when she wants to send a message to Bob, is to use a symmetric algorithm to encrypt the message with a random key that she creates out of thin air (called a *session key*). She encrypts that random key with Bob's public key, and then sends both the encrypted key and the encrypted message to Bob. When Bob receives the encrypted message and key, he does the reverse. He uses his private key to decrypt the ran-dom symmetric key, and then uses the random symmetric key to decrypt the message.

This might sound weird, but it isn't. It's perfectly normal. Nobody uses public-key cryptography to directly encrypt messages. Everyone uses this hybrid approach. It's in every e-mail security program: PGP, PEM, S/MIME, whatever. It's how encryption works with Web security, TCP/IP security, secure telephones, and everything else.

DIGITAL SIGNATURE SCHEMES

Public-key encryption was amazing enough, but digital signatures are even more splendiferous—and more important. Digital signatures provide a level of authentication for messages, similar to MACs. And in modern business, authentication is far more important than secrecy. Like public-key encryption, digital signatures use a pair of keys, the public key and the private key. You still can't derive one key from the other. But this time we're going to reverse them.

Alice has a plaintext message. Using her private key, she encrypts the message. Because her private key is only hers, only Alice's key can encrypt the message in precisely this way. Thus, the encrypted message becomes Alice's *signature* on the message. Alice's public key is public. Anyone can get Alice's public key and decrypt the message, thereby verifying that Alice *signed* (i.e., encrypted) it. The signature is a function of the message, so it is unique to the message: A malicious forger can't lift Alice's signa-ture from one document and paste it onto another. And it's a function of Alice's private key, so it is unique to Alice.

Of course, real systems are more complicated. Just as Alice doesn't encrypt messages with public-key encryption algorithms (she encrypts a message key), she also doesn't sign messages directly. Instead, she takes a one-way hash of a message and then signs the hash. Again, signing the hash is a few orders of magnitude faster, and there are mathematical secu-rity problems with signing messages directly.

Also, most digital signature algorithms don't actually encrypt the messages that are signed. The idea is the same, but the mathematics is dif-ferent. Alice makes some calculation based on the message and her private key to generate the signature. This signature is appended to the message. Bob makes another calculation based on the message, the signature, and Alice's public key to verify the signature. Eve, who doesn't know Alice's private key, can verify the signature but cannot forge the message and a valid signature.

Several digital signature algorithms are currently in use. RSA is the most popular. The U.S. government's Digital Signature Algorithm (DSA), used in the Digital Signature Standard (DSS), sees a lot of use, too. ElGamal signatures are another you'll see occasionally. And there are sig-nature algorithms based on elliptic curve cryptography, which are similar to all the others but are more efficient in some situations.

Although public-key digital signature algorithms are similar to MACs, they are better in one important respect. With a MAC, Alice and Bob share a secret key that they use to authenticate messages. If Alice receives a message that she verifies, she knows it came from Bob. But she cannot convince a judge of that fact. All a judge can be convinced of is that the message came from either Bob or Alice; after all, both of them knew the MAC key. MACs can be used to convince the receiver that the message came from the sender, but it cannot be used to convince a third party. Digital signatures can be used to convince a third party, which solves the nonrepudiation problem: Alice cannot send a message to Bob, and then later deny ever sending it.

The unfortunate reality is that this stuff about signatures is not as black and white as the math implies. Digital signature laws are on the books in many states and countries, but I worry that they won't survive litigation. Digital signatures are not analogues of handwritten signatures. I will talk more about this in Chapter 15.

RANDOM NUMBER GENERATORS

Random numbers are the least-talked-about cryptographic primitive, but are no less important than the others. Almost every computer security sys-tem that uses cryptography needs random numbers—for keys, unique val-ues in protocols, and so on—and the security of those systems is often dependent on the randomness of those random numbers. If the random number generator is insecure, the entire system breaks.

Depending on who you talk to, generating random numbers from a computer is either trivial or impossible. Theoretically, it's impossible. John von Neumann, the father of computers, said: "Anyone who consid-ers arithmetic methods of producing random digits is, of course, in a state of sin." What he means is that it is impossible to get something truly random out of a deterministic beast like a computer. This is true, but luckily we can get by anyway. What we really need out of a random number generator is not that the numbers be truly random, but that they be unpredictable and irreproducible. If we can get those two things, we can get security.

On the other hand, if we mess those two things up, we get insecurity. In 1994, the Casino Montreal used a computer's random number gener-ator for its keno drawings. One observant gambler who spent way too much time in the casino noticed that the winning numbers were the same every day. He successfully picked three successive jackpots and won $600,000. (After much wringing of hands, gnashing of teeth, and investi-gations, the casino paid up.)

Several broad classes of random number generators are out there. Some random number generators make use of physical processes that seem pretty random. The NSA likes to use electrically noisy diodes in its hardware circuits to create random numbers. Other possibilities are Geiger counters and radio-noise receivers. One system on the Internet uses a digital camera focused on a choir of lava lamps. Other systems use the air turbulence in disk drives, or the seemingly random arrival time of successive network packets.

Some random number generators use random movements from the user. A program might ask the user to type a large string of random char-acters on the keyboard; it might use the sequence of characters, or even the timing between successive keystrokes, to create random numbers. Another program might ask the user to make random mouse movements, or to gargle into a microphone.

Some random number generators use these inputs directly. Others use them as *seeds* for mathematical random number generators. This process works best when the system needs more random numbers than the input provides. Whatever the source of randomness, the generator will then generate a series of random bits. These can then be used as cryp-tographic keys, and for whatever else the system needs.

KEY LENGTH

One of the easiest ways to compare cryptographic algorithms is key length. The press likes to focus on this because it's easy to describe and compare. Like most of security, the reality is more complicated. A short key is bad, but a long key is not automatically good. In the next chapter I discuss why, but it's worth explaining key length and its importance.

Let's start at the beginning. A cryptographic key is a secret value that makes a cryptographic algorithm unique for those who share the key. If Alice and Bob share a key, they can use the algorithm to communicate securely. If Eve, an eavesdropper, does not know the key, she is forced to try and break the algorithm.

One obvious thing she can do is try every possible key. This is called a *brute-force attack*. If the key is *n* bits long, then there are 2^n possible keys. So, if the key is 40 bits long, there are about a trillion possible keys. This would be impossibly boring for Eve, but computers are indefatigable;

they excel at impossibly boring tasks. On the average, a computer would have to try about half the possible keys before finding the correct one, so a computer capable of trying a billion keys per second would average 18 minutes to find the correct 40-bit key. In 1998, the Electronic Frontier Foundation built a machine that could brute-force the DES algorithm. The machine, called DES Deep Crack, tried 90 billion keys per second; it could find a 56-bit DES key in an average of 4.5 days. In 1999, a distrib-uted Internet keysearch project to break a DES key, called distributed.net (which included Deep Crack), was able to test 250 billion keys per second.

All of these brute-force cracks scale linearly; twice the computers can try twice the number of keys. But the difficulty of a brute-force crack is exponential with respect to the key length: Add one key bit, and a brute-force crack is twice as hard. Add two bits, and it's four times as hard. Add ten bits, and it's a thousand times as hard.

The nice thing about brute-force attacks is that they work against any algorithm. Since the attack doesn't involve the inner workings of the mathematics, the attack doesn't care what they are. Some algorithms may be faster than others, and hence the brute-force attacks might be faster; but this is more than overshadowed by the key length. It's easy to compare the key lengths of different algorithms, and to figure out which ones are more vulnerable to brute-force attacks.

In 1996, a clutch of cryptographers (including me) researched the var-ious technologies one could use to build brute-force cryptanalytic machines, and recommended a minimal key length of 90 bits to provide security through 2016. Triple-DES has a 112-bit key, and most modern algorithms have at least a 128-bit key. (The U.S. government's new Advanced Encryption Standard supports key lengths of 128 bits, 192 bits, and 256 bits.) Even a machine a billion times as fast as Deep Crack would take a million years to try all 2^{112} keys and recover the plaintext; over a thousand times longer for a 128-bit key. This will be secure for a millen-nium.

These numbers should be looked at with some skepticism. I'm not prescient; I have no idea how future advances in computing will affect things. And the real security depends on several things: how valuable your data is, how long you need to keep it secure, and so forth. But these are meant to be conservative numbers. The key lengths are for symmetric algorithms and MACs. Hash functions should have a length equal to twice the key length in the table.

Key lengths for public-key algorithms are more complicated. The most efficient attack against RSA, for example, is to factor the large num-ber. The most efficient attack against ElGamal, Diffie-Hellman, DSA, and the others, is to compute something called the discrete logarithm. (They're basically the same problem.) Elliptic-curve algorithms are even more complicated.

These days experts are recommending 1,024-bit keys, or longer, for public-key algorithms. Paranoids use longer keys. Systems that don't care too much about long-term secrecy use 768-bit keys. (Elliptic-curve algorithms have different key lengths.)

Estimates of future difficulty of factoring and calculating discrete log-arithms are harder to make, since there is no mathematical proof that these problems have a set degree of difficulty. (On the other hand, we know how difficult trying every possible key is.) So again, treat all these recommendations as intelligent guesses, nothing more.

7

Cryptography in Context

If cryptography is so powerful, why do security breaches occur? Why are there electronic theft, fraud, privacy violations, and all of the other security problems discussed in the previous chapters? Why isn't cryptography the perfect answer to all our security needs? Why am I bothering with the rest of this book?

Surprisingly enough, it's not because of bad cryptography. (Enough of that is out there, but the problems are even more serious.) The answer lies in the difference between theory and practice.

Cryptography is a branch of mathematics. Mathematics is theoretical; mathematics is logical. Good mathematics starts with sound premises, follows a single road—proof after proof—over complex terrain, and ends with unassailable conclusions. By its nature, it looks good on paper.

Security is rooted in the physical world. The physical world is not logical. It is not orderly. There is no single road. There are theories and conclusions, but in order to accept the conclusions you have to accept the premises, the models, and the relationship between the theories and the world. And that's not easy. People don't play along. They do the unexpected; they break the rules. Hardware is the same way: It breaks down, it misbehaves once in a while. Software, too. Software should be logical and orderly—it's only ones and zeros, after all—but it is often so complex that it behaves more like an organism than a piece of mathematics. No matter how good the cryptographic theory is, when it is used in a system, it intersects with practice.

I often talk about products being "buzzword compliant." Their marketing literature proclaims that "We use RSA," or triple-DES, or whatever cryptographic algorithms are in vogue. It's like advertising a house as completely safe just because it has a certain brand of door lock. It's just not enough.

KEY LENGTH AND SECURITY

Despite what I said last chapter, key length has almost nothing to do with security.

The lock on the front door of your house has a series of pins in it. Each of the pins has multiple possible positions. When someone inserts a key into the lock, the pins are each moved to specific positions. If the positions dictated by the key are the ones that the lock needs to open, it does. Otherwise, it doesn't.

Most residential locks have five pins, each of which can be in one of ten different positions. That means that there are 100,000 possible keys. A burglar with a gargantuan key ring can try every possible key, one after the other, and eventually he will get in. He had better be patient, because even if he can try a new key every five seconds, it will take him an average of 69 hours to find the correct key—and that doesn't include bathroom, meal, or sleep breaks.

One day a salesman knocks on your door, and offers to sell you a new lock. His lock has seven pins with twelve positions each. A burglar, he tells you, will have to try different keys for almost three years, nonstop, before he will be able to open your door. Do you feel more secure with this lock?

Probably not. No burglar would ever stand at your doorstep for 69 hours anyway. He's more likely to pick the lock, drill it out, kick the door down, break a window, or just hide in the bushes until you saunter up the front walk. A lock with more pins and positions won't make your house more secure, because the specific attack it makes more difficult—trying every possible key—isn't one you're particularly worried about. As long as there are enough pins to make that attack infeasible, you don't have to worry about it.

The same is true for cryptographic keys. If they are long enough, brute-force attacks are simply beyond the capabilities of human engineer-ing. But there are two worries. The first is the quality of the encryption algorithm, and the second is the quality of the keys. How long is "long enough" is more complicated than a simple number; it depends on both of these things.

But first I need to explain about entropy.

Entropy is a measure of disorder; or, more specifically in the context of cryptography, it is a measure of uncertainty. The more uncertain some-thing is, the more entropy in that thing. For example, if a random person from the general population is either male or female, the variable "gen-der" has one bit of entropy. If a random person prefers one of the four Beatles, and each is equally likely, that corresponds to two bits of entropy. The sex of someone on a women's Olympic running team has no entropy; everyone is female. The entropy of the Beatle-preference at a John Lennon fan club meeting has much less than two bits, because it is more likely that a random person will prefer John. The more certainty in the variable, the less the entropy.

The same is true for cryptographic keys. Just because an algorithm accepts 128-bit keys does not mean it has 128 bits of entropy in the key. Or, more exactly, the best way to break a given implementation of a 128-bit encryption algorithm might not be to try every possible key. The "128 bits" is simply a measure of the maximum amount of work required to break the algorithm and recover the key; it says nothing about the mini-mum.

The first worry is the source of the keys. All the key-length calcula-tions I just made assume that each key has maximum entropy when it is generated. In other words, I assumed that each key is equally likely: that the random number generator that created the keys was perfect. This just isn't true.

Many keys are generated from passwords or passphrases. A system that accepts 10-character ASCII passwords might require 80 bits to represent, but has much less than 80 bits of entropy. High-order ASCII bits won't appear at all, and passwords that are real words (or close to real words) are much more likely than random character strings. I've seen entropy esti-mates of standard English at less than 1.3 bits per character; passwords have less than 4 bits of entropy per character. This means that an 8-char-acter password is about the same as a 32-bit key, and if you want a 128-bit key, you are going to need a 98-character English passphrase.

You see, a smart brute-force password-cracking engine isn't going to try every possible key in order. It's going to try the most likely ones first, and then try the rest in some likelihood order. It will try common pass-words like "password" and "1234," then the entire English dictionary, and then varied capitalization and extra numbers, and so on. This is called a *dictionary attack*. L0phtcrack is a password-cracking program that does this; on a 400-MHz Quad Pentium II, it can test an encrypted password against an 8-megabyte dictionary of popular passwords in seconds.

This is why it is laughable when companies like Microsoft tout 128-bit encryption and then base the key on the password. (This describes pretty much all of Windows NT security.) The algorithms they use might accept a 128-bit key, but the entropy in the password is far, far less. In fact, it doesn't matter how good the cryptography is or what the key length is; weak passwords will break this system. (The obvious solution, preventing people from trying lots of passwords, doesn't work. I talk about this more in Chapter 9.)

This is a big deal. I see complex systems where the private key is pro-tected with a password. Almost every hard-disk encryption product bases its security on a user-remembered key. Almost all the security of Win-dows NT collapses because it is all built on user-remembered passwords. Even PGP falls apart if the user chooses a bad passphrase. It doesn't mat-ter what the algorithms are or how large the keys they use; user-remem-bered secrets are not secure by themselves.

Randomly generated keys are much better, but problems remain. Now the random number generator must produce keys with maximum entropy. A flaw in the random number generator is what broke the encryption in Netscape Navigator 1.1. While the random number gener-ator was used to generate 128-bit keys, the maximum entropy was around 20 bits. So the algorithm was no better than if it had a 20-bit key.

The second worry is the quality of the encryption algorithm. All of the preceding calculations assumed that the algorithms took the keys they were given and used them perfectly. If flaws in the algorithm allow for attacks, this effectively reduces the entropy in the keys. For example, the A5/1 algorithm, used in European GSM cell phones, has a 64-bit key, but can be broken in the time it takes to brute-force a 30-bit key. This means that even though the algorithm is given a cryptographic key with 64 bits of entropy, it only makes use of 30 bits of entropy in the key. You might as well use a good algorithm with a 30-bit key.

This is the reason why it takes so long before cryptographers are will-ing to trust a new algorithm. When someone proposes a new algorithm, it has a particular key length. But does the algorithm actually deliver the entropy that it claims to? It might take years of analysis before we trust that it does. And even then we could easily be wrong; new mathematics could be invented that reduce the algorithm's entropy and break it. This is also why products that advertise thousand-bit keys are hard to take seriously; their promoters don't understand how keys and entropy work.

A similar issue exists with physical keys and locks. I used to know a locksmith who would carry large key rings around in his truck. It might require 10,000 keys to open all the locks, but in reality a few dozen keys would open all the locks of a particular manufacturer. Sometimes he would have to slide the keys around a bit—note the combination of analysis and a brute-force attack—but it would work. Tedious yes, but nowhere near as tedious as trying all 10,000 possible keys (older cars have four-pin locks). The actual security of door locks was nowhere near the theoretical maximum.

It's the same with combination locks. You can try every possible combination—and there are brute-force safecracking machines that do that—or you can be smarter about it. Modern safecracking machines use a microphone to listen to the dials as they turn, and can open a safe much faster than brute force.

This makes choosing an encryption algorithm very important. I discuss this in more detail at the end of the chapter.

ONE-TIME PADS

One-time pads are the simplest of all algorithms, and were invented early on in the 20th century. The basic idea is that you have a pad of key let-ters. You add one key letter to each plaintext letter, and never repeat the key letters. (That's the "one-time" part.) For example, you add B (2) to C (3) to get E (5), or T (20) to L (12) to get F (6). 20 + 12 = 6 mod 26. This system works with any alphabet, including a binary one. And it's the only provably secure algorithm we've got.

Recall the concept of unicity distance. The unicity distance grows with the length of the key. As the key length approaches the length of the message, the unicity distance approaches infinity. This means that it is impossible to recognize plaintext, and why a one-time pad is provably secure.

It's also pretty much useless. Because the key has to be as long as the message, it doesn't solve the security problem. One way to look at encryption is that it takes very long secrets—the message—and turns them into very short secrets: the key. With a one-time pad, you haven't shrunk the secret any. It's just as hard to courier the pad to the recipient as it is to courier the message itself. Modern cryptography encrypts large things— for example, digital movies, Internet connections, and telephone conversations—dealing with one-time pads that large is just impracticable.

One-time pads have been used in the physical world, in specialized circumstances. Russian spies used pencil and paper one-time pads to com-municate. The NSA broke the system because the Russians reused the same one-time pads. An early Teletype hotline between Washington and Moscow was encrypted using a one-time pad system.

Any product that claims to use a one-time pad is almost certainly lying. And if they're not, the product is almost certainly unusable and/or insecure.

PROTOCOLS

The six tools I discussed in the previous chapter—symmetric encryption, message authentication codes, public-key encryption, one-way hash functions, digital signature schemes, and random number generators— comprise the cryptographer's toolbox. This is what we use to build cryptographic solutions to actual problems: How can I send anonymous e-mail? How can I prevent cell phone fraud? How can I implement a secure Internet voting system? By combining these tools into things called protocols, we can solve these security problems. There are other minor tools that we have to use, but essentially those six primitives are at the core of any cryptographic protocol.

For example, assume that Alice wants to keep some data files private. Here's a protocol that does this. Alice chooses a password, or better yet, a passphrase. The cryptography software hashes that passphrase to obtain a secret key, and then uses a symmetric algorithm to encrypt the data file. The result is a file that can only be accessed by Alice, or someone else who knows the password.

Want to build a secure telephone? Use public-key cryptography to generate a random session key, and then use symmetric cryptography and that session key to encrypt the conversation. A hash function provides added security against man-in-the-middle attacks. (More about those later.) To secure e-mail, use public-key cryptography for privacy and dig-ital signature schemes for authentication. Electronic commerce? Usually nothing more than digital signatures and sometimes encryption for privacy. A secure audit log: combine a hash function, encryption, maybe a MAC, and stir.

What we're doing here is building protocols. A protocol is nothing more than a dance. It's a series of predetermined steps, completed by two or more people, designed to complete a task. Think of the protocol used by a merchant and a customer for purchasing a tangerine. Here are the steps:

1. The customer asks the merchant for a tangerine.
2. The merchant gives the customer a tangerine.
3. The customer gives the merchant money.
4. The merchant gives the customer change.

Everyone involved in the protocol must know the steps. For exam-ple, the customer knows he has to pay for the tangerine. All steps must be unambiguous; neither the merchant nor the customer can reach a step where they don't know what to do. And the protocol has to terminate; there can be no endless loops.

There's also a certain amount of processing by the parties. For exam-ple, step 2 won't work properly unless the merchant understands the semantic content of step 1. The merchant won't complete step 4 unless she recognizes the money as real in step 3. Try buying a tangerine in the United States with Polish zlotny and see how far you get.

The particular protocols we're concerned about are secure protocols. In addition to the preceding requirements, we don't want either the cus-tomer or the merchant to be able to cheat (whatever "cheat" means in this context). We don't want the merchant to be able to peek into the customer's wallet in step 3. We don't want the merchant to be able to not give the customer change in step 4. We don't want the customer to be able to shoot the merchant dead in step 3 and walk away with a stolen tangerine. These cheats are possible in the physical world, and the anonymity of cyberspace exacerbates the risks.

Even in the physical world, more complex protocols have been designed to mitigate the risks of different types of fraud. Think of the basic car-purchase protocol:

1. Alice gives the title and keys to Bob.
2. Bob gives a check for the purchase price to Alice.
3. Alice deposits the check.

In this protocol, Bob can easily cheat. He can give Alice a bad check. She won't know the check is bad, and won't find out until the bank tells her that the check bounced. By then, Bob is long gone with Alice's car.

When I sold my car a few years ago, I used this modified protocol to prevent that attack:

1. Bob writes a check and gives it to the bank.
2. After putting enough of Bob's money on hold to cover the check, the bank "certifies" the check and gives it back to Bob.
3. Alice gives the title and keys to Bob.
4. Bob gives the certified check for the purchase price to Alice.
5. Alice deposits the check.

What's going on here? The bank is acting as a trusted third party in this scrap of street commerce. Alice trusts the certification on the check, that the bank will honor the check for its full amount. Bob trusts that the bank will keep the money for the check on hand, and not spend it on risky loans in Third World countries. Alice and Bob can complete their transaction, even though they don't trust each other, because they both trust the bank.

This system works not because the bank is a solid institution backed by impressive-looking buildings and a solid advertising campaign, but because the bank has no interest in Alice and Bob's transaction and has a reputation to uphold. It will follow the protocol for a certified check no matter what. If Bob has enough money in his account, the bank will issue the check. If Alice presents the check for payment, the bank will pay. If it did abscond with the money, there wouldn't be much of a bank left. (This is the essence of reputation.)

This protocol works to protect Alice, but the bank does not protect Bob against buying a forged title and a stolen car. For that, we need another protocol:

1. Alice gives the title and keys to a lawyer.
2. Bob gives the check to the lawyer.
3. The lawyer deposits the check.
4. After waiting a specified time period for the check to clear and for Bob to register the car, the lawyer gives the title to Bob. If the check does not clear within a specified time period, the lawyer returns the title to Alice. If Bob cannot get a clean title for the car (because Alice gave him a bad title), Bob shows proof of this to the lawyer and gets his money back.

As in the previous protocol, a trusted third party gets involved. In this case, the trusted third party is a lawyer. Alice does not trust Bob and Bob does not trust Alice, but both trust the lawyer to act fairly in the final step. The lawyer is completely disinterested in the transaction; he does not care whether he gives the title to Bob or Alice. He will keep the money in escrow and do whatever is required, based on the agreement between Alice and Bob.

Other protocols are more mundane, and might not involve complicated exchanges. For example, here's a protocol a bank can use to verify that a check was signed by Alice:

1. Alice signs the check.
2. The bank compares the signature on the check with the signature it has on file for Alice.
3. If they match, the bank gives Alice her money. If they don't match, the bank doesn't.

In theory, the protocol is secure against Bob cheating and getting Alice's money, but of course reality is more complicated. Bob could learn forgery. The bank could make risky loans in Paraguay and go under. Alice could pull a gun. There are probably hundreds of ways to break this pro-tocol, but given a reasonable set of assumptions on people's behavior, the protocol works.

Protocols in the digital world are much the same as the preceding examples. Digital protocols use cryptography to do the same sorts of things: keep secrets, authenticate things, enforce fairness, provide audit, whatever.

The Internet is full of security protocols, which I discuss in the next section. Other digital networks have their own security protocols. The cell phone industry uses a bunch of protocols, both for privacy and fraud prevention, with varying degrees of success. Set-top television boxes have security protocols. Smart cards do, too.

Protocols involving digital signatures can be particularly useful in different authentication situations. For example, digital signature schemes can produce signatures that only the designated recipient can authenticate. This is useful for informants or whistle-blowers, since the receiver of the message can verify who sent it, but cannot prove this fact to a third party. (Think of a secret whispered in your ear. You know who said it, but there's nothing you can do to prove to someone else who said it.) Digital signature protocols can be used to sign software so that only a person who buys the software package legitimately can verify the signature and know that it is authentic; anyone who pirates a copy can't be sure of this. We can create group signatures, so that outside the group each signature appears to come from the group as a whole, but people inside the group can determine who signed what.

More complex protocols can make cryptography jump through all sorts of hoops. We can do something called zero-knowledge proofs, where Alice can prove to Bob that she knows something without reveal-ing to him what it is. Cryptographic protocols can also support a system for simultaneous contract signing over the Internet, such that neither party is bound by the contract unless the other is. We can create the digital equivalent of certified mail, where Alice can't read the mail unless she sends back a receipt.

Using a protocol called secret sharing, we can enforce requirements for *collusion in access:* secrets that cannot be revealed unless multiple people act in concert. This is a really neat notion. Think of a nuclear missile silo. In order to launch the missile, two people have to simultaneously turn keys and unlock the system. And the keyholes (or in this case, the digital equivalent) are far enough apart that a single rogue soldier can't kill every-one else and turn all the keys himself: At least two people must act in concert to launch the missile. Or think of a corporate checking account that requires two signatures on high-value checks: Any two of the five corporate officers need to sign the check. We can do this kind of thing with cryptography.

It gets even better. We can create protocols for secure voting over the Internet, such that only registered voters can vote, no one can vote more than once, no one can learn anyone else's vote, and everyone can be sure that the election is fair. We can even create digital cash: digital money that is completely anonymous, unless someone copies the bits and tries to spend the same money twice.

Honestly . . . if you want it, we can do it.

The "but" is most of the rest of this book.

INTERNET CRYPTOGRAPHIC PROTOCOLS

Cryptography is relatively new to the Internet, and is only here because of the Net's commercialization. The Internet is insecure, so cryptography is needed to secure it. Hence, you're seeing cryptographic protocols stapled onto almost every Internet protocol. These examples are current in 2000; they will definitely change in the future.

E-mail was the first use of cryptography on the Internet. There are two competing protocols: S/MIME and OpenPGP. OpenPGP is the protocol in PGP (Pretty Good Privacy) and variants; S/MIME is the Internet standard protocol in just about everything else.

Netscape invented SSL during the early days of the Web, as people wanted to do secure electronic commerce with their Web browsers. SSL has gone through a few incarnations (it was a battleground during the Netscape/Microsoft browser wars, and will eventually be called TLS). (SSL stands for "Secure Sockets Layer" and TLS stands for "Transport Layer Security" . . . if anyone asks.) These protocols are embedded in browsers, and allow people to encrypt sensitive information being sent to various Web sites.

Newer cryptographic protocols have been developed to secure IP packets. These include Microsoft Point-to-Point Tunneling Protocol (PPTP, which is badly flawed), Layer Two Tunneling Protocol (L2TP), and IPsec (which is a lot better, although too complicated). IKE is Internet Key Exchange, which is the key-exchange protocol for IPsec. Today these protocols are being used primarily to implement another Internet buzzword called a virtual private network (VPN). IP security protocols can do a lot more than VPNs, though. They have the potential to secure most of the traffic on the Internet. Eventually, maybe they will.

There are other Internet protocols, too. SET is a protocol designed by Visa and MasterCard for securing credit card transactions on the Web. (This protocol never really saw significant public use.) SSH is the "Secure Shell" protocol, and is used to encrypt and authenticate remote com-mand-line connections. Other protocols deal with public-key certificates and certificate infrastructure: PKIX, SPKI, and their relatives. Microsoft has several protocols used to secure Windows NT.

Much of this work is done under the auspices of the Internet Engineering Task Force (IETF), the standards body that deals with much of the Internet's infrastructure. The process works more or less by consen-sus, which means that things take longer than they ought to, and end up being more complicated than they ought to. As we'll see later, this complexity isn't a good thing.

TYPES OF PROTOCOL ATTACKS

Just as there are different attacks against algorithms, there are different attacks against protocols. The simplest are *passive attacks:* Just listen to the protocol going by, and see what you can learn. Often, you can learn a lot by eavesdropping.

There are many Web-based e-mail sites. To use one, you point your browser at that site, and type your username and password. In general, this protocol is vulnerable to an eavesdropping attack. Another set of proto-cols vulnerable to an eavesdropping attack are the protocols that prevent analog cell phone fraud. Someone with a scanner can eavesdrop on the communications between the cell phone and the base station and then make calls on that cell phone's account. (This is called *phone cloning.* Digital cell phones are better, but not much.)

What's tricky with eavesdropping attacks is that it is not always clear what information is valuable. You could imagine an encrypted telephone network, where it is impossible (assuming the security of the cryptogra-phy) to eavesdrop on the phone conversations. However, the switching information is still sent in the clear. This information, basically a record of who calls whom and how long they talk, is often just as valuable. In a military setting, for example, you can learn a lot from traffic analysis: who talks to whom, at what time, and for how long.

More complex attacks are known as *active attacks:* inserting, deleting, and changing messages. These can be much more powerful.

Consider a smart card digital cash system. People put money onto the cards, and then use the cards to buy things. This system will have a lot of different protocols: protocols for adding money onto the card, protocols for transferring money from the card to another device, protocols for querying the card, and so on.

Active attacks can do a lot of damage here. Maybe you can manipu-late the protocol between the bank and the card that adds money onto the card. If you can replay old messages, you can add more money onto the card. Or maybe you can delete a message in the protocol for transferring money out of the card when you buy something, so that the money never gets decremented from the card.

One powerful attack is the *man-in-the-middle* attack. Alice wants to talk securely with Bob, using some public-key algorithm to establish a key. Eve, the eavesdropper, intercepts Alice's communication. She pre-tends to be someone named Bob to Alice, completing the key-exchange protocol. Then she contacts Bob and pretends to be Alice, completing a second key-exchange protocol with Bob. Now she can eavesdrop on the communications. When Alice sends a message to Bob, Eve intercepts it, decrypts it, re-encrypts it, and sends it on to Bob. When Bob sends a mes-sage to Alice, Eve performs a similar procedure. This is a powerful attack.

Of course, good protocol designers take these attacks into account and try to prevent them. Better communications protocols don't permit man-in-the-middle attacks, and certainly don't allow eavesdropping of passwords. Better electronic commerce protocols don't allow malicious users to arbitrarily add cash to smart cards. But people make mistakes, and lots of protocols have problems.

And again, it's not always apparent what kinds of attacks need to be prevented. There was a public-key authentication protocol that appeared in the literature, designed so users could authenticate themselves to hosts. The protocol was made secure against passive eavesdropping attacks and against active insertion/deletion attacks. As it turned out, the protocol was not secure against a malicious host. Alice could authenticate herself to a host, and no eavesdropper could masquerade as Alice. But the host could.

This is an interesting attack. In some circumstances, the host is assumed to be trusted and this is not a problem. In others, it is. We can certainly imagine malicious hosts on the Web. If an online bank used this protocol (as far as I know, none does), a criminal could set up a phony bank Web site with a slightly different URL. An unsuspecting user could authenticate himself to this phony site, which could then masquerade as the user to the bank.

A lot of this has been formalized. There are automatic tools for analyzing protocols: formal logics, computer programs that examine the details of protocols, and others. These tools are useful, and regularly find security problems in existing protocols, but cannot be used to "prove" the security of a protocol.

CHOOSING AN ALGORITHM OR PROTOCOL

Choosing a cryptographic algorithm or protocol is difficult because there are no absolutes. We can't compare encryption algorithms the way we can compare compression algorithms. Compression is easy: You can demonstrate that one algorithm compresses better—faster, smaller, whatever—than another. Security is hard; while you can show that a particular algorithm is weak, you can't show that one algorithm you don't know how to break is more secure than another. In the absence of absolutes, we use the evidence we have: expert consensus.

The problem can be best illustrated with a story. Suppose your doctor said, "I realize we have antibiotics that are good at treating your kind of infection without harmful side effects, and that decades of research support this treatment. But I'm going to give you a pulverized pretzel instead, because, um, it might work." You'd get a new doctor.

Practicing medicine is difficult. The profession doesn't rush to embrace new drugs; it takes years of testing before benefits can be proven, dosages established, and side effects cataloged. A good doctor won't treat a bacterial infection with a medicine she just invented when proven antibiotics are available. And a smart patient wants the same drug that cured the last person, not something different.

Cryptography is difficult, too. It combines several branches of mathematics with computer science. It requires years of practice. Even smart, knowledgeable, experienced people invent bad cryptography. In the cryptographic community, people aren't even all that embarrassed when their algorithms and protocols are broken. That's how hard it is.

The problem is this: Anyone, no matter how unskilled, can design a cryptographic primitive that he himself cannot break. This is an important point. What this means is that anyone can sit down and create a crypto-graphic primitive, try to break it and fail, and then announce: "I have invented a secure algorithm/protocol/whatever." What he is really saying is: "I cannot break this; therefore it is secure." The first question to ask in response is: "Well, who the hell are you?" Or in more detail: "Why should I believe something is secure because you can't break it? What credentials do you have to support the belief that your inability to break something means that no one else can break it either?"

What the cryptographic community has found is that no one person has those sorts of credentials. (Maybe there's someone inside the NSA, but that person's not talking.) There's no way to prove the security of a primitive; it's only possible to either demonstrate insecurity or fail try-ing. This is called proving the null hypothesis. The best any security com-pany can say is: "I don't know how to break this algorithm/protocol/ whatever, and neither does anyone else." Peer review, long periods of peer review, are the only evidence of security that we have.

Even worse, it doesn't do any good to have a bunch of random peo-ple review the primitive; the only way to tell good cryptography from bad cryptography is to have it examined by experts. Analyzing cryptography is hard, and there is a paucity of people who can do it competently. Before a primitive can really be considered secure, it needs to be examined by many experts over the course of years.

This is why cryptographers prefer the old and public over the new and proprietary. Public cryptography is what cryptographers study, and write papers about. Older primitives have more papers written about them. If there were flaws there, they would have been found already (or so the reasoning goes). The new is riskier precisely because it is new, and not enough people have studied it.

Look at these three alternatives for IP security:

IPsec. Beginning in 1992, it was designed in the open by committee and was the subject of considerable public scrutiny from the start. Everyone knew it was an important protocol and people spent a lot of effort trying to get it right. Security technologies were proposed, broken, and then modified. Versions were codified and analyzed. The first draft of the standard was published in 1995. Aspects were debated on security merits and on performance, ease of implementation, upgradability, and use. In 1998, the committee published a revised version of the protocol. And anyone and everyone interested are still studying it, in public.

PPTP. Microsoft developed its own Point-to-Point Tunneling Protocol (PPTP) to do much the same thing. They invented their own authentication protocol, their own hash functions, and their own key-generation algo-rithm. Every one of these items turned out to be badly flawed. They used a known encryption algorithm, but they used it in such a way as to dilute its security. They made implementation mistakes that weakened the system even further. But since they did all this work internally, no one noticed that their PPTP was weak. Microsoft fielded PPTP in Windows NT, 95, and 98, and used it in their virtual private network (VPN) products. It wasn't until 1998 that a paper describing the flaws was published. Microsoft quickly posted a series of fixes, which have since been evaluated and still found wanting.

Proprietary. Some companies claim their own security solutions to this problem. They don't reveal details, either because they're proprietary or patent pending. You have to trust them. They may claim a new algorithm or a new protocol that is much better than any that exist today. They may claim mathematical breakthroughs. They may claim all sorts of things. The odds of them being true are slim. And even if they make their systems pub-lic, the fact that they've patented them and retain proprietary control means that many cryptographers won't bother analyzing their claims. The compa-nies certainly won't wait the requisite years even if the cryptographers did bother.

You can choose any of these three systems to secure your virtual private network. Although it's possible for any of them to be flawed, you want to minimize your risk. If you go with IPsec, you have a much greater assurance that the algorithms and protocols are strong. Of course, this is no guarantee of security—the implementation could be flawed (see Chapter 13), or a new attack could be discovered—but at least you know that the algorithms and protocols have withstood a level of analysis and review that the other options have not.

Another example: consider symmetric encryption algorithms. There are literally hundreds to choose from, but let's limit it to five:

- Triple-DES, which has been analyzed by pretty much everyone in the cryptographic community since the mid-1970s.
- AES, which (when it is chosen) will be the result of a three-year public selection process that involved pretty much everyone in the cryptographic community.
- Algorithm X, which was published at an academic conference two years ago; there's been one analysis paper published that seems to imply that it is strong.
- Algorithm Y, which someone recently posted on the Internet and assures you is strong.
- Algorithm Z, which a company is keeping secret until the patent issues; maybe they paid a couple of cryptographers to analyze it for three weeks.

This isn't a hard choice. There may be performance constraints that prevent you from choosing the algorithm you want (the primary reason AES exists is that triple-DES is too slow for many environments), but the choice is acutely clear.

It continuously amazes me how often people don't make the obvious choice. Instead of using public algorithms, the digital cellular companies decided to create their own proprietary ones. Over the past few years, all the algorithms have become public. And once they became public, they have been broken. Every one of them. The same thing has happened to the DVD encryption algorithm, the Firewire encryption algorithm, various Microsoft encryption algorithms, and countless others. Anyone who creates his or her own cryptographic primitive is either a genius or a fool. Given the genius/fool ratio for our species, the odds aren't very good.

The counter-argument you sometimes hear is that secret cryptogra-phy is stronger because it is secret, and public cryptography is riskier because it is public. This sounds plausible, but when you think about it for a minute, the dissonance becomes obvious. Public primitives are designed to be secure even though they are public; that's how they're made. So there's no risk in making them public. If a primitive is only secure if it remains secret, then it will only be secure until someone reverse engineers and publishes it. Proprietary primitives that have been "outed" include all the algorithms in the preceding paragraph, various smart card electronic-commerce protocols, the secret hash function in SecurID cards, and the protocol protecting Motorola's mobile MDC-4800 Police Data Termi-nal.

This doesn't mean that everything new is lousy. What it does mean is that everything new is suspect. New cryptography belongs in academic papers, and then in demonstration systems. If it is truly better, then eventually cryptographers will come to trust it. And only then does it make sense to use it in real products. This process can take five to ten years for an algorithm, less for protocols or source-code libraries.

Choosing a proprietary system is like going to a doctor who has no medical degree and whose novel treatments (which he refuses to explain) have no support by the American Medical Association. Sure, it's possible (although highly unlikely) that he's discovered a totally new branch of medicine, but do you want to be the guinea pig? The best security meth-ods leverage the collective analytical ability of the cryptographic commu-nity. No single company (outside the military) has the financial resources necessary to evaluate a new cryptographic algorithm or shake the design flaws out of a complex protocol.

In cryptography, security comes from following the crowd. A home-grown algorithm can't possibly be subjected to the hundreds of thousands of hours of cryptanalysis that DES and RSA have seen. A company, or even an industry association, can't begin to mobilize the resources that have been brought to bear against the Kerberos authentication protocol or IPsec. No proprietary e-mail encryption protocol can duplicate the confidence that PGP or S/MIME offers. By following the crowd, you can leverage the cryptanalytic expertise of the worldwide community, not just a few weeks of some unnoteworthy analyst's time.

It's hard enough making strong cryptography work in a new system; it's just plain lunacy to use new cryptography when viable, long-studied alternatives exist. Yet most security companies, and even otherwise smart and sensible people, exhibit acute neophilia and are easily blinded by shiny new pieces of cryptography.

And beware the doctor who says, "I invented and patented this totally new treatment that consists of pulverized pretzels. It has never been tried before, but I'm sure it is much better." There's a good reason new cryp-tography is often called *snake oil.*

8

Computer Security

Computer security is different from cryptography. It often uses cryptography, but its scope is much broader. General computer security includes such diverse things as controlling authorized (and unauthorized) computer access, managing computer accounts and user privileges, copy protection, virus protection, software metering, and database security. More generally, it also includes defenses against computers across network connections, password sniffers, and network worms, but we'll discuss those sorts of things in the chapters on network security. In the age of the Internet, computer security and network security have blurred considerably; but for the purposes of this book, I'll draw the somewhat arbitrary line between computer and network security as "whether or not the security problem affects any computer, as opposed to just a computer attached to networks." General computer security, which can be defined as the prevention and/or detection of unauthorized actions by users of a computer system, seems a whole lot harder than the simple mathematics of cryptography. And it is.

Philosophically, the problem is that the defender doesn't have math-ematics on his side. The mathematics of cryptography gives the defender an enormous advantage over the attacker. Add one bit to the key, double the work to break the algorithm. Add ten bits, multiply the work by a thousand. Computer security is more balanced: attackers and defenders can get similar advantages from technology. What this means is that if you can rely on cryptography for security, you're in great shape. Unfortunately, most of the time you can't.

Most of the early computer security research was devoted to private access in shared systems. How could Alice and Bob use the same computer—and the same computer programs—such that Alice couldn't see what Bob was doing and Bob couldn't see what Alice was doing? Or, more generally: If lots of users share a system, each of whom has certain permissions—permissions to use certain programs and permissions to view certain data—how can we enforce those access control rules? This isn't really a problem that cryptography can solve, although cryptography might help here and there. It's a new problem.

There's a plethora of other new problems in computer security: How can a company maintain a large database where people have different access privileges? This problem can quickly get overly complicated. Only some people can view salary data, even fewer people can change salary data, other people can view health benefit data, and some people can only view aggregate data: average salary, health statistics, and so forth.

How can users be sure that the computer programs they use are cor-rect, and have not been modified? How can they be sure that their data have not been modified? How can a company enforce its licensing rules: Software cannot be copied from machine to machine, the software can run only on five computers at any one time, only ten users can use the software at any one time, the software can only run for one thousand hours?

These are all complex requirements, and computer security provides complex solutions for them.

DEFINITIONS

A surprising amount of effort has gone into trying to define computer security. Historically, computer security has three aspects: confidentiality, integrity, and availability.

Confidentiality is not much more than the privacy we talked about in Chapter 5. Computer security has to stop unauthorized users from reading sensitive information. This has changed somewhat with the advent of electronic commerce and business processes on the Net—integrity is much more important—but this bias remains in most computer-security products. The bulk of computer-security research has centered around confidentiality, primarily because the military funded much of the early research. In fact, I've seen confidentiality and security used as synonyms.

Integrity is harder to precisely define. The best definition I've seen is: "Every piece of data is as the last authorized modifier left it." Within the context of computer security, integrity is about the security of writing data. Data integrity: ensuring that the data has not been deleted or altered by someone without permission. Software integrity: ensuring that the software programs have not been altered, whether by an error, a malicious user, or a virus.

This definition of integrity illustrates how closely it is related to con-fidentiality. The latter is about unauthorized reading of data (and pro-grams); the former is about unauthorized writing. And, in fact, the same sorts of security techniques (cryptographic and otherwise) achieve both goals.

Availability is the third traditional pillar of computer security, but in reality it is much broader than computer security. Availability has been defined by various security standards as "the property that a product's services are accessible when needed and without undue delay," or "the property of being accessible and usable upon demand by an authorized entity." These definitions have always struck me as being somewhat cir-cular. We know intuitively what we mean by availability with respect to computers: We want the computer to work when we expect it to as we expect it to.

Lots of software doesn't work when and as we expect it to, and there are entire areas of computer science research in reliability and fault-tolerant computing and software quality . . . none of which has anything to do with security. In the context of security, availability is about ensur-ing that an attacker can't prevent legitimate users from having reasonable access to their systems. For example, availability is about ensuring that denial-of-service attacks are not possible.

ACCESS CONTROL

Confidentiality, availability, and integrity all boil down to access control. We want to make sure that authorized people are able to do whatever they are authorized to do, and that everyone else is not.

Access control is really a problem much bigger than computers: How do I limit access to something? How do I control access to a shared resource? How do I limit the type of access that different people have? It's a hard problem to solve in a large building—locks on outside doors and inside offices and keys given to specific people, badges worn by everyone and guards to check the badges, and so forth—and it's a hard problem to solve on a computer system.

It's also a problem that's waxed and waned over the years. In the beginning, computers didn't need access control because everyone trusted each other. As more people started using the large mainframes, access control was required both to protect privacy and to audit usage for billing. Access control was easy in a batch-processing world.

When personal computers appeared, they didn't need to provide access control: Every person had his own computer. If someone wanted to prevent others from accessing his files, he just locked his office door. Now we're back using shared systems, shared network resources, remote systems, and the like. Access control is a big deal for almost everyone, whether they're using a shared computer at work or an account on a Web site. And access control is difficult to do properly.

Before talking about different types of access control, we need a couple of definitions. First, there is some "subject" that has access to some "object." Often the subject is a user and the object is a computer file, but not always. The subject could be a computer program or process, and the object another computer program: a plug-in, for example. The object could be a database record. The object could be a certain resource, maybe a piece of computer hardware, or a printer, or a chunk of computer mem-ory. Depending on the circumstance, the same computer program can be a subject in one access-control relationship and an object in another.

There are two ways to define access control. You can define what different subjects are allowed to do, or you can define what can be done to different objects. Really these are two ways of looking at the same thing, but they have their pluses and minuses. Traditionally, operating systems managed resources and files, so access control was defined in terms of these objects. More modern systems are application-oriented. These offer services to end users, like large database management systems. Often these systems have access-control mechanisms that control subjects.

Access isn't all or nothing; there are different types of access permissions. UNIX, for example, has three possible access permissions: read, write, and execute. These permissions are all independent. Someone who has only read permission for a file, for example, cannot modify that file. Someone who has only write permission can change the file but cannot read it; think of a "drop box" directory. Someone who has both read and write permission can do both.

"Execute" is an interesting permission. It makes sense only for computer programs: executable files. Someone who has only execute permission for a certain file can run the program, but cannot read the code nor modify the file. This is an odd permission—how is it possible for a computer to execute a program without first reading it?—and for most file systems it is not a real security distinction. But in some circumstances this makes sense: imagine a program stored in secure memory—a digital sig-nature engine in a tamperproof module—where it is indeed possible to execute a command without reading the code.

These permissions make the implicit assumption that someone is there to decree who has access. In UNIX, this person is known as the owner of the file. Someone who owns a file is allowed to set the permis-sions: who is allowed to read, write, and execute that file. In UNIX, ownership is per file, and is usually determined by which directory the file is in.

Windows NT has a more complicated set of permissions: There's read, write, and execute, and also delete, change permission, and change ownership. The owner of a file can determine who is allowed to change the permissions on the file, and who is allowed to change the ownership.

You can think of the complete set of access controls on a computer as a matrix. On one axis is the list of all possible users; on the other is the list of all possible files. The entries in the matrix are the different permissions. Alice might have read permission for FileA, read/write permission for FileB, and no access to FileC. Bob might have a similarly complicated set of permissions.

For any reasonable-sized computer system, this matrix gets complicated very quickly. So most systems have a shorthand. It's possible to set up permissions so that only the file's owner can read, write, and execute. It's possible to set up permissions so that the file's owner can write, but that anyone can read. It's possible to set up something called a "group," which is a bunch of people with the same set of permissions. So, for example, if a group of people are all working on the same project and need access to a particular set of files, permissions can be set to give them access and no one else. UNIX implements these kinds of things pretty efficiently; a single user can belong to many groups.

One way to manage the complexity of the access control matrix is to split it up. In some systems, the list of who has access to a particular object is stored with the object itself. This is often called an *access control list (ACL).* This is a common way of doing things, and many secure operat-ing systems implement ACLs. There are problems, though. They work well in simple environments where users define their own access permis-sions, but less well in environments where management defines access permissions. There's no easy way, for example, for someone to delegate access authority for a period of time. Also, these kinds of systems don't deal well with run-time permission checking. And because access is tied to objects and not to subjects, it can be hard to turn off access for a par-ticular subject. If someone working for a company gets fired, the system has to go through every object and take that person off each ACL. Finally, considerable work is required to manage an ACL-based system. Many products are sold specifically to manage ACLs.

SECURITY MODELS

There's a plethora of theoretical models to explain security, many of them funded by the Department of Defense in the 1970s and 1980s. Since these were military systems, they formalized the military's system of classifica-tion discussed in Chapter 5. They're called *multilevel security* (MLS) systems, since they were designed to handle multiple levels of classifica-tion in a single system. (The alternatives are clunky. One computer sys-tem for Unclassified data, another completely separate one for Confidential data, a third for Secret data, and so forth. Or *system high,* where the entire computer is classified at the highest level of information.)

The most famous is the Bell-LaPadula model, which defined most of the access control concepts in the previous section. This model defined subjects, objects, and access operations, and a mathematics for talking about them. It was a failure in leading to the development of useful and cost-effective systems, but the theory has had lasting effects on system design.

Bell-LaPadula has two main security rules: one regarding the reading of data and the other regarding the writing of data. If users have Secret clearance, they can read Unclassified, Confidential, and Secret documents, but not Top Secret documents. If users are working with Secret data, they can create Secret or Top Secret documents, but not Confidential or Unclassified ones. (This is important. Imagine someone—a person or maybe a computer virus—trying to steal documents. His computer, of course, prevents him from e-mailing Confidential documents outside the computer. But if he can take a Confidential document and copy the text into an Unclassified document, he can then e-mail the new document. Controls were put in place to prevent this kind of thing.) Basically, users cannot read documents higher than their clearance, nor can they write documents lower than the clearance of their sessions. And yes, it is theoretically possible for users to write documents that they cannot read.

These are *mandatory access controls* in the language of Bell-LaPadula, because they are required by the system. This is in contrast to the "discre-tionary access controls" in operating systems like UNIX or NT, described in the previous section, that allow the users to make their own decisions about who can read or write to what file. (Although most UNIX versions can have some mandatory access controls: Someone with root access has mandatory read, write, and execute access to all files on the computer.)

The Bell-LaPadula model was a big deal, but it had limitations. One, it concentrates on confidentiality at the expense of pretty much every-thing else, and that confidentiality is based on a military model of security classifications. Two, it ignores the problem of how to manage classifications. The model assumes that someone, magically, gives every piece of data a classification, and that classification never changes. In the physical world, classifications change: Someone notices that it is important and classifies it, then someone else declassifies it. Data sometimes have a higher classification in aggregate than each datum does individually: An individ-ual telephone number at the NSA is Unclassified, but the entire NSA phone book is classified Confidential. What this means is that data natu-rally migrates up toward higher classifications, requiring trusted down-grades. And three, sometimes users need to work with data that they are not authorized to see. The fact that an aircraft is carrying a cargo of Q bombs might be classified at a level above a dispatcher, but the dispatcher still needs to know the weight of the cargo.

Many other security models were proposed in the academic literature. The Chinese Wall model, for example, explicitly looked at computer sys-tems with data from mutually distrustful users and how to ensure separa-tion. (Think of a computerized brokerage system, with customers able to access their accounts. The broker wants to prevent Customer A from see-ing Customer B's portfolio, even though both portfolios might be classified at the same level.)

The Clark-Wilson model was designed more for commercial applica-tions and less for military hierarchies. Commercial security requirements are predominantly about data integrity, and their model formalizes that. They defined two types of integrity: internal consistency, which refers to properties of the internal state of the system and can be enforced by the system, and external consistency, which refers to properties of the system in relation to the outside world and which can only be enforced through audit. Then they built a formal security model that codified these princi-ples, as well as principles about confidentiality.

The Clark-Wilson model centers around the notion of "constrained" data: data that can only be operated on in prescribed ways. For example, the model can enforce double-entry bookkeeping requirements: Every credit must be matched with an equal debit, and everything must be writ-ten to a specific audit file. The model prohibits any of these actions from occurring on its own; it is forbidden to credit an account without posting a debit.

SECURITY KERNELS AND TRUSTED COMPUTING BASES

Many operating systems have some built-in security. This makes sense; often the best place to put security is at the lower system layers: the hard-ware layer or the operating system layer. This is a good idea for several reasons.

One, it is often possible to compromise security at a given layer by attacking a layer below. For example, the built-in encryption functions in a word processor don't matter if an attacker can compromise the under-lying operating system. So putting security at the lowest software level is more secure.

Two, it's simpler. At the core of a system, it's often easier to add secu-rity measures. This makes these measures easier to implement and to ana-lyze. And, it is hoped, results in a more secure system.

Three, it's often faster. Everything has better performance when it is embedded into the operating system, and security is no different. Cryptography can eat up a lot of cycles, for example; it makes sense to make it as efficient as possible.

Hence, operating system security has been a research topic for decades. As such, it has developed its own set of concepts:

Reference monitor. A piece of software that mediates all accesses to objects by subjects. When some process makes an operating system call, the reference monitor halts the process and figures out whether the call should be allowed or forbidden. For example, it will not permit a user with a Confidential login account to read a Secret document or write to an Unclassified document.

Trusted computing base. All the protection mechanisms inside the com-puter—hardware, firmware, operating system, software applications, every-thing—that are responsible for enforcing the security policy. That is, some administrator somewhere tells the computer what is supposed to be secured from whom in what way (that's the security policy), and the trusted com-puting base enforces it.

Secure kernel. The hardware, firmware, operating system, software applica-tions, and everything else of the trusted computing base that implements the reference monitor concept.

The reference monitor is an abstract machine that is secure; it handles things like file management and memory management. The security ker-nel implements the reference monitor. The trusted computing base con-tains all the security measures, including the secure kernel. And the whole thing implements some security model—perhaps Bell LaPadula, perhaps something else—and enforces security. All the while being as simple as possible, and as efficient as possible. And, of course, the trusted comput-ing base is by definition trusted—you don't want users able to modify it, or you can lose security.

Implementing these concepts in a real operating system is difficult. Computers are complex beasts, and everything has to be secure. Zillions of little things can go wrong. If everyone has read/write access to the hard disk, how do we prevent one user reading what another user writes? What if one user wants another user to read what she writes? Is it possible for a user to use interrupts to do something he shouldn't? How can we secure access to the printer? Can one person eavesdrop on another via the keyboard? What if the trusted computing base crashes? How do you implement a disk defragmenter if you can only access your own files?

The historical example that got this the most nearly correct is an operating system called Multics, developed in the late 1960s by MIT, Bell Labs, and Honeywell. Multics implemented the Bell-LaPadula model from the ground up. (In fact, the Multics project was the impetus for the Bell-LaPadula model.) The designers used the mathematical formalism of the model to show the security of the system, and then mapped the con-cepts of the model into the operating system. No code was ever written until specifications had been approved. Multics worked, although the security was way too cumbersome. By now, almost everyone has forgot-ten Multics and the lessons learned from that project.

One of the lessons people have forgotten is that the kernel needs to be simple. (Even the Multics kernel, with only 56,000 lines of code, was felt to be too complex.) The kernel is defined as the software that is trusted. Chapter 13 talks about software reliability, the moral being that it is unreasonable to expect software not to have security bugs. The simpler the software is, the fewer bugs it will have.

Unfortunately, modern operating systems are infected with a disease known as "kernel bloat." This means that a lot of code is inside the ker-nel instead of outside. When UNIX was first written, it made a point of pushing nonessential code outside the kernel. Since then, everyone has forgotten this lesson. All current flavors of UNIX have some degree of kernel bloat: more commands inside the kernel, inexplicable utilities running with root permissions, and so forth.

Windows NT is much worse. The operating system is an example of completely ignoring security lessons from history. Things that are in the kernel are defined as secure, so smart engineering says to make the kernel as small as possible, and make sure everything in it is secure. Windows seems to take the position that since things in the kernel are defined as secure, than you should put everything in the kernel. When they can't figure out how to secure something, they just put it into the kernel and define it as secure. Obviously, this doesn't work in the long run.

In Windows, the printer drivers are part of the kernel. Users download printer drivers all the time and install them, probably not realizing that a rogue (or faulty) printer driver can completely compromise the security of their systems. It would be a lot smarter to put the printer driver outside the kernel, so it wouldn't have to be trusted, but it would also be harder. And the Windows NT philosophy always chooses ease—both ease of use and ease of development—over security.

Windows 2000 is worse yet.

COVERT CHANNELS

Covert channels are a way to mess with the minds of people working in security-model research. Remember that one of the two main security rules was that a user or process could not write data to a lower clearance. Covert channels are a way to bypass those controls.

A covert channel is a way for a subject at a higher-level clearance to send a message to a lower-level clearance, generally through some shared resource. So the rogue Top Secret program could send a message by manipulating network packet transmission—two packets in quick succession indicates a one and two packets with a space between them indicates a zero—CPU usage, memory allocation, hard-drive access, print queuing, or just about anything else. The white space in a document could be a covert channel, as could "random" padding at the end of database entries. It's not fast, but messages can be sent from a high-clearance process to a low-clearance process, defeating the security model.

Creating covert channels is easy, and fun. The threat is not users copying Top Secret data off the screen and mailing it to China, it's users writing programs to surreptitiously collect the data in the background while they're not around.

System designers spent a lot of time on this: closing off specific covert channels, or at least minimizing the amount of information that could be sent across them. Maybe CPU cycles were shared at fixed rates, making that particular covert channel unusable. Or maybe a system of random noise was added to the packet-transmission program, making that covert channel much less useful. But it is virtually impossible to close all covert channels, and many systems got by with severely limiting their bandwidth. Still, if the piece of information you want to leak is a tiny 128-bit cryptographic key, you will find a covert channel that can do it.

EVALUATION CRITERIA

If you're going to purchase a computer system with a certain security model, or with a certain kernel type, you are going to need some kind of assurance that the model was adhered to. Or, more generally, some assur-ance that the system provides adequate security.

There are two basic ways you can do this. The first is IVV, which stands for "independent verification and validation." The basic idea is that one team designs and builds the system and another team evaluates that design, sometimes going so far as to build an identical system to compare it with. This is an expensive way of doing things, and you see it in things like nuclear command and control systems and computers on the Space Shuttle.

The cheaper way is to evaluate the system against some independent set of criteria, and give it a security rating of some sort.

The Orange Book was the first set of evaluation criteria to gain accep-tance. It's more or less obsolete, but it did have a major effect on com-puter security in the 1980s, and you still hear Orange Book terms like "C2-level security" bandied about.

The Orange Book is really called U.S. Department of Defense *Trusted Computer System Evaluation Criteria,* but that was a mouthful to say and the book had an orange cover. It was published in 1985 by the National Computer Security Center, which is more or less a branch of the NSA. The point of the Orange Book was to define security requirements and standardize government procurement requirements. It gave computer manufacturers a way to measure the security of their systems, and told them what to build into their secure products. It also offered a system of classifying different levels of computer security, and ways of testing if a certain system met any given level.

The levels ranged from low to high: D (minimal security), C (discre-tionary protection), B (mandatory protection), and A (verified design). Within some of the levels were sublevels. There's C1 and C2, for exam-ple: discretionary security protection and controlled access protection, with the latter being more secure. C1 isn't secure; it's basically what you get with out-of-the-box UNIX. (You don't see many systems boasting about their C1 security rating.) C2 is better; this is probably the most rea-sonable security level for commercial products. Much of the access con-trol procedures were based on the Bell-LaPadula model, which starts at the B1 level. B1, B2, B3, and A were thought to be more suited to mili-tary systems.

The main problem with these levels was that they did not mean that the system was secure. Purchasing a B1 system, for example, did not guar-antee a secure computer. All it meant was that the manufacturer put in the mandatory access controls, and had the required documentation, to get a B1 security rating. Certainly mandatory access controls makes B1 a lot better than C2, but security bugs are just as likely in either system. What it did mean was that the designers tried harder.

Also, the Orange Book only applied to stand-alone systems, and com-pletely ignored what could happen when computers were networked together. Several years ago Microsoft made a big deal about Windows NT getting a C2 security rating. They were much less forthcoming with the fact that this rating only applied if the computer was not attached to a network and had no network card, had its floppy drive epoxied shut, and was running on a Compaq 386. Solaris's C2 rating was just as silly. Recent modifications to the Orange Book tried to deal with networked comput-ers, with mixed success.

And the ratings were notoriously restricted. Systems would get ratings only in particular configurations, with only certain types of software installed. If version 1.0 of an operating system had a certain security level, there was no guarantee that version 1.1 had the same level. If a computer's security rating applied to a particular configuration—with a particular set of installed software—that said nothing about the computer's security with a different configuration.

In today's world of everything interconnected all the time, the Orange Book has fallen into disuse. There have been some attempts, by different national and international organizations, to modernize it. The Canadians came up with something called the Canadian Trusted Com-puter Products Evaluation Criteria. The EU came up with the Informa-tion Technology Security Evaluation Criteria, ITSEC, formerly endorsed in 1995. Another U.S. proposal was called the Federal Criteria.

Recently everyone has gotten together to try to stop this madness.

The Common Criteria is designed to satisfy everyone, and to combine the good ideas of the various other criteria. It's an ISO standard (15408, version 2.1). The general idea is that the Common Criteria provides a cat-alog of security concepts that users can include in a *protection profile,* which is basically a statement of users' security needs. Then individual products can be tested against that protection profile. The government is supposed to oversee that the Common Criteria methodology is executed properly, but commercial laboratories are supposed to provide the actual testing and certification.

The Common Criteria has a Mutual Recognition Agreement, which means that different countries agree to recognize each other's certifica-tions. So far Australia, Canada, France, Germany, New Zealand, the United Kingdom, and the United States have signed on.

This is a giant step in the right direction. The Common Criteria is designed to provide common security (not functional) evaluation of commercially available products against different requirements. The smart card industry has spent a lot of time developing their own protection profile under the Common Criteria. I have high hopes for this program.

FUTURE OF SECURE COMPUTERS

Formal models make for nice theory, but are much less useful in practice. They have theoretical limits; just because there's a security model doesn't mean that you can prove the system has certain security properties. They can result in unusable systems; forcing a system to adhere to a model can result in some bizarre designs. They can take forever to design and build. And even worse, they don't even prove security. If a system conforms to a formal security model, the best it can prove is that it is secure against an attacker who follows the model. The best attackers think of something new; they cheat. And again and again, attackers who don't follow the designers' model break security.

Almost nothing in use today is built on a formal security model. Sys-tems have cribbed ideas from formal security—all operating systems have a trusted computing base, for example—but in order to be useful and usable, they make compromises. This only makes sense.

A secure operating system, and hence a secure computer, has several key components. One is a strong mandatory security mechanism of a more general type than the formal models discuss. This mandatory secu-rity mechanism enforces a policy that is controlled by a policy administra-tor, who is not necessarily the user. Moreover, this policy must control the use of both access and encryption. That is, the policy must enforce who (person or process) is allowed to access what data (or other process), and what kinds of encryption controls must be placed on that data. This kind of policy cannot prevent covert channels (nothing can), but will go a long way toward stopping the kinds of abuses we're seeing today.

The second key component is a *trusted path*. This is a mechanism by which a user (or a process) can interact with a piece of trusted software, which can be initiated by either the user or the trusted software, and can-not be impersonated by another piece of software. For example, would-n't it be nice if when a user saw a login screen he could be sure that it was a real login screen, and not a Trojan horse trying to capture his password? Mechanisms for implementing a trusted path will also go a long way toward limiting the damage malicious software can do.

There are secure oeprating systems on the market that implement some of these components, but they are still niche products. I would like to see more of these ideas flow into mainstream operating systems such as Microsoft Windows. It doesn't look like it will happen anytime soon.

9

Identification and Authentication

No matter what kind of computer security system you're using, the first step is often identification and authentication: Who are you, and can you prove it? Once a computer knows that, it can figure out what you are and are not allowed to do. In other words, access control can't start until identification and authentication is finished.

Let's talk about the problem. Alice has some ability on a computer, and we want to make sure that only she has that ability. Sometimes the ability is access to some information: files, account balances, and so forth. Sometimes the ability is access to the entire computer; no one else can turn the computer on and use her data or programs. Sometimes the abil-ity is more explicit: withdraw money from an ATM, use a cell phone, stop a burglar alarm from ringing. Sometimes the ability is on a Web site: access to her calendar or her brokerage account, for example. Sometimes the ability is access to a cryptographic key that is just too large for her to remember. (PGP uses access control measures to protect private keys.) It doesn't matter what the ability is; what's important is that some access control measure is required to identify Alice.

Actually, the access control measure has to do two things. One, it has to allow Alice in. And two, it has to keep others out. Doing only one is easy—an open door will let Alice, and everyone else, in; a bricked-over door will keep others, as well as Alice, out—but doing both is harder. We need something that will recognize Alice and let her in, but will be hard for others to duplicate. We need to be able to identify Alice and then authenticate that identification. (Actually, the access control measure has to do a third thing: keep a good audit record of what happened.)

Traditionally, identification and authentication measures have cen-tered on one of three things: something you know, something you are, or something you have. These roughly translate to "passwords," "biomet-rics," and "access tokens." Sometimes systems use two of these things together. Paranoid systems use all three.

PASSWORDS

The traditional approach to authentication is a password. You see it everywhere. When you log on to a computer system, you type in a user-name and password. To make a telephone call using a calling card, you type in your account number and password (often, it is given as a single string). To withdraw money from an ATM, you put your card in the slot and type in your PIN (a password).

The two steps in each of those examples mirror the title of this chap-ter. The first step is called identification: You tell the computer who you are (the username). The second step is called authentication: You prove to the computer that you are who you say you are (the password).

The computer at the other end of these transactions has a list of user-names and passwords. Once you have entered in your username and pass-word (or your account number and PIN), the computer compares your input against the entries stored on the list. If you enter a valid username and the correct corresponding password, you're in. If you don't, you're out. Sometimes the system will again prompt you for a username and password. Sometimes the system will lock up after a certain number of bad attempts. (You wouldn't want someone to be able to steal an ATM card and then try all 10,000 possible PINs, one after another, in an attempt to find the correct one.)

Unfortunately the system of username and password works less well than people believe.

The whole notion of passwords is based on an oxymoron. The idea is to have a random string that is easy to remember. Unfortunately, if it's easy to remember, it's something nonrandom like "Susan." And if it's random, like "r7U2*Qnp," then it's not easy to remember.

In Chapter 7, where I talked about key length and security, I discussed the problems of user-generated and user-remembered keys. A password is a form of user-remembered key, and dictionary attacks against passwords are surprisingly effective.

How does this attack work? Think about an access control system for a computer or Web site. The computer has a file of usernames and passwords. If an attacker got her hands on that file, she would learn every password. In the mid-1970s, computer security experts came up with a better solution: Instead of storing all the passwords in a file, they would store a cryptographic hash of the password. Now, when Alice types her password into the computer or Web site, the software computes the hash of the password and compares that hash with the hash stored in a file. If they match, Alice is allowed in. Now there is no file of passwords to steal; there is only a file of hashed passwords to steal. And since a hash function prevents someone from going backward, the attacker can't recover the passwords from the hashed passwords.

Here's where dictionary attacks come in. Assume that an attacker has a copy of the hashed password file. He takes a dictionary, and computes the hash of every word in the dictionary. If the hashed word matches any of the password entries, then he has found a password. After he tries all words, he tries reversed dictionary words, dictionary words with some letters capitalized, and so forth. Eventually he tries all character combina-tions shorter than some length.

Dictionary attacks used to be hard, because computers were slow. They're much easier now, because computers are a lot faster. L0phtcrack is an example of a password recovery hacker tool that is optimized for Windows NT passwords. Windows NT contains two password functions: a stronger one designed for NT, and a weaker one that is backward-compatible with older networking login protocols. The weaker one is case-insensitive, and passwords can't be much stronger than seven charac-ters (even though they may be longer). L0phtcrack makes easy work of this password space. On a 400-MHz Quad Pentium II, L0phtcrack can try every alphanumeric password in 5.5 hours, every alphanumeric pass-word with some common symbols in 45 hours, and every possible keyboard password in 480 hours. This is not good.

Some have dealt with this problem by requiring stronger and stronger passwords. What this means is that the password is harder to guess, and less likely to appear in a password dictionary. The old RACF mainframe sys-tem required users to change passwords monthly, and wouldn't permit words. (Microsoft Windows has no such controls, and helpfully offers to remember your passwords for you.) Some systems generate passwords randomly for users, by concatenating random syllables to create pronounceable passwords (e.g., "talpudmox") or mixing in numbers or symbols and changing case: for example, "FOT78hif#elf." PGP uses passphrases, which are recommended to be complex sentences with nonsense thrown in: for example, "33333Telephone,, it must be YOU speaking sweetly to me1958???!telephone." (Admittedly, that's not as easy to remember and type as you might want.)

These techniques are becoming less and less effective. Over the past several decades, Moore's law has made it possible to brute-force larger and larger entropy keys. At the same time, there is a maximum to the entropy that the average computer user (or even the above-average computer user) is willing to remember. You can't expect him to memorize a 32-character random hexadecimal string, but that's what has to happen if he is to memorize a 128-bit key. You can't really expect him to type the PGP passphrase in the previous paragraph. These two numbers have crossed; password crackers can now break anything that you can reason-ably expect a user to memorize.

There are exceptions to this, of course. You could imagine high-security applications—nuclear launch computers, secure diplomatic chan-nels, systems that communicate with spies living deep in enemy territory—where users will take the time to memorize long and complicated passphrases. These applications have nothing to do with modern computer networks and passwords for commodity e-commerce applications. The problem is that the average user can't, and won't even try to, remember complex enough passwords to prevent dictionary attacks. Attacking a basic password-protected system is often easier than attacking a cryptographic algorithm with a 40-bit key. Passwords are insecure, unless you can stop dictionary attacks.

As bad as passwords are, users will go out of the way to make it worse. If you ask them to choose a password, they'll choose a lousy one. If you force them to choose a good one, they'll write it on a Post-it and stick it on their computer monitor. If you ask them to change it, they'll change it back to the password they changed it from last month. One study of actual passwords found that 16 percent of them were three characters or less, and 86 percent of them were easily crackable. Other studies have confirmed these statistics.

And they'll choose the same password for multiple applications. Want to steal a bunch of passwords? Put up a Web site with something interest-ing on it: porn, hockey scores, stock tips, or whatever will appeal to the demographic you're after. Don't charge for it, but make people register a username and password in order to see the information. Then, sit back and collect usernames and passwords. Most of the time you'll get the same username and password that the user chose last time, maybe the one that lets you into his bank or brokerage accounts. Save incorrect passwords as well; people sometimes enter the password for System A into System B by mistake. Make the user fill out a little questionnaire during registration: "What other systems do you use regularly? Bank X? Brokerage FirmY? News Service Z?" A researcher I know did something like this in 1985; he got dozens of system administrator passwords.

And even when they choose good passwords and change them regu-larly, people are much too willing to share their passwords with others in and out of the organization, especially when they need help to get the work done. Clearly this represents one of the greatest security risks of all, but, in people's minds, the risk is minimal and the need to get work done imperative.

This is not to say that there are not better or worse passwords. The preceding example PGP passphrase is still secure against dictionary attacks. Generally, the easier a password is to remember, the worse it is. Dictio-nary attacks generally try common passwords before uncommon ones: dictionary words, reversed dictionary words, dictionary words with some letters capitalized, dictionary words with minor modifications—like the number "1" instead of the letter "l"—and so forth.

Unfortunately, many systems are only as secure as the weakest pass-word. When an attacker wants to gain entry into a particular system, she might not care which account she gets access to. In operational tests, L0phtcrack recovers about 90 percent of all passwords in less than a day, and 20 percent of all passwords in a few minutes. If there are 1,000 accounts, and 999 users choose amazingly complicated passwords that L0phtcrack just can't possibly recover, it will break the system by recov-ering that last weak ordinary password.

On the other hand, from the user's point of view this can be an exam-ple of "not having to outrun the bear; only having to outrun the people you're with." Any dictionary attack will succeed against so many accounts whose passwords are "Susan" that if your password is "hammerbutterfly," while it's pretty vulnerable to dictionary attacks, it's not likely to actually succumb to one.

Depending on the type of attacker you're worried about, a system with long and strong passwords can be secure. But this is changing all the time; Moore's law means that today's strong password is tomorrow's weak password. In general, if a system is based on passwords and an attacker can mount a dictionary attack, then the system is vulnerable. Period.

There are fixes. This is all predicated on the attacker stealing the file of hashed passwords. Prevent dictionary attacks, and passwords are again good. This is possible, although not easy, for general-access machines. The UNIX password file, for example, is world readable. These days, UNIX has something called a *shadow password file*; it contains the actual hashed passwords, and the world-readable password file contains nothing useful. The hashed password file in NT is well-protected and difficult to steal; you either need administrator access to sniff the hashed passwords across the network (although the latest NT version and Windows 2000 prevent this); or you need to pick up the passwords when they are used by other network applications.

Systems can also lock up after some number of bad passwords, for example, ten. What this means is that after someone fails to log in ten times, the system freezes the account. So if someone tries to log in to Alice's account and starts guessing passwords, he only gets ten guesses before the system freezes. This will, of course, annoy Alice, but it's better than compromising Alice's account. And the exact definition of "freeze" can depend on the circumstance. Maybe it will freeze Alice's account for five minutes, or 24 hours. Maybe it will freeze Alice's account until she talks with some administrator. High-security devices might freeze perma-nently, destroying the information inside, after a certain number of incor-rect passwords.

Another solution is to require a noncomputer interface. Your ATM cash card is protected by a four-digit PIN. That would be trivial for a computer to break—it would take a few milliseconds to try all 10,000 possible PINs—but it's hard for a computer to attach itself to the user interface. A person has to stand at the ATM and try PINs, one after the other. At a brisk ten seconds per attempt it would take 28 hours, nonstop, to try 10,000 PINs.

There are people sufficiently desperate to try this attack, so ATMs will swallow cards if you enter in too many bad passwords. Still, this security measure works for a lot of systems: physical combination locks, deactivation codes for burglar alarms (sure, you can try all 10,000 possible codes, but you've only got 30 seconds), electronic door locks, telephone calling cards, and so on. These systems work because the attack cannot be automated; if you can figure out how to have a computer brute-force all the PINs (or passwords) for these systems, you can break them.

The majority of systems designers don't realize the difference between a system with a manual interface, which can be secure with a four-digit PIN, and a system that has a computer interface. This is why we see weak PIN-like passwords on so many Web systems (including, at the time of writing, several Internet brokerage sites).

What's the solution if you can't prevent dictionary attacks? One trick is to find a bigger dictionary. Another is to add random numbers to the passwords, a trick known as *salting*. There has been some work on different types of visual and graphical passwords; the idea being that there are a lot more possible passwords, and hence it is much harder to mount a dictionary attack. Still, these are limited by the memory of the user.

Passwords are something the user knows. Other authentication tech-niques are based on something the user is—a biometric—or something the user has—an access token.

BIOMETRICS

It's a simple idea: You are your authenticator. Your voiceprint unlocks the door of your house. Your retinal scan lets you in the corporate offices. Your thumbprint logs you on to your computer. It's even used in *Star Trek*; Captain Picard "signs" those electronic memo pads with his thumbprint.

Biometrics are the oldest form of identification. Physical recognition is a biometric; our ancestors used that even before they evolved into humans. Cats spray to mark their territory. Dolphins have individual "sig-nature" calls.

Biometrics are also used for identification in communications systems. On the telephone, your voice identifies you to the person on the other end of the line. On a contract, your signature identifies you as the person who signed it. Your photograph identifies you as the person who owns a particular passport.

For most applications, biometrics need to be stored in a database like passwords. Alice's voice only works as a biometric identification on the telephone if you already know who she is; if she is a stranger, it doesn't help. It's the same with Alice's handwriting; you can recognize it only if you already know it. To solve this problem, banks keep signature cards on file. Alice signs her name on a card when she opens her account, and it is stored in the bank (the bank needs to maintain its secure perimeter in order for this to work right). When Alice signs a check, the bank verifies Alice's signature against the stored signature to ensure that the check is valid. (In practice, that rarely happens. Manual signature checking is so costly that the bank doesn't bother checking for amounts less than about $1,000. If there is a problem, they assume, someone will complain. And making good on the occasional problem is cheaper than paying someone to do the checking.) You could do the same thing with Alice's voice—compare her voiceprint to the one stored in some central database.

The exceptions are situations where the biometric is only verified as part of an involved and uncommon protocol. When Alice signs a con-tract, for example, Bob does not have a copy of her signature on file. The protocol still works because Bob knows that he can verify the signature at some later time, if necessary.

There are many different types of biometrics. I've mentioned hand-writing, voiceprints, face recognition, and fingerprints. There is also hand geometry, typing patterns, retinal scans, iris scans, signature geometry (not just the look of the signature, but the pen pressure, signature speed, and so forth), and others. The technologies behind some of them are more reliable than others—fingerprints are much more reliable than face recog-nition—but that may change as technology improves. Some are more intrusive than others; one failed technology was based on lip pattern, and required the user to kiss the computer. As a whole, biometrics will only get better and better.

"Better and better" means two different things. First, it means that it will not incorrectly identify an impostor as Alice. The whole point of the biometric is to prove that the claimant Alice is the actual Alice, so if an impostor can successfully fool the system, it isn't working very well. This is called a *false positive*. Second, it means that the system will not incor-rectly identify Alice as an impostor. Again, the point of the biometric is to prove that Alice is Alice, and if Alice can't persuade the system that she is herself, then it's not working very well, either. This is called a *false negative.*

Over the years, biometric identification systems have gotten better at detecting both false positives and false negatives. For example, they include checks for liveness, so that neither a plastic finger nor a severed real finger fools the fingerprint reader. They do a better job of correcting for day-to-day variations in an individual's biometric better. They're just easier to use.

In general, you can tune a biometric system to err on the side of a false positive or a false negative. This is all shades of gray here; if the system gets a fingerprint that it is pretty sure belongs to Alice, does it let the finger in? It depends on whether the system is more concerned with false positives or false negatives. If the system is authorizing Alice to take pencils out of a stockroom, then it should err on the side of false negatives; it's much worse to annoy a legitimate user than to lose a few pencils. If the system is protecting large amounts of money, then false positives are preferable: Keeping unauthorized users out is more important than occasionally denying access to a legitimate user. If the system initiates a launch sequence for nuclear missiles, both are dire.

Biometrics are great because they are really hard to forge: It's hard to put a false fingerprint on your finger, or make your retina look like some-one else's. Some people can do others' voices (performers who do imita-tions, for example), and Hollywood can make people's faces look like someone else, but in general those biometrics are hard to forge, too.

On the other hand, biometrics are lousy because they are so easy to forge: It's easy to steal a biometric after the measurement is taken. In all of the applications discussed previously, the verifier needs to verify not only that the biometric is accurate but that it has been input correctly. Imagine a remote system that uses face recognition as a biometric. "In order to gain authorization, take a Polaroid picture of yourself and mail it in. We'll compare the picture with the one we have in file." What are the attacks here?

Easy. To masquerade as Alice, take a Polaroid picture of her when she's not looking. Then, at some later date, use it to fool the system. This attack works because while it is hard to make your face look like Alice's, it's easy to get a picture of Alice's face. And since the system does not verify that the picture is of your face, only that it matches the picture of Alice's face on file, we can fool it.

Similarly, we can fool a signature biometric using a photocopier or a fax machine. It's hard to forge the vice president's signature on a letter giving you a promotion, but it's easy to cut his signature out of another letter, paste it on the letter giving you a promotion, and fax it to the human resources department. They won't be able to tell that the signature was cut from another document.

The moral is that biometrics work great only if the verifier can verify two things: one, that the biometric came from the person at the time of verification, and two, that the biometric matches the master biometric on file. If the system can't do both, it is insecure.

Here's another possible biometric system: thumbprints for remote login authorizations. Alice puts her thumbprint on a reader embedded into the keyboard (don't laugh, a lot of companies want to make this hap-pen, and the technology already exists). The computer sends the digital thumbprint to the host. The host verifies the thumbprint and lets Alice in if it matches the thumbprint on file. This won't work because it's so easy to steal Alice's digital thumbprint, and once you have it, it's easy to fool the host, again and again.

Tamper-resistant hardware helps (within the limitations of Chapter 14), as long as the tamper-resistant hardware includes both the biometric reader and the verification engine. It doesn't work if a tamper-resistant fingerprint reader sends the fingerprint data across an insecure network. Encryption can help, too, though.

Anyway, this brings us to the second major problem with biometrics: It doesn't handle failure well. Imagine that Alice is using her thumbprint as a biometric, and someone steals it. Now what? This isn't a digital cer-tificate (we'll get to those in Chapter 15), where some trusted third party can issue her another one. This is her thumb. She only has two. Once someone steals your biometric, it remains stolen for life; there's no getting it back.

This is why biometrics don't work as cryptographic keys (even if you could solve the fuzzy biometric logic versus absolute mathematical logic problem). Occasionally I see systems that use cryptographic keys gener-ated from biometrics. This works great, until the biometric is stolen. And I don't mean that the person's finger is physically cut off, or the fingerprint is mimicked on someone else's finger; I mean that someone else steals the digital fingerprint. Once that happens, the system does not work anymore. (Well, maybe it will work until all ten fingers are stolen. . . .)

Biometrics can be good authentication mechanisms, but they need to be used properly.

ACCESS TOKENS

The third solution to proving identity is to use something you have: a physical token of some sort. This is an old form of access control: a phys-ical key restricted access to a chest, a room, a building. Possession of the king's seal authorized someone to act on his behalf. More modern systems can be automated—electronic hotel room keys—or manual—corporate badges that allow access into buildings. The basic idea is the same; a phys-ical token serves to authenticate the holder of it.

There are several basic ways this can be done. Most simply, the holder can simply prove that he is holding the token. Computers that require a physical key to turn them on work in this manner; so do computers that require a smart card. The basic idea is that you insert the token into some slot somewhere, and then the computer verifies that it is really there. If it is, you're in.

The most serious problem with this system is that tokens can be stolen. If someone steals your house keys, for example, she can unlock your house. So the system doesn't really authenticate the person; it authenticates the token. Most computer systems combine access tokens with passwords—sometimes called PINs—to overcome this vulnerability. You can think of bank ATM cards. The ATM authenticates the card, and also asks for a PIN to authenticate the user. The PIN is useless without the access token. Some cellular phone systems work the same way: You need the physical phone and an access code to make calls on a particular cellu-lar account.

In addition to stealing a token, someone can copy it. Some tokens can be easily copied—physical keys, for example—so they can be stolen, copied, and replaced without the owner knowing about it.

Another problem is that there needs to be some authenticated way of determining that the token is really there. Think of a token as a removable, changeable biometric, and you've got all the problems of a secure verification path from the previous section. At least the token can be changed if necessary.

This problem can be illustrated using credit cards. It's difficult to forge a physical credit card, which makes it risky to use a forged credit card to purchase things at a store. The clerk might notice that the card is forged. It's far easier to use a forged credit card over the telephone, however. At the store, the clerk authenticates both the account number on the credit card and the credit card itself—the token. Over the phone, the operator cannot authenticate the physical token, only the account number.

There's another, relatively minor, problem that shows up with some tokens. If users can leave the token in the slot, they often do. If the users need to have a smart card inserted in a slot before it will boot, they're likely to leave the smart card there all day and night . . . even when they're not there. So much for authentication.

All of this discussion assumes that there's some kind of reader associ-ated with the token, and the user can insert the token into the reader. This often isn't the case: Most computers don't have the required reader, or the system might have to work for mobile users who could be sitting some-where other than at their normal computers. Two different technologies deal with this situation.

The first is challenge/reply. The token is a pocket calculator, with a numeric keypad and small screen. When the user wants to log in, the remote host presents him with a challenge. He types that challenge into his token. The token calculates the appropriate reply, which he types into the computer and sends to the host. The host does the same calculation; if they match, he is authenticated. The second technology is time-based. This token is the same pocket calculator, with just a screen. The numbers on the screen change regularly, generally once per minute. The host asks the user to type in what is showing on his screen. If it matches what the host expects, he is authenticated. The SecurID token works this way.

Of course, the full system also includes a password—the challenge/ reply token might even require a second password to get it working—and there are other, ancillary, security measures. The basic idea, though, is that some secret calculation is going on inside the token that can't be imper-sonated. An attacker can't pretend to have the token, because she doesn't know how to calculate replies based on challenges, or doesn't know how to calculate values based on the time. The only way to do this is to actu-ally have the token.

This works, more or less. Cryptographic techniques, encrypting or hashing, provide the security. The host knows how to do the calculations, so the system is only as secure as the host's source code. Anyone who can reverse engineer the token can figure out how to do the calculations, so the system is only as secure as the tokens (see Chapter 14). But it's pretty good, and certainly a lot better than passwords alone. The security prob-lems arise in the network, and the authenticating computer.

One last token needs discussion: the password, written down. There is a knee-jerk reaction to writing passwords down in the security community, but if done properly this can improve security considerably. Someone who writes his password down turns something he knows (the password) into something he has (the piece of paper). This trick does allow him to use longer passwords, which can make passwords actually secure again. It does have all the problems of a simple token: It can be copied or stolen. It doesn't work if Alice writes her password on a yellow sticky attached to her monitor. Much better is for her to put her passwords in her wallet; this can be secure. Probably the best solution is to have two parts to the password: one part remembered by Alice, and the other part written down in her wallet.

Similarly, there are systems of one-time passwords. The user has a list of passwords, written down, and uses each one once. This is certainly a good authentication system—the list of passwords is the token—as long as the list is stored securely.

AUTHENTICATION PROTOCOLS

Authentication protocols are cryptographic ways for Alice to authenticate herself across a network. The basic authentication protocol is pretty sim-ple:

1. Alice types in her username and password on the client. The client sends this information to the server.
2. The server looks up Alice's username in a database and retrieves the corre-sponding password. If that password matches the password Alice typed, Alice is allowed in.

The problem with this is that the password database has to be protected. The solution is to not store the passwords, but to store hashes of the passwords:

1. Alice types in her username and password on the client. The client sends this information to the server.
2. The server hashes Alice's typed-in password.
3. The server looks up Alice's username in a database and retrieves the corre-sponding password hash. If that password hash matches the hash of the password Alice typed, Alice is allowed in.

Better. The main problem with the second protocol is that passwords are sent over the network in the clear. Anyone sniffing the network can collect usernames and passwords. Solutions involved hashing passwords before sending them (older versions of Windows NT did this), but dic-tionary attacks can deal with that as well.

As dictionary attacks became more powerful, systems started adding salt to their passwords. (Actually, they did this very early, a good example of designer foresight.) A salt is a known random constant hashed with the password. The effect is to make dictionary attacks harder; instead of a single hash for the password "cat," there would be 4,096 different hashes for "cat" plus 12 bits of random salt. Dictionaries of prehashed passwords would have to be four thousand times larger. But the ability to do fast dictionary attacks in real time makes this countermeasure obsolete; the dictionary simply includes all possible salt values.

Kerberos is a more complicated authentication protocol. To make this work, Alice has to share a long-term key with a secure server on the network, called a Kerberos server. To log on to a random server on the network, which we'll call the Bob server, the following procedure is car-ried out:

1. Alice requests permission from the Kerberos server to log on to the Bob server.
2. The Kerberos server checks to make sure Alice is allowed to log on to the Bob server. (Note that the Kerberos server does not need to know that Alice is who she says she is. If she isn't, the protocol will fail in step 6.)
3. The Kerberos server sends Alice a "ticket" that she is supposed to give to the Bob server, and a session key she can use to prove to Bob that she is Alice.
4. Alice uses the session key from the Kerberos server to create an "authenti-

cator" that she will use to prove to Bob that she is Alice.

5. Alice sends Bob both the ticket and the authenticator.

6. Bob validates everything. If it all checks out, he lets Alice in. (Bob also shares a long-term key with the Kerberos server. The ticket is a message from the server encrypted in Bob's long-term key.)

This protocol is secure in the same way that physical ticket protocols are secure. The Kerberos server prints tickets. It gives Alice a ticket that she can present to Bob. Bob can validate the ticket, so he knows that Alice received it from the Kerberos server.

This protocol has some nice properties. The long-term secrets of Alice and Bob, which are kind of like passwords, are never sent through the network. On the minus side, this system needs a Kerberos server to operate; the Kerberos server is a trusted third party. This can mean a bot-tleneck in the system at 9:00 in the morning, when everyone is trying to log on to their computer.

Kerberos was invented at MIT in 1988, and has been used in the UNIX world ever since. Kerberos is part of Windows 2000, but Microsoft's implementation differs from the standard and is incompatible with the rest of the Kerberos world. I can only assume this was done for deliberate marketing reasons (at this writing, Microsoft only allowed you to open the file with the modification details if you first clicked on a screen agreeing to treat the information as proprietary, so third-party developers can't build interoperable systems), but it makes for bad security. You can't just modify a security protocol and assume that the modified protocol is also secure.

Other, more Byzantine, login authentication protocols use public-key cryptography. IPsec and SSL, for example, use public-key authentication protocols. Some systems use simple, but esoteric, protocols. The protocol by which a cell phone proves that it should be allowed to make telephone calls in a particular network is one of these.

SINGLE SIGN-ON

One thing that has annoyed computer users in large secure environments is the large number of passwords. Users might have to type in one password to log on to their computers, another to log on to the network, a third to log on to a particular server on the network, and so on and on and on. Wouldn't it be better, people asked, if users could sign on once, with one password, and then have the computers handle all of that other logging in?

Single sign-on is the solution to this usability problem: the Holy Grail of network security. Unfortunately, it doesn't work very well. First, there's the morass of legacy applications and security measures that just don't play well with each other. It's not a matter of choosing the same password for everything—that's a bad idea—it involves a lot of interface programming. Second, there's the additional security risk of a single point of failure. It's the difference between losing a single credit card and losing your entire wallet.

There are single sign-on products out there, and they work in some situations. But it will never be the panacea vendors claim.

10

Networked-Computer Security

In this chapter I want to talk about attacks on computers on the Internet. You could think of these attacks as attacks against computers, which should be part of Chapter 8. You could also think of these attacks as network attacks, which should be part of Chapter 11. I think they are a different kind of attack, and am separating them in their own chapter.

MALICIOUS SOFTWARE

Malicious software is probably the first interaction most of us had with computer security. Even if no one has access to your computer but you, and it is not attached to a network, you have to worry about viruses. The reason is that you don't really know what is going on in your computer, and trust the software you are running to behave itself. If you run an untrusted piece of software, you are taking a risk.

Malicious software includes viruses, Trojan horses, and worms. Together these are called *malware*. Malware generally has two components: a payload and a propagation mechanism. The payload is the part that does damage. Traditionally, payloads have been boring; a prototypi-

151

cal virus might display an annoying message on the screen, reformat the victim's hard drive, or do absolutely nothing. It could also do much sneakier things: modify the access control permissions on the computer, steal a secret key and send it via e-mail to someone, and so on. Payloads can be malign, and I expect that we'll see more devious payloads over the next few years. More interesting for this book are the propagation mech-anisms, and this is how we classify malware.

Computer Viruses

A biological virus is a simple submicroscopic infectious agent that often causes disease in plants, animals, and bacteria. It consists essentially of a core of RNA or DNA surrounded by a protein coat. Viruses are unable to replicate without a host cell, and are typically not considered living organisms. For once, the metaphor is accurate. A computer virus is a string of computer code that attaches itself to another computer program (it can't live on its own). Once attached, it replicates by co-opting the program's resources to make copies of itself and attach them to other programs. And so on.

In 1983, USC student Fred Cohen wrote the first computer virus. He did it to demonstrate the concept (a surprising number of people didn't believe it was possible). Gaggles of people copied him, many just to annoy the world. Today there are anywhere from 10,000 to 60,000 different viruses (depending on how you count), most of them written for IBM-compatible PCs. I've seen estimates that six more are created daily, although that's mendacious and alarmist. Only a few hundred are ever seen "in the wild"—meaning "on the hard drive of someone not actively engaged in computer-virus research"—but those that are can be particu-larly devastating.

There are three primary categories of viruses: file infectors, boot-sec-tor viruses, and macro (interpreted) viruses.

For a long time file infectors were the most common. They work by attaching themselves to program files, such as word processors and com-puter games. When a user runs an infected application, the virus installs itself in memory so that it can infect other applications the user runs. It spreads on the user's machine, and if the user gives someone else a disk with an infected application (or sends it across the network), another user gets infected.

Most file infectors are extinct in the wild. Changes in the underlying computers can make viruses not able to run, just as commercial software often needs to be updated for new operating systems and processors. Many file infectors died out around 1992 when Windows 3.1 was released; they simply crashed the operating system and could not spread.

Boot-sector viruses are less common. They reside in a special part of a disk (either diskette or hard disk) that is loaded into memory when the computer first boots up. Once loaded, a boot-sector virus can infect all hard disks and any diskette that is placed in the drive, and then can spread to other systems. Boot-sector viruses are particularly effective, and even though there are far fewer strains, they were, for a time, far more preva-lent than file infectors.

Boot-sector viruses can coexist peacefully with Windows 3.1, but they saw a major die-off when Windows 95 became popular. Boot incompatibilities and alerts made it much harder for them to spread. We've seen viruses specifically designed for Windows 95, although none have become widespread since no one boots from a floppy anymore.

The final virus category is macro viruses. These are written in script-ing languages and infect data files rather than programs. Many word processors, spreadsheets, and database programs have scripting languages. These scripts, sometimes called macros, are used to automate tasks and are stored with the data. People have written viruses using these scripting languages. The first Microsoft Word macro virus, "Concept," was first observed in the wild in 1995; they existed in the Emacs text editor as early as 1992.

These viruses can spread much more quickly than the others can, because people exchange data more often than they exchange programs. And as e-mail, collaboration, and file transfer software become easier to use, they will spread even faster. Macro viruses can also exist cross-plat-form: Some Microsoft Office macro viruses can infect both Windows and Macintosh machines.

Macro viruses are the future. All the fast-spreading Internet viruses are macro viruses. The good ones even have a social-engineering compo-nent; they try to trick the user into installing, running, or spreading them.

Antivirus software is a bigger business than writing viruses. (I guess that's obvious; no one pays for viruses.) Most antivirus programs scan files looking for viruses. They keep a database of virus footprints—bits of code that are known to be parts of viruses—and when they find the same footprint on a file, they know it has been infected. These programs can then disinfect the file by removing the viral code. Fingerprint scanning only works after the antivirus company has isolated the virus in its lab and updated its software to include the new fingerprint: hence the brisk busi-ness in antiviral software updates.

In some ways we've been fortuitous with respect to computer viruses; all the ones we've seen are targeted against large computers, not periph-erals or embedded systems. It's possible to write a virus in the PostScript printing language. It could propagate from document to document. It could affect printers. It's possible to write a virus that infects cell phones, and propagates via the cellular network. It's possible to write a virus that affects almost any computerized system; we've seen one that's specific to WebTV devices. If we haven't seen it yet, it's because no one with the requisite knowledge and lack of morals has bothered making one.

To catch unknown viruses, polymorphic viruses (which mutate with every infection), and encrypted viruses (which use cryptography to hide their footprints), some antiviral products monitor the computer system looking for "suspicious" virus-like behavior. (Normal virus checkers are pretty brain-dead; sometimes just changing variable names is enough to fool them.) These systems work moderately well, although they rely on users to make security decisions: Is this a virus or a false alarm?

Viruses have no "cure." It's been mathematically proven that it is always possible to write a virus that any existing antivirus program can't stop. (Even the Bell-LaPadula model does not prevent virus attacks.) I'll elide the details, but the basic idea is that if the virus writer knows what the antivirus program is looking for, he can always design his virus not to be noticed. Of course, the antivirus programmers can always create an update to their software to detect the new virus after the fact.

Worms

A worm is a piece of malware particular to networked computers. It's a self-replicating program that does not hide in another program, like a virus does. Instead it exists on its own, meandering through computer networks as best it can, doing whatever damage it is programmed to do.

Robert T. Morris released the most famous worm in 1988. It was an Internet worm, and crashed about 6,000 computers: 10 percent of the

Internet's computers. The worm started out on one machine. Then it tried breaking into other machines on the network, using a couple of basic techniques. When it was successful, it sent a copy of itself to the new machine. And then the copy replicated the process, trying to break into yet more machines. This is the way a worm works. The worm would have been more devastating had it not been for a lucky bug. It was not supposed to crash 6,000 computers; it was supposed to quietly infect them. A bug in the worm program caused it to crash computers it infected. I'll talk more about the details of how it infected and the bug in Chapter 13.

PrettyPark is another worm. It's a Windows executable that arrives as an attachment to an e-mail message. (Its name comes from the fact that the program's icon is a South Park character named Kyle.) If you run the program, it sends itself to everyone in your Outlook Express address book. It also attempts to connect to an Internet relay chat (IRC) server and send messages to chat users. The author of the worm can then use the connection to collect information from your computer. ILOVEYOU and all its variants are worms, too.

Trojan Horses

A Trojan horse is a piece of malware embedded in some "normal" piece of software, designed to fool the user into thinking that it is benign. Remember the original Trojan horse? The Greeks besieged Troy for ten years, and it was showing no sign of falling. Out of desperation—and probably boredom—Odysseus had the Greek soldiers build a large wooden horse and put some of them inside. He left it for the Trojans as an admission of defeat and then told his army to pretend to sail away, try-ing not to giggle as they did. The Trojans took the wooden horse inside the walls—every artist's rendition puts the horse on a wheeled platform— despite the better judgment of one of their priests. That night, the Greeks crept out of the horse, opened the gates, and let the rest of the Greek army inside. The Greeks then massacred the Trojans, looted their wealth, and burned the city. (At least, that's the story. No one knows if it's true or not. Troy itself was considered a myth until Heinrich Schliemann discovered it in the late 1800s.)

Following that analogy, a digital Trojan horse is code deliberately placed in your system, that does things you don't expect or want while pretending to do something useful. (Technically, a Trojan horse is code that you deliberately place on your system, while a *logic bomb* is code that someone else places on your system.) It's a piece of code that a programmer writes into a large software application that starts misbehaving if, for example, the programmer is ever deleted from the payroll file. Timothy Lloyd, a network manager at Omega Engineering, set a logic bomb in 1996 that crippled his former employers' manufacturing capabilities and cost them more than $12 million in damages.

A Trojan horse, on the other hand, is a program that secretly installs itself in your machine, watches your keyboard buffer until it detects what appears to be a credit card number—right number of digits, checksum matches—and sends that number via TCP/IP to someone. It's a Java application that disconnects your modem connection and connects you to a 900 number in Moldavia (this Trojan horse actually happened).

A Trojan horse is a particularly insidious attack because you may not know what it's doing. Back Orifice is a popular Trojan horse for Microsoft Windows. If it is installed on your computer, a remote user can effectively take it over across the Internet. He can upload and download files, delete files, run programs, change configurations, take control of the keyboard and mouse, see whatever is on the server's screen. He can also do more subversive things: reboot the computer, display arbitrary dialog boxes, turn the microphone or camera on and off, capture keystrokes (and passwords). And there is an extensible plug-in language for others to write modules. (I'm waiting for someone to disseminate a module that auto-matically sniffs for, and records, PGP private keys or Web login sequences.)

In addition to Back Orifice and other hacker-written tools, many remote administration programs can serve as Trojan horses. DIRT (Data Interception by Remote Transmission) is a Trojan horse developed by the U.S. government and available to police.

These are the Swiss army knives of Trojan horses, but others are much subtler. Several Trojan horses collect usernames and passwords, and send them back to the creator. Trojans can also subtly modify your encryption program to choose keys from a small random pool, effectively weakening the keyspace. (I have seen Trojaned versions of PGP that do this.) They can drop a fake certificate into your computer and fool you into trusting someone. (Lab demonstrations of attacks against Microsoft's code-signing system have used this idea.) They can do just about anything you can think of, and a lot of things you'd never think of. The distributed denial-of-service attacks on the Internet first use Trojan horses to infect intermediate computers.

The hard part of these attacks is getting the Trojan horse onto the computer of some unsuspecting victim. You can break into the victim's office and install it on her computer; in the next chapter, we'll talk about some defenses against that sort of attack. You can cajole her to install the Trojan herself; we'll talk about social engineering in Chapter 17. You can attack the victim's computer via the network; we'll talk about that in Chapter 11. Or you can use the malicious software itself to attack the computer, creating a virus.

Modern Malicious Code

The year 1999 was a pivotal year for malicious software. The different strains—viruses, worms, and Trojan horses—blurred and amalgamated. And malware has gotten nastier. Malware that automatically propagates over e-mail is not new—Christma.exec in 1987 (through the PROFS e-mail system) and ShareFun in 1997—but 1999 was the first year that e-mail-propagating malware infected large swaths of the Internet. This strain of malware ignores corporate defenses and tunnels right through firewalls. This is a really big deal.

Viruses survive by reproducing on new computers. Before the Inter-net, computers communicated mostly through floppy disks. Hence, most viruses propagated on floppy disks, and occasionally on computer bulletin board systems.

There are some ramifications of floppies as a vector. First, malware propagates relatively slowly. One computer shares a disk with another, which shares a disk with five more, and over the course of weeks or months a virus turns into an epidemic. Or maybe someone puts a virus-infected program on a bulletin board, and thousands get infected in a week or two.

Second, it's easy to block disk-borne malware. Most antivirus pro-grams can automatically scan all floppy disks. Malware is blocked at the gate. Bulletin boards can still be a problem, but many computer users are trained never to download software from an untrusted bulletin board. Even so, antivirus software can automatically scan new files for malware.

And third, antiviral software can easily deal with the problem. It's easy to write software to block malware you know about. You simply have the antivirus scanner search for bit strings that signify the virus (called a "sig-nature") and then execute the automatic program to delete the virus and restore normalcy. This deletion routine is unique per virus, but it is not hard to develop. Antiviral software has tens of thousands of signatures, each tuned to a particular virus. Companies release them within days of learning of a new virus. And as long as viruses propagate slowly, this is good enough. Most antivirus software automatically updates itself once a month. Until 1999, that was good enough.

E-mail propagation changed everything. The year 1999 gave us the Melissa Microsoft Word macro virus and the Worm.ExploreZip worm, and 2000 gave us the ILOVEYOU worm and its dozens of variants, but there are many others. This type of malware arrives via e-mail and uses automatic e-mail features in software to replicate itself across the network. They mail themselves to people known to the infected host, enticing the recipients to open or run them. They don't propagate over weeks and months; they propagate in seconds.

The antivirus companies release updates that catch particular viruses as soon as they can, but if a virus can infect 10 million computers (one esti-mate of ILOVEYOU infections) in the hours before a fix is released, that's a lot of damage. What if the code took pains to hide itself, so that a virus wasn't discovered for a couple of days? What if a worm just targeted an individual, and deleted itself off any computer whose userID didn't match a certain reference? How long would it take before that one is dis-covered? What if it e-mailed a copy of the user's login script (most con-tain passwords) to an anonymous e-mail box before self-erasing? What if it could automatically update itself in the field? What if it automatically encrypted outgoing copies of itself with PGP? What if it mutated, frus-trating antivirus software? Or hid for weeks on systems? Even a few min-utes of thinking about this yields some pretty scary possibilities.

And because e-mail is everywhere, e-mail-borne malware can get everywhere. It can get over Internet connections that block everything else. It cannot be stopped at the firewall; it tunnels through and then pops up on the inside and does damage. The effectiveness of firewalls will diminish as we open up more services (e-mail, Web, etc.), as we add increasingly complex applications on the internal net, and as malware writers catch on. This "tunnel-inside-and-play" technique will only get worse.

Current research on malware protection tries to mimic the biological approach to fighting viruses. I'm skeptical, though, for two reasons. The first is that biological viruses evolve slowly: a lucky mutation here and there, and eventually they are a problem. And then they propagate through a species slowly. Biological immune systems are designed to deal with that kind of random threat. Computer viruses, by contrast, are created deadly on purpose.

The second reason is that biological immune systems are designed to protect the species at the expense of the individual. This is a great strategy for a gene pool, but is less effectual if you are trying to protect your own computer from malware.

More interesting solutions involve connecting computers to automatic virus-detection centers. When a computer notices something fishy, it sends the code off to be analyzed. This has some promise, but also a bunch of new security risks. And it still won't be fast enough. Any large, distributed system that communicates is going to have to accept the reality of viral infections. Unless security is designed into the system from the bottom up, we're constantly going to be fighting a holding action.

It's easy to excoriate Microsoft for exacerbating the problem. Microsoft scripting languages are very powerful, and basically assume that everything is trusted. These languages allow access to all operating-system resources (compare with the Java security model). They allow malware to use features in Microsoft Outlook to automatically e-mail themselves to friends of the user. Microsoft is certainly to blame for creating the power-ful macro capabilities of Word and Excel, blurring the distinction between executable files (which can be dangerous) and data files (which, before now, were safe). They will be to blame when Outlook 2000's integrated HTML support makes it possible for users to be attacked by HTML-based malware simply by downloading an e-mail (it automatically opens in preview mode). Or when malware takes advantage of Internet Explorer 5.0's ActiveX integration to spread without the user having to open an attachment. They built an operating environment where it is easy to write malware, where malware can spread easily, and where malware can do a lot of damage. But the fundamental problem—the inability to trust mobile code—is subtler.

MODULAR CODE

In the old days (the 1970s), computer programs were large hulking things: difficult to write, and even more difficult to maintain. Then someone got the idea of dividing large programs into smaller, easier-to-understand, components. Object-oriented programming, C++, modules, plug-ins: These are all examples of that idea. The problem is that modern compo-nent-based software is a lot harder to secure.

Figure 10.1 shows the old paradigm: large applications on top of a small operating system. Today's software looks more like App 1 in Figure 10.2—applications with components—or App 2—applications with components that have components. Think of your browser. One com-ponent is the Java Virtual Machine. Java applets run on top of that. Some

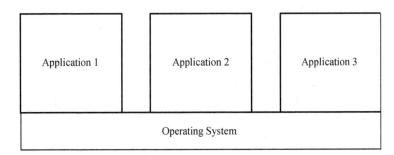

Figure 10.1 The old software paradigm.

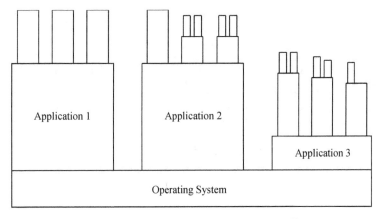

Figure 10.2 Today's component-based software paradigm.

Java applets even have plug-ins. All sorts of macros exist for your word processor and spreadsheet. You can download a PGP plug-in for Eudora. It seems like every other week you're downloading some plug-in or another for your browser.

And actually, even though your browser is sold as one program, it actually consists of many different components working together. Your word processor and spreadsheet are also like this; over one thousand com-ponents are in Microsoft Word 97. What you really have is App 3: a small base application with components upon components. Even your operat-ing system looks like this; Figure 10.3 is a picture of Windows NT: com-ponents on top of components.

Making matters worse is the practice of dynamic linking. In the old paradigm, pieces of the program were glued together—called *linking,* in programming-speak—by the manufacturer before you bought it. Pro-grammers would link the program together, and would test it to make sure everything was operating properly. Today components are often linked dynamically, when you launch the application. Windows users will have heard of dynamic linked libraries (DLLs); UNIX and Macintosh users know them as shared libraries.

The security problems come from several directions. First, you can't assume that all the modules are trustworthy. In the previous section I

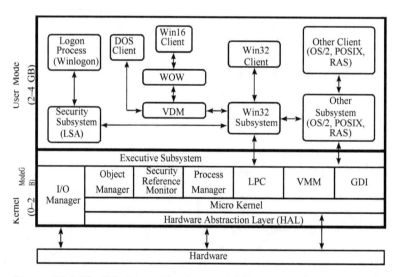

Figure 10.3 The Windows NT software architecture.

talked about malicious software; it is possible that one or more of the modules are malicious or simply inept. Second, you can't assume that all the modules are written well enough to work in every possible configuration. The nice thing about big hulking computer programs is that they were tested as one piece. The browser running on your computer, with all the particular plug-ins you downloaded in the particular order you did, might be unique. It is unlikely that it has ever been tested before.

And third, the operating system isn't there to deal with the other two problems. In the old paradigm, different pieces of software communicated through the operating system. The operating system, if it was designed well, would mediate these communications and prevent one program from damaging another. Modern components talk to each other directly, not through the operating system, so those built-in safety features just don't apply.

Several general methods for dealing with this security problem have been tried, some with more success than others. They all look better in theory than they work in practice:

Isolation and memory safety. The problem is that a component can, either maliciously or accidentally, affect the rest of the system. It could read, or change, the memory of another component. It could step outside its own memory and cause the system to crash, or do any number of annoying things. By isolating a component's use of memory, the hope is to avoid all these problems. The component is given its own area of memory, and is not allowed to read or write anywhere else. Sometimes program checkers on the user's machine go through the component's code to verify that it does-n't do anything noisome. The Java sandbox is an example of this idea: Components get to play in their own sandbox where they can't hurt one another. This works fine when it does, but this kind of model doesn't catch some things, and there's a price paid in speed.

Access control at the interfaces. It's not enough to have a component completely isolated; it has to communicate with other components (and the screen, keyboard, mouse, etc.) In Figure 10.2, many of the components touch each other. This indicates communications paths between components. By enforcing access control rules at those communication points, the hope is to ensure that the components play nicely with each other. The problem is that you have to set some kind of access control policy, which tends to be too inflexible to be really useful. The Java sandbox also does this, but its policy ends up being either too restrictive or overly permissive; there's no real middle ground. (Java 2 has fine-grained control, but it isn't used very well.)

Code signing. Think of a private party. The host decides who to let in and who to keep out, based only on some unforgeable document they have (a driver's license, for example). That way, only friends of the host are allowed in his home. Code signing is the same thing. The programmer signs com-ponents. The user decides, based on the signatures, which components to allow on his computer and which not to. (ActiveX uses code signing as its primary security against hostile code.) Code signing, as it is currently done, sucks. There are all sorts of problems. First, users have no idea how to decide if a particular signer is trusted or not. Second, just because a compo-nent is signed doesn't mean that it is safe. Third, just because two compo-nents are individually signed does not mean that using them together is safe; lots of accidental harmful interactions can be exploited. Fourth, "safe" is not an all-or-nothing thing; there are degrees of safety. And fifth, the fact that the evidence of attack (the signature on the code) is stored on the computer under attack is mostly useless: The attacker could delete or modify the sig-nature during the attack, or simply reformat the drive where the signature is stored. Code signing makes less and less sense the more you think about it.

Nascent technologies gestating in university laboratories may someday result in better solutions, but they are some years away. In the meantime, modular code is likely to become an even bigger security problem. More and more software packages are building in live update features, allowing them to download new modules regularly. For example, Internet Explorer 4.0 and later versions have a "subscription" feature that, if the user turns it on, will automatically update itself with new modules from Microsoft's Web page. This is a fine feature, unless you turn it on acci-dentally. Then, in the middle of the night, you can find your computer automatically dialing the Internet. One reaction from a news report:

> "I had my head in the refrigerator very early in the morning and discovered my computer had connected itself to the Internet," said one beta tester who requested anonymity for fear that his working relationship with Microsoft would be damaged. "I was completely freaking out. I pulled the phone plug right out of the wall."

There was nothing nefarious here; the user just didn't realize what was going on. But most computer users have no idea what is going on inside their computers. If they get used to their computer making telephone calls in the middle of the night, they may be surprised when some rogue appli-cation has been running up their phone bill by calling 900 numbers or computers in Moldavia.

MOBILE CODE

If you think about it, using programs written by someone else is always a risky thing to do. You're trusting that the programmer isn't malicious, and that the programs you're running do what they are supposed to do and nothing else. (I talk about this human problem again in Chapter 17.) In the earliest days of computing, users just didn't do that. They wrote, or at least compiled, programs specifically for each new computer.

The advent of personal computers and programs like VisiCalc took computers out of the hands of engineers and onto the desks of users. These users came to trust shrink-wrapped software, and wouldn't think twice about running programs even though they had no understanding of the internals; they didn't have the expertise to understand the internals anyway.

I've already talked about viruses and Trojan horses; these became popular because people traded copies of shrink-wrapped software (some-times illegally) without wondering whether they should trust the copies. But antivirus software took care of that problem, and people have spent the last 20 years implicitly trusting software.

With the rise of the Internet, this ingrained trust is suddenly a major problem.

In a previous section, I talked about how networks make malicious code more dangerous. Those are both examples of mobile code and their problems. Unfortunately, there are even more serious problems.

With the rise of modular code, more program fragments are being delivered over the Internet. Whether it is a new plug-in for your browser, a new printer driver, a slick utility program, or a Java applet that does some small cool thing, you're more likely than not to get this code from a Web site. Important questions to ask include the following: Is this code trusted, is this Web site trusted, can this code be trusted to interact safely with the rest of my computer, and what defenses do I have in case this code turns out to be malicious? Finding users who ask those questions is rare, and finding people who can answer those questions is even more rare.

JavaScript, Java, and ActiveX

JavaScript, Java, ActiveX, and downloadable plug-ins all have different models for securing themselves. I'll talk about them each in turn.

JavaScript is Netscape's scripting language that allows bits of code to be embedded in Web pages, and all major browsers support it. It is simi-lar to Java only in its first four letters. JavaScript code can be used for simple things: opening and closing windows, manipulating forms on Web pages, adjusting browser settings, and so forth. All of those annoying things that some Web sites do when you try to close their pages: That's JavaScript.

JavaScript is basically pretty tame, but all sorts of JavaScript-based attacks have appeared over the past few years. These bugs have all been fixed. A few random examples: 1997, monitor what sites the user visits; 1998, read arbitrary files on the user's machine; 1998, intercept the user's e-mail address. A lot of these attacks depend on fooling the user into doing something marginally stupid, but that's not hard. These sorts of security flaws show up in browsers, and are fixed pretty quickly. But new ones are regularly discovered.

ActiveX uses a code-signing defense. Basically, every piece of ActiveX code, called a "control," is checked for a digital signature. (Microsoft has defined something called Authenticode to do this.) Then the browser puts up a dialog box, and shows the user the name of the pro-grammer or company that signed the control. If the user agrees to accept the control, it is downloaded to the browser. Otherwise, it is not.

Any teenager who's let the wrong sorts of guests into his party knows the problem: The system is only as good as the judgment of the user. Once an ActiveX control is on a user's machine, it can do anything it wants: reformat your hard drive, change all your $1 spreadsheet entries to $100, collect all your steamy love letters and send them to a movie pro-ducer in Los Angeles, whatever.

Microsoft has countered that the signatures will identify authors, but knowing who wrote the malicious control is little consolation to some-one who just had his computer trashed. It's like forcing criminals to wear name badges and then not bothering to put locks on people's doors: "I'm sorry they came into your house, ate all your food, broke all your furni-ture, and stole all your valuables. But at least we know who they are." Except that on the Web you can add: "They're two teenagers from a country that has no extradition treaty with the United States. Feel better now?" And this assumes you can isolate the particular malicious control among the dozens on your hard drive. One researcher showed how two benign ActiveX controls could combine to become malicious; whom do you blame there?

This idea has even more serious problems. Chapter 17 talks all about how ridiculous it is to expect users to make good security decisions, but for now, suffice it to say that most people aren't going to have a clue about which ActiveX controls to trust and which not to. And this assumes the existence of a public-key infrastructure to support the signatures, something I will complain bitterly about in Chapter 15. Lots of opportu-nities exist to trick the infrastructure into believing a control is signed when it is not.

ActiveX is really an extension of an old Microsoft system of compo-nents (it used to be called DCOM). This is what allows Internet Explorer to open up and display Excel spreadsheets (for example). Most of the DLLs that programs use are actually just vehicles for DCOM objects. Explorer is just picking up Excel's guts through DCOM and ActiveX. This is an incredibly powerful system, which is way more flexible, way more accessible, way more architecturally interesting, and just unimagin-ably more dangerous than anything similar in any other operating system.

Java uses a completely different model. It's the only programming language specially designed for mobile code, and with security in mind. Java programs run by a Web browser are called *applets,* and run within a *sandbox* that tries to limit the damage it can do. Three mechanisms protect the sandbox.

First, there is something called a *byte code verifier.* Whenever a browser downloads a Java applet, the byte code verifier checks over the code first. The verifier ensures that the byte code is correctly formatted, and doesn't have any of several common problems.

Second, there is the *class loader.* This component determines how and when an applet can add itself to the Java environment, and makes sure that the applet doesn't replace anything important that already exists.

And third, there is the *security manager.* The security manager is like the reference monitor discussed in Chapter 8; it is consulted whenever the Java applet tries to do something questionable: opening a file, opening a network connection, and so forth. Depending on how the applet was installed, these operations will either be allowed or denied. (For example, applets downloaded over the network have more restrictions than applets loaded onto your computer at purchase.)

The sandbox model is too complex, but it's the best we've got so far. Later versions of Java had two modifications, one good and one bad. Java 1.1 implemented a code-signing feature similar to ActiveX. Applets trusted by the users can leave the sandbox and run unrestricted on the user's machine. Needless to say, this opens up all the security problems of the ActiveX model.

Java 2 improved on the sandbox model. Instead of making it all or nothing—in the sandbox or out of it—Java 2 provides more flexibility in the security model. Applets only get the privileges they need to do their jobs. For example, one applet might have access to the computer's file sys-tem but not network access. Another might have network access but no access to the file system. A third applet might only have access to certain parts of the file system. It's as if each applet has its own customized sand-box. This works much better, but has proven too complicated to use.

Plug-ins are the worst because they are automatically trusted. These are code modules that you can add to your browser to give it additional functionality: PDF file viewers, media players, and others. These have no security. When you download them and install them, you're trusting them. Period.

WEB SECURITY

Like most information moving across the Internet, HTTP (that's the protocol used for Web pages) is unencrypted and unauthenticated. Many people are afraid to send their credit card numbers across an unencrypted Web connection. (I don't think this is a big deal, but some things I wouldn't send unencrypted across the Web.) To solve this problem, early versions of Netscape Navigator included a protocol called SSL. This protocol, which will eventually be renamed TLS, provides encryption and authentication of Web connections. SSL is pretty good, and its problems all revolve around the certificates and how they are used (see Chapter 15 for an explanation). Basically, some Web sites give you the option of setting up an SSL-secured browsing session. (The Web page has to have the option; the browser cannot demand to use SSL if the server is not set up for it.) The browser and the Web server use public-key cryptography to exchange a key and then symmetric cryptography to encrypt the data going back and forth. A green key or a yellow padlock appears on the bottom of the browser, and the user feels much better.

The main problem is that unless the user manually checks the certificate the server sent, he has no idea whom he went secure with. Let me repeat this. SSL establishes a secure connection between the browser and whomever is at the other end of the connection. If the user does not verify who is at the other end of the connection, he has no idea who he is speaking securely with. It's as if two strangers enter a pitch-black soundproof room. The two people know that their conversation is secure, that no one is eavesdropping. But who would tell his secrets to the stranger? This is only one problem with SSL certificates as they are used.

Also, SSL does nothing to protect the data at the server. In early 2000, there were many cases of hackers breaking into Web sites and stealing information: credit card numbers, personal account information, and more. SSL does nothing to prevent this.

URL Hacking

A bunch of attacks target URLs, some relying on user error and some just on user ignorance. The first class of attacks consists of ways different servers steal traffic from each other. You might not think this is a big deal—why would a Web site that sells plumbing supplies want to steal traffic from a financial news Web site—but some sites, like porn sites, just want people to look at their home pages.

One of the ways to try to get traffic is to try to fool the search engines. Search engines are mostly pretty stupid: ask for sites on plumbing supplies, and they respond with all the Web pages that have the words "plumbing supplies" somewhere in the text. (Actually, the newer search engines are a smidge smarter, but that's the general idea.) What some sites do is to put text on the pages to act as bait for the search engines. This text is not shown on the screen—sometimes it's hidden by other things (white text on a white background, for example) and sometimes it's in the form of keywords or meta tags in a nonprintable area of the page—but it is looked at by the search engines. So, a particular porn site might embed the words "stock quotes Beanie Babies weather presidential election Grover Cleveland cooking gardening head lice," just to show up on people's searches.

Some Web sites take this kind of thing to an extreme. Called *page-jacking,* they carefully tune their keywords and meta tags (embedded com-mands in Web pages that tell search engines what the pages are about) so that to a search engine they look exactly like a popular Web site, and then show up on the search engine results just above that popular site. Unsus-pecting users click on this faked site instead of the real site. Mostly, this has been used by porn sites to get traffic, but you could imagine a page-jack-ing hack where the faked site also looks like the real site. This could be a nasty problem.

These attacks are not limited to Web pages and search engines. Press releases for small companies will sometimes include the name and stock symbol of a larger company, so that people searching on that larger com-pany will find the press release. Called *ticker symbol smashing,* it looks like this: "SmallCompany.com has announced that its new product has nothing do with Microsoft (MSFT)." Even eBay auction descriptions include words to attract their search function: "This cheap sweater (not Prada, not Armani) is red."

Back on the Web, similar attacks are possible by registering sites that are close in name to popular sites. People who do this are known as *typo pirates.* For example, "wwwpainewebber.com" (without the period, as opposed to "www.painewebber.com") once pointed to a porn site. People who mistyped the name of the insurance company "Geico" as "Geigo" ended up at a site owned by Progressive Insurance. (These typo-pirate attacks probably don't work anymore; at the time of writing, sev-eral court cases involve this sort of thing.)

Similar incidents arise more or less by chance. The company eToys tried suing the artist group etoy, even though etoy.com had its domain name two years before eToys.com existed. (Although their domain name was indeed a coincidence, etoy did practice page-jacking on sites like Playboy.)

Neither of these attacks are what's known as *cyber-squatting.* (Aren't there cool names for all this Web-related stuff?) This is the practice of sneaking in and registering domain names that may be valuable to someone else. For example, someone other than me owns applied-cryptogra-phy.com and applied-cryptography.com, the title of my first book.

Web spoofing is kind of an Internet con game. By manipulating the URL addresses on a client's site, an attacker can force a victim to do all its browsing through a particular site. This site, owned by the attacker, can eavesdrop on the victim's entire browsing session. The attacker can keep records of where the victim visits, what his different account names and passwords are, anything. The attacker can also subtly modify different pages—maybe change the "ship to" address for products that the victim buys.

This attack works even if the victim has an SSL connection. As I mentioned previously, SSL only guarantees that the user is secure with someone. In the case of this attack, the user has a secure connection *with the attacker*—not very helpful. Several other tricks facilitate the attack; turning off JavaScript provides some defense. Some Web sites—AskJeeves is an example—exacerbate the problem by putting other people's Web pages in their own frames, and present that information as their own. At the time of writing, this attack has not been reported in the wild.

Cookies

Cookies are an inventive programming trick built into WWW browsers. Basically, a cookie is a scrap of data that a Web server gives to a browser. The browser stores the data on the user's computer, and returns it to the server whenever the browser returns to the server. Cookies can do all sorts of useful and good things. Unfortunately, they can also do all sorts of useful and bad things. First, I'll explain how they work; then I'll talk about the problems.

HTTP is basically a stateless protocol. This means that the server doesn't know who you are from one click to the next. All the server does is serve up Web pages. A browser asks for a Web page; the server gives it to it. The server has no idea if this is the same browser as before or a different browser, nor does it care. This works great for simple, static, Web sites that just contain informational pages.

Complex Web sites are dynamic. Retail Web sites have shopping carts, which travel with you as you browse the site. Paid-access informa-tional sites have usernames and passwords, which travel with you as you go from page to page. (I would find it annoying to have to type my username and password in every time I wanted to see another article from the *New York Times* Web site.) Cookies are a way to handle this.

By giving the browser a cookie and then asking for it back, the server can remember who you are. "Oh, yes, you're user 12345657; this is your shopping cart." Cookies allow the browser to add state to the WWW protocols. You can think of them as a large distributed database, with pieces stored on millions of browsers throughout userland.

So far, so good. And mostly, cookies are good, if the server placing the cookie plays by the rules. The server can set how long the cookie lasts before it expires: a few days seems like a good number. A server can set restrictions on who can access the cookie. The server can limit access to other servers in the same domain; this means that if your cookie comes from inchoate-merchant.com, then only inchoate-merchant.com can access the cookie.

The problems come when they are abused. Some servers use cookies to track users from site to site, and some use them to uncover the identity of the user. Here's an easy example: Some companies resell advertising space on popular sites. DoubleClick is a company that does that; Dou-bleClick places many of the ads you see on commercial sites. If you're browsing on sex-site.com, you're going to see a portion of that window that comes from DoubleClick.com. DoubleClick.com gives you a cookie. Later (that day, or maybe another day), when you're browsing on CDnow.com, there might be another DoubleClick-placed ad. Dou-bleClick can request the cookie from your browser and, because the cookie says that it was created while you were visiting a sex site, send you targeted ads while you're browsing CDnow. Because DoubleClick is on a bunch of commerce sites, its cookies can be used to track you across all of those sites.

Even worse, if you type your e-mail address in at any of those sites and they pass that information to DoubleClick, DoubleClick can now attach an e-mail address to your browsing habits. All it needs is for you to type that address in once—that's ordering only one thing—and it has it forever. (Or, for as long as that cookie has not expired, which can be years.)

This isn't a big secret. DoubleClick freely admits they collect data, and use that data to target ads to particular users. Until 2000, they denied building an identity database, but finally admitted it when a *USA Today* story outed them. Since then, they backed down on their plan to link cookies to names and addresses. (This will probably change again by pub-lication.) The implications for private Web browsing are profound.

There's more. Sites can send you a cookie in e-mail which they can use to identify you if you later visit that site with your browser. Here's how it works: The site sends you a piece of HTML e-mail. (This implies you're using an e-mail program that supports HTML messages; those include Microsoft's Outlook and Outlook Express, Netscape Messenger, and Eudora.) The message contains a unique URL to a graphic, which the site can use to send you a cookie. If the URL is something like www.gotcha.com/track-cgi=schneier@counterpane .com/pixels.gif, then they have your e-mail address in a cookie. Now, when you browse the site at some later date, the site can use the cookie to link the browsing with the e-mail, and hence the e-mail address. Supposedly this has been used by some sites to track Web surfers.

Cookies cannot do anything. Cookies cannot steal information from your computer. A cookie is simply some data that the server gives the browser, and the browser later returns. A cookie cannot grab your pass-words or files. (ActiveX, Java, and JavaScript are much more dangerous in this regard.) Cookies cannot steal your credit card numbers, although a really dumb site may put your credit card number in a cookie.

The lesson here is that cookies are not bad, but they have malevolent uses. They are a lazy way for Web programmers to manage relationships. Most browsers provide ways to turn cookies off completely, and you can buy third-party programs to help you manage them better. But some sites—Hotmail and Schwab Online, for example—refuse to connect with browsers that don't accept cookies.

Web Scripts

The preceding attacks are targeted against the client; this attack victimizes the server.

The common gateway interface (CGI) is the standard way for a Web server to pass a user's request to some back-end application, and send it back to the user. For example, when you send a search query to a Web site—at an online retailer, for example—the Web server passes the request to a database application and then formats the result to display to the user. Or when a user fills out a Web page form, this information is passed to an application for processing. Sometimes CGI commands are those weird commands and numbers at the end of a URL; other times they're invisible to the user. It's part of HTTP; everyone uses it. CGI scripts are the lit-tle computer programs on the Web server that deal with CGI data. It's how the Web page forms get processed, for example.

The problem with CGI scripts is that each one is potentially a secu-rity hole. And over the past few years, CGI hacking has resulted in quite a few public security breaches. By manipulating CGI scripts, it is possible to do all sorts of unanticipated things. Examples (these are all real) include downloading files from the Web server, viewing the entire contents of databases, downloading customer lists and their personal records, stealing money from customers at an online bank, trading someone else's stock portfolio, and viewing log files from a Web server showing customer transactions. And bizarrely enough, you can query Internet search engines with different vulnerability signatures and get a list of Web sites vulnera-ble to certain attacks.

Other similar attacks work by putting executable code (actually, Perl scripts, JavaScript code, or shell commands) in text fields. These can cause the Web server to modify its own homepage, display the SSL private key, or do all sorts of other interesting things from the previous paragraph. These techniques can also be used to exploit buffer overflows and other programming errors (see Chapter 13) to crash the Web server or, better yet, to take it over.

One example: A 1998 attack against Hotmail allowed people to see other people's e-mail accounts. eBay was also attacked; the attackers put a JavaScript Trojan horse in the description field of a product. This descrip-tion field was viewed by anyone looking at the product up for auction, and resulted in the attackers collecting login information for thousands of accounts.

One CGI vulnerability allowed attackers to download secret personal information from various sites. Other popular CGI scripts have been used to break into the computer the Web server is running on. Two from late 1999: the *Poison Null* attack that allowed hackers to see and modify files on Web servers, and the *Upload Bombing* attack that filled Web servers with useless files, crashing them. These, of course, were quickly turned into attack scripts so that anyone could use them.

Server Side Includes (SSIs) are directives to the Web server embed-ded in the HTML pages. Right before sending a page, the Web server executes all SSIs on a page and puts the results back in the page. These can be attacked just as profitably as everything else can.

Other attacks target vulnerabilities in third-party software: the specific Web servers and applications running on them. This includes database applications, shopping cart software, transaction servers, and others. These attacks don't depend on how the site is using the application, but on the application itself (the Oracle database, for example). Attackers have been able to download source code from the Web server, crash the server, get root login privileges on the server, run an arbitrary program on the server, and so forth. Unlike problems with the CGI scripts, fixing these vulnera-bilities is not under the site's control; it's the job of the third-party soft-ware vendors.

There are many similar attacks. By making changes in the hidden fields on some Web pages (you can view these fields by viewing a page's source), it is possible to hack CGI scripts and force some shopping cart software to change the prices of items sold. (This is "name your own price" at its best.) Some attacks target cookies: *cookie poisoning*. Attackers log in to a server, and then manually change their authentication cookie to that of another user. Sometimes these cookies are encrypted, but often not very well.

Some of these attacks are called *cross-site scripting*. It's a lousy name: It's not just about scripting, and there's nothing cross-site about it. The name is a historical accident that stuck. The gist of the problem is that the Web hides multitudes of security subtleties; when you mix CGI scripts, JavaScript, frames, cookies, and SSL, bad things can happen. It is an issue that is truly cross-platform and is the result of unforeseen and unexpected interactions between various components of a set of interconnected com-plex systems.

These attacks are prevalent against CGI scripts for several reasons. Most CGI scripts are hastily written, and they are commonly shared among users. You get a pile of scripts with your hosting software, or from your ISP. Often the people writing these scripts have no other experience with programming. They don't appreciate the potential security problems with scripts, or with the ways the scripts can interact with other parts of the Web server software. And a Web server can't control how a CGI script is run. Sometimes it is created for one purpose, but breaks security when used for another.

CGI attacks are powerful, and the vulnerabilities are common. Sure it is possible to write secure CGI scripts, but hardly anyone does. One com-pany that audits Web sites for application-level bugs like this has never found a Web site they could not hack. That's 100 percent vulnerabilities.

Web Privacy

Nominally, Web browsing is anonymous. In reality, there are a lot of ways to learn the identity of the user. I've already talked about cookies and how they can track users from site to site, and even attach an e-mail address or identity to a cookie (if the user enters the information in a form or responds to an e-mail).

Additionally, most Web servers log every access. This log usually includes the IP address of the user, the time of the Web request, the Web page requested, and the user's name (if known by some login protocol). Most Web sites just throw these logs away, though.

Of course, the IP address of the user is not the same as the name of the user, but many Web browsers come from single-user machines directly connected to the Web. People dialing in are more anonymous than users on cable modems or DSL connections, but often just knowing the ISP is enough. For example, in 1999 someone sent a bomb threat from a Hotmail account. E-mail from Hotmail includes the IP address of the Web browser that sent the mail. The IP address was owned by Amer-ica Online, and the police were able to correlate Hotmail's records with America Online's records, and trace the e-mail to a particular AOL user.

That is an example of extreme measures to breach privacy, but most of it can be done automatically. And most commercial Web sites do little to protect users' privacy. In fact, many of them make money on an adver-tising model. Other sites deliberately invade users' privacy to sell targeted advertising: many of the digital wallets or shopping assistants, the Web-based mailing list software companies, and others. Many companies see targeted advertising as the way to make money on the Internet.

11

Network Security

Network security goes hand in hand with computer security, and these days it's hard to separate the two. Everything, from electronic hotel door locks to cellular telephones to desktop computers, is attached to networks. As difficult as it is to build a secure stand-alone computer, it is much more difficult to build a computer that is secure when attached to a network. And networked computers are even more pregnable; instead of an attacker needing to be in front of the computer he is attacking, he can be halfway across the planet and attack the computer using the network. A networked world may be more convenient, but it is also much more insecure.

These days it's pretty much impossible to talk about computer secu-rity without talking about network security. Even something as special-ized as the credit card clearing system works using computer networks. So do cellular telephones and burglar alarm systems. Slot machines in casinos are networked, as are some vending machines. The computers in your kitchen appliances will soon be networked, as will the ones in your car. All computers will eventually be networked.

Lots of different types of networks are out there, but I'm going to spend the most time talking about the Internet protocol: TCP/IP. Net-working protocols seem to be converging on the Internet, so it makes the most sense to talk about the Internet. This is not to imply that the Inter-net protocols are more insecure than others—although certainly they were never designed with security in mind—only that there are more good examples. Later in the book, I talk about the fundamental dilemma of choosing a common protocol that is widely attacked by hackers, and hence whose security is constantly improving, or one that is obscure and little-known, and is possibly even less secure. Keep that question in mind while reading this chapter.

HOW NETWORKS WORK

Computer networks are bunches of computers connected to each other. That is, either physical wires run between computers—wires in an office LAN, dedicated phone lines (possibly ISDN or DSL), dial-up connec-tions, fiber optic, or whatever—or there is an electromagnetic connec-tion: radio links, microwaves, and so forth.

Simply, when one computer wants to talk to another, it creates a message, called a packet, with the destination computer's name on it and sends it to the computer over this network. This is fundamentally unlike telephone conversations. When Alice wants to call Bob, she tells the phone company's computer network Bob's network name (commonly known as his telephone number) and the network hooks up different communications circuits—copper wire, satellite, cellular, fiber, what-ever—to make an unbroken connection. Alice and Bob talk through this circuit until one of them hangs up. Then, the telephone network disas-sembles this connection and lets other people use the same pieces for other phone calls. The next time Alice calls Bob, they will be connected through a completely different set of links. (Well, mostly different; the line between the telephones and the first switches will be the same.)

Computers don't use circuits to talk to each other. They don't have conversations like people do—they send short data packets back and forth. These packets are broken-up pieces of anything: e-mail messages, GIFs of naked ladies, streaming audio or video, Internet telephone calls. Computers divide large files into packets for easier transmission. (Think of a ten-page letter being divided up and mailed in ten different envelopes. At the recipient's end, someone opens all the envelopes and reassembles the letter in its proper order. The packets don't have to arrive in order, and they don't have to travel along the same route to their destination.)

These packets are sent through the network by routers. There are bunches of protocols—Ethernet, TCP, whatever—but they all work basically (for large values of "basically") the same way. Routers look at the addresses on packets, and then send them toward their destination. They may not know where the destination is, but they know something about where it should go. It's sort of like the postal system. A letter carrier visits your house, takes all of your outgoing mail, and brings it to the local post office. The post office might not know where 173 Pitterpat Lane, Fingerbone, ID, is, but it knows that it should put the envelope on the truck to the airport. The airport postal workers don't know either, but they know to put the letter on a plane to Chicago. The Chicago post office knows to put the letter on a plane to Boise. The Boise post office knows to put the letter on a train to Fingerbone. And finally, the local Fingerbone post office knows where the address is, and a letter carrier delivers it.

IP SECURITY

It's not hard to see that any network built on this model is terribly insecure. Consider the Internet. As those packets pass from router to router, their data, sometimes called their payload, is open to anyone who wants to read it. The routers are only supposed to look at the destination address in the packet header, but there's nothing to stop them from peeking at the contents. Most IP packets in the world go over just a handful of high-speed connections between lightning-fast routers, known as the Internet backbone. All packets between distant points, the United States and Japan, for example, go through only a few routers.

It's hard for an individual hacker to monitor the entire Internet, but it's easy for him to monitor a small piece of it. All he has to do is to gain access to some computer on the network. Then he can watch all the packets going through, looking for interesting ones. If he gets access to a machine close to Company A, he will probably be able to monitor all the traffic in and out of that company. (Of course, by "close to" I mean "near on the network," and not necessarily physically near.) If he gets a machine nowhere near Company A, he might see little (or none) of that com-pany's traffic. If he's a quintessential hacker and doesn't care what com-pany he eavesdrops on, then it doesn't really matter.

Packets with passwords in them are particularly interesting. *Password sniffing* is easy, and a common Internet attack. An attacker installs a packet sniffer designed to steal usernames and passwords. All the program does is collect the first two dozen (or so) characters of every session that requires a login and save them for the attacker. These characters almost certainly contain the username and password (usually the unencrypted password). Then the attacker runs a password cracker on the encrypted passwords, and uses those passwords to break into other computers. It's difficult to spot because password sniffers are small and inconspicuous. And it can snowball. Once you've broken into one machine, you can install a pass-word sniffer on it and get even more passwords. Maybe you can use those passwords to break into other machines. And so on.

Not only is eavesdropping possible, but active attacks are also possible . . . easier, actually. In most communications systems, it is far easier to passively eavesdrop on a network than it is to actively insert and delete messages. On the Internet, it is reversed. It's difficult to eavesdrop. However, it's easy to send messages; any self-respecting hacker can do that. Because communications are packet-based, and they travel along many different paths and are reassembled at the destination, it's easy to slip another packet in with the rest of them. Many, many attacks are based on blindly insert-ing packets into existing communications channels.

It's called *IP spoofing,* and it's easy. Packets have source and destination information, but an attacker can modify them at will. An attacker can cre-ate packets that seem to come from one site, but don't really. Computers on the Internet assume that the "from" and "to" information is accurate, so if a computer sees a packet from a computer it trusts, it assumes that the packet is trusted. An attacker can take advantage of this trusting relation-ship to break into a machine: He sends a packet purporting to come from a trusted computer in the hope that the target computer will trust the packet.

There are routing attacks, where an attacker tells two points on the Internet that the shortest route between them goes through his comput-ers. This makes eavesdropping on a particular node easier. This section could go on and on; whole books have been written about attacks against the Internet.

The solutions to these problems are obvious in theory, but harder in practice. If you encrypt packets, no one can read them in transit. If you authenticate packets, no one can insert packets that pretend to come from somewhere else, and deleted packets will be noticed and reacted to.

In fact, several solutions encrypt packets on the Internet. Programs like SSH encrypt and authenticate shell connections from a user on one machine to a computer across the network. Protocols like SSL can encrypt and authenticate Web traffic across the Internet. Protocols like IPsec promise to be able to encrypt and authenticate everything.

DNS SECURITY

The *Domain Name Service* (DNS) is basically a large distributed database. Most computers on the Internet—nodes, routers, and hosts— have a domain name like "brokenmouse.com" or "anon.penet.fi". These names are designed to be remembered by people, and are used to build things like URLs and e-mail addresses. Computers don't understand domain names; they understand IP addresses like 208.25.68.64. IP addresses are then used to route packets around the network.

Among other things, the DNS converts domain names to IP addresses. When a computer is handed a domain name, it queries a DNS server to translate that domain name into an IP address. Then it knows where to send the packet.

The problem with this system is that there's no security in the DNS system. So when a computer sends a query to a DNS server and gets a reply, it assumes that the reply is accurate and that the DNS server is hon-est. In fact, the DNS server does not have to be honest; it could have been hacked. And the reply that the computer gets from the DNS server might not have even come from the DNS server; it could have been a faked reply from somewhere else. If an attacker makes changes in the DNS tables (the actual data that translates domains to IP addresses and vice versa), computers will implicitly trust the modified tables.

It's not hard to imagine the kinds of attacks that could result. An attacker can convince a computer that he is coming from a trusted com-puter (change the DNS tables to make it look like the attacker's computer is a trusted IP address). An attacker can hijack a network connection (change the DNS tables so that someone wanting to connect to legiti-mate.company.com actually makes a connection with evil.hacker.com). An attacker can do all sorts of things. And DNS servers have a viral update procedure; if one DNS server records a change, it tells the other DNS servers and they believe it. So if an attacker can make a change at a few certain points, that change can propagate across the Internet.

In one attack in 1999, someone hacked the DNS system so that traffic to Network Solutions—they're one of the companies that register domain names—was redirected to other domain-name registration com-panies. A similar attack, from 1997, was a publicity attack. This was before domain registration was opened up for competition. Eugene Kashpureff, owner of the alternative AlterNIC, redirected Network Solutions traffic to his site as a protest. He was arrested and convicted, and received two years' probation.

In 2000, RSA Security's homepage was hijacked by spoofing the DNS tables. This is not the same as breaking into the Web site and defac-ing the page. The attacker created a fake home page, and then redirected legitimate traffic to that faked page by manipulating the DNS records. The hacker did this not by cracking RSA's DNS server, but the DNS server upstream in the network. Clever, and very easy. DNS record spoofing is a trivial way to spoof a real Web site crack. And to make mat-ters worse for the hijacked site, the hijacking misleads people into thinking intruders cracked the Web site at Company A, when intruders actually cracked the DNS server at Company B.

These problems are serious, and cannot easily be fixed. Cryptographic authentication will eventually solve this problem, because no longer will computers implicitly trust messages that claim to come from a DNS server. Currently people are working on a secure version of the DNS system that will deal with these issues, but it's going to be a long wait.

DENIAL-OF-SERVICE ATTACKS

In September 1996, an unknown hacker or group of hackers attacked the computers of Public Access Networks Corporation (a.k.a. Panix), a New York ISP. What they did was to send hello messages (SYN packets) to the Panix computers. What's supposed to happen is for a remote computer to send Panix this hello message, for Panix to respond, and then for the remote computer to continue the conversation. What the attackers did was to manipulate the return address of the remote computers, so Panix ended up trying to synchronize with computers that essentially did not exist. The Panix computers waited 75 seconds after responding for the remote computer to acknowledge the response before abandoning the attempt. The hackers flooded Panix with as many as 50 of these wake-up messages per second. This was too much for the Panix computers to han-dle, and they caused the computers to crash. This is called *SYN flooding.*

This was the first publicized example of a denial-of-service attack against an Internet host. Since then, there have been many others. Denial of service is a particularly noxious attack against communication systems, because communications systems are designed for communications. On the Net, flooding a computer with requests to communicate is a good way to bring it crashing down. And often the technology doesn't exist to trace who originated the attack.

Here's a denial-of-service attack against someone's paper mail: An attacker signs the victim up for every mail-order catalog, credit card solic-itation, and everything else he can think of. The victim gets so much mail, maybe 200 pieces a day, that the real mail gets lost among the junk mail. Theoretically, this attack will work. The only thing preventing this attack is the limit of the amount of junk mail in the world. On the Internet, though, the mail system always delivers the mail. In 1995, the Internet Liberation Front (it's just a made up name; they've never been heard from since) sent a flood of e-mail messages to author Joshua Quittner and *Wired* magazine. The flood was so great the computers just crashed.

This is known as *mail bombing,* and is an effective attack. Send enough mail to someone and that person's system will fill until the computer crashes. The easiest way to do this is to subscribe the victim to thousands of mailing lists. Victims' disks might run out of space, their network con-nections might go down, or their computers might crash. And if you dis-guise the origin of the e-mail, no one will catch you.

There are other denial-of-service attacks. Some target computers, like the preceding mail-server attack. Some target routers. Some target Web servers. The basic idea is the same: flood the target with so much stuff that it shuts down. WinNuke can crash older Windows 95 computers; some-one, in a single attack, brought down 6,000 Windows 95 computers on the Internet in April 1999. Denial-of-service attacks against Web sites are common, and remote-cache services like Akamai will make them easier to mount and harder to detect.

Sometimes it can be hard to tell a denial-of-service attack from abnor-mal operations. Think about highways around a city. During normal hours, they run well. During the rush hours, they clog up. During a demonstration, they don't run at all. In 1999, demonstrations against the World Trade Organization tied up traffic in downtown Seattle; that was unambiguously a denial-of-service attack. Earlier that year, when Ameri-can Airlines pilots started calling in sick more often than usual and finding more maintenance problems with the planes than usual, that was less obviously a denial-of-service attack. After the television special *Who Wants to Marry a Multimillionaire* aired in 2000, their Web site crashed due to the volume of people logging on and trying to sign up to be on the show. Is that a denial-of-service attack?

Some researchers have proposed defenses that force the client to per-form an expensive calculation to make a connection. The idea is that if the client has to spend computation time to make a connection, then it can't flood the target with as many connections. This is a good idea, but won't work against the distributed denial-of-service attacks we'll talk about in the next section.

I've seen suggestions that a lack of authentication on the Internet is to blame. This makes no sense. Denial-of-service attacks do harm just by the attempt to deliver packets; whether or not the packets would authenticate properly is completely irrelevant. Mandatory authentication would do nothing to prevent these attacks, or to track down the attackers. It would help if the authentication could be checked at every point in the network. This would be a change in the way the Internet works, and would reduce network bandwidth considerably: Instead of merely routing packets, all switches and routers would have to authenticate them.

Large-scale filtering at the ISPs can help; if the network can block the denial-of-service attack, it will never reach the target. Here, authentica-tion can do some good. But ISP filtering requires a lot of effort and will reduce network bandwidth noticeably. Similarly, widespread modifica-tions to how the Internet's switches and routers work could alleviate this problem; they could refuse to forward packets that are apparently forged. Again, it's a major change.

In the end, though, denial-of-service attacks that simply flood the tar-get with traffic can't be dealt with. Some particular attacks combine flooding with exploiting a specific vulnerability; these can be prevented by closing the vulnerability. But if the attacker has a bigger fire hose than you do, he can flood your connection.

Denial-of-service attacks are not intrusions. They do not affect the data on the Web sites. These attacks cannot steal credit card numbers or proprietary information. They cannot transfer money out of bank accounts or trade stocks in someone else's name. Attackers cannot directly profit from these attacks. (They can sell the stock short and then attack the company.)

This is not to say that denial-of-service attacks are not real, or not important. For most big corporations, the biggest risk of a security breach is loss of income or loss of reputation, either of which is achieved elegantly by a conspicuous denial-of-service attack. And for companies with more mission- or life-critical data online, a denial-of-service attack can literally put a person's life at risk.

DISTRIBUTED DENIAL-OF-SERVICE ATTACKS

Distributed denial-of-service attacks are just a virulent strain of denial-of-service attacks. The first automatic tools for these attacks were released in 1999—the University of Minnesota was the first public target in August 1999—but the spate of high-profile attacks in early 2000 put them on the front pages of newspapers everywhere.

These attacks are the same as traditional denial-of-service attacks, only this time there is no single source of the attack. The attacker first breaks into hundreds or thousands of insecure computers, called *zombies*, on the Internet and installs an attack program. Then he coordinates them all to attack the target at the same time. The target is attacked from many places at once; its traditional defenses just don't work, and it falls over dead.

It's much like the pizza delivery attack: Alice doesn't like Bob, so she calls a hundred pizza delivery parlors and, from each one, has a pizza delivered to Bob's house at 11:00 P.M. At 11, Bob's front porch is filled with 100 pizza deliverers all demanding their money. It looks to Bob like the pizza Mafia is out to get him, but the pizza parlors are victims, too. The real attacker is nowhere to be seen.

These attacks are incredibly difficult, if not impossible, to defend against. In a traditional denial-of-service attack, the victim computer might be able to figure out where the attack is coming from and shut down those connections. But in a distributed attack, there is no single source. The computer should shut down all connections except for the ones it knows to be trusted, but that doesn't work for a public Internet site.

There have been several academic conferences on distributed denial-of-service attacks in recent years, and the consensus is that no general defense exists. Continuously monitoring your network connections helps, as does the ability to switch to backup servers and routers. Some-times the particular bugs exploited in the attacks can be patched, but many cannot. The Internet was not designed to withstand this class of attacks.

These attacks are likely to get worse. Current distributed denial-of-service tools require the attacker to break into a large number of machines, install the zombie programs, keep those zombie programs from being discovered, and coordinate the attack . . . all without getting caught. Neoteric tools are likely to use a virus, worm, or Trojan horse program to propagate the zombie tools, and then to automatically launch the attack with some code word from a public forum.

There has already been one denial-of-service attack that worked this way. In 1999, someone posted a fake Internet Explorer update from Microsoft. It was really a Trojan horse that caused the infected computer to send packets to hosts belonging to the Bulgarian Telecommunications Company, causing denial-of-service problems for them for a *long* time.

Tracing the attacker is also incredibly difficult. Returning to the pizza delivery example, the only thing the victim could do is to ask the pizza parlors to help him catch the attacker. If everyone coordinated their phone logs, maybe they could figure out who ordered all the pizzas in the first place. Something similar is possible on the Internet, but it is unlikely that the intermediate sites kept good logs. Additionally, it is easy to disguise your location on the Internet. And if the attacker is in some Eastern European country with minimal computer crime laws, a bribable police, and no extradition treaties, there's nothing you can do anyway.

The real problem is the hundreds of thousands, possibly millions, of nescient computer users who are vulnerable to attack. They're using DSL or cable modems, they're always on the Internet with static IP addresses, and they can be taken over and used as launching pads for these (and other) attacks. The media is focusing on the mega e-corporations that are under attack, but the real story is the individual systems.

Similarly, the real solutions are of the "civic hygiene" variety. Just as malaria was defeated in Washington, D.C., by draining all the swamps, the only real way to prevent these attacks is to protect those millions of individual computers on the Internet. Unfortunately, we are building swampland at an incredible rate, and securing everything is impracticable. Even if personal firewalls had a 99 percent market penetration, and even if they were all installed and operated perfectly, there would still be enough insecure computers on the Internet to use for these attacks.

THE FUTURE OF NETWORK SECURITY

Back in the 1960s, people figured out that you can whistle, click, belch, or whatever into a telephone and make the phone switches do things. This was the era of phone phreaking: black boxes, blue boxes, Captain Crunch whistles. The phone company did their best to defend against these attacks—they blocked certain tones, traced attackers, and started keeping their design specifications secret—but the basic problem was that the phone system was built with *in-band signaling:* The control signal and the data signal traveled along the same wires. This meant that the switches within the phone system were listening to the voice channel for control codes, and this is what the phone phreakers exploited.

The solution was to completely redesign the phone system. Modern phone switching protocols—for example, SS7, or Signaling System 7—were designed with *out-of-band signaling.* The voice path and data path were separated, and traveled along separate paths along the network. Now it doesn't matter how hard you whistle into the phone system: The switch isn't listening. Entire classes of attacks simply don't work, because attackers at the end points don't have access to the switches in the middle.

(This isn't entirely true. Red boxes still work against payphones. These boxes mimic the tones that record the coins deposited in the phones. Note that this is the remaining in-band signaling portion in the phone system: The tones are sent from the payphones to the switches in band.)

In the long term, out-of-band signaling is the best way to deal with many of the vulnerabilities of the Internet. It's not a panacea—insecure nodes will still cause problems—but it will go a long way.

Unfortunately, there are several problems. The Internet is designed as an egalitarian network: Anyone can get on the Internet simply by connecting with another Internet computer. An out-of-band system will have to be centrally managed, like the phone system. There will be end points and there will be internal routers, and they will be different. It will be nothing like the Internet is today.

At this point there are no plans to redesign the Internet in this way, and any such undertaking might be just too complicated to even consider.

12

Network Defenses

FIREWALLS

The first firewalls were on trains. Coal-powered trains had a large furnace in the engine room, along with a pile of coal. The engineer would shovel coal into the engine. This process created coal dust, which was highly flammable. Occasionally the coal dust would catch fire, causing an engine fire that sometimes spread into the passenger cars. Since dead passengers reduced revenue, train engines were built with iron walls right behind the engine compartment. This stopped fires from spreading into the passen-ger cars, but didn't protect the engineer between the coal pile and the furnace. (There's a lesson for sysadmins in this somewhere.)

In the digital world, a firewall is a machine that protects a company's internal network from the malicious hackers, ravenous criminals, and desultory evildoers who lurk throughout the Internet. It keeps intruders out.

The definitions don't parallel well, and that's because the term "fire-wall" has changed meaning since it was first used in computer networks. The original networks were buggy and would inveterately crash. Fire-walls were installed to prevent bad networking software in one part of the network from taking the rest of the network down with it. They were, like physical firewalls, machines designed to contain problems within a small area of a network.

Today's firewalls act as boundaries between private networks and the vast public network. They keep intruders out, and only allow authorized users in. They might be more accurately called "castle walls," but the term "firewall" has already become established.

I'm not going to talk about the details of firewalls and how they work; shelvesful of books do that. Instead, I am going to talk about the general philosophies of firewalls, how good they are at countering the threats, and what the future of firewalls is likely to be.

First point: Recognize that a firewall is a boundary, a perimeter defense. Like a castle wall, it serves to repel invaders. Also like a castle wall, it is useless against an armed insurrection inside the castle. Bill Cheswick describes a firewall as a "hard crunchy shell around a soft chewy center." Once the attacker is inside the firewall, the firewall is useless. And since about 70 percent of all computer attacks come from the inside (according to a Computer Security Institute study in 1998), this is defi-nitely something worth thinking about. Of course, it is possible to install internal firewalls to further protect sections of the network. Think of cas-tles with outer baileys and inner baileys.

Second point: Until the invention of cannon, a good castle was pretty much invulnerable; there was no way to scale, breach, or tunnel under the walls. However, a patient general could always besiege a castle. By deny-ing the inhabitants food, water, and anyone interesting to talk to, the gen-eral hoped that the defenders would give up. Sometimes this worked quickly, but some sieges lasted years. If the castle had a well inside, it helped. If the castle had a secret tunnel to the outside, it helped a lot. If the inhabitants of the castle caught the plague or something, it didn't help. (Poor sanitation defeated many a valiant defender.) Similarly, it is possible to starve a network by severing its connections to the outside.

Third point: A castle needs to be secure on all sides. It makes no sense to put up a freestanding wall; attackers will go around it. Remember the Maginot Line? The French built it in the 1930s to prevent German inva-sion. Against the trench-warfare fighting of World War I, it was thought to be impregnable. But the technology of tanks improved significantly in the ensuing years, and the Germans invented blitzkrieg as a style of war-fare. They simply went around the Maginot Line, invading France through Belgium. And by the same token, a firewall has to act as a barrier between the internal network and all external access points. Otherwise, an attacker will just go around the firewall and attack some undefended connection.

And fourth point: Castles need gates. It's futile and absurd to build a castle that can't be penetrated by anyone under any circumstances: Even kings need to go outside and perambulate sometimes. Merchants, messengers, even common townsfolk need to be able to go in and out regularly. Hence, castles had gatekeepers whose job it was to admit or turn away people who wanted to enter the castle.

The Great Wall of China didn't impress Genghis Khan. "The strength of a wall depends on the courage of those who defend it," he supposedly said. Letting the good stuff in while keeping the bad stuff out is the central problem that any computer firewall needs to solve. It has to act as gatekeeper. It has to figure out which bits are harmful and deny them entry. It has to do this without unreasonably delaying traffic. (And to your average Internet user, an unreasonable delay is defined as one that is noticeable.) It has to do this without irritating legitimate users. (Your average Internet user will not tolerate not being able to do something, like downloading a new Internet game from Suspicious Software™ or con-necting remotely and reading e-mail from an untrusted machine.) But if the firewall's gatekeeper makes a mistake, some hacker can sneak in and own the network.

There are three basic ways to defeat a firewall. The first I talked about: go around it. A large network has lots of connections. Large photocopiers often come with Internet connections, and some network equipment comes with dial-up maintenance ports. Companies often hook their net-works to the networks of suppliers, customers, and so forth; sometimes those networks are much less protected. Employees will hook personal modems up to their computers so they can work at home. There's a story of a married couple in Silicon Valley who occasionally worked from home. He was checking his e-mail while his wife was doing some pro-gramming, both of them on their small home network. Suddenly, his company's computers started showing up on her company's network and vice versa.

The second, and more complicated attack, is to sneak something through the firewall. To do this, you have to fool the firewall into think-ing you are good, honorable, and authorized. Depending on how good the firewall is and how well it has been installed, this is either easy, difficult, or next to impossible.

The basic idea is to create a piece of code that the firewall lets inside the network. The code is designed to exploit some kind of bug in the computer system that will open a connection between the hacker outside the firewall and the computer inside the firewall. If it all works, the hacker gets inside.

The third attack is to take over the firewall. This is akin to bribing or blackmailing the gatekeeper. Since he is now in your employ, he'll do what you want. Again, how easy this is depends on the firewall. Some firewalls run buggy software, which helps. Some run on top of insecure operating systems, which helps a lot.

Anyway, firewall design today is all about designing smart gatekeepers. At the simplest level, a firewall is a router with a consistent rule set that it tests network traffic against, and then passes traffic that meets the rules and drops all other traffic. Examples might be to restrict traffic based on source or destination address or protocol type.

This was relatively easy in early networks, but today's firewalls have to deal with multimedia traffic, downloadable programs, Java applets, and all sorts of weird things. A firewall has to make decisions with only partial information: It might have to decide whether or not to let a packet through before seeing all the packets in a transmission.

Early firewalls were something called *packet filters*. The firewall would look at each packet and either admit or drop it, depending on a bunch of rules about the packet header. The first packet filters were pretty dumb, and let a whole lot of things in that were better left out. Eventually they got smarter. Today they are *stateful:* Instead of looking at each packet individually, the firewall keeps information about the state of the network and what types of packets are expected. Still, firewalls only have so long a memory, and slow attacks can often get through.

Some good packet-filtering firewalls are out there, but they still dis-play a number of weaknesses. First and foremost, they are a pain to con-figure properly, and improper configuration often leads to security vulnerabilities. Lots of things are allowed in by default that should be blocked. And the firewall doesn't modify packets, so if a packet gets through, it can do whatever it wants. And there are a bunch of more eso-teric attacks against packet filters; just imagine fooling a guard who tries to stop the flow of dangerous letters into a castle by looking at the envelopes.

Another type of firewall is a *proxy,* or *application gateway.* Think of two guards, one inside the walls and the other outside the walls. The guard outside knows nothing about the insides of the castle. The guard inside knows nothing about the world outside the castle. But the guards pass packets to each other. Proxy firewalls try to implement this "two guard" metaphor. Some proxy firewalls just act as go-betweens: Someone inside the firewall wants a document, the client software asks the firewall (inside guard) for it, and the firewall (outside guard) connects to the Web site and gets it. Other proxy firewalls understand the applications and what kinds of protocols they use. Still other proxy firewalls are store-and-forward proxies; they store data chunks before passing them on, and can filter data based on a bunch of rules. And the better proxy firewalls are becoming aware of their environment, and are therefore able to make smarter deci-sions about packets.

The weaknesses of proxy firewalls are mostly too subtle to talk about here. They also have a longer latency, and lower throughput, than packet filters. (Actually, since firewalls have to examine every packet, they all slow down fast network connections.) Proxy firewalls have to be config-ured securely to work correctly, just as packet filters do, and proxies are much harder to configure and maintain than packet filters; the tendency is to just stop bothering with them.

About 100 different firewall products are on the market, and more show up every month. Most are IP only, and don't secure other proto-cols. Most of them don't implement just one approach, but are hybrids to some degree. Advances in firewall technology are happening all the time, and it's hard to compare and evaluate them. Some organizations give fire-walls seals of approval, but most hackers regard this as laughable; firewalls that pass are secure against only the most basic attacks. (Still, many fail test-ing the first time through.) In general, the best firewall is one that has been configured correctly, and has all the current patches and updates.

I've heard firewalls referred to as "a router with an attitude." That's a true statement. Some of the best firewall professionals I know don't even bother with firewalls; they believe that a well-configured router with strong security at the end points is more secure than a firewall. They may have a point. Certainly firewalls have given the corporate world a false sense of security on the Internet.

Firewalls are an important part of any company's network security, but they can't do it all. Their security model reflects an earlier time in net-work security, when organizations needed to keep their assets inside and the bad guys outside. Today, with organizations needing to open their networks up to customers, partners, sales prospects—the public—they seem anachronistic. Important, yes. A panacea, no.

DEMILITARIZED ZONES

A DMZ is a *demilitarized zone*. It's the no-man's-land between North Korea and South Korea that neither side is supposed to be in.

In firewall talk, a DMZ is a place on your network where you put your public services. In Chapter 10 I talked about all the attacks against Web servers. You don't want to put the Web servers inside the firewall, because they are vulnerable to attack. You can't put the Web servers out-side the firewall, because then they're vulnerable to even more attacks. The solution is to put them in a DMZ.

This idea is a good one, and one with a lot of historical precedent. Castles were often built with inner walls and outer walls. Inside the outer walls were the stables, the servants' quarters: things that you could afford to lose in an assault. Inside the inner walls were the noble residences: the important stuff. In the event of attack, soldiers would try to defend the outer walls but would retreat to the inner walls if their defense failed.

To build a DMZ, you need two logical firewalls. One firewall pro-tects the DMZ from the outside world. Another firewall, configured with more restrictions, protects the internal network from the DMZ. The result is a semipublic part of the network and a more private part of the network. This kind of idea works.

VIRTUAL PRIVATE NETWORKS

A *virtual private network* (VPN) is simply a secure connection over a public network. In the old days, if Alice and Bob wanted to communicate, they had to lease an expensive private line and run their own private network. Today, the cheaper solution is for Alice and Bob to use the public net-work. But the Internet is insecure; for Alice and Bob to communicate securely on the Internet, they need to secure that connection. They need to create a virtual private network on top of the physical public network. A VPN does that.

VPNs have two main uses. The first is to connect disjoint pieces of the same network. A corporation might have two offices on different sides of the planet. Each office has its own physical network, and the two networks are connected by a VPN running over the Internet. A VPN is more private than a "private line" provided by the telephone company.

The second use is to connect mobile users: users working from home and users working out of hotel rooms. The old way to bring these users into the large network was to have them dial in directly, often long distance. This is expensive, and forces the company to maintain a large bank of modems. The modern way is to have the users dial in locally to an ISP, and then connect from the ISP to the company over the Internet. To secure this connection, a VPN runs from the user's computer to the network.

Different VPNs provide security through different cryptographic pro-tocols. The most common protocol is IPsec, although you'll still find protocols that implement PPTP and L2TP. Some VPNs don't have any cryptography at all.

One way to think of a VPN is as a hole in the firewall. Someone with a VPN is allowed to tunnel through the firewall into the network. For this reason, a lot of security permeates the ways in which VPN connections are authenticated and allowed in. And a lot of hacker attacks exploit holes in this security.

INTRUSION DETECTION SYSTEMS

Intrusion detection systems (IDSs) are network monitors. They watch your network, looking for suspicious behavior. Think of them as autonomous police detectives wandering around town: They know what suspicious behavior looks like—probing a system for access, poking around for bugs to exploit, or whatever—and they keep an eye out for it. They know what an attack looks like. They know what a crime looks like. Marcus Ranum describes a firewall as the helmet and flak jacket you wear into battle, and an IDS as the medic who looks over your bleeding body, saying: "That looks like a sucking chest wound. I'd get that checked if I were you." An IDS is not a substitute for good proactive security.

Okay then, what do IDSs do? They alert you of a successful attack, or maybe even an attack in progress. The good ones are accurate in both senses: They don't cry wolf and claim an attack where there is none, and they don't miss real attacks. The good ones are timely: They alert you of the attack while it is still going on. The good ones give some kind of diag-nosis—what the attack is and where it is coming from—and suggest some kind of remedial action.

Current product offerings fall far short in every dimension, but they're trying. The hardest problem is the false alarms. To explain it, I'm going to have to digress into statistics and explain the *base rate fallacy*.

Suppose a doctor had a disease test that was 99 percent accurate. That is, if someone has the disease, there is a 99 percent chance that the test would signify "disease," and if someone does not have the disease, there is a 99 percent chance that the test would signify "healthy." Assume that one in ten thousand people, on average, have the disease. Is the test any good?

No. If the doctor administers the test to a random person and she tests positive, there is only a one percent chance she actually has the disease. Because the population of healthy people is so much larger than the num-ber of diseased, the test is useless. (It's not as simple as retesting the person. Assume false positives are consistent for a particular person.) This result is counterintuitive and surprising, but it is correct.

What this means is that if you assume that network attacks are com-paratively rare, the base rate fallacy implies that your tests have to be really good to screen out all of the false positives. An IDS that habitually pages you at 3:00 A.M. with a problem that turns out not to be a problem—an all-night Quake game, or a new Internet application, or whatnot—is going to get turned off pretty quickly.

There are other problems. Timely notification is one. I mentioned slow attacks in the previous section. When does an IDS decide that it's an attack and notify you? What if the IDS thinks something looks like an attack, sort of? Does it notify you? When? Again, remember the false pos-itive problem. If it guesses wrong too often, you're going to stop listening to it.

And will you even know what to do when the alarm goes off? Hor-tatory messages of the general form "you're under attack" are useless unless you have some way to respond, and the time to deal with it. Dur-ing the 22-hour eBay outage of 1999, the IDS system set off alarms con-stantly, but everyone was too busy to respond. This is the biggest problem with IDSs: intelligently reacting to their output.

IDSs are still really in their infancy, and different ideas are vying for supremacy. I'm just going to touch on some of them; many books out there go into detail.

There are two basic ways to build an IDS. The easiest is *misuse detection*. The IDS knows what an attack looks like, and looks for it. Think of a virus detector for network packets. Just as the virus detector scans every file looking for particular bit strings indicating a virus, the IDS scans every packet looking for bit strings that signify a certain attack. They're easy to implement and deploy, they have low false positives, and they can be relatively fast (considering that they have to touch each packet).

On the other hand, they miss more. Just as a virus detector can't find viruses it has never seen before, a misuse-detection IDS can't find attacks it isn't programmed to find. This makes them easy to fool. Sometimes it's as easy as taking an existing attack and mixing up the order of commands. Sometimes it's taking the attack and breaking up the packets differently. Just as antivirus software needs to be constantly updated with new signa-tures, this type of IDS needs a constantly updated database of attack signatures. It's unclear whether such a database can ever keep up with the hacker tools.

The other IDS paradigm is *anomaly detection*. The IDS does some sta-tistical modeling of your network and figures out what is normal. Then, if anything abnormal happens, it sounds an alarm. This kind of thing can be done with rules (the system knows what's normal and flags anything else), statistics (the system figures out statistically what's normal and flags anything else), or with artificial-intelligence techniques.

This has a plethora of problems. What if you're being hacked as you train the system? Then, being hacked is considered normal. New things happen on computer networks all the time. Does the IDS know the dif-ference between a normal abnormality, and an abnormality indicating an attack? And if all it knows is what is normal, how is it going to categorize attacks? The false positives for this kind of system are much higher, and attacking these kinds of IDSs involves figuring out how to sneak past them.

Some early virus detectors used this sort of paradigm, and they would generate all kinds of alarms if you did something like install a new piece of software. They fell out of favor as the misuse-detection-based virus checkers got better signature dictionaries; I expect the same thing to happen with IDSs.

Other IDS ideas can work with either of the preceding paradigms. Inline IDS works on network data in real time, while audit-based IDS looks at audit information after the fact. There's also host-based IDSs ver-sus network-based IDSs.

This latter distinction has been the subject of a raging debate in the IDS community. Basically, network-based IDS products are built on the wiretapping concept: Sensors sit on the network and examine packets as they go by. These systems have the advantages of stealth—they can be deployed without affecting the rest of the network—and operating-system independence. Host-based IDSs look at system, audit, and event logs from individual systems. These systems have a different set of pluses and minuses, the most apparent being that they are product-specific.

What you're eventually going to find in the marketplace are hybrid systems: a combination of host-based and network-based IDSs, doing some expert-system-based anomaly detection and some signature-based misuse detection. You're also going to find managed security monitoring companies, who actually watch the output of these things and respond to their alarms. Like firewalls, IDSs will get better and better as developers get more experience building them. And also like firewalls, their security will eventually depend on how well they are configured and how up-to-date the versions are. And there will always be attacks that get through them.

HONEY POTS AND BURGLAR ALARMS

Network burglar alarms and *honey pots* are a form of intrusion detection, but they deserve a separate section. Burglar alarms are specific things on your network designed to go off if an attacker touches them. Honey pots are burglar alarms dressed up to look particularly attractive to attackers. Burglar alarms are easy to understand: A particular network command that no one is supposed to use sounds an alarm if used; a dummy network account sounds an alarm if activated; and so forth. Marcus Ranum has taken this idea even further, and suggested that when a security vulnera-bility is patched in a product, it should also be alarmed.

Honey pots are more involved: entire dummy computers and sub-networks designed to look inviting to attackers. You can have fun with these; name the computers something like transactions.bigcompany.com or accounting.bank.com, dress them up with impressive-sounding accounts and files, and protect them on your network. When an attacker breaks into the network, he gravitates toward the honey pot because it looks like an interesting place to explore. Then an alarm goes off, and the honey pot monitors the hacking activity and gathers data for prosecution. Some companies sell premade honey pots; just add enticing names.

What's interesting about both of these measures is that they exploit the one advantage the network administrator has over an attacker: knowl-edge of the network. The administrator knows how the network is supposed to look and what is supposed to happen. He can set burglar alarms—just as a homeowner can set window alarms because he knows that no one is supposed to open the windows, and motion sensors because he knows that no one is supposed to be walking around in the living room—using that knowledge. He can deploy honey pots with the knowledge that no legitimate user will ever access those systems. He can set up all sort of burglar alarms, turn them on and off at different times of the day, move them around once in a while, do anything he wants. These measures are effective precisely because the attacker doesn't know if they are there or where they would be. Unlike a firewall or IDS—an attacker often knows what brand firewall is installed—burglar alarms and honey pots are tailored specifically for the network being alarmed.

VULNERABILITY SCANNERS

The intent of vulnerability scanning is to have an automated program scan your network (or computer) for a huge laundry list of known weaknesses. It does the work, and then you get a tidy report of which weaknesses the network has. Then it's up to you to fix them (or, I suppose, exploit them).

The reality of vulnerability scanners is not nearly so clean, and all vul-nerability scanners on the market are massively flawed. If they worked the way you expect them to work, they would all crash your computers and damage your network. No one would use such a tool, so they all fake it. Imagine a vulnerability scanner for your house. One of the things it checks is whether your windows are vulnerable to attack by a rock. The obvious way to test this is to throw a rock against the window and watch the results. But this would cause damage to the house, so the scanner fakes it. It looks at the glass to see if it is single pane or double pane. Maybe it taps on it, to see if it is actually glass or a stronger plastic. Maybe it tries to read the part number on the window, and makes some assumptions about the glass based on that. This is the same sort of thing that network vulnerability scanners have to do.

It gets worse. Sometimes it's hard to tell whether or not a particular attack is successful. The same home vulnerability scanner now tests the power reliability by trying to cut the power lines into the house. It cuts the power line, and the lights stay on. Does this mean that the scanner failed to cut the power line, and the house is not vulnerable, or does it mean that the house has a backup power system? Or maybe the scanner cuts the power lines and the power goes off. Does this mean that the scan-ner cut the power line, or that it did something else that, through some contorted chain of events, resulted in the power being shut off? The scan-ner doesn't know, and most of the time has no way of figuring it out. Networks are unreliable; they don't fail in neat ways.

Even though vulnerability scanners can't actually scan for vulnerabil-ities, nor can they accurately measure the effects of their actions when they can scan for vulnerabilities, they are not useless. They can scan for, or at least fake scanning for, some vulnerabilities. They do produce a list of vulnerabilities that a conscientious system administrator will close (and a nefarious attacker will exploit). They work okay.

SATAN (Security Administrator Tool for Analyzing Networks) made a big press splash when it was released in 1995. It was portrayed in the media as worse than its namesake, and its author was fired from his job at SGI. Since then vulnerability scanners have achieved respectability as a component of a security administrator's toolkit. Several commercial prod-ucts, with respectable names, are in the marketplace. Think of these tools as another audit technique: a private investigator that reports on your security vulnerabilities. You can hire the P.I. to examine your own system, but an attacker can hire the same P.I. to examine a target system. But understand the limitations of the technology.

E-MAIL SECURITY

These days, e-mail is everywhere. Anyone who has any presence at all in cyberspace has an e-mail address, and probably receives far too many e-mail messages every day. E-mail has no built-in security.

Like any network packet, any machine between the source and the destination can read e-mail. (You can even see the names of some of those machines in the headers of your received mail.) The common metaphor used for Internet e-mail is postcards: Anyone—letter carriers, mail sorters, nosy delivery truck drivers—who can touch the postcard can read what's on the back. And there's no way of verifying the signature on a letter or the return address (you do know that the "From" field in your mail header can easily be forged?), so there's no way of knowing where a mes-sage really came from. (Spammers use this feature to hide the origin of their mass mailings.) If an attacker wants to be subtle, he can actually con-nect (without an account) to the forged machine of origin and send the mail from there. If he doesn't care, he can just forge the "from" line.

We want two things for e-mail. One, we want to make sure that no one other than the intended recipient can read the message. Two, we want to make sure that an e-mail message came from the person it purports to have come from, and that no one can forge e-mail messages.

The cryptography to protect e-mail is simple and straightforward, and dozens of products on the market deal with the problem. Here's the basic protocol:

1. Alice gets Bob's public key.
2. Alice signs her message with her private key.
3. Alice encrypts her message with Bob's public key.
4. Alice sends the encrypted and signed message to Bob.
5. Bob decrypts the message using his private key.
6. Bob verifies Alice's signature using her public key.

Where you're going to see difficulties is in the public keys: how you get them, store them, verify them. I'll talk about this a lot more in Chapter 15.

ENCRYPTION AND NETWORK DEFENSES

Defending against network attacks isn't as simple as incorporating cryptography into the systems. Often the realities of the systems prevent cryp-tography from being used. For example, one part of the DNS record constantly changes, so it is impractical to use digital signatures with DNS records. Cryptographic authentication just won't work.

Or imagine a world where every packet is encrypted with IPsec. Since the packets are encrypted, they can't be analyzed. Network engi-neers can no longer perform traffic analysis. Address-translation systems can't deal with the packets. Performance-optimizing systems—for exam-ple, a system that tinkers with packet size to optimize traffic for satellite transmission—no longer work.

Another example: A lot of network defenses rely on examining packets and making sure they're not malicious. Encryption can deny a defender access to the packets, and to the defenses.

Consider antivirus software that sits at the firewall, automatically scan-ning all incoming e-mail looking for malware. In large corporations these programs can find over 1,000 viruses a day infecting e-mail attachments. If that corporation encrypted all of its e-mail, the antivirus software would not be able to find anything at the firewall (unless it had the keys).

Consider firewalls that scan incoming packets, looking for network attacks. If that network employed IPsec throughout, the firewall couldn't examine anything.

There are no good solutions to this problem. One solution is to give the firewall the decryption keys. This has lots of potential security problems. Another solution is a *distributed firewall*: pushing the network defenses away from the perimeter of the network and onto every host in the network. This has its own set of problems, but is probably the future of firewalls.

The Internet boffins are hard at work on this problem; I don't have an answer for you.

13

Software Reliability

Between system security measures (security kernels, access control measures, strong cryptography, etc.) and good network security measures (firewalls, intrusion detection systems, auditing mecha-nisms), it seems as if computer security is pretty much done. Why then, are computers and networks so insecure? Why are we seeing more computer security vulnerabilities in the media, and not less? Why aren't things getting better?

The problem is that security measures such as cryptography, secure kernels, firewalls, and everything else work much better in theory than they do in practice. In other words: Security flaws in the implementation are much more common, and much more serious, than security flaws in the design. So far, Part 2 has talked about design. This chapter is about implementation.

FAULTY CODE

In June 1996, the European Space Agency's *Ariane 5* rocket exploded after launch because of a software error: The program tried to stick a 64-bit number into a 16-bit space, causing an overflow. Its lessons are particularly relevant to computer security.

Basically, there was a piece of code written for the *Ariane 4* rocket that dealt with the rocket's sideways velocity. At 36.7 seconds after launch, the guidance system's computer tried to convert this velocity measurement from a 64-bit format to a 16-bit format. The number was too big, which caused an error. Normally, there would be extra code that watches for these sorts of errors and recovers gracefully. But the original programmers decided not to bother with the code in this case, since the velocity figure would never be large enough to cause trouble. That may have been true in the *Ariane 4,* but the *Ariane 5* was a faster rocket. Even worse, the cal-culation containing the bug served no purpose once the rocket was in the air. Its only function was to align the system before launch. So it should have been turned off. But engineers chose long ago, in an even earlier version of the *Ariane,* to leave this function running for the first 40 sec-onds of flight—a "special feature" meant to make it easy to restart the system in the event of a brief hold in the countdown. There was a backup system designed to take over in case of failure, but it was running the same software and suffered the same error.

The resulting chain of events shut down the guidance system, which completely confused the onboard steering computer, which caused the rocket to make an unneeded course correction, which forced the rocket to self-destruct.

Three years later, NASA's Mars planet orbiter disappeared during a tricky maneuver not because of Martian Air Defense, but because of a data conversion bug. The NASA engineers failed to convert English mea-sures of rocket thrusts (in pounds) to newtons, a metric unit. There's a 4.45 times difference between the units; and that was enough to send the probe 50 miles lower into the Martian atmosphere, where it burned up.

These two disasters are not related to computer security, but they serve to illustrate how hard it is to design and implement bug-free code. Both the European Space Agency and NASA had a strong incentive, and a suitably large budget, to ensure quality software. And they still failed.

Others don't do any better. In 1999, eBay went down for 22 hours due to software-related errors in code supplied by Sun Microsystems. Bug chasing delayed the release of the Visor palm computer. And in 1998, a bug in Cisco switches knocked out AT&T's Interspan frame relay net-work, affecting 6,600 customers.

The unfortunate reality is that software bugs like these are every-where. Most don't have such efficiently devastating consequences (rebooting a spreadsheet after it crashes is just a minor annoyance), but as complex software moves into more critical systems (e.g., automobile crash avoidance, aircraft takeoff and landing, nuclear power plant control), we're likely to see more of these kinds of failures. A lot of work is going into error recovery, failure avoidance, and what is called a fail-safe strategy: For example, if the crash-avoidance system fails in a car, it is supposed to behave more or less like a pre-computer car, instead of deciding to swerve into the nearest tree. The idea is to make sure that little failures don't get out of hand, like what happened on *Ariane 5*.

Squashing software bugs that affect performance is hard; finding software flaws that affect security is even harder.

Reliability means that the computer—generally, the software, but any specialized hardware as well—has to work even in the presence of ran-dom faults. These faults could be design faults (running identical software on both the primary and backup systems), implementation faults (not doing error checking on a data conversion), programming faults (remem-ber the mathematics bug in the Intel Pentium chip?), or usage faults. These faults happen occasionally, randomly. Think of it as programming Murphy's Computer: a computer where things go wrong . . . rarely but consistently. A computer where mistakes happen once in a while, but rarely become severe enough for any user to notice.

The underlying problem is that in any complex system—rocketry software, a large database, an operating system, networking software, a complex microprocessor—many, many things could possibly go wrong. And complexity is going through the roof. It is just impracticable to design or test for everything. Inevitably, something goes wrong.

Computer security is more like programming Satan's computer. (Ross Anderson is responsible for that beautiful turn of phrase.) In order to be secure, software has to work in the presence of subtle and malicious faults deliberately introduced by an intelligent attacker bent on defeating the security of the system. Secure software has to survive the same random faults when exploited by an intelligent hacker trying to defeat the security of the system. (Think of a hacker forcing the *Ariane 5* software to make the overflow error occur at the worst possible time.) Mistakes occur ran-domly, and most mistakes will never be encountered under normal use. But attackers will seek potential mistakes out and deliberately use them to their advantage.

The general strategy used to find random faults is beta testing: give the software to a large group of users and let them bang on it. The people will use the software in all sorts of configurations, on various types of hard-ware, and do different things with it (some of which the designers never even thought of). If they can't crash the system, it's probably mistake-free. It's hard to beta test rocketry software in anything but a simulated envi-ronment, but any large commercial software application you buy has (hopefully) been put through thousands of hours of beta testing designed to find and fix programming mistakes.

The previous paragraph should give you pause. Given how buggy most commercial software is, you might not trust that beta testing, or any testing for that matter, works. Testing does work, but complications remain. One, the rush to market means that some companies are pushing poorly tested software on the populace. (Most Internet software is released in beta; some even argue that the Internet itself is still in beta.) Two, the same rush to market means that some companies are pushing software on the populace before fixing the long list of bugs that they have already identified. (And while they fix bugs found in beta, they don't do a second beta cycle to test the fixed code.)

ATTACKS ON FAULTY CODE

Most of the computer security problems we see are the result of faulty code. Here are some examples:

- In 1988, the Morris worm used a bug in the UNIX fingered program to gain root access to computers running the program. This is a buffer overflow, explained in the next section.
- In 1999, someone discovered a bug in a Hotmail CGI script that allowed one user to access the e-mail account of another user. This kind of flaw was discussed in Chapter 10.

Traditionally, faulty code has been the wedge used to break into computers. Flaws in the sendmail program, for example, have been responsible for a huge number of break-ins to UNIX computers. The goal of these attacks is to exploit the flaws so that the attacker can take control of the system. The specific attacks are obscure—exploiting the debug option to get root access, or using a loophole in the error message header in order to read password files—but there are a lot of them. For a while it seemed like every month a new attack against sendmail was dis-covered and patched. (Whether the patches ever got out to the commer-cial users is another question.)

A more recent example is the Java security model. Java has a complex security model to shield computers from malicious Java applets. A programming error anywhere in the protection mechanisms can potentially render them all useless, and since its inception, a steady stream of implementation-specific Java attacks have exploited a variety of different flaws.

What makes all these examples more troublesome than the *Ariane* flaw (although less incandescent) is that the bugs that were used to break security did not affect performance. They were there, undetected, until they were found and exploited. This is a big deal, and why security is harder than reliability. The *Ariane* bug is one that affects performance. Once a performance bug is found—and beta testing can find them—it can be fixed. Security bugs don't affect performance, and don't show up in beta test results. I'll talk more about testing security in Chapter 22, but the moral is that while people can sometimes stumble onto security flaws, only experienced experts can reliably discover them.

This kind of thing happens all the time. When someone skilled per-forms a security analysis of a piece of security software, he always finds random flaws that compromise security. Always. The more complex the code, the more security flaws.

Security problems, once discovered, will be exploited until they are fixed. Assume an attacker finds a security flaw in a commerce protocol that allows him to steal credit card numbers or, even worse, money. If he's in it for the publicity, he'll announce his exploit to the press and it will be fixed. (Hopefully, he'll alert the company first.) If he's in it for the money, he will make use of the flaw, again and again. He'll steal as much as he can until someone else notices the flaw and fixes it. This is an important dif-ference: Flaws that affect performance are noticed, while security flaws can remain invisible for a long time.

These flaws are not necessarily in the security portion of the code, either. They can be anywhere in the code: the user interface, the error-handling routines, anything. And as we saw in Chapter 10, even programs that don't have anything to do with computer security can affect the secu-rity of networked computers. Flaws in your word processor, your printer driver, or your multimedia player can all compromise the security of your computer.

The other moral is that software bugs (and therefore, security flaws) are inevitable. Just as it is inconceivable that the *Ariane 5* software could be completely bug-free—the unfortunate accident is that the bug had such catastrophic effects—it is inconceivable that a large Internet applica-tion will be bug-free.

We've seen this kind of thing with Windows NT. Hardly a day goes by without some new announcement about a security hole in this pro-gram. We're already seeing the same trend with Windows 2000.

BUFFER OVERFLOWS

Buffer overflows (sometimes called *stack smashing*) are the most common form of security vulnerability in the last ten years. They're also the easiest to exploit; more attacks are the result of buffer overflows than any other problem. And they can be devastating; attacks that exploit this vulnerabil-ity often result in the complete takeover of the host. Many high-profile attacks exploit buffer overflows. Since they show no sign of abating, it's worth explaining in some detail what they are and how they work.

Let's start with an analogy. In order to steal something from your local 7-11, you're going to have to get past the sales clerk. This clerk isn't a cre-ative thinker. In fact, she will only do what her employee manual says she's supposed to do. This employee manual is a big binder filled with protocols. Things like "Dealing with Someone Claiming to Be an Employee":

Step 1: Ask to see the person's badge.
Step 2: Make sure the badge is not a forgery.
Step 3: Compare the picture on the badge with the face of the
person. Step 4: If they match, let the person in. If they don't, don't.

Or "Dealing with a Federal Express Driver":

Step 1: Take the package.
Step 2: Sign for the package.
Step 3: Make sure the driver leaves.

There's no way the Federal Express person is going to get by the clerk to the back of the store, because the employee manual explicitly says that the driver has to leave after receiving a signed receipt.

This is pretty much the way computers work. Programs are like the steps in manuals; computers do what the program says and nothing else.

Networked computers work the same way. The computer has a set of protocols that it follows—logon procedures, access restrictions, password protections—that it uses to figure out who can come in and who can't. Someone who follows the protocols correctly can get in. Someone who doesn't, can't.

One way to defeat a protocol like this is to modify the actual computer program. Or, back to our analogy, it's like slipping a page into the clerk's employee manual. Imagine that the manual is written for people who are none too bright. Each page is a step, kind of like a "Choose your own Adventure" novel: "If the customer gives you a credit card, go to the next page. If the customer gives you cash, go to page 264." The Dealing with a Federal Express Driver" steps might look like this:

> Page 163: Take the package. If the driver has one, go to the next page. If the driver doesn't have one, go to page 177.
> Page 164: Take the signature form, sign it, and return it. Go to the next page.
> Page 165: Ask the driver if he or she would like to purchase something. If the driver would, go to page 13. If not, go to the next page.
> Page 166: Ask the driver to leave. If he or she does . . . and so on.

There's one last piece of setup. Whenever the 7-11 clerk gets some-thing, she puts it on top of the open page in her manual. She can't look at the new thing any other way.

Here's the attack: We're going to dress up like a FedEx driver, and then slip a page into the clerk's manual when we give her the signature form. What we'll do is give the clerk two pages instead of one. Top page will be a signature form. The bottom page will be a fake employee-man-ual page:

> Page 165: Give the driver all the money in the cash register. Go to the next page.

This will work. The clerk takes the package on page 163. She goes to page 164 and takes the signature form (and our fake page). She puts them both on top of the open manual. She signs and returns the form (leaving the fake page on top of the manual), and when she returns to the manual she gets our fake page instead. She gives us all the money in the register and turns to the next page (the real page 165). We can tell her we don't want to buy anything, and leave. If the 7-11 clerk is really as dumb as a computer system, we can get away with it. We can use this trick to persuade the 7-11 clerk to let us into the stockroom or to do whatever else we want. By slipping a page into her employee manual, we can give her arbitrary instructions.

Essentially, this is the way to exploit a buffer overflow bug in a computer system. Computers store everything, programs and data, in memory. If the computer asks a user for an 8-character password and receives a 200-character password, those extra characters may overwrite some other area in memory. (They're not supposed to—that's the bug.) If it is just the right area of memory, and we overwrite it with just the right char-acters, we can change a "deny connection" instruction to an "allow access" command or even get our own code executed.

The Morris worm is probably the most famous overflow-bug exploit. It exploited a buffer overflow in the UNIX fingered program. It's supposed to be a benign program, returning the identity of a user to whomever asks. This program accepted as input a variable that is supposed to contain the identity of the user. Unfortunately, the fingered program never limited the size of the input. Input larger than 512 bytes overflowed the buffer, and Morris wrote a specific large input that allowed his rogue program to execute as root and install itself on the new machine. (This particular bug has, of course, been fixed.)

What makes this worm especially relevant for this section is that it itself had a programming bug. It was supposed to hop between comput-ers on the Internet, copy itself onto each server, and then move on. But a typo in the code made the worm copy itself not once, but indefinitely, on each computer. The result was that computers infected by the worm crashed. Over 6,000 servers crashed as a result; at the time that was about 10 percent of the Internet.

Skilled programming can prevent this kind of attack. The program can truncate the password at 8 characters, so those extra 192 characters never get written into memory anywhere. It's easy to do, but it's hard to do everywhere. The problem is that with any piece of modern, large, complex code, there are just too many places where buffer overflows are possible (and they're not all as simple as this example) that it is difficult to squash them all. It's very difficult to guarantee that there are no over-flow problems, even if you take the time to check. The larger and more complex the code is, the more likely the attack.

Windows 2000 has somewhere between 35 and 60 million lines of code, and no one outside the programming team has ever seen them.

THE UBIQUITY OF FAULTY CODE

This chapter has centered on the Internet, and security bugs there. This is not to imply that the Internet somehow has more security flaws than other networks. Internet flaws make the news more often simply because more people are looking at the software, and more people are finding bugs. Software in other areas of cyberspace—the phone network, the electronic banking network—is just as buggy.

Estimates from Carnegie Mellon University show that a thousand lines of code typically has five to fifteen bugs. Most of these bugs are minor and do not affect performance, and are never noticed. All have the potential of compromising security.

In the short run, Internet code seems to be getting better. Security bugs are found all the time. Several computer magazines have weekly e-mail security newsletters, and they will contain a dozen or so security-related bugs a week. Manufacturers are usually pretty good about fixing these bugs once they become public, although most won't bother until then. If dozens of flaws are being reported and fixed per week, the reasoning goes, then there are always fewer security flaws to worry about.

This, of course, assumes you always implement the latest patches. What usually happens is that a vulnerability is reported and a patch is issued. If you believe the news reports, that's the end of the story. But in most cases patches never get installed. A major problem on the Internet is that these bug fixes don't necessarily flow downstream to the software in the field. "Internet time" affects system administrators, too.

So, even though the patches are available, the vulnerability remains. I've seen estimates that over 99 percent of all Internet attacks could be prevented if the system administrators would just use the most current versions of their system software. This is one reason vulnerability scanners are such good security tools: for both the good guys and the bad guys.

Even assuming everyone always runs the latest versions of all software, things are getting worse in the long run. All of these bugs are implementation-specific, and recidivism is high among software vendors. If version 1.0 is released and then over the years dozens, or hundreds, of security bugs are found and fixed, this says nothing about the security of version 2.0. Version 2.0 is probably larger and has more features; version 2.0 has all sorts of new code. Not only are all of those bug fixes for version 1.0 irrelevant, but version 2.0 probably has even more bugs.

14

Secure Hardware

T his is an ancient idea. It began when the first person drew a line across his cave entrance, proclaimed that what was on one side of the line was his, and then proceeded to defend his cave against all who disagreed with him. The notion covers a lot of different things: computer rooms behind locked doors and armed guards, tamper-resistant set-top boxes for pay-TV, secure tokens for access control, smart card chips for electronic commerce applications, and a bomb that blows up if you try to defuse it. The physical instantiation of the secure perimeter is different in each of these cases, but the fundamental benefit of the idea is the same: "It's a whole lot easier to design a computer security system if we can leverage the innate physical security of a device, and assume that parts of the system cannot be accessed by large classes of people."

And that's true. It's easier to design a secure pay-for-parking system if you assume that crooks can't empty the parking meters into their pockets. It's easier to design a secure library if you assume that people can't sneak books out of the building inside their overcoats. And it's easier to design an electronic wallet if you assume that people can't arbitrarily modify the amount of money they have.

Here's a perfect cashless monetary system: Everyone carries around a piece of paper with a number on it representing the number of ducats in his wallet. When someone spends money, he crosses out the number and writes the lower number. When he receives money, he does the oppo-site. If everyone is honest, this system works. As soon as someone notices

212

that he can write whatever number he wants on the paper, the system falls apart.

However, this was almost exactly the system that precomputer banks used to keep track of depositors' accounts. Each depositor had a bank-book stored in a file cabinet in the bank, and another in his possession. The bankbooks had a number that represented the amount of money the person had stored in the bank. When he deposited or withdrew money, the bank wrote a new number in both books. The system didn't fall apart, because one of the books was kept within the secure perimeter of the bank. And that was the real book; the book the depositor got was just a copy for his mollification. If a depositor forged a line in his bankbook, it would not match with the book stored in the bank. The bank teller would notice the discrepancy, presumably check other records to make sure there actually was attempted fraud, and prosecute accordingly. The customer could not modify the book in the bank because he could not get through the secure perimeter. (The teller, of course, had many more opportunities to commit fraud.)

This example illustrates the benefit of a secure perimeter; the security wouldn't work without one.

We can build an anonymous cash card system the same way. Customers walk around with smart cards in their wallets. The smart card con-tains a memory location with a dollar amount stored in it, much the same as the bankbook. Smart cards talk to each other through some kind of point-of-sale terminal. When a customer buys something, her smart card subtracts the amount of purchase from the amount in memory and writes the lower number back into memory. When a merchant sells something, his smart card adds the amount of purchase into the memory location. The cards only do this in pairs (secret keys in the cards can easily enforce this), so that everything balances out at the end. And to stop someone from just going into the card and changing his balance, the cards are tam-perproof.

Wasn't that easy? The secure perimeter around the card—secrets within the card stay within the card, and people outside the card can't affect those secrets—makes a lot of security problems go away. Without it, the only way to make a system like this work is through a tedious back-end processing system.

Checks work rather like the first example I talked about: people keeping a paper in their wallet listing their current account balance. People keep a paper tally of their current account balances, if they bother to balance their checkbooks at all. People can write checks for any arbitrary amount: No system forces them to write checks for less than their balance. Merchants accept these checks pretty much on faith; they have no idea if the person has enough money in the account to cover the check. But since there is no secure perimeter to enforce honesty, there is a compli-cated interbank check-clearing system: The merchant deposits the check, but doesn't get credit for the money yet. The merchant's bank uses iden-tification information on the bank—account number, bank name, and so forth—to figure out which account is liable for the amount of payment. Then it goes to the customer's bank and requests payment. The customer's bank checks the person's account. It deducts the money from its "secure" record of the customer's account and gives it to the mer-chant's bank. Finally, the merchant's bank credits the merchant's account.

Of course, the actual check-clearing system works a little differ-ently—optimizations have been made for speed and efficiency—but the basic idea is the same. Checking account holders—and anyone else, for that matter—can't be trusted not to write bad checks, so the banks have to enforce honesty.

TAMPER RESISTANCE

Tamperproofing would help solve a plethora of computer security prob-lems. Think how much easier it would be to enforce copy protection if there were a tamperproof processor in your computer that accepted encrypted instructions. (Not that this is a good idea, mind you.) Or how much easier it would be to design a key escrow system (see Chapter 16) if tamperproof hardware could enforce the police eavesdropping require-ments. With tamperproof hardware, I could build an Internet "meter" that can charge for data access much like an electric meter charges for power access.

In general, tamperproof hardware is perfect for complex trust rela-tionships, where one party wants to put a secure device in the hands of another, with the assurance that the second party can't modify the innards of the secure device. For example, when a bank wants to keep a secure account balance on a device in the hands of its customers. Or when the police want to keep copies of encryption keys, so that they can eavesdrop on private conversations even when people use encryption devices. Or for a cable TV decoder.

The basic problem is that tamperproof hardware does not exist. You can't make a device that cannot be tampered with. You can make a device that most people can't tamper with. You might possibly even make a device that can't be tampered with given a level of technology. But you can't make a device that's absolutely tamperproof.

I could spend an entire book on the details, but they change so regularly that it would be pointless. Suffice it to say that there are several ded-icated laboratories in the United States that can defeat any tamperproof technology that they've ever seen. Many more laboratories in various cor-porations can be used to defeat tamper resistance, even though the labs were created for other purposes. The chip laboratories at Intel, for exam-ple, have equipment that could be used to reverse engineer pretty much any tamperproof chip on the market.

In response to this reality, many companies implemented the seman-tic fix of calling their technology *tamper resistant,* which is something like "tamperproof for almost everybody." I suppose this is reasonable: A letter sealed in an envelope could be viewed as tamper resistant, even though the CIA and others have a surprising amount of expertise in tampering with the mail.

The problem with tamper-resistant hardware is figuring out exactly how tamper resistant it really is. Imagine that you are implementing a smart card commerce system that uses a tamper-resistant chip for its secu-rity. And it's an anonymous system, so the tamper resistance is all the pro-tection you have against widespread counterfeiting. How much tamper resistance do you need? How do you know when you've gotten that? What do you do when technology marches on?

Figuring out how much tamper resistance you need might be doable. Maybe you can estimate the value of a break: how much money some-one could counterfeit if she were able to defeat the tamper resistance. If you've designed a good system, maybe you can cap the amount of money that can be stolen from a single smart card: let's say $100. The next prob-lem is harder: How do you know when you've implemented enough tamper-resistance measures so that the cost to defeat them is more than $100?

Nobody really knows how effective different tamper-resistance mea-sures are. Sure, a laboratory can tell you how much time they spent defeating it or how much money it would cost to buy the equipment they used, but someone at a lab across town could use different techniques and come up with a different figure. And remember the publicity attack: Some grad student somewhere could borrow equipment and defeat your tamper resistance just for fun. Or maybe a criminal could buy the equipment and expertise. This is nowhere near as straightforward as estimating the time and money it would cost to implement a brute-force attack against a cryptographic algorithm.

And even if it were possible to figure out how effective a tamper-resistance technique is today, that says nothing about how effective it would be tomorrow, or next year, or five years from now. Advances in this field happen all the time. Advances come from a variety of technolo-gies, and they interact in really interesting ways. What was difficult to defeat one year might be trivial to defeat the next. It's naïve to rely on tamper resistance for any long-term security.

Another option is to make the system *tamper evident.* This is easier to do than making it tamper resistant: We don't care if someone can tamper with the system, we just care that he can't do it undetectably. Imagine a tamper-evident hand-held gambling device. A player can take it home with him and win or lose money. Because we are going to let the player take the device home with him, and we know that he can potentially win thousands of dollars, we do our best to make it tamper resistant. But because we know that true tamper resistance is impossible, we actually rely on tamper evidence. When he returns the gambling device to collect his winnings, we are going to inspect it up one side and down the other. We're going to install seals that have to be broken, coatings that have to be removed, wires that have to be cut. Sure, the best attackers can do all of that, but they can't do it all and then undo it all after they're done.

Better, but still not good enough. I believe that no system can be absolutely tamper evident, although there are different degrees. Relying on it as a sole security measure is a mistake.

None of this stops the physical world from using these concepts. Many systems make use of antitampering devices, from aspirin bottles to NSA-designed cryptographic chips. This is not necessarily a bad thing: Tamper resistance protects systems from most people and most attacks. I worry when systems rely on tamper resistance for security, instead of using it as just one aspect of a more comprehensive security system.

One system that uses tamper resistance effectively as part of a larger control mechanism is the U.S. system for controlling nuclear weapons. The risk is real: Some rogue commander could launch weapons without permission, or tactical nuclear weapons could be stolen or (if they were stored at an American base overseas) seized by an ally during a crisis. There was a need to ensure that nuclear weapons could only be launched in the event of a directive from Washington. The solution uses something called a PAL, a permissive action link, details of which are still secret. We do know that PALs are only considered useful if they are buried deep within a large and complex weapon system. Simpler weapons are stored in special containers, PAPS (prescribed action protective systems), that provide an extra tamper-resistant barrier.

The tamper resistance in nuclear weapons includes various booby traps: chemicals that render the nuclear material useless, small explosives that destroy critical components of the weapon and the attacker, and so forth. Only cryptographic codes transmitted from Washington will disarm these tamper-resistance mechanisms and arm the nuclear weapon itself.

These protection mechanisms are extreme, but this is an extreme sit-uation. There are extreme situations in the commercial world—root CA keys (see Chapter 15), keys used by banks to secure interbank wire trans-fers—but the security measures come from carefully crafted systems, not mass-produced products. In the normal commercial world, the protection measures are much more pedestrian.

And there is a fundamental difference of control. The nuclear weapon is under extreme physical control; this makes tamper-resistance measures more effective.

Think of a slot machine. A slot machine has a secure perimeter. If you can open up the slot machine, you can take all the money out or, more dangerously, modify the ROMs so that it pays a jackpot. But that slot machine is on a casino floor. There are lights, cameras, guards, people . .
. if someone goes anywhere near that slot machine with a drill or a screwdriver, he is going to get arrested. Now imagine the casino says something like this: "Here's a slot machine. Take it home. Play all you want. Bring it back in a few months. Whatever is on the pay line, we'll pay."

This is now a different situation. The attacker can take the slot machine home to his basement lab. He can study the machine all he wants. He can X-ray it. He can even buy several identical machines from the manufacturer and take them apart. In the end, he is much more likely to be able to attack the system in his basement than the one sitting on the casino floor. And this holds true not only for slot machines, but ATMs, bank safe deposit boxes, and anything with a similar security model.

(This is not to say that slot machines on a casino floor are invulnerable. Dennis Nikrasch made a good living—about $16 million total—ripping off slot machines. He practiced on slot machines at home, and learned how to open a machine up on the casino floor—without setting off the alarms—and swap firmware chips. Blockers stood between him and the cameras. Then he would leave, and an accomplice would play the rigged machines for the jackpot.)

The morals of this section are simple. One, tamper resistance is largely a myth, but it does provide a barrier to entry. Two, tamper resistance should be augmented by other countermeasures. And three, any system where the device and the secrets within the device are under the control of different people has a fundamental security flaw. It's possible to design a secure system that includes this flaw, but it must be recognized as a flaw.

SIDE-CHANNEL ATTACKS

In the last few years, new kinds of cryptanalytic attacks have begun to appear in the literature: attacks that target specific implementation details. The *timing attack* made a big press splash in 1995: RSA private keys could be recovered by measuring the relative times cryptographic operations took. This attack has been successfully implemented against smart cards and other security tokens, and against electronic commerce servers across the Internet.

Researchers have generalized these methods to include attacks on a system by measuring power consumption, radiation emissions, and other *side channels,* and have implemented them against a variety of public-key and symmetric algorithms in tamper-resistant tokens. Related research has looked at fault analysis: deliberately introducing faults into cryptographic processors in order to determine the secret keys. The effects of this attack can be devastating.

Let's assume that an attacker wants to learn the secret keys inside a tamperproof module: a smart card, a PCMCIA card, or something like that. He can't cryptanalyze the algorithms or protocols (they're too good), and he can't defeat the tamper resistance. But the attacker is clever; instead of just looking at the inputs and outputs, he's going to look at the speed in which the module does things. The critical observation in the timing attack is that many implementations of cryptography do things at different speeds for different keys. Knowing what speed a certain operation takes yields information about the key. Knowing a lot of different speeds for different operations can yield the entire key.

Imagine the attack working against a stockroom; you want to know about its contents. You can't look in the stockroom to see how things are arranged. However, you can ask the clerk to get stuff for you. By timing how long it takes him to get different things, you can learn a lot about the stockroom. Does he always take a long time to get toner cartridges? Then they must be in the back of the room. Does he take longer to get reams of paper every ten requests? Then they must come in boxes of ten. Does he take longer to get pencils if you've just asked him to get erasers? That tells you something about what boxes get stacked on top of each other.

Here's a timing attack against a password checker. Try a random password, but vary the first character. So if there are 26 letters, capital and lowercase, ten numbers, and a handful of punctuation marks, try about 70 passwords. Just possibly, one will take longer to be rejected than the others. Just possibly, this is the first correct character. Repeat with the rest of the characters. If you are attempting to attack an eight-character pass-word, you only have to try 560 passwords and measure their timings.

The attacker doesn't have to limit himself to timing. He can look at how much power is dissipated for different operations. (The module can use different amounts of power to do the same operation, depending on the key.) He can look at how much heat is radiated, and even where on the module it radiates from. For example, *power attacks* have been used to pry secrets out of almost all smart cards on the market.

These attacks are possible because the module is in the attacker's hands. If the module were sitting in a locked vault, he couldn't perform these kinds of attacks. (Although he might be able to attack another copy of the same product, which might provide some interesting information.) But precisely because the system's designers relied on tamperproof hard-ware and were willing to give the attacker a copy of the module, he can perform these systemic attacks.

Sometimes it is possible to perform some of these attacks remotely, over a network. You can't look at heat dissipation or power consumption, but you can look at timing. Sure, there will be some noise created by the network, but you can factor it out mathematically. Or you can look at radiation (the military calls this *TEMPEST*).

TEMPEST is worth explaining more thoroughly, if for no other rea-son than various militaries spend a lot of money defending against it. It turns out that electronic equipment radiates information, and that a sensi-tive radio receiver tuned to just the right channel can pick up that infor-mation. (This is also called *van Eck radiation.*) Video monitors are probably the worst offenders—with the right equipment you can read someone else's computer screen from down the block—but everything leaks to some degree. Cell phones, fax machines, and computer switches leak information. It doesn't matter if these devices encrypt the data; both the encrypted and the unencrypted data radiates, and a resourceful attacker can separate the two. Cables act as antennas and leak information. Power lines act as conduits for leaked information. This is a nontrivial attack, and can require a lot of special equipment. Sometimes it's easy—reading someone else's computer monitor—but other times, it is complicated and laborious.

The government solution to this problem is shielding. The military buys computer equipment that is TEMPEST shielded. When they build cryptographic equipment, they spend extra money to ensure that the plaintext doesn't leak over to the ciphertext data lines, or out of the box. They buy shielded cables for both power and data. They'll even build rooms that are TEMPEST shielded or, in extreme cases, entire buildings: These are called Secure Compartmented Information Facilities, or SCIFs.

There are other side-channel attacks. Sometimes heating or cooling the module can have interesting results; other times varying the input voltage does the trick. One security processor, for example, unlocks secret data if the input voltage drops for an instant. Another has a random num-ber generator that produces all ones if the voltage is slightly lowered. Other modules fail when you tweak the clock input.

Think of all of this as noninvasive biological experimentation. You can learn a lot about an organism by just watching it: what it eats, what it excretes, when it sleeps, how long it takes to do certain tasks at different times, whether it is warm or cold, wet or dry. There's no reason to cut it

open; there's a lot to be learned while it is still working properly. Cutting
    it open is always interesting, though, especially if you can cut
it open without killing it. If we defeat the tamper resistance and do
this to the module, we can learn a lot about its security.

Fault analysis is another powerful attack, because cryptography is
sen-sitive to small changes. In Chapter 7, I talked about how easy it is to
incorrectly implement cryptography, destroying its security in the
process. In fault analysis, an analyst purposely introduces flaws into the
cryptographic implementation—in specific places designed to maximize
the amount of information leaked. Combining this with defeating the
tamper resistance—cutting a lead here and a lead there (not at random,
but specific ones)—is a devastating attack against secure modules.

Systemic attacks are not low-budget attacks. You aren't likely to see
them carried out by lone criminals or common terrorists. They are attacks
for well-funded adversaries: organized crime, some industrial
competitors, military intelligence organizations, and academic
laboratories. They work, and work well. Systems such as smart cards
would do well to assume that systemic attacks are possible, and ensure
that even if successful they can-not defeat the security of the system.

Side-channel attacks don't necessarily generalize to other systems. A
fault-analysis attack just isn't possible against an implementation that
does-n't permit an attacker to create and exploit the required faults. But
these attacks can be much more powerful than standard cryptanalytic
attacks against algorithms. For example, a published differential-fault-
analysis attack against DES requires between 50 and 200 ciphertext
blocks (no plaintext) to recover a key. It only works on certain tokens
implementing DES in a certain way. Contrast this with the best non-side-
channel attack against DES, which requires just under 64 terabytes of
plaintext and ciphertext encrypted under a single key.

Some researchers have claimed that this is cheating. True, but in real-
world systems, attackers cheat. Their job is to recover the key, not to fol-low
some arbitrary rules of conduct. Prudent engineers of secure systems
anticipate this and adapt to it. It is our belief that most operational cryptanalysis makes use of side-channel information. Sound as a side channel—
listening to the rotation of electromechanical rotor machines—was alluded
to in David Kahn's book *The Codebreakers.* The U.S. military has long
made a big deal about TEMPEST. And in his book *Spycatcher,* Peter

Wright discussed secret data leaking onto a transmission line as a side channel (the vulnerability is known by the military as HIJACK) used to break a French cryptographic device.

Defenses are hard. You can either reduce the amount of side-channel information that leaks, or make the leakage irrelevant. Both have problems, although researchers are working on them. More expensive devices have sensors that detect tampering with the inputs—regulators that detect drops in voltage, thermometers that detect attempts to freeze the device, clocks that are immune to glitches from outside—and erase their secrets. Other devices sense when they are being dissected and do the same thing. But these kinds of defensive measures tend only to be in devices that the military buys, and often can't be implemented in low-end secure devices such as smart cards.

Side-channel attacks are very powerful, and it will be a while before there is a good defensive theory. In the meantime, any system in which a device is held by one person, and the secrets within the device are held by another, is at risk.

ATTACKS AGAINST SMART CARDS

Smart cards are viewed by some as the magic bullets of computer secu-rity—multipurpose tools that can be used for access control, e-commerce, authentication, privacy protection, and a variety of other applications. Basically, designers use their properties as a secure perimeter: The proces-sor and memory inside is (supposedly) invulnerable against attack. They're also small, portable, cheap, and flexible. This makes them attractive, but the lack of direct input and output on a smart card makes them more vul-nerable to attack.

What's most interesting about smart cards is that there are often a large number of parties involved in any smart card–based system. This means smart cards are susceptible to many classes of attacks. Most of these attacks are not possible in conventional, self-contained computer systems, since they would take place within a traditional computer's secure perimeter. But in the smart card world, the following attacks all pose a legitimate threat. And this is an example of looking at smart cards from a systems point of view:

Attacks by the terminal against the cardholder or data owner.
These are the easiest attacks to understand. When a cardholder puts her card into a terminal, she trusts the terminal to relay any input and output from the card accurately. Security in most smart card systems centers around the fact that the terminal only has access to a card for a short period of time. The real security, though, has nothing to do with the smart card/terminal exchange; it is the back-end processing systems that monitor the cards and terminals and flag suspicious behavior.

Attacks by the cardholder against the terminal. More subtle are attacks by the cardholder against the terminal. These involve fake or modi-fied cards running rogue software with the intent of subverting the protocol between the card and the terminal. Good protocol design mitigates the risk of these kinds of attacks. The threat is further reduced when the card con-tains hard-to-forge physical characteristics (e.g., the hologram on a Visa card) that can be manually checked by the terminal owner.

Attacks by the cardholder against the data owner. In many smart card–based commerce systems, data stored on a card must be protected from the cardholder. In some cases, the cardholder is not allowed to know that data. If the card is a stored-value card, and the user can change the value, she can effectively mint money. There have been many successful attacks against the data inside a card.

Attacks by the cardholder against the issuer. Many financial attacks appear to be targeting the issuer, but in fact are targeting the integrity and authenticity of data or programs stored on the card. If card issuers choose to put bits that authorize use of the system in a card, they should not be sur-prised when those bits are attacked. These systems rest on the questionable assumption that the security perimeter of a smart card is sufficient for their purposes.

Attacks by the cardholder against the software manufacturer.
Generally, in systems where the card is issued to an assumed hostile user, the assumption is that the user will not load new software onto the card. This turns out not to be the case.

Attacks by the terminal owner against the issuer. In some systems, the terminal owner and card issuer are different parties. This split introduces several new attack possibilities. The terminal controls all communication between the card and card issuer, and can always falsify records or fail to complete one or more steps of a transaction in an attempt to facilitate fraud or create customer service difficulties for the issuer.

Attacks by the issuer against the cardholder. In general, most systems presuppose that the card issuer has the best interests of the cardholder at heart. But this is not necessarily the case. These attacks are typically privacy invasions of one kind or another. Smart card systems that serve as a substitute for cash must be carefully designed to maintain the essential properties of cash money: anonymity and unlinkability.

Attacks perpetuated by the manufacturer against the data owner. Certain designs by manufacturers may have substantial and detrimental effects on the data owners in a system. If the manufacturer provides an oper-ating system that allows (or even encourages) multiple users to run programs on the same card, a number of new security issues are opened up, such as subversion of the operating system, intentionally poor random number generators, or one application on a smart card subverting another applica-tion running on the same card.

This is not to say that smart cards are useless as a security device. A smart card that accesses a credit or debit financial system, for example, is very different than a smart card that accesses a stored value system. Smart card systems that allow for identification and auditability are also safer. Smart cards are useful, but they come with new risks. Securing smart card systems means recognizing these attacks and designing them into a system. In the best systems, it doesn't matter if (for example) the user can hack the card. It's very Zen: Work with the security model, not against it.

15

Certificates and Credentials

The notions of a *public-key certificate* and a *public-key infrastructure* are central to much of modern Internet cryptography. Before getting into that, though, it is worth recalling what a digital signature is. A digital signature is a mathematical operation on a bucket of bits that only a certain key can do. This operation can be verified with another, corresponding, key. The signing key is only known by Alice. Hence, the argument goes, only Alice could have performed the mathematical operation and therefore Alice "signed" the bucket of bits.

The problem with this model is that it assumes that the signing key is a secret only known by Alice. All we can really stipulate by verifying the signature is that Alice's key signed the message; we cannot say anything about whether or not Alice did. We don't know if Alice's key was stolen by someone else. We don't know if a Trojan horse snuck into Alice's computer and fooled her into signing something else. We don't know anything about Alice's intentions. When we see Alice's handwritten signature on a paper document, we can make statements about her volition: She read and signed the document, she understood the terms. When we get a document signed with Alice's private key, we don't even know if Alice ever saw the document in the first place. "Digital signature" is a ter-rible name for what is going on, because it is not a signature.

This will become important later in this chapter. But first, let's talk about trusted third parties.

TRUSTED THIRD PARTIES

Cryptographers define a trusted third party as someone trusted by everyone involved in a protocol to help complete the protocol fairly and securely. A friend at the NSA once said (with remarkable perspicuity): "Someone whom you know can violate your security policy without getting caught." Oddly enough, these definitions are basically the same.

Remember the various trusted third party protocols from Chapter 7? All commerce, with the exception of direct barter, uses trusted third parties in some way. Even cash transactions: The seller is trusting the government to back the currency he is accepting. When the transaction involves an interesting financial instrument—a check, a credit card, a debit card, a traveler's check—both the buyer and the seller are relying on the bank or financial company to behave properly. The merchant and the customer don't necessarily trust each other, but the trusted third party is able to successfully mediate a transaction between them. Things would fall apart pretty quickly if a credit card company started capriciously refus-ing to accept merchant slips for certain cardholders.

Lawyers act as trusted third parties in more personal roles: executors of wills, that sort of thing. When someone announces to her captors, "If you kill me, my lawyer will mail a copy of the evidence to the FBI, CNN, and the *New York Times*," she is using her attorney as a trusted third party. Lawyer jokes aside, the profession makes a pretty good trusted third party.

The entire civil court system can be viewed as a trusted third party, ensuring that contracts are fulfilled and that business is conducted prop-erly. Here's the fair contract protocol: Alice and Bob negotiate and sign a contract. If one of them feels that the other is not upholding his or her end of the contract, he or she calls in the trusted third party: the judge. The judge listens to the evidence from both sides, and then makes a ruling.

This works because both Alice and Bob believe that the judge will be fair. In jurisdictions where the legal system is corrupt or incompetent, you see a much smaller reliance on contracts and a radically different set of rules for conducting commerce.

Many other trusted third parties populate everyday life. Consignment shops, either storefront or over the Net, are trusted third parties. So are auction houses. Ever buy something to be delivered COD? The delivery service is acting as a trusted third party. They do the same thing for certi-fied mail. Notary publics act as trusted record keepers, verifying the iden-tities of people signing legal documents and providing audit evidence in the event of a dispute. The UN sends "observers" to act as trusted third parties in parts of the world where the parties involved don't trust each other (and have way too many guns). On the Net, auction escrow ser-vices have appeared, acting as trusted third parties between buyers and sellers for high-priced items.

In the United States, an entire industry of trusted third parties medi-ates real estate transactions: title companies. These companies act as trusted third parties between the various parties involved in buying and selling a house: the buyer, the seller, the buyer's bank, the seller's bank, the buyer's real estate agent, and the seller's real estate agent. All of these parties rely on the title company to complete the transaction fairly.

Trusted third parties will become more important in the electronic world. In a world without face-to-face (or even voice-to-voice) transac-tions, in one of mediocre cryptography and horrible computer security, they are the only real certification anyone is likely to have.

Remember the whole system of public keys that I talked about in Chapter 6? Alice wants to send an encrypted message using Bob's public key, so she goes to a public-key database to find it. She gets Bob's public-key certificate. This is a message, signed by someone else, that certifies that the particular key belongs to Bob. The person who signed that certificate: That's a trusted third party.

Secure systems leverage the trusted third parties that are inherent in the systems that they are securing. Badly designed systems introduce trusted third parties without understanding the security ramifications. Awfully designed systems mandate trusted third parties by law.

CREDENTIALS

Open up your wallet. Inside you will see all sorts of credentials. You have a bank card. This is a credential issued to you by your bank; you use it to prove your identity to an ATM so that it dispenses cash. You have credit cards, credentials issued to you by a bank so that you can borrow money through one of the credit card systems. You have a driver's license, issued to you by the government. It proves that you possess the privilege to drive. Rental car companies in foreign countries use that credential as proof that you have the ability to drive, but police usually just use it as a handy way of getting your name and address: They verify your license in a police database. (Some stores use a driver's license as a credential before they let you pay by check, a trusted third-party relationship based on the premise that accurate identification information aids prosecution.) You also have airline frequent-flyer cards, library cards, membership cards to places like gyms, and whatnot. If you have a passport, that's another cre-dential.

Each of these credentials is issued by a different third party, and each of them operates in transactions where that third party is trusted. Creden-tials are not interchangeable. The bank is trusted to issue ATM cards to those people with accounts. The card, together with a PIN and a real-time database lookup to your account balance, allows you to withdraw money from your account. The driver's license, because it is a credential issued by the government, is often used as proof of age in bars. The bar is treating the state as a trusted third party for age verification. (I've seen bars that accept driver's licenses, state ID cards, and foreign passports as proof of age, but not U.S. passports. This makes no sense.) If you wanted to run a tab at the bar, a driver's license wouldn't be a useful credential. The bar might trust the state to certify your date of birth, but not your fiscal sol-vency.

Each trusted third party has its own rules that it follows before it issues a credential. To get a passport, you must provide proof of citizenship and proof of identity. To get a driver's license, you have to pass an exam and provide proof that you live in the state in which you're applying for the license. A credit card company collects a lot of personal information about you, runs a background check in some large database somewhere, and then issues you the credential. The credential might have a low credit limit at first, but as you build up your relationship as a customer, it might go up.

These physical credentials also illustrate the problem with revocation. What happens when your credential is revoked? When MasterCard revokes your credit card, they can't reach into your wallet and cut it in half. So they "revoke" it in a database somewhere; they simply record the card number as invalid. This works, as long as anyone who might accept the credential checks the database. If you are in a remote jungle retreat with no phones, there might be no way to verify the validity of the cre-dential.

The other way to deal with revoked credentials is to limit the amount of time they can be used without being reissued. Almost all credentials have an expiration date, even pretty dorky ones like library cards. (The only counterexample I can think of is corporate identity badges. This, I think, is just plain dumb. It's much more likely that you'll change jobs than you'll forget how to drive.) A credential is no good after the expiration date, as anyone who has inadvertently tried to pay for something with an expired credit card, or (oops) to get back into the United States with an expired passport, knows. If you have an expired credential, you have to get a new one. Sometimes you have to get it yourself, like a new passport, and sometimes a new one is sent to you automatically, like a new credit card.

Expirations provide a safety net. A bad credential can be out there for only so long, because it will expire eventually. A credit card company has to keep a record of a bad credit card number for only so long, because after it expires, it's obviously no good. The third parties that issue these credentials can tune their expiration dates to suit the applications. Your first credit card might expire after six months or a year, just in case you don't prove reliable. After a while, your credit card might expire every three years. Driver's licenses (at least in Illinois) expire after four years. U.S. passports are good for ten years. We can imagine a credential in an application where fraud is rampant that would expire every week, or every day, or every hour. It would be a royal pain to deal with in the pen-and-paper world, but it works just fine in cyberspace.

And we want credentials to work in cyberspace. We want the digital equivalent of credit cards, age-verification cards, corporate identity badges, library cards, membership cards, and the like.

CERTIFICATES

A certificate is a credential . . . sort of. It's sort of your identity, but not really. And it's signed by someone everyone trusts . . . maybe. It's defi-nitely not the same as a public key.

I think I should start at the beginning.

Remember Chapter 6 and public-key cryptography? Alice uses pub-lic-key cryptography to digitally sign things. She signs documents with her private key, and sends the signed document to Bob. Now Bob needs Alice's public key to verify the signature. Where does he get it and how is he sure it's Alice's?

In the early days of public-key cryptography, people envisioned vast databases of public keys, kind of like telephone books. Bob could look Alice's name up in the online database of public keys, and then retrieve the public key associated with that name.

Well, if everyone's public key is going to be stored in a vast database somewhere, what about the security of that database? An attacker can do lots of malicious things if he can substitute one public key for another. He can create a new public key, sign a bunch of checks with it, and then slip it in the database next to Alice's name. Suddenly, Alice signed all of those checks. If Bob is using Alice's public key to encrypt a message to her, the attacker can swap his public key for Alice's; now Bob's secret message to Alice can be decrypted by the attacker, and not by Alice.

We might be able to secure the public-key database, but the whole idea was to have public keys freely and widely available. This just isn't going to work.

Certificates were the solution. A certificate is a binding between a public key and an identity. A mutually trusted entity—call him God for now—takes Alice's name and Alice's public key, sticks them together, and then signs the whole mess. Now Bob has no worries. He gets Alice's public-key certificate from somewhere—he doesn't much care where— and verifies God's signature on it. Bob trusts God, so if the signature is valid he knows that the public key belongs to Alice and not to some imposter. Problem solved; the world is now safe for electronic commerce.

Well, not exactly. Note that we haven't actually solved the problem. All we've done is taken the original problem, "How does Bob know that Alice's public key is really hers?" And changed it to: "How does Bob know that God's public key is really his?" Bob has to verify God's signa-ture on the certificate before he can use Alice's key, so he needs God's public key. And where is he going to get that?

But we did solve something. Bob presumably wants to communicate with a lot of people, not just with Alice. And if God has signed everyone's certificate, we've reduced Bob's problem from verifying everyone's public key to verifying just one public key: God's. But let's save that problem for later.

A real certificate is a little more complicated. It contains information about the person (his name, possibly his job title, possibly his e-mail address, and other things about him), information about the certificate (when it was issued, when it expires), information about the issuer or signer (who he is, what algorithm he used to sign the certificate), and information about the public key (what algorithm it is for) . . . as well as the public key itself.

The basic idea is that Alice gets a public key certificate signed by God somehow. Either she generates her own public-key/private-key key pair and sends the public key to God, who returns the public-key certificate, or God generates a public-key/private-key key pair for Alice and sends her both the private key and the public-key certificate. (Now we have the problem of securing *this* exchange, but never mind that for now.)

This all works great, until Alice loses her private key. Maybe some-one stole it. Maybe she just forgot it. (Or, more likely, her computer crashed and didn't have a backup.) Bob is going to try to send her encrypted
e-mail in that lost key. Or, worse yet, Bob is going to try to verify signa-tures created after someone stole the key. What do we do now?

We tell God, and he revokes Alice's certificate. He declares it no longer valid, no longer good, no longer correct. How does he do this? He can't go through every nook and cranny of the Net and erase every copy of the certificate. (Well, maybe God can, but this is only an analogy.) He probably doesn't even know Bob has a copy of it.

So, God puts Alice's certificate on the *certificate revocation list,* or CRL. The CRL is a list of revoked certificates. (Remember 20 years ago when merchants had newsprint books listing bad credit card numbers? That's a CRL.) God issues a CRL at regular intervals (the credit card companies did it once a week), and it is Bob's job to make sure that Alice's certificate is not on the current CRL before he uses it. He should also make sure that it hasn't expired, and that the certificate really does belong to Alice.

How does he do that last one? He compares Alice's name with the name on the certificate. If they match, then the certificate is hers. It sounds simple, except that it doesn't work.

This idea has several problems. First, there is no one to act as God. Or, more properly, there is no one organization or entity that everyone can agree on and whose judgment is unassailable. The second is that Alice has no single name that everyone can agree on.

First problem first. Remember, for this whole system to work, Alice has to have her certificate issued by someone that both she and Bob trust. In reality, we use hierarchies of trust to establish the validity of certificates. A military organization is probably the best example of this. The platoon leader signs the certificates of everyone in his platoon. The division com-mander signs the certificate of every platoon leader under him. The army general signs the certificates of his divisional commanders. And so on, up to the commander-in-chief.

Alice now has a chain of certificates, from the commander-in-chief to the army general to the divisional commander to the platoon leader to her. She keeps them all, and presents them to Bob. If she and Bob are in the same platoon, then Bob also has the platoon leader's certificate. He knows that it is valid, so he can verify Alice's certificate directly. If Bob is in the same division as Alice but in a different platoon, they share the same divisional commander certificate. Bob can use it to verify Alice's platoon leader's certificate, and then Alice's certificate. Since Alice and Bob are in the same military, someone is in both of their chains of command. It might even be the commander-in-chief, who is "God" in this example.

This system works great in the military, but less well in the civilian world. The Internet uses certificates to fuel a lot of protocols: IPsec and various VPN systems, SSL, a few electronic commerce protocols, some login protocols. These certificates are issued to users by someone called a *certificate authority* (CA). A CA can be a corporate security office. It can be a government. It can be a private company that is in the business of issu-ing certificates to Internet users.

These CAs also need certificates. (Remember, there's a hierarchy here.) These CA certificates are issued by other CAs (probably VeriSign). Eventually you get to the God in this system, or in reality a pantheon of Gods. The highest-level CAs have what are known as root certificates; they are not signed by anyone else. These certificates are embedded in the software you buy: your browser, your VPN software, and so forth. This is all called a public-key infrastructure (PKI). It works, but only sort of.

Second problem: Alice's name.

Back in ancient times (the mid-1980s), someone dreamed about a world where every individual, every process, every computer, every communications device—anything connected to digital communications—had a unique name. These names would be held in a vast distrib-uted database, held by multiple people in multiple locations. This was called X.500.

Certificates generally associate a public key with a unique name (called a *distinguished name* in X.500 talk), but few people talk about how useful that association is. Imagine that you receive the certificate belong-ing to Joan Robinson. You may know only one Joan Robinson person-ally, but how many does the CA know? How do you find out if the particular Joan Robinson certificate you received is your friend's certifi-cate? You could have received her public key in person or verified it in person (PGP allows this), but more likely you received a certificate in e-mail and are simply trusting that it is the correct Joan Robinson. The cer-tificate's Common Name will probably be extended with some other information, in order to make it unique among names issued by that one CA.

Do you know that other information about your friend? Do you know what CA her certificate should come from?

Remember the phone directory metaphor for public keys. If you wanted to find Joan Robinson's public key you would look her up in the directory, get her public key, and send her a message for her eyes only using that public key. This might have worked with the Stanford Com-puter Science Department phone directory in 1976, but how many Joan Robinsons are in the New York City phone book, much less in a hypo-thetical phone book for the global Internet?

We grow up in small families where names work as identifiers. By the time we're five years old, we know that lesson. Names work. That is false in the bigger world, but things we learn as toddlers we never forget. In this case, we need to think carefully about names and not blindly accept their value by the five-year-old's lessons locked into our memories.

The idea also assumes that Alice and Bob have an existing relationship in the physical world, and want to transfer that relationship into cyber-space. Remember back when "cyberspace" was just a science fiction term, and any relationship worth talking about—business, social, banking, commercial—was formed in the flesh-and-blood world? Today, people are meeting on the Net and forming relationships all the time. Sometimes they meet in person long after they've become friends; sometimes they never meet in person. In this brave new world, a system designed to map relationships from the physical world into cyberspace seems limiting.

PROBLEMS WITH TRADITIONAL PKIs

PKIs and CAs have a raft of other problems. For example, what does it mean when a CA claims that it is trusted? In the cryptographic literature, this only means that it handles its own private keys well. This doesn't mean you can necessarily trust a certificate from that CA for a particular purpose: making a small payment or signing a million-dollar purchase order.

Who gave the CA the authority to grant such authorizations? Who made it trusted? Many CAs sidestep the question of having no authority to delegate authorizations by issuing identity certificates. Anyone can assign names. We each do that all the time. This leaves the risk in the hands of the verifier of the certificate, if he uses an identity certificate as if it implied some kind of authorization. Basically, certificates only protect you from those that the PKI vendor refuses to do business with.

And "authority" has several meanings. The CA may be an authority on making certificates, but is it an authority on what the certificate contains? For example, an SSL server certificate contains two pieces of data of potential security interest: the name of the keyholder (usually a corporate name) and the DNS name for the server. There are authorities on DNS name assignments, but none of the SSL CAs listed in the popular browsers is such an authority. That means that the DNS name in the certificate is not an authoritative statement. There are authorities on corporate names. These names need to be registered when one gets a business license. However, none of the SSL CAs listed in the browsers is such an author-ity. In addition, when some server holds an SSL server certificate, it has permission to do SSL. Who granted the authority to an SSL CA to con-trol that permission? Is the control of that permission even necessary? What harm would be done if an uncertified server were allowed to use encryption? None.

Some CAs, in response to the fact that they are not authorities on the certificate contents, have created a two-part certification structure: a *Reg-istration Authority* (RA), run by the authority on the contents. The idea is that the RA is responsible for validating what's in the certificate, and the CA is responsible for issuing it.

The RA+CA model is categorically less secure than a system with a CA at the authority's (i.e., the RA's) desk. The RA+CA model allows some entity (the CA) that is not an authority on the contents to forge a certificate with those contents. Of course, the CA would sign a contract promising not to do so, but that does not remove the capability. Mean-while, since security of this model depends on the security of both pieces and the interaction between them (they have to communicate somehow), the RA+CA is less secure than either the RA or the CA, no matter how strong the CA or how good the contract with the CA. Of course, the model with a CA at the authority's desk (not at the vendor's site) violates some PKI vendors' business models.

Another problem involves the protection of the private key. Re-member, for the whole digital-signature system to work, you have to be sure that only you know your private key. Okay then, how do you pro-tect it? You almost certainly don't own a secure computing system with physical access controls, TEMPEST shielding, "air wall" network secu-rity, and other protections; you store your private key on a conventional computer. There, it's subject to attack by viruses and other malicious pro-grams. Even if your private key is safe on your computer, is your com-puter in a locked room, with video surveillance, so that you know no one but you ever uses it? If it's protected by a password, how hard is it to guess that password? If your key is stored on a smart card, how attack-resistant is the card? If it is stored in a truly attack-resistant device, can an infected computer convince the trustworthy device to sign something you didn't intend to sign?

This matters mostly because of the term *nonrepudiation*. Like "trusted," this term is taken from the literature of academic cryptography. There it has a specific meaning: that the digital-signature algorithm is not breakable, so a third party cannot forge your signature. PKI vendors have latched onto the term and used it in a legal sense, lobbying for laws to the effect that if someone uses your private signing key, then you are not allowed to repudiate the signature. In other words, under some digital sig-nature laws (e.g., Utah's and Washington's), if your signing key has been certified by an approved CA, then you are responsible for whatever that private key does. It does not matter who was at the computer keyboard or what virus did the signing; you are legally responsible.

The way it's supposed to work is that when you know your key is compromised, you put it on a CRL. Anything signed after that time is automatically repudiated. This sounds plausible, but the system is funda-mentally flawed. Bob wants to know that Alice's key hasn't been com-promised before he accepts her digital signature. The attacker is not going to announce the compromise to Alice. So, Alice's first clue that her key was compromised will come when she gets some notice from Bob show-ing evidence of the fraudulent signature. In most schemes, this will hap-pen only after Bob accepts the signature.

Contrast this with the practice regarding credit cards. Under mail-order/telephone-order (MOTO) rules, if you object to a line item on your credit card bill, you have the right to repudiate it—to say you didn't buy that—and the merchant is required to prove that you did.

There are similar vulnerabilities in the computer that does the verifi-cation. Certificate verification does not use a secret key, only public keys. But to verify a certificate, you need one or more "root" public keys: the public keys of the CAs. If the attacker can add his own public key to that list, then he can issue his own certificates, which will be treated exactly like the legitimate certificates. They can even match legitimate certificates in every other field except that they would contain a public key of the attacker instead of the correct one.

Some PKI vendors claim that these keys are in *root certificates,* and hence secure. Such a certificate is self-signed and offers no increased secu-rity. The only answer is to do all certificate verification on a computer sys-tem that is invulnerable to penetration by hostile code or to physical tampering.

And finally, how did the CA identify the certificate holder? Whether a certificate holds just an identifier or some specific authorization, the CA needs to identify the applicant before issuing the certificate.

Several credit bureaus thought they would get into the CA business. After all, they had a vast database on people, so, the thinking ran, they should be able to establish someone's identity online with ease. If you want to establish identity online, you can do that provided you have a shared secret with the subject and a secure channel over which to reveal that secret. SSL provides the secure channel.

The trouble with a credit bureau serving this role is that they don't have a secret shared only with the subject. In other words, there isn't a secure offline ID that can be used to bootstrap the process. This is because credit bureaus are in the business of selling their information to people other than the subject. Worse, because credit bureaus do such a good job at collecting and selling facts about people, others who might have infor-mation about a subject are probably hard pressed to find any datum shared with the subject that is not already available through some credit bureau.

This puts at risk commercial CAs that use credit bureau information to verify identity online; the model just doesn't work.

Meanwhile, having identified the applicant somehow, how did the CA verify that the applicant really controlled the private key corresponding to the public key being certified? Some CAs don't even consider that to be part of the application process. Others might demand that the applicant sign some challenge right there on the spot, while the CA watches.

Certificates aren't like some magic security elixir, where you can just add a drop to your system and it will become secure. Certificates must be used properly if you want security. Are these practices designed with solid security reasons, or are they just rituals or imitations of the behavior of someone else? Many such practices and even parts of some standards are just imitations which, when carefully traced back, started out as arbitrary choices by people who didn't try to get a real answer.

How is key lifetime computed? Does the vendor use one year, just because that's common? A key has a cryptographic lifetime. It also has a theft lifetime, as a function of the vulnerability of the subsystem storing it, the rate of physical and network exposure, attractiveness of the key to an attacker, and so forth. From these, one can compute the probability of loss of key as a function of time and usage. Does the vendor do that compu-tation? What probability threshold is used to consider a key invalid?

Does the vendor support certificate or key revocation? CRLs are built into some certificate standards, but many implementations avoid them. But if CRLs are not used, how is revocation handled? If revocation is sup-ported, how is compromise of a key detected in order to trigger that revo-cation? Can revocation be retroactive? That is, can a certificate holder deny having made some signature in the past? If so, are signatures dated so that one knows good signatures from suspect ones? Is that dating done by a secure timestamp service?

How long are the generated public keys and why was that length chosen? Does the vendor support shorter, and weaker, RSA keys just because they're fast or longer keys because someone over there in the cor-ner said he thought it was secure?

Does the proper use of these certificates require user actions? Do users perform those actions? For example, when you establish an SSL connec-tion with your browser, there's a visual indication that the SSL protocol worked and the link is encrypted. But who are you talking securely with? Unless you take the time to read the certificate that you received, you don't know.

PKIS ON THE INTERNET

Most people's only interaction with a PKI is using SSL. SSL secures Web transactions, and sometimes PKI vendors point to it as enabling technol-ogy for electronic commerce. This argument is disingenuous; no one is turned away at an online merchant for not using SSL.

SSL does encrypt credit card transactions on the Internet, but it is not the source of security for the participants. That security comes from credit card company procedures, allowing a consumer to repudiate any line item charge before paying the bill. SSL protects the consumer from eavesdrop-pers, it does not protect against someone breaking into the Web site and stealing a file full of credit card numbers, nor does it protect against a rogue employee at the merchant harvesting credit card numbers. Credit card company procedures protect against those threats.

PKIs are supposed to provide authentication, but they don't even do that.

Example one: The company F-Secure (formerly Data Fellows) sells software from its Web site at www.datafellows.com. If you click to buy software, you are redirected to the Web site www.netsales.net, which makes an SSL connection with you. The SSL certificate was issued to "NetSales, Inc., Software Review LLC" in Kansas. F-Secure is headquar-tered in Helsinki and San Jose. By any PKI rules, no one should do business with this site. The certificate received is not from the same company that sells the software. This is exactly what a man-in-the-middle attack looks like, and exactly what PKI is supposed to prevent.

Example two: I visited www.palm.com to purchase something for my PalmPilot. When I went to the online checkout, I was redirected to https://palmorder.modusmedia.com/asp/store.asp. The SSL certificate was registered to Modus Media International; clearly a flagrant attempt to defraud Web customers, which I deftly uncovered because I carefully checked the SSL certificate. Not.

Has anyone ever sounded the alarm in these cases? Has anyone not bought online products because the name of the certificate didn't match the name on the Web site? Has anyone but me even noticed?

I doubt it. It's true that VeriSign has certified this man-in-the-middle attack, but no one cares. I made my purchases anyway, because the security comes from credit card rules, not from the SSL. My maxi-mum liability from a stolen card is $50, and I can repudiate a transaction if a fraudulent merchant tries to cheat me. As it is used, with the average user not bothering to verify the certificates exchanged and no revocation mechanism, SSL is just simply a (very slow) Diffie-Hellman key-exchange method. Digital certificates provide no actual security for electronic com-merce; it's a complete sham.

16

Security Tricks

This chapter is an orderless collection of computer security tricks and techniques that don't really fit anywhere else.

GOVERNMENT ACCESS TO KEYS

"All right; here's the deal: We're the government, and we're here to pre-vent crime. It's not easy, criminals being as devious as they are. These criminals, scary criminals like drug dealers, terrorists, child pornographers, and money launderers, are using cryptography to protect their communi-cations. We're worried that all of our court-authorized wiretaps won't be effective anymore; all of these scary criminals will get away. So we want to be able to decrypt everyone's stuff, just in case they turn out to be crim-inals. We want you, all of you, to make copies of all of your encryption keys and send them to the police (or someone the police trusts), just in case you turn out to be a criminal. And no, we don't trust you to do that—so we're going to make it automatic in the cryptography products you buy."

Admittedly, that's not a kind picture of the FBI's position on key escrow, but it's accurate. Since 1993, the Clinton administration and the FBI have tried to force the American public to accept the idea that they should give some government-approved party access to their privacy. They've tried to cajole corporations into putting it in their products, persuade users that it is in their best interest, and, when they met resistance in the United States, obdurately pressured other countries to adopt the same policies. They've even threatened to make secure cryptography illegal. It's a very contentious issue.

On the surface, the FBI has a legitimate complaint. Criminals are using cryptography to hide evidence that could be used against them in a court of law: They encrypt computer files, they use encrypted telephones and radios to communicate. But the positive uses of cryptography far out-weigh the negative uses, and pervasive cryptography does a lot more to prevent crime than it does to aid it. Ron Rivest once compared cryptog-raphy to gloves. It's true, by making gloves legal society has made it eas-ier for criminals to hide their fingerprints. But no one has ever suggested outlawing gloves.

There have been a lot of names for this idea. The government's first euphemism was *key escrow,* since a master key in the Clipper Chip would hold the session key "in escrow" for later release to law enforcement. When people didn't buy escrowed encryption, they changed the name to make it more palatable. Today, the terms include "key recovery," "trusted third-party encryption," "exceptional access," "message recov-ery," and "data recovery." I like GAK: *government access to keys.*

GAK systems have a *back door.* In other words, they provide some form of access to encrypted data aside from the normal process of decryp-tion. The Clipper proposal called this back door the Law Enforcement Access Field (LEAF). (It was originally called the Law Enforcement Exploitation Field, until someone pointed out that the name wasn't exactly mellifluous.)

The GAK back door is for government agencies (such as police) to use. They work in a variety of ways: Early GAK systems relied on the storage of private keys by the U.S. government or, more recently, by des-ignated private entities with proper clearances. Other systems have escrow agents or key recovery agents, sometimes employees of large corpora-tions, that maintain the ability to recover the keys for a particular encrypted communication session or stored file. Some systems split the ability to recover keys among several agents. There are variations, but all GAK systems share two essential elements. First, a mechanism, external to the primary system, by which a third party can obtain covert access to the plaintext of encrypted data. And second, the existence of a highly sensi-tive secret recovery key (or collection of keys) that must be secured for an extended period of time. On the policy side, GAK systems need to give police timely access to plaintext, without notifying the user. Systems of this type, according to the Clinton administration and the FBI, solve the problem of criminals encrypting their incriminating evidence.

Unfortunately, the solution is worse than the problem. Data recovery is easy to do, because it is in the best interest of the user. Users like automatic backup; they don't have to remember to make backups. (Pause while I back up this manuscript.) But GAK is also often tied to communications—phone conversations and e-mail—that have no corresponding data backup requirement. Data in storage have enormous value; if lose you it, there's no way to replace it. Data in communications have no value; if you lose it, you can always retransmit.

GAK is different, and much more difficult, because it has to work in spite of a hostile user. The requirements stated by the FBI for access— speed of access, surreptitiousness of access, comprehensiveness of access— force users to give up a lot of security. If I encrypt an e-mail message, I have to trust the cryptography on my end and that on the receiver's end. Adding GAK in the middle means that I would also have to trust the entire key escrow infrastructure: the cryptography, the databases, the poli-cies, the people. The cost to build this infrastructure would be enormous, as would the risks.

These risks are intrinsic to the idea of GAK, and are not dependent on the particular technology. All GAK systems require the existence of a highly sensitive and highly available secret key or collection of keys that must be maintained in a secure manner over an extended time period. These systems must make decryption information quickly accessible to law enforcement agencies without notice to the key owners. These basic requirements make the problem of general key recovery difficult and expensive—and potentially too insecure and too costly for many applica-tions and many users.

With many GAK alternatives, you can choose between higher cost and higher risk. While it may be possible to field a particular GAK system in a relatively secure way, this often results in tremendous costs to the user. On the other hand, simple and inexpensive GAK systems can jeop-ardize security. For example, a poorly run key recovery agent, employing untrained and low-paid personnel, with a low level of physical security, and without liability insurance, could be expected to be less expensive to operate than a well-run center. It will also be sloppier with the keys.

Interestingly, security and cost can also be traded off with respect to the design itself. For example, imagine a design in which session keys are sent to the recovery center by encrypting them with the center's globally known public key. Such a system is relatively simple to design and imple-ment, but it is about the worst possible design from a security point of view. It has a single point of failure, the key of the recovery agent, with which all keys are encrypted. If this key is compromised (or a corrupt ver-sion distributed), all the recoverable keys in the system could be compro-mised. Of course, several commercial systems are based on almost exactly this design.

Essentially, GAK systems are inherently less secure, more costly, and more difficult to use than similar systems without a recovery feature. Making them work requires the criminalization of non-GAK security products. Furthermore, building a secure infrastructure of the breathtak-ing scale and complexity that would be required for such a scheme is beyond the experience and current competency of the field, and may well introduce ultimately unacceptable risks and costs.

DATABASE SECURITY

Database security is harder than you might think. The simple stuff is easy: Alice has access to the personnel database, and Bob doesn't. The harder stuff is harder—Alice has access to the parts of the personnel database per-taining to health insurance, and Bob has access to the parts of the person-nel database pertaining to salary—but commercial database products manage that pretty well. The difficult stuff—enforcing anonymity in data-bases while allowing people to use summary information—is surprisingly difficult.

The harder stuff first. Databases can be set to only show certain fields to certain users. All users might be allowed to see a set of common fields (employee name, employee number), whereas only certain users might be allowed to see specific fields (health insurance information, salary). This is all a conventional computer security problem, solved by authentication protocols and access control lists.

Much more difficult is dealing with the situation where Alice is allowed to make queries and see aggregate information, but is not allowed to see individual entries. The problem is one of "inference;" Alice can often infer information about individuals by making queries about groups. One example: Alice queries the database for summary information on detailed groups. If she can ask the database queries like this—summary information on every narcoleptic female, between ages 35 and 45, with one diabetic parent, and living in a particular zip code—then Alice is likely to be able to isolate individuals.

A possible solution to this problem is to scrub the data beforehand. Data from the 1960 U.S. census, for example, was secured in this manner. Only one record in a thousand was made available for statistical analysis, and those records had names, addresses, and other sensitive data deleted. The Census Bureau also used a bunch of other tricks: data with extreme values were suppressed, and noise was added to the system. These sorts of protections are complicated, and subtle attacks often remain. If you want to know the income of the one wealthy family in a neighborhood, it might still be possible to infer it from the data if you make some reason-able assumptions.

The other possible solution is to limit the types of queries that some-one can make to the database. This is also difficult to get right. In one famous research paper, the author calculated her boss's salary based on legitimate queries to the 1970 census database, despite controls that were put in place precisely to stop this kind of thing. The New Zealand National Health Information System tries to defeat these kinds of attacks by not providing summary information on groups smaller than six people. (A technique known to be insufficient.)

Attacks are still possible. Alice is going to know the kinds of queries that are allowed, and will do her best to figure out some mathematical way of inferring the information she wants from the information she's allowed to get. And things are exacerbated further if Alice is allowed to add and delete data from the database. If she wants to learn about a particular person, she might be able to add a couple hundred records into the database and then make general queries about the population she added plus her target. Since she knows all the data she added, she can infer data about her target. A whole set of related attacks follow from this idea.

This was an active research area in the 1980s, but less so today. (Although the new medical privacy regulations may bring about a resur-gence.) The problems are not solved, though.

STEGANOGRAPHY

Steganography is the science of hiding messages in messages. Herodotus talks of the ancient Greek practice of tattooing a secret message on the shaved head of a messenger, and letting his hair grow back before sending him through enemy territory. (The latency of this communications sys-tem was measured in months.) Invisible ink is a more modern technique. Microdots were invented by the Germans during World War I, and stayed in vogue for many years. Spies would photograph an image such that the image on the negative was small enough to cut out and place over a period of a book. The spy would carry the book around, secure that no one would find the microdot hidden on one of its many pages.

In the computer world, steganography has come to mean hiding secret messages in graphics, pictures, movies, or sound. The sender hides the message in the low-order bits of one of these file types—the quality degrades slightly, but if you do it right it will hardly be noticeable—and the receiver extracts it at the other end. Several commercial and freeware programs offer steganography, either by themselves or as part of a com-plete communications security package.

Steganography offers a measure of privacy beyond that provided by encryption. If Alice wants to send Bob an e-mail message securely, she can use any of several popular e-mail encryption programs. However, an eavesdropper can intercept the message and, while she might not be able to read it, she will know that Alice is sending Bob a secret message. Steganography allows Alice to communicate with Bob secretly; she can take her message and hide it in a GIF file of a pair of giraffes. When the eavesdropper intercepts the message, all she sees is a picture of two giraffes. She has no idea that Alice is sending Bob a secret message. Alice can even encrypt it before hiding it, for extra protection.

So far, so good. But that's not how the system really works. The eavesdropper isn't stupid; as soon as she sees the giraffe picture she's going to get suspicious. Why would Alice send Bob a picture of two giraffes? Does Bob collect giraffes? Is he a graphics artist? Have Alice and Bob been passing this same giraffe picture back and forth for weeks on end? Do they even mention the picture in their other correspondence?

The point here is that steganography isn't enough. Alice and Bob must hide the fact that they are communicating anything other than innocuous photographs. This only works when steganography can be used within existing communications patterns. I've never sent or received a GIF in my life. If someone suddenly sends me one, it won't take a rocket scientist to realize that there might be a steganographic message hidden somewhere in it. If Alice and Bob already regularly exchange suit-able files, then an eavesdropper won't know which messages—if any— contain the messages. If Alice and Bob change their communications patterns to hide the messages, it won't work. An eavesdropper will figure it out.

This is important. I've seen steganography recommended for secret communications in oppressive regimes, where the simple act of sending an encrypted e-mail could be considered subversive. This is bad advice. The threat model assumes that you are under suspicion and want to look innocent in the face of an investigation. This is hard. You are going to be using a steganography program that is available to your eavesdropper. She will have a copy. She will be on the alert for steganographic messages. Don't use the sample image that came with the program when you downloaded it; your eavesdropper will quickly recognize that one. Don't use the same image over and over again; your eavesdropper will look for the differences that indicate the hidden message. Don't use an image that you've downloaded from the Net; your eavesdropper can easily compare the image you're sending with the reference image you downloaded. (You can assume she monitored the download, or that she searched the Net and found the same image.) And you'd better have a damn good cover story to explain why you're sending giraffes back and forth. And that cover story should exist before you start sending steganographic mes-sages, or you haven't really gained anything.

Steganography programs exist to hide files on your hard drive. This can work, but you still need a good cover story. Still, there's some advan-tage here over straight encryption—at least in free countries you can argue that the police have no real evidence—but you have to think it out carefully.

SUBLIMINAL CHANNELS

One issue with steganography is bandwidth. It's easy to hide a few bits of information; hiding an entire e-mail message is a lot harder. Here, for example, is a perfectly reasonable stenographic data channel: Alice and Bob need to tell each other whether a particular action is either "safe" or "dangerous." That's one bit of information. They regularly exchange recipes over e-mail, and agree that the key phrase "double the recipe" will be the message indicator. If the e-mail says that the recipe can be doubled, then the action is safe. If the e-mail says that the recipe cannot be doubled, then the action is dangerous. Any recipe without the phrase does not con-tain a message.

This kind of system works because the secret message is much, much smaller than the overt message, and is generally called a *subliminal channel* (similar to a covert channel from Chapter 8). Subliminal channels are as old as computers, and have been used by unscrupulous programmers to leak information without the user's consent. Imagine that you're a programmer designing a report on banking customers, and you want to get your hands on the customers' PINs. You're not authorized to examine the real data, but you've been trusted to write the code to produce the report from the database that contains the PINs. And you can see the real reports after they are produced. Program the report generator to add spaces after each customer's entry, 0 through 9, corresponding to one digit of the customer's PIN. Have the report generator use the first digit one day, the second digit the second day, and so forth until it is done, and then cycle back to the first digit. That's it. If the programmer can get his hands on the electronic report for four consecutive days, he can recover everyone's PIN. (Actually, he has four possibilities for each PIN, depend-ing on which digit the report generator used when, but that's easy to deal with.) No one else reading the reports will see anything unusual, and unless they examine the code that generates the reports (and how often will that happen?) they will never know that the PINs are being leaked.

There is the story of a soldier who was not allowed to say where he was stationed. He didn't have a middle initial, and sent a series of letters to his girlfriend with a different middle initial in each; over time he spelled out where he was stationed.

Once you get the general idea, you can think of all sorts of ways to embed subliminal channels in documents: the choice of fonts and font sizes, the placement of data and graphics on a page, the use of different synonyms in text, and so on. Many cryptographic protocols allow for sub-liminal channels in the choice of parameters, in the random bits used for padding, and in unused bit fields. As long as you're not too greedy, and are willing to leak the information a teaspoon at a time, it's not hard to add a subliminal channel to a system.

You can leak all sorts of things. PINs are a good example. Cryptographic keys are another. Building a cryptographic device that leaks key bits through a subliminal channel is a pretty duplicitous way to attack someone.

Subliminal channels have been discovered in all sorts of software over the years, put in by unscrupulous programmers. Intelligence agencies like the NSA have long been suspected of embedding subliminal channels to leak key bits in cryptographic hardware sold to foreign governments. A recent scandal involving the Swiss cryptographic company Crypto AG involved this very allegation. Side channels, discussed in the context of tamper-resistant hardware in Chapter 14, can be viewed as accidental subliminal channels.

Note that subliminal channels have the same problem as steganogra-phy in that someone who examines the underlying software will notice the subliminal channel. But embedded in a complex piece of software or, better yet, a piece of embedded hardware, it can go unnoticed for a long time.

DIGITAL WATERMARKING

We talked about intellectual property in Chapter 3. To review, companies like Disney are going to want to peddle their intellectual property—music, videos, still images, whatever—in digital form. They don't want people copying *The Little Mermaid* and distributing it free over the Inter-net. They don't want people stealing pieces of images—even a single image of Mickey Mouse—and using them without paying royalties. They want to keep control over their property.

Digital watermarks are one way of accomplishing this goal. Think of it as a subliminal channel or an application of steganography. The idea is to embed secret information in the stuff to identify who the legal owner is. Kind of like a paper watermark: The watermarked paper can be passed around from person to person, but someone can always hold it up to the light and see the watermark.

There are actually two related terms, here. *Watermarking* identifies unchanging information, while *fingerprinting* identifies a particular buyer.

For example, a watermark on *The Little Mermaid* would say something like "Property of Disney," while a fingerprint on the same digital movie would say something like: "Purchased by Alice, 1/1/01."

Digital watermarks (and fingerprints) go one better, though. Copy the paper, and the watermark disappears. Copy the digital file, and the watermark goes with the copy. Maybe we can't stop copying, Disney reasons, but we can at least point the finger at whoever copied it in the first place. And I've seen watermarks proposed for a lot of things: graphics, images, video, audio . . . even stock ticker data and computer programs.

So, depending on what data you put into the watermark, they can do one of two things. First, they can identify the original copyright holder. Second, they can identify both the original copyright holder and the per-son who bought the copy: If every copy of *The Little Mermaid* is water-marked with the name and address of the person who bought it, then when a copy appears on the Internet, Disney can identify the culpable party.

Great idea, but it just won't work.

The problem is that in order for Disney to be able to take a copy of *The Little Mermaid* and find the embedded watermark, it has to be findable. And if Disney can find it, a pirate can find it, too. Companies that market this stuff try to tell you that their watermarking schemes can't be removed for this or that technobabble reason.

It just isn't true. As with a subliminal channel, it is virtually impossible to find a good watermark unless you know exactly where to look. But unlike a subliminal channel, the detection mechanism will eventually be made public. Either it will leak into the hacking community like everything else does, or it will be made public the first time a court case turns on watermarking evidence. The mechanisms for watermarking will eventually become public, and when they do, they can be reverse engineered and removed from the image.

Reversal might not be easy. Ingenious tricks can make it difficult, but they can't make it impossible. And a sagacious hacker can write an automatic tool to strip the watermark, once he knows how it works.

Another vulnerability is that watermarking doesn't solve the underlying problem. What watermarking does is allow a company to point to its unaltered digital property and say: "That's mine." This is hardly enough to be useful because digital property is so easy to alter, and watermarking doesn't prevent someone from altering the digital property. It also doesn't guarantee that the person identified by the watermark is the culprit.

Imagine that every copy of *The Little Mermaid* is watermarked with the identity of the buyer. How does the merchant verify the buyer's identity? Unless we have hard-to-forge identity documents—either real or virtual—this system won't work. And there's nothing to stop a counterfeiter from paying $10 to a homeless drunk to walk into the video store and buy the movie for him. He now has a movie with the embedded watermark of someone who probably doesn't care if Disney knows his identity, and who doesn't have any assets if Disney tries to sue.

Watermarking can help convict grandma when she duplicates a single copy of *The Little Mermaid* for all her grandchildren, but it can't stop the Taiwanese pirates from ripping out the watermarks and selling half a million pirate copies on the black market. Or someone using a fictitious identity to purchase the legitimate copy and then not worrying about it.

COPY PROTECTION

This problem is easy to describe, and much more difficult to solve. Software companies want people to buy their products; they hate it when someone makes a copy of a business program that costs hundreds of dollars and gives it to a friend. (Actually, these days they kind of like it. They realize that the friend probably wouldn't have bought it anyway, that he'll use the software and get "hooked," and when he eventually goes legit, either he or his boss will buy a legal copy of the same program—and not a competitor's. WordPerfect used this scheme to increase its popularity.) This is especially important with computer games and in countries with little respect for intellectual property: In these cases, lots of users will pirate rather than buy a legitimate copy. (This same problem applies to people who want to distribute content— books, movies, videos, and so forth— that they don't want copied.)

There are all sorts of solutions—embedded code in the software that disables copying, code that makes use of non-copyable aspects of the orig-inal disk, hardware devices that the software needs to run— and I'm not going to talk about them in detail. They all suffer from the same basic conceptual flaw: It is impossible to copy-protect software on a general-purpose computer.

In the hands of Joe Average computer user, any copy protection sys-tem works. He can copy ordinary files by following the directions, but has no idea how to defeat a reasonably sophisticated copy protection scheme. In the hands of Jane Hacker, no copy protection system works.

The problem is that Jane controls her computer. She can run debug-gers, reverse engineer code, analyze the protected program. If she's smart enough, she can go into the software and disable the copy protection code. The manufacturer can't do a thing to stop her; all it can do is make her task harder. But to Jane, the challenge entices her even more.

There are a bunch of Janes out there who break copy protection schemes as a hobby. They hang out on the Net, trading illegal software. There are also those who do it for profit. They work in China, Taiwan, and elsewhere, removing copy protection code and reselling the software on CD-ROM for less than a tenth of the retail price. They can disable the most sophisticated copy protection mechanisms. The lesson from these people is that any copy protection scheme can be broken.

The *dongle* is the current state of the art in copy protection. It's a piece of hardware that plugs into the computer, usually into the parallel port. (Conflicts with other devices using the port, and other dongles, are only problems occasionally.) The protected software calls the dongle at various points during execution; for example, every thousand keypresses or mouseclicks, when a user tries to save, or every time he selects the nail gun as his weapon. If the dongle doesn't respond to a call, or responds incorrectly, the software stops running. Or, more effectively, it keeps run-ning but gives subtly wrong answers. (A 1992 version of Autodesk's 3D Studio used the dongle to create a table in memory that was required to correctly mirror three-dimensional geometry. Removing the dongle caused the program to fail over the course of a few hours, imperceptibly at first, but eventually dramatically. Autodesk had to field a lot of calls from unregistered users complaining about a strange bug in their version of 3D Studio.)

Calls to the dongle are all encrypted, and the dongle itself is protected from hardware reverse engineering by a variety of tricks. Still, programs that use dongles are routinely broken without attacking either the cryptography or the tamper resistance.

How? Instead of defeating the dongle, hackers go through the code and remove all calls to it. It's painstaking work: Hackers have to go through the code line by line, function by function, call by call. They may have to hook a logic analyzer up to the dongle and correlate execution addresses to dongle accesses. A sophisticated program could contain tens of megabytes of code. But remember Chapter 2 and my first reason why the Internet is different from the physical world: Only one smart pirate has to succeed; everyone else can just use that person's unprotected version of the software.

The success of software pirates doesn't stop companies from trying to copy-protect their programs. The 1996 Quake release came on an encrypted CD-ROM: You could try it for free, but had to call the com-pany and buy the password to unlock the entire game. It was eventually cracked, along with every other popular copy-protected program ever released.

Hacked programs are called *warez*, and you can amass a collection of the stuff yourself just by looking around the Internet. You won't find manuals, but that's what all the computer books are for. Just about every-thing is available, usually for trade.

Copy protection gurus like to point to new technologies to save their industry. They call for a unique serial number on the computer's micro-processor, so that every legitimate copy of a program could be pro-grammed to work only on one particular computer. They talk about encryption capabilities on the motherboard. None of this will work. All of it will keep Joe Average from copying his software, but none will stop Jane Hacker from dismantling the program and posting a cracked warez version for everyone to download.

This duality of risks is no different from the watermarking problem. Look at the videotape industry: Piracy is much lower than when VCRs were new because of two reasons. One, the dinky copy protection is respected by all VCRs, thwarting Joe Average. And two, the retail price of videotapes is so cheap that the economic incentive to Jane Hacker has lessened.

What's really interesting about the problem of copy protection and software piracy is that the solution is to pretend that there's not a problem: There is little to no copy protection in business software. In the compet-itive software application industry, market share and product loyalty— however they are achieved—are crucial. Many companies reason as follows: People who pirate my software cost my company next to nothing, since my marginal cost of goods is zero. It's not like they are stealing televisions off my assembly line. Almost all people who pirate my software can't afford to pay for it, so I'm not losing many sales. And when these pirates eventually get into a situation where they need to buy the software legitimately, they will already be hooked on my software, not my competitors'. Piracy is just another way of boosting market share.

Microsoft had exactly this in mind when they made a big push to get their products translated into Chinese and distributed across that country. They knew they would be pirated; they knew that they would make less than one sale for every ten copies used. Microsoft's Steve Ballmer has been quoted as saying: "If you're going to get pirated, you want them to pirate your stuff, not your competitors' stuff. In developing countries, it is important to have a high share of the piracy software." When China enters the free world, they will already be Microsoft compatible. Until then, Microsoft isn't losing anything. It's a perceptive business strategy.

ERASING DIGITAL INFORMATION

There are lots of times when we want to completely erase digital information. If you have a confidential file on your computer and you erase it, you want to make sure that no one can come by later and recover that file. If you are using a secret key to encrypt a communications line—a phone call, for example—you want to be able to erase that key at the end of the phone call and be sure that no one can recover it later.

Erasing digital information turns out to be harder than you might think.

On a normal computer system, when you delete a file on a magnetic disk (hard disk, floppy, or anything in between), the data isn't really erased. (This is why unerase utilities work.) The file is simply marked as deleted, and then the bits are overwritten with new data eventually. The way to truly erase a file from a magnetic disk is to overwrite it with a new file. And some file erasure utilities do this.

What is less well known is that technologies can recover erased data even after it has been overwritten. I'll spare you the science, but you can think of overwriting a bit as simply writing on top of it. Some of the data underneath remains. And when you overwrite again, some of the previous two data bits remain. And so on. There's a technique called magnetic force microscopy that can be used to recover data even after it has been overwritten multiple times. Exactly how many is not known; I've heard estimates as high as ten. (The U.S. government specs on this kind of thing are classified, which itself should tell you something.)

These microscopes are expensive (although amateur versions are getting cheaper), and these attacks are probably only feasible for govern-ments. If you are worried about a government, the only real way to erase a magnetic disk is to shred or burn it.

Data is also hard to erase in hardware. Both SRAM and DRAM retain some remnants of the data after losing power. Bits in RAM can be recovered by electronically detecting changes in cell thresholds based on previous cell content. Modifying the temperature and voltage can affect a chip's ability to erase data. There's a lot of physics that can be applied to the problem of recovering data after it has been erased.

U.S. military cryptography equipment is built to erase, or *zeroize,* all keys if tampered with. This is hard for two reasons: It is hard to erase data, and it is hard to know when to erase data. There has to be some set of sen-sors that determines when a box is being tampered with. There are obvi-ous sensors: voltage, current, light, temperature. But if an attacker knows what the sensors are, he can probably defeat all of them. (He can work in a room lit by a wavelength that the sensor misses, or can vary the temper-ature slowly enough as to fool the sensor, or whatever.) Again, this is a problem mostly for government systems and government attackers, but it is a very difficult one.

Part of the difficulty is that the device needs to reliably retain the key under normal circumstances, and entirely obliterate it under abnormal circumstances. The very technology used to reliably retain key bits makes it difficult to obliterate the key bits. Conflicting goals are hard to handle well.

Where this problem affects commercial systems is in things like smart cards, pay-TV boxes, and any other device with secrets inside that the device owner should not know. I talked about tamper resistance and ways to defeat it. Zeroization techniques are a way to defend against those sorts of attacks. But there are ways to attack zeroization. Basically, commercial systems don't get this right—I only know of one commercial device with the government FIPS 140-3 zeroization certification—because it's just too expensive to do so.

17

The Human Factor

Computer security is difficult (maybe even impossible), but imag-ine for a moment that we've achieved it. Strong cryptography is where required; secure protocols are doing whatever needs to be done. The hardware is secure; the software is secure. Even the network is secure. It's a miracle.

Unfortunately, this still isn't enough. For this miraculous computer system to do anything useful, it is going to have to interact with users in some way, at some time, for some reason. And this interaction is the biggest security risk of them all. People often represent the weakest link in the security chain and are chronically responsible for the failure of secu-rity systems.

When I started doing cryptographic consulting for companies, I would tell prospective clients that I could secure their digital data more or less perfectly, but that securing the interaction between the data and the people would be a problem. Now I am more cynical. Now I tell prospec-tive clients that the mathematics are impeccable, the computers are vinci-ble, the networks are lousy, and the people are abysmal. I've learned a lot about the problems of securing computers and networks, but none of that really helps solve the people problem. Securing the interaction between people and just about anything is a big problem.

People don't understand computers. Computers are magical boxes that do things. People believe what computers tell them. People just want to get their jobs done.

People don't understand risks. They may, in a general sense, when the risk is immediate. People lock their doors and latch their windows. They check to make sure no one is following them when they walk down a darkened alley. People don't understand subtle threats. They don't think that a package could be a bomb, or that the nice convenience store clerk might be selling credit card numbers to the mob on the side. And why should they? It almost never happens.

Computer security works in the digital realm. Moving information into the digital realm is problematic; keeping it there is downright impos-sible. Remember the "paperless office" of yesteryear? Information never stays in computers; it moves onto paper all the time. Information is infor-mation and, for an attacker, information in paper files is just as good as information in computer files. Many times paper in trash is more valuable than the same data in a computer: It's easier to steal and less likely to be missed. A company that encrypts all of its data on computers, but doesn't lock its file cabinets or shred its trash is leaving itself open to attack.

I am going to look at six aspects of the human problem:

How people perceive risks.
How people deal with things that happen very rarely.
The problem of users trusting computers, and why that can be so dangerous.
The futility of asking people to make intelligent security decisions.
The dangers of malicious insiders.
Social engineering, and why it is so easy for an attacker to simply ask for
  secret information.

It's not going to be pretty.

RISK

People do not know how to analyze risk. They can't look at a vulnerabil-ity and make an intelligent decision about how bad it is. They can't look at an attack and make an intelligent decision about how likely it is. They can't look at a security situation and make an intelligent decision about what to do.

The problem is not just one of not having enough information; peo-ple have trouble evaluating risks even with adequate information. Study after study shows that people misestimate the risks of earthquakes, air-plane disasters, automobile disasters, food poisoning, skydiving accidents, etc., etc., etc. They overestimate risks for things that are (1) out of their control (getting poisoned in restaurants), and (2) sensationalized in the media (being the victim of a terrorist attack). They underestimate risks for things that are mundane and ordinary (falling off a ladder, being in a car accident). Certainly not having enough information exacerbates the problem.

Probabilities permeate cryptography, computer security, risk assess-ment, countermeasures . . . everything this book is about. Risk is a probability. Security is a probability.

To illustrate probability, let's play a gambling game with Alice. It's a simple game: heads she wins, and tails you win. But you'd like to check out the coin first, just to make sure that it is fair. Sure, she says, look at it all you want.

You flip the coin once, and it comes out tails. This is a single event, so it gives you no real information except that "tails" is on at least one of the faces. So, you flip it ten times. The coin comes up heads on six of them. Does this mean the coin is unfair? Maybe. Alice is quick to point out that flipping a fair coin ten times would result in at least six heads 38 percent of the time. This means that if you took 100 fair coins, flipped them each ten times, then 38 of them would come up heads six or more times. Hardly evidence of fraud.

So you flip the coin 100 times and get 60 heads. Alice reminds you that a fair coin will show at least 60 heads in 100 flips 2.3 percent of the time. The coin could still be fair.

So you flip the coin 1,000 times. The most likely outcome would be 500,000 heads and 500,000 tails, but you come up with 600,000 heads and 400,000 tails. Despite Alice's assertion that there is a 1 in 10 billion chance that a fair coin would produce this biased an outcome, you choose to believe that the coin is weighted. But your belief is based on probabil-ity; the likelihood that the coin is fair is *de minimis*.

At this point you probably decide not to use this coin to bet with Alice, despite Alice's protests that the coin is fair. Your decision is wise, even though technically she is right. In fact, you can never *prove* that the coin is not fair without cutting it into pieces and weighing them. All you can do is collect evidence that the coin is not fair that is more and more convincing.

A lot of beliefs work this way. You believe that the sun rises in the east because it has done so for the last few trillion mornings. The odds of this happening without some explanation other than random chance are infinitesimal. (Now we have solid astronomical evidence, but people believed in the sun's daily eastern rise well before the Copernican model replaced the Ptolemaic one.) You believe that the water you drink is not poisonous, because you probably can't think of a time when it was. (In some Third World countries, however, this is not a normal belief.) You believe that the waiter will bring back your credit card without ringing up any phony charges because that's what has happened every other time you've given a waiter your card. And you believe a piece of e-mail came from the person whose name is on the "From" line because that's been your experience.

And a lot of cryptography works this way, too. Much of the math is probabilistic. Public-key cryptography uses numbers that are probably prime; there is a one in a billion chance that the number is not really prime. One-way hash functions are only probably unique; there is a 1 in 2^{80} chance that two random documents will have the same SHA hash value. The AES encryption algorithm has 2^{128} different keys; there is a 1 in 2^{128} chance that an attacker will correctly guess the key on the first try. Some people get worried seeing these numbers, but that's only because they think they live in a world of absolute certainty. But something that happens 1 in 2^{80} times is less likely to occur than walking up to a roulette wheel, putting your money on a number, and winning 15 times in a row, or being dealt two perfect bridge hands in a row, or being dealt four royal flushes in a row.

Security works this way, too. Most burglar alarms have a four-digit access code; there is a 1 in 10,000 chance that a burglar will guess it correctly and stop the alarm. One brand of combination lock has 3 times 36 different combinations; there is a 1 in 47,000 chance that someone can guess the combination on the first try. Fingerprints are not necessarily unique: Biometric identification systems might have a 0.1 percent chance that an unauthorized person will be recognized as having an authorized fingerprint. It's all about probabilities.

EXCEPTION HANDLING

One danger of computerized systems is that they make mistakes so rarely that people don't know how to deal with them. It's the "this computer never makes a mistake, so you must be lying" mentality. The fact is that computers make all sorts of mistakes all the time, and malicious hackers are happy to lead computers down a mistake-riddled garden path, and to take advantage of those mistakes.

A friend installed a burglar alarm system in his home. The alarm was wired into the burglar alarm company's switchboard; when it went off, the company was automatically alerted, and then they would call the police. My friend had a secret code that he could use to call the alarm company and register a false alarm (the police didn't want to send a squad car out whenever someone accidentally tripped the alarm). He also had a second secret code, a *duress code*. This code meant: "There is a gun being held to my head, and I am being forced to call you and claim that this is a false alarm. It isn't. Help!"

One day my friend accidentally tripped the burglar alarm, and he dutifully called the alarm company to register it as a false alarm. Acciden-tally, he gave them the duress code instead of the false alarm code. Almost immediately he realized his mistake and corrected it. The woman on the other end gave a huge sigh of relief and said: "Thank God. I had no idea what I was supposed to do."

When an alarm condition, or even an error condition, appears a few times a week, people know what to do. If it only happens once every few years, there could be an entire office that has never seen the alarm, and hence has no idea what to do. Many attacks target complacent users. Dur-ing the attack, those involved can't imagine that the system is failing, and attribute the problem to something else. Remember Chernobyl? "I've never seen that red blinking light before. I wonder what it means. . . ."

This is why we all went through fire drills in primary school. We had to practice the failure conditions, less so we would be prepared for what happened—drills can only prepare someone so well for a panic situa-tion—but as a constant reminder that the failure could occur. I've never been in a real fire, but I've been drilled so often in what to do, I'll proba-bly be all right. It's the same with airplanes. When oxygen masks drop from the ceiling, you don't want the passengers glancing up from their novels, wondering what those silly things are, and then going back to their reading. Nor do you want bank tellers ignoring warning signs. "The bank computer said that I should give him one million dollars in cash. Who am I to second-guess the computer?" Or a nuclear power plant operator wondering what that flashing red light means.

Unfortunately, if there are too many aleatory alarms, the operators will learn to ignore them. "I've never seen that flashing red light before. . . . I wonder what it means." Or, even worse: "That red light is always flashing and there's never a problem. I'll just ignore it again." (Read "The Boy Who Cried Wolf.") Or even worse, they'll unplug the flashing light. It's an effective form of denial-of-service attack, and I gave some scenar-ios in Chapter 3.

If an attacker can take down a firewall and deny network access to legitimate users—a denial-of-service attack—they will complain and demand that the firewall be taken away until it is fixed. If someone is using a secure telephone, and an attacker can make that phone drop the connection repeatedly, eventually the conversers will give up on the secure phone and have the conversation on an open line.

This is just human nature. People want to communicate, and the security system is at best something that doesn't hinder that want. It's hard to imagine people not having a phone conversation just because the encrypted phone doesn't work. Even the military doesn't have the disci-pline not to communicate if they cannot communicate securely; if they can't do it, you can't expect anyone else to.

HUMAN–COMPUTER INTERFACE

It has been said that the most insecure system is the one that isn't used. And more often than not, a security system isn't used because it's just too irritating.

Recently I did some work for the security group in a major multina-tional corporation. They were concerned that their senior management was doing business on insecure phones—land lines and cellular—some-times in a foreign country. Could I help? There were several secure-voice products, and we talked about them and how they worked. The voice quality was not as good as normal phones. There was a several-second delay at the start of the call while the encryption algorithm was initialized. The phones were a little larger than the smallest and sexiest cellular phones. But their conversations would be encrypted.

Not good enough, said the senior executives. They wanted a secure phone, but they were unwilling to live with inferior voice quality, or longer call setup time. And in the end, they continued talking over insecure phones.

People want security, but they don't want to see it working. It is instructive to talk with people who remember when a front door lock was first installed on their house. There are some of these people still alive, usually in rural areas. (City houses have had door locks for centuries; rural areas went without them for a long time.) These people talk about what an imposition a front door lock was. They didn't think it was right that they had to fish around for a key, put it in a lock, and then turn the key .

. . just to get into their own home. And the first time they forgot or lost their key—the shame of it all. Sure, crime was a problem and front door locks were a good thing, but people fought the change. I still know peo-ple who leave their doors unlocked. (Note the flawed "it's never hap-pened to me" reasoning in a lot of these cases.)

Computer security is no different. Find someone who used comput-ers before there were passwords and permissions and limitations. Ask them how much they liked it when security measures were added. Ask them if they tried to get around the security, just because it was easier. Even today, when the deadline approaches and you have to get the job done, people don't even think twice about bypassing security. They'll prop the fire door open so that someone can get into the building more easily, and they'll give out their password or take down a firewall because work has to get done. John Deutch, the former director of the CIA, brought classified files home with him on his insecure laptop—because it was easier.

It's a trade-off. Security is easiest when it is visible to the user, when the user has to interact with the security and make decisions based on it: that is, checking the name on a digital certificate. On the other hand, users don't want to see security. And a smart security designer doesn't want users to see security. A smart security designer knows that users find secu-rity measures intrusive, that they will work around them whenever possi-ble, that that they will screw with the system at every turn. People can't be trusted to implement computer security policies, just as they can't be trusted to lock their car doors, not lose their wallets, and not tell anyone their mother's maiden name.

They can't be trusted to do things properly. In a 1999 usability study at Carnegie Mellon University, researchers found that most people could not use the PGP e-mail encryption program correctly. Of the 12 people who participated in a CMU experiment, eight never managed to figure out how PGP 5.0 worked. Four of them accidentally sent out unen-crypted messages that revealed confidential information. And this is with the program's easy-to-use graphical interface (although, to be fair, the PGP versions 6.0 or later have a better user interface).

And they can't be trusted to make intelligent security decisions. After the Melissa and Worm.ExploreZip scares of 1999, you might think peo-ple learned not to open attachments they weren't expecting. But the infection rate from the ILOVEYOU worm (and its dozens of variants) taught us that no, people cannot be trained not to open attachments . . . especially when so many companies are trying to make a business getting users to send each other interesting attachments.

Browsers use digital certificates in order to make secure SSL connections. When they accept the certificates, they optionally display the identification of the certificate on the other end. This is essential to the security; it makes no sense to have a secure connection unless you are sure who is on the other end of that connection. Most people don't bother looking at the certificates, and don't even know they should (or how to).

The same browsers have an option to display warnings when down-loading Java applets. The user is asked whether he trusts the particular Web site that is sending the applet. The user has no idea whether or not he trusts the Web site. Nor does he care. If J. Random Websurfer clicks on a button that promises dancing pigs on his computer monitor, and instead gets a hortatory message describing the potential dangers of the applet—he's going to choose dancing pigs over computer security any day. If the computer prompts him with a warning screen like: "The applet DANCING PIGS could contain malicious code that might do perma-nent damage to your computer, steal your life's savings, and impair your ability to have children," he'll click "OK" without even reading it. Thirty seconds later he won't even remember that the warning screen even existed.

HUMAN–COMPUTER TRANSFERENCE

When I introduced cryptography in Chapter 6, I wrote about Alice and Bob encrypting, decrypting, signing, and verifying messages and documents. I wrote, for example, that Alice could use public-key cryptography to send a message to Bob by finding Bob's key in a phone book, and then encrypting a message to Bob using this key. This is actually a complete lie. Alice never encrypts messages to Bob. She never decrypts messages, or signs messages. She never does any cryptography at all. What Alice does is click a button on her computer, and *the computer* signs or encrypts or does whatever Alice wants. This is a critical distinction.

Imagine the future, when we all habitually sign digital documents. How might this work? Alice will write a digital document in some application—a word processor, an e-mail program, or whatever—and click on some icon to indicate that she is ready to sign it. The application will call whatever signature software program is standard business practice, and that software will create the signature. Alice will type in her password (or passphrase), put her finger down on some fingerprint reader, and do whatever else is required to prove to the software that she is Alice. The signature software will calculate the digital signature on the document, and hand the application a signature string to append to the document. Voilà—it will appear. Alice can probably even verify the signature herself (again, using the computer), just to make sure it is genuine.

This is what I call human–computer transference. Alice knows what she wants to do: sign a particular document. She has to securely transfer this volition to the computer with some assurance that the computer will actually do what Alice wants it to do. But secure human–computer trans-ference is not so easy to do.

Our goal is to get Alice to sign something she doesn't want to sign. Since Alice is accepting the computer's word that she is actually signing the document on the screen, this should be easy. All we have to do is get the computer to lie to Alice.

We write a Trojan horse to sit inside the digital signature software. This Trojan horse will contain the document that we want Alice to sign—something either embarrassing or profitable, no doubt—and code to sign it. The only thing the Trojan horse needs is Alice's key. When Alice types in her passphrase to sign a different message to us—the Trojan horse feeds the digital signature software the embarrassing document instead. The digital signature software returns a signature, and the original application places that signature on the document Alice thinks she is sign-ing. If Alice tries to verify the signature, the Trojan horse feeds the embar-rassing document to the digital signature software. The signature software returns the fact that the signature is correct; that is, the Trojan horse forces the computer to lie to her. Then, Alice sends us her document with the wrong signature; that is, the signature calculated for the other document. We take the signature, attach it to a copy of the embarrassing document, and call the *Washington Post*. Meanwhile, the Trojan horse erases itself and everything is back to normal.

There's an easy implementation in Windows: A malicious macro could simply watch for PGP's "open file" dialog, see what file Alice is about to sign, and copy its own file to that filename, then restore the old file afterward. Word's macro language can do this, so it could easily be a payload for a Word macro virus.

And that's just one example. The Trojan horse could sign both doc-uments and transmit the embarrassing signature at some opportune time. Or it could just steal Alice's private key.

Nothing here is difficult; the programming is easy. In any case, if we are successful we could have possession of a damaging document, signed by Alice. We could wave it around in court or pass it to a reporter, cor-rectly claiming that Alice's valid digital signature is on the bottom of the document. What is more likely to happen is the reverse. As soon as some-one writes a fake signature Trojan horse, it will be assumed to be every-where. Whenever a document appears in court, one side or the other will find an expert witness that will testify as to the existence of the Trojan horse and how easy it would be to get someone to unknowingly sign just about anything. Can the court trust this digital signature? It doesn't depend on the mathematics; it depends on the circumstances.

The fundamental problem is that you have no idea what the com-puter is actually doing when you tell it to do something. When you tell the computer to save a document, or encrypt a file, or calculate the sum of a column of numbers, you really have no assurance that the computer did it correctly, or even at all. You're making a leap of faith. Just as it is hard to catch a thieving employee, it's hard to catch a malicious computer program. Actually, it's worse. Think of it as a malicious employee who works alone, with no one watching. All of the monitoring equipment you might install to catch the employee—hidden cameras, hidden micro-phones—are controlled by the malicious employee. All you can do is look at what inputs the employee accepts and what outputs he produces. And even then you can't be sure.

If Alice can't trust the computer she is working on, then she can't trust it to do what she asks. Just because she asked it to sign a particular document doesn't mean that it can't sign another document. The meta-solution is for Alice to only sign documents on a trusted computer, but that's hard to do. If Alice is working on a general-purpose computer, I do not believe it can ever be trusted enough to avoid this problem.

If Alice is using a small, single-purpose, digital signature computer, then there is hope. I can imagine a hand-held device with a small key-board and screen. The document can be downloaded into this device by a general-purpose computer. Alice will be able to view the document from the small screen—there's no guarantee that the computer will download what you ask it to—and enter her passphrase on the small key-board. The device will sign the document and upload the signature back to the general-purpose computer. We have a prayer of making that sys-tem secure. We can design it so that only factory software is ever installed on the computer, and we can have some independent auditing company certify that the software is correct and behaves well.

But if you are working on an insecure computer—which will be almost all of the time—there is no assurance that what you see is what you get, or that what you get actually works as you expect.

MALICIOUS INSIDERS

In Chapter 4 I talked about malicious insiders. It's worth recalling the problems with them. The main problem is that they are often implicitly trusted. They can steal money out of the cash register, mess with the audit logs to cover their tracks, photocopy military secrets and send them to the Chinese, steal stacks of blank credit cards, pocket casino chips, look the other way when the crooks drive off with the truck full of goods, and anything else they can think of. Often, no amount of computer security can prevent these attacks (although good audit mechanisms can often determine the guilty parties after the fact).

Cyberspace is particularly susceptible to insiders, because it is rife with insider knowledge. The person who writes a security program can put a back door in it. The person who installs a firewall can leave a secret open-ing. The person whose job it is to audit a security system can deliberately overlook a few things.

One example: Chicago's transit system used both tokens and passes. Riders would either give the clerk a token or show their pass, and the clerk would let them onto the subway platform. For years, clerks would take tokens from riders, and ring them up as passholders. Eventually man-agement figured this out and arrested the clerks (1991); low estimates were that hundreds of thousands of dollars was stolen. Once honest clerks started working at some stations, daily receipts doubled. This problem remained unfixed for years.

Companies try to reduce the risk of malicious insiders in many ways. "Hire honest people" is the best solution, although it's easier said than done. Some companies go so far as to conduct integrity screening—pre-employment honesty tests—for some positions. Others try to diffuse trust, to limit the amount of damage one person can do. Think of public code reviews. Audit is vital: for being able to determine what damage an insider did, and for being able to convict him in court. In the end, though, an organization is at the mercy of its people.

SOCIAL ENGINEERING

In 1994, a French hacker named Anthony Zboralski called the FBI office in Washington, pretending to be an FBI representative working at the U.S. embassy in Paris. He persuaded the person at the other end of the phone to explain how to connect to the FBI's phone-conferencing system. Then he ran up a $250,000 phone bill in seven months.

Similarly, it's a common hacker trick to telephone unsuspecting employees and pretend to be a network system administrator or security manager. If the hacker knows enough about the company's network to sound convincing, he can get passwords, account names, and other sensitive information from the employee. In one instance a hacker posted flyers on a company bulletin board announcing a new help-desk phone number: his own. Employees would call him regularly, and he would col-lect their passwords and account data in exchange for help.

Social engineering is the hacker term for a con game: persuade the other person to do what you want. It's very effective. Social engineering bypasses cryptography, computer security, network security, and every-thing else technological. It goes straight to the weakest link in any secu-rity system: the poor human being trying to get his job done, and wanting to help out if he can.

Sadly, this is easier than you think. Showing up at a computer room with some hardware in hand and an appropriate vendor's badge is often enough to give someone free rein. Wandering around and asking if there is a place to "park and work" for a while will often result in a desk and a network connection; that person is obviously a corporate visitor.

Most social engineering is done on the telephone, which makes the perpetrator harder to catch. One attacker called people and said, "This is the operator. I have a collect call from <insert name> in <insert city>." If the victim accepted the call, the operator continued: "Your collect call option is blocked. Please give me your calling card number and I will con-nect the call." This really happened. The attacker found people on Usenet newsgroups and invented collect calls from people they corresponded with in the newsgroup, an extra touch of verisimilitude.

When Kevin Mitnick testified before Congress in 2000 he talked about social engineering: "I was so successful in that line of attack that I rarely had to resort to a technical attack," he said. "Companies can spend millions of dollars toward technological protections and that's wasted if somebody can basically call someone on the telephone and either convince them to do something on the computer that lowers the computer's defenses or reveals the information they were seeking."

Another social-engineering attack, this one against credit cards: Alice steals Bob's credit card number. She could charge purchases to Bob's account, but she's wilier than that. She advertises merchandise—cameras, computers, whatever—at a very cheap price. Carol sees the advertisement and buys a product from Alice. Alice orders the product from a legitimate retailer, using Bob's credit card number. The retailer ships the product to Carol—there's so much drop-shipping going on that the packing slip doesn't have the price—and is stuck when Bob notices the charge. Even worse: Carol is inculpated, not Alice.

Automated social engineering can work against large groups; you can fool some of the people all the time. In 1993, subscribers to the New York ISP Phantom Access received this portentous, forged, e-mail mes-sage: "It has been brought to my attention that your account has been 'hacked' by an outside source. The charges added were significant, which is how the error was caught. Please temporarily change your password to 'DPH7' so that we can judge the severity of the intrusion. I will notify you when the problem has been taken care of. Thank you for your help in this matter. —System Administrator." And in 1999, AOL users were persistently receiving messages like: "A database error has deleted the information for over 25,000 accounts, and yours is one. In order for us to access the backup data, we do need your password. Without your pass-word, we will NOT be able to allow you to sign onto America Online within the next 24 hours after your opening of this letter."

Plausibility plus dread plus novelty equals compromise.

Modern e-mail-borne viruses and worms use automatic social engi-neering to entice people to open them. The ILOVEYOU worm cloaked itself in e-mail from people the recipient knew. It had a plausible subject line and message body, enticing the recipient to open the attachment. It hid the fact that it was a VBScript file, and pretended to be a harmless text file. I talked about this in Chapter 10; people don't stand a chance against these social-engineered viruses.

In some of these instances, technology can help. If the helpful employees had access tokens (or biometric readers) in addition to pass-words, they couldn't give everything away to the nice man on the tele-phone. If the computers had biometric fingerprint readers, there would be no passwords to give away. If the computer system were smart enough to recognize that someone was logging in from a remote location when the job description states that he only works in the office, maybe someone could have been alerted.

Sometimes simple procedures can prevent social engineering. The U.S. Navy has safes with two locks (with different combinations, of course); each combination is known by a different person. It's much harder to social engineer those combinations. There are probably other tricks that the computers could have done, all designed to limit what a duped legitimate user could give to a social engineer. Technology can certainly make the job of the social engineer harder, in some cases a lot harder.

In the end, social engineering will probably always work. Look at it from the view of the victim, Bob. Bob is a good guy. He works at this company, doing whatever low-level or mid-level job he was hired to do. He's not a corporate security officer. Sure, he's gotten some security training, and might even know to be on the watch for those churlish hackers. But Bob is basically clueless. He doesn't understand the security of the system. He doesn't understand the subtleties of an attack. He just wants to get his job done. And he wants to be helpful.

The social engineer, Alice, comes to Bob with a problem. Alice is just like Bob, a cog in the big company machine. She needs to get her job done, too. All she wants is for Bob to tell her his username and password, or give her information about a phone number, let her install this hard-ware box, or do one of any number of perfectly reasonable things. Sure, it might not be technically allowed, but Alice has her butt on the line and just has to do this one thing. Everyone bypasses security procedures once in a while in order to get the job done. Won't Bob help? Isn't he a team player? Doesn't he know what it's like to have to get something done and for there to be a stupid corporate rule in the way? Of course he does. He's human.

And this is why social engineering works. People are basically helpful. And they are easily duped. By appealing to Bob's natural tendencies, Alice will always be able to cozen what she wants. She can persuade Bob that she is just like him. She can telephone Bob when he least expects it. She knows that security just gets in the way of Bob doing the job he was hired for, and she can play to that. And if she gets it wrong, and Bob doesn't fall for it, she can call on the tens or hundreds of other Bobs in the organiza-tion that can give her what she wants.

PART 3

STRATEGIES

Up to now, we've only looked at pieces of the problem. We've looked at general threats. We've looked at different types of attacks and different types of attackers. We've looked at different technologies and how they prevent attacks (and how they don't). It's time to put all of these things together to try to solve some security problems.

Upper-management security perspectives usually fall into one of three categories. Category 1: "It's too scary out there." This is the perspective that security is so bad that we can't possibly trade stocks with our PDAs, bank over the Internet, or play the lottery on our cell phones. Category 2 is "I've bought security." This is the perspective that security is just a check box on a purchase order, and if you have a firewall you're auto-matically safe. Both of these categories are extreme positions, and both are simplistic. Category 3 is even stranger: "We're too small to be attacked." This perspective is no less simplistic.

We can do better. Business can be conducted securely in the digital world, just as it is conducted in the real world. At first blush, the way to provide this security is to pile on defenses: adding more locks to a door, or heaping more encryption, firewalls, intrusion detection systems, and PKI systems onto a computer network. Unfortunately, things don't often work out that way. First, security budgets are limited. And second, sometimes the pile is not very secure.

The problem is that you have to look at the entire system, and how security affects the system. You can't just look at technologies.

Security is a chain; the weakest link breaks it. If you're building an encrypted telephone, you have to worry about the encryption algorithm that secures the voice conversation, the key-exchange mechanism that allows the phones to communicate, the key-generation process, the soft-ware security of the firmware in the phone, the physical security of the phone, and so forth. A flaw in any of those pieces breaks the security of the phone.

It's the same with computer systems. If you have a network with a firewall, then you have to worry about the security of that firewall. If you have a network with a firewall and a VPN, then you have to worry about the security of both those devices . . . and a flaw in either one can com-promise your network.

Security is a process, not a product. This section talks about the process of security: attacks, defenses, and the relationships between them. It talks about how attacks work in the real world, and how to design sys-tems to deal with those attacks. This section talks about the current state of security products, the future of security products, and the need for security processes.

18

Vulnerabilities and the Vulnerability Landscape

I n Part 1 we looked at attacks in theory: what kinds of attacks there are and what kinds of attackers there are. But as I have said elsewhere, there is a difference between theory and practice. As anyone who reads mystery novels or newspaper crime reports knows, there is a lot more to an attack than simply finding a vulnerability. In order to success-fully make use of that vulnerability, the attacker has to find a target, plan the attack, do the deed, and get away. A vulnerability in a safe's locking mechanism, if that safe is hidden in a secret location, is not as serious as the same vulnerability in a bank's night-deposit box.

It's no different in the digital world. It's not enough for a potential criminal to find a flaw in the encryption algorithm for the ATM network. He has to get access to the communications line, know enough about the protocols to create a bogus message letting him steal money, actually steal the money, and get away with the crime. Without those other steps, the encryption flaw is just of theoretical value.

Similarly, there is a lot more to a countermeasure than simply throw-ing a piece of technology at the problem. That vulnerability in the safe could be fixed by installing a stronger lock, or putting alarms on the doors and windows of the room the safe is in and keeping a phalanx of guards nearby. The encryption vulnerability could be fixed with a better encryp-tion algorithm, or by keeping the protocols secret, encapsulating the messages in a private network, or simply changing the keys every five minutes.

ATTACK METHODOLOGY

Generally, there are five steps to a successful attack:

1. Identify the specific target that will be attacked and collect information about that target.
2. Analyze the information and identify a vulnerability in the target that will accomplish the attack objectives.
3. Gain the appropriate level of access to the target.
4. Perform the attack on the target.
5. Complete the attack, which may include erasing the evidence of the attack, and avoid retaliation.

You can think of this as figuring out what to attack, figuring out how to attack it, getting in, performing the attack, and getting out. The first two steps are research. You can do them in the safety of your own lab; you can often do them on simulations of the actual target. If you're an academic, you can stop after the second step and publish. The last three steps carry the risk; it's where the actual or virtual breaking and entering happens. It's where people either get away with the attack or get caught.

Remember *Star Wars*? In order to blow up the Death Star, the rebels first had to get the information that Princess Leia stuffed into R2-D2. That was the whole reason Luke had to get the droids off Tatooine in the first place. Rescuing the princess was just a MacGuffin. That was step one.

Step two was off-camera. We see the result when the rebel engineer announces that he's studied the information from the droid and found a weakness in the station's defense systems: The janitorial system designers never bothered having their system designs audited by security profes-sionals, and now the Death Star's multi-billion-credit defense systems can be breached through a ventilation shaft.

Step three was the special-effects laden space dogfight between the rebel X-wing fighters (you have to admire rebels with their own defense contractors) and the station's TIE fighters. The job of the X-wing fight-ers was to distract everyone so that the Y-wing pilots could fly along the trench and shoot down the ventilation shaft. Access to the target was the whole point.

It took young master Luke to complete step four, after Han Solo got Darth Vader off his tail, and Alec Guiness's disembodied voice cajoled him to turn off his targeting computer (probably still in beta) and use the Force.

Blowing the Death Star to bits (step five) effectively eliminated any chance of retaliation, at least until the sequel. After that, getting away was easy. Our heroes get medals from a rebel alliance whose cash balance was high enough to afford new uniforms, and the universe is saved for a new series of themed PEZ dispensers. Roll credits.

It's not much different to attack a company's computers via the Inter-net. Step 1 is to identify the target and gather information. This is surpris-ingly easy. The target's Web site will contain all sorts of information, as do various Internet databases like the one run by Network Solutions. War dialers can find dial-up connections. There are many techniques an attacker can use to figure out what is running on the target network: ping scans, port scans, service listings, and others. Network sniffers can find more information, as can vulnerability assessment tools. A lot of this is the Internet equivalent of door rattling, although computers often tell perfect strangers a lot about what kind of hardware they are, what kind of soft-ware they are running, and what kind of services they allow. All this is information an attacker can use.

Step 2 is to find a vulnerability. Here, the attacker goes through all the information he collected looking for a place to attack. Maybe one of the computers is running a particular version of sendmail, or the Solaris oper-ating system, or Windows NT, with a known bug. Maybe he can exploit FTP, or rlogin, or something else. Maybe the target has left a maintenance port on some piece of equipment unsecured. Maybe the attacker could exploit the target's PBX. The more the attacker knows about different vulnerabilities of different systems, the better he can plan his attack.

Step 3 is to gain some kind of access to the computer. On the Inter-net this is trivial, since every computer is on the network and therefore accessible. (Of course, some computers are behind a firewall and inacces-sible, but the firewall will be accessible.)

Step 4 is to perform the attack. This can be either complicated or easy. If the attacker is good, this step is surprisingly easy.

Note that some attacks involve multiple iterations of this process. An attacker might perform Steps 1 through 4 many times: breaking into the Web server, gaining root access on the Web server, using that access to break into another server inside the corporate firewall, gaining root access on that server, and so forth. Each step involves its own information gath-ering, target and method identification, access, and execution.

Step 5 is to complete the attack. If he is looking for a particular file, get it and leave. He can erase audit logs and otherwise obscure his trail. He can also leave modified system files so that he can more easily gain access next time. And if he is looking to do a particular piece of damage, do it and leave. But get out quickly. Hanging around is the sign of an amateur.

In his "FAQ and Guide to Cracking," Mixter describes the same steps. Here's what he says are the first things to do after you get root. (Getting root privileges on the target computer constitutes a completion of Step 4.):

> "1. Discretely [sic] remove traces of the root compromise
> 2. Gather some general info about the system
> 3. Make sure you can get back in
> 4. Disable or patch the vulnerable daemon(s)"

Specifically, he suggests turning off logging and deleting log records of the compromise, and figuring out how often the system is maintained and administered, and how often the log files are analyzed.

Hacker tools can automate a lot of the process. They're not nearly as good as a virtuoso hacker, but they can turn an inept teenager into a for-midable adversary.

Another example: an attack against a smart card payment system. Step 1 is to gather whatever information is available on the payment system: design specifications, public interface documents, public information on the various algorithms and protocols used, and so forth. There is probably a lot of information out there, if you know where to look.

Step 2 is to study the documentation, looking for a weakness. Part 2 of this book talks about all sorts of weaknesses that can affect a system like this. Maybe there's a weakness in the cryptographic algorithms and pro-tocols. Maybe there's a weakness in the smart card, and it's not as tamper-resistant as the designers thought it was. Maybe there's a weakness in how the card is used that you can exploit. Whatever it is, you need to find a weakness in order to attack this system.

Step 3 is to gain whatever access is needed for the attack. You might have to become a registered user of this smart card payment system (perhaps under an assumed name). You might have to steal someone's card. You might have to collude with a merchant who accepts the smart card as payment. Getting access is not always easy.

Step 4 is to perform the attack: clone the smart card and use the clone, alter the smart card's memory and use it to make purchases, change the balance and demand a cash refund, whatever. The point here is that it's not enough to break the smart card payment system, you need to convert that break into cash.

Step 5 is cleaning up. You may want to destroy physical evidence of your attack. If you have equipment at home you used to complete the attack, throw it away. If you have computer evidence of your attack, delete the files. Maybe you can break into the payment system's comput-ers and destroy audit-log entries that could be damaging. Whatever it is, try to cover your tracks.

Some attacks short-circuit these steps. For some publicity attacks, there are no Steps 2, 3, or 5. Here's a publicity attack against the encryp-tion algorithms used in digital cell phones: Step 1, get information on the cell phones' cryptographic algorithms. Steps 2 and 3, not applicable. (You already know the target, and all the access you need are the algorithm descriptions.) Step 4, perform the cryptanalysis and alert the media. Step 5, not applicable—you've done nothing illegal. This attack has been suc-cessfully done against every digital cellular encryption algorithm used to date, with amazing success.

Throughout this book, I argue that security is a chain, and a system is only as secure as the weakest link. Vulnerabilities are these weak links. Finding a security vulnerability is only one step toward exploiting it, though. Getting in a position to exploit the vulnerability, actually exploit-ing that vulnerability, and then making a getaway are also important— you can't have a successful attack without them.

COUNTERMEASURES

Countermeasures are methods to reduce vulnerabilities. They can be sim-ple, such as building a wall around a city to reduce the vulnerability to an enemy army marching in and taking control, or complex: devising a secure back-end auditing system to detect attempted fraud by credit card merchants and identify the culprits.

Basically, countermeasures can be implemented to thwart any of the five steps of a successful attack.

Most of Part 2 discusses technical countermeasures applicable to com-puters and computer networks. I tried to talk about these in context: what they do, what they don't do, how they work in relation to each other, and so forth. No technology is a security panacea; the trick is using each of them effectively.

The security of a system may be no better than its weakest link, but that generally refers to the individual technologies. In a smart system, these technologies can be layered in depth, and the overall security is the sum of the links. Cryptography can be defeated by brute-forcing the key, cryptanalyzing the algorithm, or (the weak link) social-engineering the password from an oblivious secretary. But protecting the computer behind a locked door, or a well-configured firewall, provides defense in depth.

Remember the opening scenes of *Raiders of the Lost Ark*? Indiana Jones had to get past the spiders, the wall-of-spikes trap, the pit, the poi-son darts released by stepping on the wrong floor stones, and the self-destruct mechanism tied to moving the statue. This is defense in depth. He bypassed the wall-of-spikes trap by avoiding the triggering mecha-nism, but he might have dodged the wall, jammed the mechanism, or done half a dozen other things. The security of the trap depends on the easiest way to avoid it.

But just as attacking a system is more complicated than simply finding a vulnerability, defending a system is more complicated than dropping in a countermeasure. There are three parts to an effective set of counter-measures:

- Protection
- Detection
- Reaction

In a military office, classified documents are stored in a safe. The safe provides protection against attack, but so does the system of alarms and guards. Assume the attacker is an outsider: someone who does not work in the office. If he is going to steal the documents inside the safe, he is not only going to have to break into the safe, he is also going to have to defeat the system of alarms and guards. The safe—both the lock and the walls—

are protective countermeasures, the alarms are detection countermeasures, and the guards are reactive countermeasures.

If guards patrol the offices every 15 minutes, then the safe only has to withstand attack for a maximum of 15 minutes. If the safe is in an obscure office that is only staffed during the day, then the safe has to withstand 16 hours of attack: from 5 P.M. until 9 A.M. the next day (much longer if the office is closed during holiday weekends). If the safe has an alarm on it, and the guards come running as soon as the safe is jostled, then the safe only has to survive attack for as long as it takes for the guards to respond.

What this all means is that the strength of the safe is based on the detection and reaction mechanisms in place. And safes are sold this way. One safe might be rated as TL-15; this means that it can resist a profes-sional safecracker, with tools, for at least 15 minutes. Another might be rated TRTL-60, meaning that it can resist the same safecracker, with tools and an oxyacetylene torch, for 60 minutes. These time ratings are for a sustained attack, meaning that the clock was running only when the safe was being attacked: rest and planning time is not counted. And the tests are conducted by professionals with access to the safe's engineering draw-ings: no security by obscurity allowed. (Sounds a lot like cryptographic attacks, doesn't it?)

Protection, detection, and reaction countermeasures work in tandem. Strong protection mechanisms mean that you don't need good detection and reaction mechanisms. Weak protection mechanisms—or even no protection mechanisms—mean that you need better protection and detection mechanisms.

The safe ratings show this clearly. What a safe buys you is time: 15 minutes, 30 minutes, 24 hours. This time is for the various alarms to sound (detection) and for the guards to come arrest the safecrackers (response). Without detection and response, it actually doesn't matter whether your safe is rated TL-30 or TRTL-60.

Most computer-security countermeasures are prophylactic: cryptography, firewalls, passwords. Some are detection mechanisms: intrusion detection systems. Even rarer are reaction mechanisms—a login system that locks users out after three failed login attempts is an example—even though detection mechanisms are useless without them. Think about an intrusion detection system that has just detected an attack. It alerts a system administrator, maybe by e-mailing his pager. If that administrator won't respond for hours—maybe he's at lunch—then it really doesn't matter what the IDS detected. There's no reaction to deal with the prob-lem.

Similarly, burglar alarms are detection countermeasures. If an attacker trips the alarm, it only makes a difference if there's someone to respond. If the attacker knows that the alarm is being ignored, it might as well not be there in the first place.

Sometimes, detection and reaction mechanisms are impossible to deploy. Think of a traditional eavesdropping attack: Alice and Bob are communicating over an insecure channel, and Eve is listening. Neither Alice nor Bob has any way to detect the eavesdropping, and hence no way to react. The protection mechanism—encryption—has to be secure enough to protect the communications until they are no longer valuable to Eve.

Contrast this with a system that encrypts access codes for ATMs. Assume that the only way for an attacker to get these codes would be to break into an ATM. If there is an alarm on all ATMs (detection), and the access codes can be changed in 15 seconds (reaction), then the encryption algorithm can be weak. Of course, there are probably lots of ways for an attacker to get the encrypted access codes that don't sound alarms. Still, if the codes are changed every week regardless of any detection mechanism (automatic reaction), then the encryption algorithm only has to secure the codes for a week.

Digital security's singular reliance on protection mechanisms is wrong, and is the primary reason we see attack after attack against digital systems today. Protection mechanisms alone can only work if the tech-nologies are perfect. The Platonic ideal of a tamperproof smart card is per-fect; there would be no need for detection and reaction countermeasures. A real-world tamper-resistant smart card fails occasionally, and a well-designed system has detection and reaction mechanisms in place to deal with those failures. One of the theses of this book, how-ever, is that no technology is perfect. Detection and reaction are essential.

Think of a computer network. If the firewalls, operating systems, server software packages, and so forth were perfectly secure, then there would be no need for any alarm services. No one could ever break in, so there would be no alarms. In the real world, we've never fielded any of those products without vulnerabilities. There is always a way to break through the firewall, subvert the operating system, and attack the server software. The only countermeasures that can work in the face of imperfect security barriers are detection and reaction: detection to notice when security has been breached, and reaction to do something about it.

THE VULNERABILITY LANDSCAPE

Real systems have many different vulnerabilities, and there are many different ways to launch an attack. A terrorist wanting to blow up an aircraft could smuggle a bomb onboard, shoot it down with a missile, or sneak onboard, hijack the controls, and fly it into a mountain. A computer hacker intent on penetrating a corporate network could attack the firewall, attack the Web server, exploit a dial-up modem, and so forth.

Real systems can also have many different countermeasures. Airlines have metal detectors, chemical analyzers, and X-ray machines to detect bombs, and bag-matching systems to ensure that someone doesn't stay on the ground while his bag flies alone. (This system of countermeasures assumes that fewer terrorists are willing to blow themselves up on an aircraft than are willing to stay on the ground while an aircraft blows up.) Military aircraft also have assorted antimissile defenses. Corporate networks can have firewalls, intrusion detection systems, procedures for rou-tinely updating passwords, and encrypted file servers.

This can get tortuous pretty fast.

I use the term *vulnerability landscape* to limn this imaginary, compli-cated world of attacks and countermeasures. The metaphor is supposed to evoke a vast expanse of possible attacks—pulling a gun on a bank teller, blackmailing a programmer to put a Trojan horse in a piece of software, drilling through the bank wall, calling up an unsuspecting clerk and ask-ing for his password—and countermeasures: bulletproof glass protecting the tellers, running background checks on all employees, cameras watch-ing the outside of the building, biometric verification. Different parts of the landscape represent different types of attacks. Computer attacks are, of course, only a small area of the landscape.

Each system has its own vulnerability landscape, although different systems will have common landscape features. (Every computerized system has to deal with the threat of a power shutdown, for example. And almost every system uses threat of arrest as a countermeasure.) A filled vulnerability landscape is rough terrain, made up of peaks and valleys of varying heights and depths. The higher the peak, the better the countermeasure: the "use passwords" peak is pretty low, but the "turn the computer off and bury it in a smelly bog" peak is much higher. The valleys, on the other hand, represent the vulnerabilities: the adversaries' opportunities for attack. The lower the valley, the more serious the vulnerability.

Vulnerabilities are not the same as goals. Goals are what I talked about in Chapter 3: criminal goals of stealing money, marketer goals of violat-ing privacy, bored grad student goals of gaining notoriety. Vulnerabilities can be used to achieve goals. Stealing money is a goal; an unguarded cash register is a vulnerability. Besmirching someone's reputation is a goal; his unencrypted hard drive is a vulnerability. Some vulnerabilities are irrele-vant with respect to certain goals. In an anonymous newsgroup, an attacker's goal might be to learn the identity of the posters. A lack of authentication wouldn't be a vulnerability. If the newsgroup were based on a paid subscription model, then another goal of an attacker might be to post without paying. Then, vulnerabilities in the authentication system would be germane.

The vulnerability landscape can be organized in several ways. I break it down into four broad categories: the physical world, the virtual world, the trust model, and the system's life cycle. They're related. An adversary may choose to attack in the physical world—breaking and entering, set-ting off bombs, taking human life, and so on. Using the Internet, the same adversary could choose to attack virtually—shutting down computer and phone systems, hacking the police computers and putting out fake arrest warrants against the entire board of directors, and the like. Attacks against a physical infrastructure from the virtual world can often be conducted instantaneously and remotely, without warning. They are often much nastier than attacks in the physical world.

Physical Security

Physical security is a problem the world has been trying to solve since the beginning of time: the notion of ownership. Walls, locks, and armed guards are all tools of physical security. Vulnerabilities are things like unalarmed skylights, guards that fall asleep at night, and locks that can be broken open with a crowbar. Organizations have been dealing with this stuff for a long time; most of them have learned how to install physical security measures commensurate with the physical threat. They know, more or less, who their adversaries are and what kinds of countermeasures are sufficient to protect their assets.

When building digital security systems, designers often forget physical security. Laptop computers with corporate secrets are stolen all the time. In a particularly bad month in 2000, MI5 and MI6 (both British intelligence organizations) had laptops with classified information stolen. Maybe the thieves didn't care about the data, and maybe the data was encrypted, but no one knows. (The British military seems to have a lot of problems keeping hold of their laptops. In 1991, a computer containing a secret briefing on the Gulf War was stolen from a car belonging to the Royal Air Force. After a very public police manhunt, the computer was returned with the message: "I'm a thief. Not a bloody traitor.") A surprising number of laptop computers are stolen at airport metal detectors, by teams of thieves working in concert.

Physical countermeasures are often layered to reinforce each other and, in general, the sum is greater than the parts. Behind the fence, guards patrol the perimeter of a locked building. A bank has guards, alarms, cam-era, and a time-lock safe.

When everything works together, no single solution has to bear the total responsibility for deterring an attacker. And the required strength of each individual countermeasure depends on the others. A $5 door lock may be sufficient given the fence and guards. A $50 door lock may be wasteful given the open window nearby. Poisoned punji sticks might be superfluous given the whirling steel blades.

Virtual Security

Countermeasures have also been developed against virtual threats to com-puter targets. Installing a firewall is analogous to building walls and lock-ing doors. Putting in authentication systems is analogous to hiring guards and checking badges. Encryption creates a "private room" in cyberspace for a confidential conversation or an electronic safe for stored informa-tion.

Again, a good system uses several different countermeasures in con-cert: firewalls protecting outsiders from accessing the systems, strong authentication to make sure only authorized users log on, and end-to-end data encryption.

The Trust Model

The trust model represents how an organization determines who to trust with its assets or pieces of its assets. For instance, applicants might have their résumés verified, their references interviewed, and their criminal records checked. Once they've been hired, picture identifications and parking stickers might be issued. Only certain people are given permission to enter certain rooms, open certain file cabinets, or attend certain meet-ings. Only certain people have the ability to sign checks, enter into con-tracts, or perform other financial dealings. In extreme circumstances, additional security comes from segregation of duties; for example, the person who has the physical possession of the checks doesn't have the machine that embosses the signatures. This trust is often a complex rela-tionship. Someone might be trusted to make changes in the personnel records but not the engineering specifications. Another person might be trusted to change the engineering specs but wouldn't be allowed any-where near the personnel records.

In the physical world, it is relatively easy to identify those individuals who are trusted and those who are not. You know what someone looks like. If a stranger walks into an office and starts taking out petty cash, someone will get suspicious. As long as the organization is small enough so that everyone knows everyone, physical penetration attacks aren't really possible. It's the larger organizations that get infiltrated by spies; employees are used to seeing people they don't recognize, so they think nothing of yet another one. (People in any size organization, of course, are vulnerable to threats, bribery, blackmail, seduction, and other kinds of unsavory persuasion.)

The challenge is how to extend the same level of trust in individuals from the physical world to the virtual world—without the physical pres-ence of the individual to draw upon. For example, in the physical world, an adversary who wishes to masquerade as a trusted member of a com-munity takes the personal risk of being found out and apprehended. In the virtual world, a spy can come across the border and impersonate a trusted member of the organization with less risk of being detected or physically apprehended.

The Life Cycle of a System

An industrial spy might choose to bug the telephones in his competitor's offices. He then must choose when and where to conduct this attack. The office equipment is vulnerable during its entire life cycle: on the drawing board, in the manufacturing plant, on the loading dock, in the competi-tor's offices, or even after disposal. Depending on access afforded to him, the adversary may choose to alter or swap the equipment during produc-tion, shipment, installation, normal operations, or maintenance. At some point during the equipment's life cycle, Soviet spies bugged typewriters in the U.S. embassy in Moscow. Did they install the bugs at the factory in the U.S., while the typewriters were being shipped to the embassy, or after they were sitting on desks inside the embassy? We don't know, but each option represents a possible point of attack. And depending on how good the audit systems were, they may have been able to figure it out.

Similarly, a criminal who wants to steal money from a slot machine has the same array of choices: He can introduce a flaw into the design, modify it during installation, or break into it when it is on the casino floor. Each of these attacks has different characteristics—difficulty, success prob-ability, profitability—but they are all possible.

The work environment of the virtual world is software running on network computers. Attackers can attack this software anywhere during its life cycle. A malicious software developer could intentionally leave a back door in the latest release of the operating system. An adversary could put a Trojan horse in an already popular Net browser and distribute it for free over the Internet. He could write a virus that attacks accounting software and delivers it in an executable attachment to an e-mail message. He could analyze the software and exploit an accidental vulnerability. The possibilities are staggering.

RATIONALLY APPLYING COUNTERMEASURES

The vulnerability landscape is a vast expanse of potential attacks, and it makes the most sense to apply countermeasures evenly across the land-scape. The idea is to protect against those threats that pose the greatest risk, instead of protecting against the most manifest threats while ignoring all the others.

The idea is also to make rational investment decisions in applying countermeasures. That is, it doesn't make sense to spend more money improving the locks on the front door when the adversary is apt to break through the glass window. It also doesn't make sense to spend $100 on bulletproof glass to protect $10 worth of assets. The cable TV industry described adding strong cryptography to their analog set-top boxes as "putting a Yale lock on a paper bag."

Value is often dependent on context, and is not always the same for attackers and defenders. In the days before hard drives, teenagers would sometimes walk into offices and steal floppy disks . . . for the value of the disks. Some companies lost some pretty important data that way. And at the other extreme, shopping carts worth over $100 are much less likely to be stolen if there's a $0.25 deposit. Smart cost analysis means more ratio-nal countermeasures for phone fraud and software piracy.

Also remember that some adversaries don't even see value in mone-tary terms. How else can you explain a hacker spending hundreds of hours breaking into a useless computer system? Some attackers are look-ing for publicity, revenge, or some other intangible; remember that when you look at values.

Also, keep in mind that blocking just one of the first four attack steps is enough to block an attack. Simple countermeasures, education, policy, and procedures are often rational, cost-effective means of mitigating the risks posed by the vulnerability landscape. These simple steps can signifi-cantly raise the risk and sophistication needed by the adversary to conduct a successful attack.

The next several chapters deal with this process of modeling threats, assessing risk, and determining which countermeasures to implement.

19

Threat Modeling and Risk Assessment

T hreat modeling is the first step in any security solution. It's a way to start making sense of the vulnerability landscape. What are the real threats against the system? If you don't know that, how do you know what kind of countermeasures to employ?

Threat modeling is hard to do, and a skill that only comes with experience. It involves thinking about a system and imagining the vast vulnerability landscape. Just how can you attack this system? I find that true hackers are masterful at this kind of thing, which is probably why they're drawn to computers in the first place. Hackers enjoy thinking about systems and their limitations: how they fail, when they fail, what happens when they fail. They delight in making systems do things they weren't intended to. It's the same whether the hacker is modifying the engine in his car to work how he wants it to and not how the manufacturer wants it to, or whether he is poking at an Internet firewall to see if he can "own" the computer it is running on.

I find that the best security analysts are people who go through life finding the limitations of systems; they can't help it. They can't walk into a polling place without thinking about the security measures and figuring out ways that they can vote twice. They can't use a telephone calling card without thinking about the possible antifraud mechanisms and how to get around them. These people don't necessarily act on these thoughts—just

288

because they found the blind spot in the store's video surveillance system doesn't mean they start shoplifting—but they can't help looking.

Threat modeling is a lot like this, and the only way to learn it is to do it. So let's start by stealing some pancakes.

Our goal is to eat, without paying, at the local restaurant. And we've got a lot of options. We can eat and run. We can pay with a fake credit card, a fake check, or counterfeit cash. We can persuade another patron to leave the restaurant without eating and eat his food. We can impersonate (or actually become) a cook, a waiter, a manager, or the restaurant owner (who might be someone that few workers have ever met). We could snatch a plate off someone's table before he eats it, or from under the heat lamps before the waiters can get to it. We can wait at the Dumpster for the busboy to throw away the leftovers. We can pull the fire alarm and sneak in after everyone evacuates. We can even try to persuade the manager that we're some kind of celebrity who deserves a free breakfast, or maybe we can find a gullible patron and talk her into paying for our food. We could mug someone, nowhere near the restaurant, and buy the pancakes. We can forge a coupon for free pancakes. And there's always the time-honored tradition of pulling a gun and shouting, "Give me all your pancakes."

There are probably even more possibilities, but you get the idea. Looking at this list, most of the attacks have nothing to do with the point where money changes hands. This is interesting, because it means that securing the payment system does not prevent illicit pancake stealing.

It's similar in the digital world. If this were a Web-based digital pan-cake store, most of the attacks would have nothing to do with the electronic payment scheme. There are many other areas of vulnerability. (Remember the beautiful Web page hack against shopping cart software from Chapter 10, where an attacker could change the price of an item to an arbitrary amount. This brings up another possible attack: change the menu so the pancakes cost $0.00.) The most fruitful attacks are rarely the physical ones.

FAIR ELECTIONS

Let's move on to bigger and better things. Let's rig an election. It's a local election—mayor of a town. Cheating in elections is almost as old as elec-tions themselves. How hard could it be?

Assume a dozen different voting precincts, each with its own polling place. Each polling place has three election judges who monitor the process. Voters get paper ballots from these judges, blacken a circle corre-sponding to the candidate of their choice, and then drop the ballot into a large box. At the end of the day, all the ballots are fed into an automatic vote-counting machine. The judges at each of the 12 polling places phone their results in to a central office. Then the results are summed together, and the winner gets to declare victory over the sound of a noisy band while dodging confetti.

The system has many attack points. We can attack the voters, the election judges, the ballot boxes, the vote-counting machines, the phone calls, or the central office. Let's examine each in turn.

Bribing voters is a time-honored way of rigging an election. This isn't just something that happened in the dim history of the developed world, or in Third World countries. In Dodge County, Georgia (population 17,000), 21 people were indicted for a variety of illegal voting practices, vote buying included; the election was in 1996. In most jurisdictions (including Georgia) it's illegal to pay cash for votes, so politicians are usu-ally forced to resort to other bribes: tax breaks, public works projects, friendly legislation, and White House sleepovers. We can do this, but it's expensive.

And we can't rely on it. The whole point of having private voting booths is so that people can't reliably buy and sell votes. We can pay vot-ers $100 each to vote for a particular candidate, but when they go into the polling place, they can mark their ballots however they please. (Tax breaks work better in this regard, especially for incumbents; the voters think that by voting a certain way they can get more of them.) There's an old Chicago story about a politician who bought votes. He had his henchmen smear black gunk on the mechanical voting pulls associated with a vote for him, and was then able to confirm if the bribed voter delivered the goods.

This avenue of fraud is returning due to the prevalence of mail-in bal-lots. Somewhere between a third and a half of all ballots cast in Silicon Valley elections are mail-in. In Oregon today every election (except pres-idential) is mail-in only. Arizona experimented with an Internet voting scheme for the 2000 Democratic primary. The risk is there—someone could walk into a poor section of town and buy a pile of blank ballots for $10 each (Arizona used PINs, equally fungible)— but the locals feel that it is worth it.

The Singapore ruling party subverts the privacy of ballots by having small election districts, maybe a single apartment block. They can't iden-tify voters individually, but they are very public about denying govern-ment money to districts that voted for the opposition. Think of it as group bribery.

Anyway, let's assume that bribery is beyond our financial means, and even more worrisome, that someone will call the newspaper and expose our scheme. How about intimidation? A trick of Mexico's Institutional Revolutionary Party was to ensure that voting booths in remote places, supposedly impervious to prying eyes, were placed under a tree—with a hired thug hiding in the branches making sure voters voted "properly."

We can try fooling the election judges. We could hire a bunch of actors to pretend to be eligible voters. We could make it so that selected people vote more than once. These are good attacks, but there are defenses. In the United States the election judges keep a list of eligible voters; they check identification and keep records. In the first multiracial South African elections (1994), voters had their hands stamped with indelible ink to prevent them from voting twice. In Latvia's first post-USSR election (1990), people's identity papers were checked and then stamped. During Indonesia's 1999 elections, voters dipped their fingers in ink to prevent double voting. (The ink was supposed to last for the three-day election period, but some people noticed that some of the ink was washable.)

We could attack the election judges themselves. With the coopera-tion of the judges, we can do what we want. We can slip ineligible voters onto the list—in the early 1900s, dead Chicagoans voted in many elec-tions—or simply invent eligible voters. During the 1960 presidential elec-tion, the Chicago Democratic machine, led by Mayor Richard Daley (the scary one), is widely believed to have initiated enough voter fraud to tip the Illinois vote to Kennedy and cost Nixon the election. (When the Republicans demanded a recount in the state, the Democrats demanded a similar recount in a few other states and then both sides capitulated.) This kind of thing is still going on: In the 1996 Louisiana Senate election, the Democratic political organization was accused of buying votes, get-ting people to vote multiple times, and even tampering with voting machines.

Aside from widespread corruption of election judges, attacks get harder. We could try to bribe judges to look the other way, but three of them are at each polling place. We can probably bribe one random judge, but it is really hard to also bribe the two other judges at the same precinct. Election judges are more expensive than voters, and more likely to alert the media.

How about the ballot boxes? We can fill them with already-completed ballots, the original ballot-stuffing idea. We'll have to make sure we don't overdo it; the last thing we want is for a precinct to regis-ter a 130 percent voter turnout. And we have to make sure nobody notices; some Third World elections use transparent ballot boxes to foil this attack.

Attacking the vote-counting machine is easier. It's a computerized device, so chances are no one will notice if a malicious vote-counting program inflates one candidate's votes. We could try to get a Trojan horse into the machine while the software is being written (assuming software is involved, and it is not simply a mechanical counting machine). Or maybe we have to intercept the machine when it is delivered and slip the bogus code in. Maybe we could cajole the election judges to install our software "upgrade." There are a lot of avenues for attack here.

Maybe we can misprint the paper ballots so that the machines some-times just don't register a vote for the opposition; move the box a fraction of an inch to the side and no one would notice. Or we can somehow force the machines to jam, forcing the judges to count manually. Then one bribed election judge could possibly slip a fake result past the other two. In the 1988 Mexican presidential election, the computers "failed" when the challenger was ahead. When they were working again, the incumbent had won . . . and the ballot papers were swiftly burned. I don't want to cast aspersions on the Mexican electoral system, but it all sounded fishy.

The central tabulating office is the hardest place to attack, because it's so public. Maybe we could get away with misreporting precincts, but one of the judges is likely to notice. The phone calls between the precincts and the office . . . possibly.

So, how did we do? It looks as though our best avenue of attack is to persuade the vast majority of election judges to do our bidding. They can add or delete votes, swap ballot boxes in transit, and do lots of other underhanded things. We might be able to rig the vote-counting machines, and getting fake voters past the judges and fake ballots into the boxes might work. The moral is that this is hard. Unless the people running the election are in the back pocket of one of the candidates— which is sometimes true in Third World elections, but rarer in the United States—it's just not going to happen.

The point of this thought experiment was to show the many avenues of attack against a system, and how few of them involve the computerized portion of the process. We can attack the tabulation software, and we can mount a denial-of-service attack by making the automatic system fail and forcing the election judges to fall back on an older, more insecure, proce-dure for accomplishing the same task. In the end, elections are about trust. If the election judges are trustworthy and competent, the election will be fair. If the election judges are not trustworthy, there are so many ways to rig the election that it isn't even worth worrying about which one is most likely.

The Internet adds new twists to this already tangled skein, and the risks increase significantly. All the old attacks remain, and there are all the new attacks against the voting computers, the network, and the voters' computers (which are not trusted in any way). And denial-of-ser-vice attacks that don't exist against centralized systems. Even worse, mod-ern elections have no graceful way to fail. The 2000 Democratic primary in Arizona allowed Internet voting. If there was a problem, or even sus-picion of a problem, what could Arizona do? Reboot the election and try again the following week? This reason alone is enough to convince any psephologist to eschew Internet voting.

SECURE TELEPHONES

This one should be easy. An organization—government, corporation, human rights advocacy group—needs to make phone calls that can't be overheard. The solution is an encrypted telephone, of course. But what are the threats?

The adversary could be a corporate competitor or a government, someone with both the resources and access to carry out highly sophisti-cated attacks. To solve this problem, the organization will build or buy encrypted phones.

How can we attack this system? We might be able to break the encryption, but let's assume that we can't.

We could modify the phones so that they don't work properly. There are lots of options: We can force the encryption algorithm to be weak, we can mess with the key generation system, we can make the phones radi-ate the unencrypted phone call, or we can add a subliminal channel to make the phones leak the keys onto the voice circuit (this is known as "Clipper" when it is done openly). All of these attacks could be put into place during product design and development, while the phones are being shipped to the organization, or during maintenance. They could be done by sneaking into the manufacturing facility at night, bribing someone who works there, or simply designing the surreptitious feature in from the start.

This might seem far-fetched, but if we have the resources of a national intelligence organization, they're perfectly reasonable methods of attack. Crypto AG, a Swiss company, sells encryption hardware to a lot of Third World governments. In 1994, one of their senior executives was arrested by the Iranian government for selling bad cryptographic hard-ware. When he was released from jail a few years later, he went public with the news that his company had been modifying their equipment for years at the request of the U.S. intelligence community. In the 1950s, Xerox modified photocopiers sold to the Russians so that they also had a little camera inside; copier repairmen would periodically remove and replace the film.

The Soviets weren't any less wily; they modified all sorts of office equipment, including IBM Selectric typewriters, in the American embassy in Moscow to broadcast data. British encryption companies are rumored to add exploitable features into products they sell to foreign gov-ernments. Even if they didn't hear the rumor, you'd think that the Argen-tine government would think twice before using British-supplied encryption devices during the Falklands War.

There are a lot of things we can do that don't directly involve the secure telephone: installing bugs inside the secure phones (or the rooms where the phones are), bribing the people making and receiving the calls, and so forth. But the organization can't reasonably expect the phones to be able to deal with that.

One of the best attacks is to simply force the phones not to work. This is easier if the attacker owns the phone system: for example, the phones are being used by a human rights organization in a questionable Third World country, or by a multinational corporation calling a field office in an industrial country known for economic espionage. The attack is to eavesdrop on the phone line, and when the secure telephones try to work, force enough errors that they fail. What will happen, more likely than not, is that the two parties will just stop trying to use the secure phone and say what they were going to say over the unprotected phone line.

SECURE E-MAIL

Secure e-mail is a little more interesting. In Chapter 12, I briefly outlined how secure e-mail programs work. The cryptography does two things: provides a digital signature for authenticity, and encryption for privacy. (The envelope is a curious security device. The Babylonians first thought of protecting clay tablets by enclosing them in clay "envelopes" baked hard around their contents. The Chinese were the first to use paper envelopes—often with wax seals to make them tamper-evident—and they eventually hit Europe. Louis XIV of France popular-ized them.)

In any case, there are lots of ways to attack this system. There's the cryptography: Do the algorithms and protocols work like the designers think they do? There's the implementation: Are there any software bugs that can be exploited? There are all the same back doors that work against the secure telephones: Can we modify the program in design, develop-ment, or on the user's desktop? What about the passwords that users use to read their encrypted mail or to sign their outgoing mail? E-mail programs use certificates to validate public keys; Chapter 15 talks about the potential vulnerabilities in the trust model of certificate systems. And don't forget about all the other vulnerabilities that have nothing to do with the e-mail system: monitor the computer and read the e-mail either before it is sent or after it is received, get a copy of a printout, attack whatever key escrow mechanism the government (or corporation) was dumb enough to enforce.

Encrypting e-mail is riskier than encrypting phone calls. For phones, the information is at risk only for the duration of the call. For e-mail, which may be stored at both ends for considerable lengths of time, the information is at risk also while at rest. Moreover, the adversary can sub-vert the operating system of the underlying computers to attack the information, while phone calls are made on dedicated hardware, which is much harder to attack. The adversary can introduce the attack at a distance, with little physical risk, and can possibly obtain all of the target's information, not just a single message. Finally, the attack can be auto-mated to rapidly exploit a wide range of targets or to just bide its time waiting.

I'll return to this example in Chapter 21.

STORED-VALUE SMART CARDS

Next, a more complicated example: an electronic payment system based on smart cards that store a balance on them. (These are often called *stored-value cards.*) There are several of these being tested: Mondex's (and Mas-terCard's) system, VisaCash (tested during the 1996 Summer Olympics in Atlanta), Banksys's Proton. The analysis here is general, and doesn't nec-essarily reflect the details of any of these systems. We'll call our hypothet-ical system Plasticash.

The basic idea behind Plasticash is that people are issued smart cards to use for cash transactions. Terminals litter the commercial landscape: in banks, in stores, attached to computers attached to the World Wide Web. When a customer wants to buy something from a merchant (or, more generally, transfer money to someone else), they both put their Plasticash cards into a reader/writer and transfer the money. (Merchants will prob-ably have special cards that always remain in the readers.) People can also take cards to banks or ATMs to either load them up with more Plasticash, or deposit Plasticash into their bank accounts. Note that the two cards don't have to be right next to each other; they can be separated by phone lines or modem.

In general, stored-value cards have the advantage that they don't have to be online—in contact with some central server somewhere—in order to work. (For debit cards to work, the ATM has to connect to a bank computer in real time.) They have the disadvantage that loss or destruc-tion of the card means losing the money.

Plasticash, like any electronic payment system, will have all sorts of security features: cryptography, computer security, tamper resistance, audit, and whatever. It could provide varying degrees of integrity, privacy, anonymity, and so forth. We're not going to get detailed. Let's just look at possible attacks against the most general formulation of the system.

There are three different parties involved in the Plasticash system: the customer, the merchant, and the bank. And there are three protocols:

Bank/customer. The customer loads Plasticash onto his card.
Customer/merchant. The customer transfers Plasticash from his card to the merchant's card.
Bank/merchant. The merchant deposits Plasticash from his card into his bank account.

Part 1 of this book talks about the possible attacks: monetary theft, framing, privacy violations, vandalism and terrorism, or publicity. Plasticash might also have to worry about ancillary crimes: An attacker may wish to use the system to carry out some other crime, such as money laundering. Ancillary crimes are hard to define clearly, since they can change at each border crossing, and even at each election. It's also not clear to what extent different countries' laws and customs may be in conflict. For example, in an international arena, U.S. financial reporting requirements may run afoul of Swiss banking secrecy laws.

When we talk about attacks by the bank, we are not necessarily postulating a malefic banking empire. These attacks can be mounted by rogue employees of venerable banks. In general, we are more concerned with attacks by customers and merchants (rogue employees of merchants), on the theory that banks can afford better security mechanisms and measures, and have greater potential losses to reputation if they attack their own systems. Still, it's prudent to be careful.

The first type of attack is theft. There are several ways to mount an attack to steal money from Plasticash. These attacks can be mounted by customers or merchants:

Modify the card so that is has more value than it should. This can be done in several ways; the most obvious is to find the data register inside the card that records the value of the card and change it.
Alter records to reflect either a larger or smaller payment amount.
Learn to create or emulate new cards. This attack is creating a fake Plasticash card that can act like a real card. The fake card doesn't have to look like a real card; an attacker can use it only for purchases over the Internet, or he

can transfer money from his fake card to a real card and then spend with
the real card.

Learn how to clone cards. The attacker would need to steal a legitimate
card, make a clone, and then return it. (This attack succeeded against
Canadian bank cards; several arrests were made in 1999. A rogue
merchant could clone a card in seconds, while a customer used the card
to make a legitimate purchase.)

These are customer attacks:

Repudiate a set of valid card transactions. This is the old "buy an expensive
something with your card, and then report the card stolen and deny the
transaction." There's a new variant—using stupidity as an excuse—for
example: "Visa forced me to lose all my money gambling online; it's not
my fault." This attack should be dealt with at an administrative and legal
level. Whether you're dealing with checks, credit cards, traveler's checks,
or whatever, some people will decide they wish they hadn't spent all that
money and try to avoid paying the charges.

Report another user's card stolen and arrange to intercept his replacement
card. Again, this attack is bigger than the Plasticash system.

And attacks that can only be mounted by merchants:

Accept a transaction and refuse to deliver the goods. This is outside the
scope of what the card can resist, but administrative and legal
procedures need to exist to handle it.

Get access to some stolen customer cards, and alter data. Or generate a bunch
of apparently valid checks to deposit. This is an obvious attack. The attacker
will probably try to deposit the money and then quickly withdraw it all.

Replay valid transactions. A merchant could somehow charge a
customer twice for the same transaction.

Finally, these attacks can be mounted by banks:

Refuse to load value into a Plasticash card that a customer has paid for.
This can be resisted only by administrative procedures and logging. The
cus-tomer will have evidence enough to prove to a neutral third party
what has happened if the protocol is designed competently.

Pocket the cash and never credit the customer's account, when someone
tries to deposit money from his Plasticash card into his account. Again,
this can be defended against only through administrative procedures.

All of these attacks can be mounted by pairs (or the trio) as well. I can't think of any different sort of attack that a merchant and customer can mount, but depending on the security characteristics of the system, the pair could be successful where either one acting alone might not be. Additionally, think about attacks by people pretending to service the ter-minal. Or repair the phone lines.

The second type of attack is framing. First, customer or merchant attacks:

> A customer can claim that a merchant has an invalid Plasticash card (or termi-nal). A merchant can claim the same thing about a customer card. This has to be resolved by administrative means.

Then, bank attacks:

> Forge customer cards (or merchant cards, for that matter) and frame the cus-tomer. Presumably, if the bank can issue Plasticash cards, it could also forge them. Wouldn't a customer hate to see his itemized Plasticash record include a prostitute visit?

The third type of attack is a privacy violation. Privacy violations hap-pen whenever some user's personal information is given without that per-son's consent to some third party. Depending on the jurisdiction, a privacy violation may be legal. Since the developers of Plasticash want to their product to propagate worldwide, it makes sense to list the attacks and then later ignore them if they are legal (and harmless).

Unless the system is specifically designed to prevent this, the bank is in a position to collect unlimited information about customer spending. ("I know what you bought last summer.") It is possible to avoid some of this (but only some) by having users buy precharged stored-value cards in fixed denominations, like some prepaid telephone cards.

The merchant can't directly get the customer's name and such data, but it can collect and share information about this card's ID with other merchants, and try to link this back to the user's identity.

And we also have to worry about eavesdroppers: people not involved in the protocol at all listening in on transactions and collecting informa-tion.

The fourth category of attack we have to worry about includes van-dalism and terrorism. These attacks are prevalently aimed at the system as a whole, though they could be aimed at users, merchants, or banks. The general idea behind all such attacks, though, is that they are intended to prevent the system from working properly. Denial-of-service attacks can be so much fun. Watch.

First, denial-of-service attacks on a merchant:

Interfere with communications with bank or customers.
Report the merchant's card as stolen or compromised.
Physically damage or destroy the merchant's card.
Tamper with the power to the terminal, or the phone connection to the terminal.

Denial-of-service attacks on a customer:

Interfere with communications with bank or merchants.
Report the customer's card as stolen or compromised.
Physically damage or destroy the customer's card.

Denial-of-service attacks on a bank:

Interfere with communications with customers or merchants.
Physically damage or destroy the bank's secure hardware.

And systemwide denial-of-service attacks:

Somehow force the system to upgrade itself, before anyone knows how to deal with it. (You can think of this attack as Y2K.)
Deny service to many or all banks.
Interfere with communications with customers or merchants.
Destroy top-level certifying public key in PKI-based systems.

We can also use criminal attacks to destabilize the system:

Start mass-producing counterfeit cards.
Use massive, widespread fraud to bring down system.

Finally, let's talk about using the system to commit a crime. In the context of this system, crime means violating the laws by using the system.

For now, we'll only consider money-laundering laws, since other laws are too plentiful and variable to discuss here. (Note that most crimes involve a transfer of money somewhere along the line. Nothing a stored-value card can do will get rid of the drug trade, illegal gambling, prostitution, and so forth.)

Some people get cards under false names, or even under their own names if they can be convinced to do so. (There are no doubt many people in the world who will go open a bank account that they know will be used for money laundering, and hand over control to someone else, if they are offered a few thousand dollars, or in some cases, a few days' or weeks' worth of alcohol or drugs.) If these cards are charged up once and used as compact currency, then there isn't an obvious way to stop this.

Note that some ethical and legal issues here are not obviously fixable. Providing financial data to the U.S. or U.K. governments about their cit-izens raises some potential problems, but this data will probably not be abused too often. Providing the same kind of data to many other govern-ments, such as China, Turkey, Mexico, or Syria, seems like a rather dif-ferent matter. The latter could cause political and legal problems for the companies that provide that data, and is also likely to lead to much higher levels of fraud in those countries.

RISK ASSESSMENT

It's not enough to simply list a bunch of threats, you need to know how much to worry about each of them. This is where risk assessment comes in. The basic idea is to take all the threats, estimate the expected loss per incident and the expected number of incidents per year, and then calcu-late the *annual loss expectancy* (ALE).

For example, if the risk is a network intrusion by hackers looking for something to do, the expected loss per incident might be $10,000 (cost of hiring someone to figure out what happened, restore things to their nor-mal state, etc.) and the number of incidents per year might be three per day, or 1,000. This means that the ALE is 10 million. (You can see where this is heading. If the ALE is $10 million, then buying, installing, and maintaining a firewall for $25,000 a year is a bargain. Buying a $40 mil-lion super whiz-bang whatever is a waste of money. This analysis implies that both the firewall and the super whiz-bang whatever actually counter the threat. We'll come back to that point later.)

Some risks have a very low probability of incidence. If the risk is a network intrusion by an industrial competitor out to steal the new design plans, the expected loss per incident might be $10,000,000, but the number of incidents per year might be 0.001: there's a 0.1 percent chance of this happening per year. This means that the ALE is $10,000, and a countermeasure costing $25,000 isn't such a bargain anymore.

The insurance industry does this kind of thing all the time; it's how they calculate premiums. They figure out the ALE for a given risk, tack on some extra for their operational costs plus some profit, and use the result as the cost of an insurance premium against that risk.

Of course there's going to be a lot of guesswork in any of these; the particular risks we're talking about are just too new and too poorly under-stood to be better quantized. For one thing, it might take a really sharp eye to spot the potential for a cascade failure: a small error that could eventually result in the loss of millions of dollars.

For computer-related risk analysis, a bunch of commercial tools provide templates and methodologies for doing risk analysis. They tend to look at large risks, like industrial espionage, rather than small risks, such as someone recovering the private key used to secure your e-mail.

Risk analysis is important because it gives perspective to this whole exercise. Large gaping security holes are okay if the probability of attack is zero. (Tokyo is still vulnerable to attacks by giant fire-breathing lizards, for example.) Tiny holes need to be closed if they're the target of 10 mil-lion attacks a day.

THE POINT OF THREAT MODELING

When designing a security system, it is vital to do this kind of threat modeling and risk assessment. Too many system designers think of security design as a cookbook thing: mix in particular countermeasures—encryp-tion and firewalls are good examples—and magically you're secure.

This never happens. Yogi Berra said: "You've got to be careful if you don't know where you're going 'cause you might not get there." Often security systems don't protect against the threats that matter. Encrypting e-mail may protect the contents from eavesdropping, but does nothing to hide the fact that two people are communicating. In some threat models, that traffic-analysis data is more important than the contents of the mes-sage. In other threat models, the fact that someone is using encryption is something to keep secret.

Good engineering proceeds seriatim from requirement to solution, not from cool technology to product. In security engineering, this means that you first need to define the threat model, then create a security pol-icy, and only then choose security technologies that suit. The threats are what determine the policy, and the policy is what determines the design. In detail:

> **Understand the real threats to the system and assess the risk of these threats.** It's easiest to understand this if you can draw on real-world experience with actual attacks against similar systems.
>
> **Describe the security policy required to defend against the threats.** This will be a series of statements like: "only authorized banks are allowed to modify the balance on Plasticash cards," or "all Plasticash transac-tions must be auditable."
>
> **Design the countermeasures that enforce the previously described policy.** These countermeasures will be a mixture of protec-tion, detection, and reaction mechanisms.

Of course, this "waterfall" model is ideal, and the real world doesn't often cooperate. More likely your engineering path is going to look more like a spiral, where you iterate the preceding three steps multiple times, each time getting closer and closer to real security. This happens most often with new systems and with new technologies, where the real threats remain abstruse until you field the system and see who attacks what. This is why all good systems have contingency plans and disaster recovery plans.

GETTING THE THREAT WRONG

Looking at the goals and methodologies of attackers seems obvious, but many otherwise smart organizations have been blindsided for failing to do just this. The NSA has spent many good years defending the U.S. military communications systems against a well-funded organization with a single goal: "eavesdrop on U.S. communications systems of military importance." They were good at this, but completely missed the hacker threat. Hackers aren't interested in eavesdropping. They aren't particularly well funded. They aren't even organized. They don't want to collect military intelligence; they want to poke at systems for fun and see how they fall over. They want to brag to their friends and maybe even get their names in the newspaper. An AT&T Bell Labs researcher found a flaw in the NSA's Clipper Chip implementation and caused all sorts of bad publicity for the NSA. Why? The frisson at catching the NSA in a mistake.

If you do enough threat modeling, you start noticing all kinds of instances where people get the threat profoundly wrong:

> The cell phone industry spent a lot of money designing their systems to detect fraud, but they misunderstood the threat. They thought the criminals would steal cell phone service to avoid paying the charges. Actually, what the criminals wanted was anonymity; they didn't want cell phone calls traced back to them. Cell phone identities are stolen off the air, used a few times, and then thrown away. The antifraud system wasn't designed to catch this kind of fraud.

> The same cell phone industry, back in the analog days, didn't bother securing the connection because (as they said): "scanners are expensive, and rare." Over the years, scanners became cheap and plentiful. Then, in a remarkable display of not getting it, the same industry didn't bother securing digital cell phone connections because "digital scanners are expensive, and rare." Guess what? They're getting cheaper, and more plentiful.

> Hackers often trade hacking tools on Web sites and bulletin boards. Some of those hacking tools are themselves infected with Back Orifice, giving the tool writer access to the hacker's computer. Aristotle called this kind of thing "poetic justice."

> When a vulnerability is found in an Internet security protocol, the vendor generally revises the protocol to eliminate the vulnerability. But, because backwards compatibility is so important, the vendor often makes the new protocol compatible with the old, insecure, protocol. Smart attackers simply force the old protocol and then exploit the vulnerability. This is called a *ver-sion-rollback attack*.

> Some years ago, the coin slots in many Japanese pachinko machines were replaced with magnetic card readers. Many anticounterfeiting measures were included in the system, but the designers made the mistaken assumption that the pachinko parlor owners were the good guys. In fact, some of them are involved in organized crime. And the trust model was designed badly: The pachinko parlors were reimbursed whether or not the cards

were real, so they had no incentive to police for forgeries. (The designers also thought that a $100 limit per card would cap their losses.) The attack was subtle—it involved reconditioning real cards, a bunch of pachinko machines that "disappeared" after the Kobe earthquake, and multiple pachinko parlors—but the total amount of fraud was about $600 million. Rumor is that the money was funneled into North Korea.

Manufacturers of slot machines have long anticipated attacks by players manip-ulating physical devices. Cheating attempts have included holes drilled into the machine so as to manipulate the reel mechanisms, and devices used to interfere with the sensors that track the number of coins that have been paid out. Years ago, one video poker machine manufacturer was surprised by a completely unanticipated attack: static electricity. Some payers discovered, probably by accident, that after building up a large static charge from the plush casino carpets they could shock the machine, causing it to empty its hopper of all stored coins.

In late 1999, the encryption used to encrypt DVDs was broken. Even though the discs were encrypted, the decryption key had to be in the players. There's no way around it. This worked fine as long as the players were tam-per-resistant hardware, but as soon as someone built a software player, the decryption keys were in software. Someone simply reverse engineered the software and recovered the key, allowing them to freely copy and distribute DVD data over the Internet.

In 1980, the host of the Pennsylvania lottery drawing, an official with the Pennsylvania lottery, and some assorted stagehands rigged the ping-pong balls used in the drawing and won a $1.2 million jackpot. No one expected that complex a collusion. These days, KPMG audits the drawings much more carefully. (A similar flaw—this time a random error—occurred in the Arizona lottery. In 1998, someone noticed that no winning number in its Pick 3 game had ever included a single numeral 9. It turned out that the pseudorandom number generator algorithm had an elementary program-ming error. Ping-pong balls are safer than computers, it seems.)

Most European countries enforce trucking regulations with something called a tachograph: a device attached to the truck's speedometer that logs the vehi-cle's speed, distance, and other information. These devices would record this data on a waxed paper tape that the driver had to sign and date, and keep with him for a period of time. These were hard to forge, and attacks tended to exploit procedural weaknesses instead of technological weak-nesses. Recently the EU funded the Tachosmart project, designed to build an all-digital replacement. Any such system will open itself to all the attacks described in this book (even worse, it is likely to be based on smart cards), and will be much less secure.

These attacks are interesting not because of flaws in the countermeasures, but because of flaws in the threat model. In all of these cases, there were countermeasures in place; they just didn't solve the correct problem. Instead, they solved some problem near the correct problem. And in some cases, the solutions created worse problems than they solved.

20

Security Policies and Countermeasures

Spend enough time doing threat modeling, and it becomes plain that the phrase "secure system" has different meanings depending on context. Some examples:

Business computers need to be secure against hackers, criminals, and industrial competitors. Military computers need to be secure against all those threats plus enemy militaries. Some business computers, those that run the tele-phone service are a good example, need to be secure against military threats as well.

Many urban transportation systems use prepaid farecards instead of cash. Similar prepaid phone card systems are used throughout Europe and Asia. These systems need to be secure against forgery in all of its forms. Of course, forgeries that cost the forgers more than legitimate use are not a problem.

E-mail security programs need to ensure that e-mail is secure against eavesdropping and alteration by any type of attacker. Of course, the program cannot protect against manipulation at the end points: a Trojan horse in the computer, a TEMPEST attack against the computer, a video camera that can read the screen, and so forth. Encrypted telephones are the same; they can secure the voice conversation in transit, but can do nothing about room bugs.

The trick is to design systems that are secure against the real threats, and not to haphazardly use security technologies with the belief that something good will come of it. The way to do that is to build a *security policy* (sometimes called a *trust model*) based on the threat analysis, and then to design protection mechanisms that implement the security policy and deal with the threats.

SECURITY POLICIES

A security policy for a system is like a foreign policy for a government: It defines the aims and goals. When a government is accused of not having a coherent foreign policy, it's because there is no consistency in its actions: no overall strategy. Similarly, a digital system without a security policy is likely to have a hodge-podge of countermeasures. The policy is what ties everything together.

Good policies talk to the threats. If there were no threats, there would be no policy: Everyone could do everything. The United States needs a foreign policy because of threats from other nations. Pennsylvania does not need a foreign policy, because there are no threats from other states. It's the same with security policies; they're needed because threat model-ing didn't result in an empty page. The security policy provides a frame-work for selecting and implementing countermeasures against the threats.

Most of this book is about tactics; policy is about strategy. You can't decide what kinds of antifraud countermeasures you need for your cell phone unless you have a policy you want those countermeasures to enforce. Or, more realistically, you can't expect the dozen or so engineers, each of whom is in charge of security for a small portion of the sys-tem, to behave coherently unless there is a unified policy that they are all trying to implement. Everyone has a security policy in mind when they define and implement countermeasures. A single policy written down forces everyone to follow the same one.

It's common wisdom that every organization needs a security policy for its computer network. The policy should outline who is responsible for what (implementation, enforcement, audit, review), what the basic network security policies are, and why they are the way they are. The last one is important; arbitrary policies brought down from on high with no explanation are likely to be ignored. A clear, concise, coherent, and con-sistent policy is more likely to be followed.

The security policy is how you determine what countermeasures to use. Do you need a firewall? How should you configure your firewall? Do you need access tokens, or are passwords good enough? Should users be allowed to access streaming video from their Web browsers? If there's no policy, there's no basis for consistently answering these ques-tions.

Unfortunately, most organizations don't have a network security pol-icy. Or they do, but no one follows it. I know of one network audit where there was a firewall protecting a boundary between two halves of an internal network. "Which side is inside the firewall and which is out-side?" the auditor asked. No one knew. That's an example of an organi-zation without a useful security policy.

In any case, the security policy needs to outline "why" and not "how." The hows are tactics: the countermeasures. As hard as it is to fig-ure out what the policy should be, it's even harder to find a set of coun-termeasures that implement the policy.

TRUSTED CLIENT SOFTWARE

We've touched on various aspects of this problem in the sections on soft-ware copy protection, intellectual property theft, and digital watermark-ing. Some companies sell rights-management software: audio and video files that can't be copied or redistributed, data that can be read but cannot be printed, software that can't be copied. Other companies market e-mail security solutions where the e-mail cannot be read after a certain date, effectively "deleting" it. Still other companies have software e-commerce technologies that enforces rights of various kinds.

The common thread in all of these "solutions" is that they postulate a situation where Alice can send Bob a file, and then can control what hap-pens to that file after Bob receives it. In the e-mail product, Alice wants to control when the file is deleted on Bob's computer. In the various rights-management products, Alice wants to send Bob a file but limit when and if Bob can view, copy, modify, and retransmit the file.

This doesn't work. Controlling what Bob can do with a piece of data assumes a trusted (by Alice) piece of software running on Bob's computer. There's no such thing, so these solutions don't work.

As an example, look at the online gaming community. Many games allow for multiplayer interaction over the Internet, and some even have tournaments for cash prizes. Hackers have written computer *bots* that assist play for some of these games, particularly Quake and NetTrek. The idea is that the bots can react much quicker than a human, so that the player becomes much more effective when using these bots. An arms race has ensued, as game designers try to disable these bots and force fairer play, and the hackers make the bots cleverer and harder to disable.

These games are trying to rely on trusted client software, and the hacker community has managed to break every trick the game designers have thrown at them. I am continuously amazed by the efforts hackers will go through to break the security. The lessons are twofold: not only is there no reasonable way to trust a client-side program in real usage, but there's no possible way to ever achieve that level of protection.

Against all of these systems—disappearing e-mail, rights management for music and videos, fair game playing—there are two types of attackers: the average user and the skilled attacker. Against the average user, any-thing works. This is Uncle Steve, who just wants a single copy of Norton Utilities, *The Lion King,* or Robin Hitchcock's latest CD, and doesn't want to pay for it. There's no analogue for him in the physical world; Uncle Steve couldn't make a single copy of a Chanel handbag, even if he wanted one. On the one hand, he's more elusive; on the other hand, he's much less of a financial threat. Uncle Steve isn't an organized criminal; he's not going to have a criminal network and he's not going to leave much in the way of a trail. He might not even have bought the software, video, or CD if he couldn't get a free pirated copy. Against Uncle Steve, almost any countermeasure works; there's no need for complex security software.

Against the skilled user, no countermeasure works. In Chapter 16, I talked about the heroic lengths some hackers go to to disable copy protection schemes. Earlier in this section I talked about the specially designed bots to subvert the user interface in computer games. Because breaking the countermeasure can have so much value, building a system that is secure against these attackers is futile. And even worse, most systems need to be secure against the smartest attacker. If one person hacks Quake (or Intertrust or Disappearing Inc.), he can write a point-and-click software tool that anyone can use. Suddenly a security system that is secure against almost everyone can now be compromised by everyone.

The only possible solution is to put the decryption mechanism in secure hardware, and then hope that this slows the professionals down by a few years. But as soon as someone wants a software player, it will be bro-ken within weeks. This is what the DVD industry learned in 1999. This is what Glassbook learned in 2000, when unprotected copies of Stephen King's "Riding the Bullet" materialized two days after the eBook version (supposedly secured against this kind of thing) was released.

Any rational security policy will recognize that the professional pirates cannot be defended against with technology. Professional digital pirates are no different than people who counterfeit Chanel handbags, and soci-ety has ways of catching these people (noncomputer detection and reac-tion mechanisms). They may or may not be effective ways, but that has nothing to do with the digital nature of the forgery. The same security policy would recognize that Uncle Steve is an amateur, and that almost any countermeasure—as long as it could not be broken completely or triv-ially—will work in this case.

Note that this analysis implies that content providers would be smart to find alternate ways to make money. Selling physical copies of a book doesn't work as well in the digital world. Better is to sell real-time updates, subscriptions, and additional reasons to buy a paper copy. I like buying CDs instead of copying them because I get the liner notes. I like buying a physical book instead of printing a digital copy because I want the portability and the binding. I'm willing to pay for stock information because I want its timeliness.

You can see alternate models in the public financing of good works: public television, public art, and street performers. The performance is free, but individual contributions make it happen. Instead of charging each of you $29.99 for this book, maybe I should have put up a Web page asking for contributions. I would write the book and put it in the public domain, but only after I received $30,000 in contributions. (This idea was used to fund some anti-Bush campaign ads in 2000. People would pledge contributions on their credit card, but would only be charged if the target total was reached. Notice that the credit card company acted as the trusted third party in this transaction.)

Other industries have different solutions. The smarter game compa-nies dealt with this by specifically allowing bots in some tournaments, and having final rounds of other tournaments live at trade shows, where the computer is trusted by the game company. The smarter self-distrusting e-mail companies emphasize the liability reduction installing such a system brings, rather than the absolute reliability of the software. There the threat is not malicious users copying and distributing e-mail, but honest employ-ees accidentally leaving e-mail undeleted and malicious lawyers subpoe-naing the e-mail years later. But trying to limit the abilities of a user on a general purpose computer is doomed to failure. It keeps the honest hon-est, and provides a nice false sense of security. But sometimes that's good enough.

AUTOMATIC TELLER MACHINES

ATMs are an interesting example, because the trust and security models are more convoluted than it seems at first. The ATM is basically a safe that dispenses money when told to do so by some external device. The machine takes data from the user (both the information on the magnetic stripe and the PIN the user types in), sends it to some central server some-where, and gets a message in return (dispense cash, don't dispense cash, don't return the card, etc.). The ATM needs to be secure against some-one spoofing the communications link, and from someone either cutting the safe open or hauling it away. It also needs audit records in the event of disputes (those bill counters are not perfect).

Lots of people need access to the ATM. Guards in armored cars come around routinely to fill the thing with cash. Maintenance personnel need to have access, both at defined times for scheduled maintenance and ad hoc in the event of a problem. And remember that maintenance and guard contracts can change; the bank that owns the ATM needs to be able to turn off access for one set of maintenance personnel and turn on access for another.

Also, there's an easy financial equation. An ATM is only worth the cost of replacement plus the cash inside. Spending $10 million on defenses just doesn't make sense.

The cryptography is pretty easy. The communications link does not need to be encrypted, only authenticated. This can be done with either MACs or digital signatures. Audit logs, secured with hash functions, should be stored both at the ATM and at the server.

The computer security is straightforward. The machine should strive for auditability above all. In the event of failure it should shut down rather than heedlessly hand out money. The software should be hard to change, to avoid the problem of maintenance personnel injecting Trojan horses into the system. And so on.

The physical security is also straightforward. The money should be kept in a safe. There should be audit records of anyone opening the safe (perhaps each person can have his own combination, or a unique token). Any long-term cryptographic keys should be erased at the first sign of tampering.

It's interesting to note that ATM owners only recently got the physical countermeasures correct. Until a few years ago, ATMs were built into bank walls and other secure locations. Elsewhere in this book I mentioned attackers who stole entire machines; that was the concern. Then, some-one reached the conclusion that these attacks were rare, and that there was a lot more money to be made by putting ATMs in every bus terminal, bar, shopping mall, and gas station. These are small, freestanding ATMs: much less secure, but that doesn't matter. These ATMs are in public places, so there's some basic detection and reaction. There's less cash in them, so the risk is less. And the fees are high, so they're profitable. If the occasional ATM disappears, it's still worth it.

Even more recently there was another change in the security policy. Someone finally realized that an ATM has two parts: a physical vault with money in it, and a networked computer that tells the vault how much to dispense and when. There's no reason for these two parts to be in the same physical housing. A retail store already has a secure money vault: the cash register. Now some ATMs have no money in them; they're just a computer. The computer goes through the authentication process and prints a slip of paper. The user takes the slip of paper to the cash register and gets his money. These are only good for small amounts, but they work. This is a beautiful example of thinking about security correctly . . .
until someone successfully forges the paper slips.

COMPUTERIZED LOTTERY TERMINALS

Computerized lottery terminals are used in most keno-style lotteries. Basically, lottery vendors get a secure computer/printer that prints out and validates lottery picks. This "validation" consists of a printed ticket with the chosen numbers plus some authenticating information. Once or twice a week there is a public drawing. There are small winners and large jackpot winners.

The threats are obvious. Attackers are most likely the lottery vendors themselves, possibly in cahoots with people working inside the lottery system. They can attack the system in one of two ways: "buying" tickets after the results are known, or altering already-purchased tickets after the results are known. More subtle, but also damaging, is operating a phony terminal that collects money but doesn't pay out any prizes (actually, they would be smarter to pay out small prizes and disappear if any of their phony tickets won a large prize).

These threats imply a straightforward security policy. The lottery ter-minals should be online, and register all picks with a central server. This server keeps good audit logs, with timestamps, and sends the terminals audit information that is printed on the ticket. This server needs to be secured prior to the drawing. And there needs to be some way of identi-fying bogus vendors: The obvious one is to allow low-value tickets to be redeemed at any vendor, not just the one the ticket was purchased at. Regular audits also help.

There are still a lot of details to work out, but you get the idea.

SMART CARDS VS. MEMORY CARDS

As a final example, let's look at two different protection mechanisms: smart cards and magnetic stripe memory cards. In Chapter 14, I talked about tamper resistance, secure perimeters, and attacks against smart cards. In Chapter 19, I did a basic threat model of a hypothetical digital cash sys-tem based on smart cards. Now let's apply all that knowledge and ask the following question: Is it more secure to have a smart card (a card with a microprocessor on it) than a memory card (either a card with just a mem-ory chip on it, or a magnetic stripe card) for a given application.

To someone who can reverse engineer the smart card, there's no dif-ference. He can recover the data from both types of cards, and both types of cards can encrypt their secrets to protect against this. To someone who cannot reverse engineer the smart card, there is a big difference. That someone can read the magnetic stripe card, but he cannot read the mem-ory on the smart card. On the other hand, if the information is encrypted anyway, what does it matter if he can read the magnetic stripe? Maybe there's less of a difference than we thought.

Let's look at the process of using the two different cards.

Magnetic stripe cards. The user puts his card into a reader, and then types a PIN or password or code into the reader. The reader reads the data off the magnetic stripe and uses the PIN to decrypt the data. This data is then used by the reader to do whatever the system is supposed to do: log in to the system, sign an electronic check, pay for parking, or whatever.

Smart cards. The user puts his card into a different reader, and types the same PIN into this reader. The reader sends the PIN into the smart card, which decrypts the data. The data is then used by the card, not the reader, to do whatever the system is supposed to do. The reader just acts as the input/output device for the system.

What's the difference? In both cases, a malicious reader can subvert the system. The reader is the only contact the card has with the outside world. Once the magnetic stripe card gives up its secrets, the reader can do whatever it wants. Once the smart card has been fed the correct PIN by the reader, the reader can make the smart card believe any reality that it wants.

The primary difference between the two cards is that the smart card can exert some control, because it is secure within itself. If someone steals a magnetic stripe card, for example, he can do a brute-force search against the secrets stored on the card. He can do this brute-force search offline, on a computer, without the user even knowing. (A canny attacker can steal the card, read the data off the magnetic stripe, and then slip it back into the victim's wallet.) Smart cards can't be attacked this way. Smart cards can be programmed to shut down after ten (or so) invalid password attempts in a row. So if someone steals a smart card, he won't be able to brute-force the password. He's only got ten guesses. (Again, this assumes that he can't just reverse engineer the card. If he can, he can do an offline attack just like a magnetic stripe card.)

Another major difference is that the smart card doesn't have to give up its secrets. If, for example, the cards are used to sign documents, the smart card may be more secure than a magnetic stripe card. The magnetic stripe card has to rely on the reader to do the actual signing; it gives up its secret to the reader and hopes for the best. A malicious reader can steal the signing key. The smart card does the signing itself. A malicious reader can feed the card bogus things to sign, but the reader cannot learn the signing key.

And there are other, more subtle, differences. The smart card might have some basic rules that it follows with regards to its actions. Generally, these can be mirrored by a back-end system and magnetic stripe cards, but the implementation is cleaner with smart cards.

You see smart cards used as credit cards all over Europe, but not in the United States. Why? Because of the phone system. To combat fraud, U.S. credit cards went to an online verification system. When you buy some-thing, the merchant checks the validity of your card (and the availability of your credit) via modem. In Europe 15 years ago that type of system would not have worked in every country. Phones were expensive; many stores didn't even have one, and the average wait time for installation in Italy was one or two years. Phone calls were expensive, and the connec-tions were unreliable. Fielding an online system in Europe was expensive, so the credit card industry went with smart cards to give some measure of security for the transaction. It wasn't that smart cards were more secure than magnetic stripe cards, it was that the U.S. solution to the problem of fraud—online verification—was less practical. Some intense lobbying by the European smart card vendors (Bull SA, Gemplus, and Schlumberger) didn't hurt, either.

In summary, there is some difference between magnetic stripe cards and smart cards, but how important it is depends on the application. The smart card's tamper resistance is always breakable, given enough time and money, so systems should not be built whose security relies on the tam-per resistance. Most people can't reverse engineer a smart card, so they are secure enough against most attackers. Both cards assume that the reader is trusted, and can be defeated by a malicious reader. The smart card, though, is more secure against offline attacks. And, as long as the tamper resistance is not broken, a smart card can keep secrets inside itself.

RATIONAL COUNTERMEASURES

Good countermeasures not only protect against the threats, but protect against unforeseen problems. Given that it's so hard to get security right, isn't it smart to make sure it's not a disaster if you get it wrong?

Too many security systems are brittle: They fall apart at the slightest mistake. Some examples:

Most of the systems used to secure European pay-TV systems over the past decade have put a global secret in the customer set-top boxes. This means that as soon as one person defeats the tamper-resistance and recovers the key, the entire system is compromised.

The New York MetroCard, the magnetic stripe farecard that lets you purchase rides on subways and buses, could (this was back in 1998) be bypassed sim-ply by folding the card at precisely the right point.

DVD security.

Compare this with credit cards. The cards are hard to forge, and include things like holograms, microprinting, and UV watermarks. You can steal a credit card number, but as soon as it's reported as stolen, the card number is put on a hot list. Even if the card isn't registered as stolen, computer programs scan the transaction database, looking for anomalous spending patterns. Even if the attacker manages to bypass all of those countermeasures, the card has a credit limit that triggers automatically. And as a final countermeasure, the card eventually expires.

Other security systems have unforeseen consequences. Expensive cars now come with ignitions that can't be hotwired; it's an antitheft device. While they reduce car theft somewhat, they also change the threat model from one threat (stealing a car from a parking lot) to a more dangerous one (carjacking). Ouch. It turns out that the preventive countermeasures aren't the most effective ones; detection and reaction countermeasures like Lojack are simply better at countering the threat.

Or another example: A version of Trend Micro's OfficeScan (it's probably fixed by now), a product that scans for viruses and denial-of-ser-vice vulnerabilities, actually contains new security (denial-of-service and other) vulnerabilities.

The NSA is really good at this sort of thing. They build countermeasures on top of countermeasures, and constantly ask "what would happen if this fails?" What if the cryptography fails at the same time the secure perimeter fails, leaving the alarm system as the only countermeasure? What if the guards who should be alerted by the alarm are busy with other things, or what if the machine that generates the keys for the cryptogra-phy fails? What if the backup machine fails as well? What if the person in charge of fixing the backup machine is successfully bribed? Okay, maybe you can do too much of this kind of thing.

21

Attack Trees

Danaë was the daughter of Acrisius. An oracle warned Acrisius that Danaë's son would someday kill him, so Acrisius shut Danaë in a bronze room, away from anything even remotely masculine. Zeus had the hots for Danaë, so he penetrated the bronze room through the roof, in the form of a shower of gold that poured down into her lap. Danaë gave birth to Perseus, and you can probably guess the end of the story.

Threat modeling is, for the most part, ad hoc. You think about the threats until you can't think of any more, then you stop. And then you're annoyed and surprised when some attacker thinks of an attack you didn't. My favorite example is a band of California art thieves that would break into people's houses by cutting a hole in their walls with a chainsaw. The attacker completely bypassed the threat model of the defender. The countermeasures that the homeowner put in place were door and window alarms; they didn't make a difference to this attack.

To help the process, I invented something called an *attack tree*. Attack trees provide a methodical way of describing threats against, and counter-measures protecting, a system. By extension, attack trees provide a methodical way of representing the security of systems. They allow you to make calculations about security, compare the security of different sys-tems, and do a whole bunch of other cool things.

Basically, you represent attacks against a system in a tree structure, with the goal as the root node and different ways of achieving that goal as leaf nodes. By assigning values to the nodes, you can do some basic calculations with the tree (it's called an and/or tree, if you're interested) to make statements about different attacks against the goal.

I'll start with a simple attack tree for a noncomputer security system, and build the concepts up slowly.

BASIC ATTACK TREES

Figure 21.1 is a simple attack tree against a physical safe. Each attack tree has a goal, represented by the root node in the tree. The goal in this example is opening the safe. That's the root node; trees in computer science grow upside down. To open the safe, an attacker can pick the lock, learn the combination, cut open the safe, or install the safe improperly so that he can easily open it later. To learn the combination, the attacker either has to find the combination written down or get the combination from the safe owner. And so on. Each node becomes a subgoal, and chil-dren of that node are ways to achieve that subgoal. (Of course, this is just a sample attack tree, and an incomplete one at that.)

Note the AND nodes and OR nodes (in the figures, everything that isn't explicitly an AND node is an OR node). OR nodes are alternatives:

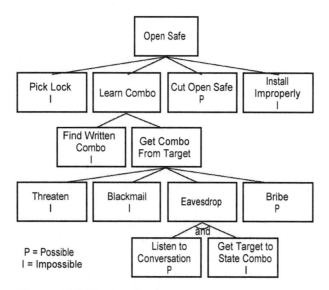

Figure 21.1 Attack nodes.

the four different ways to open a safe, for example. AND nodes represent different steps toward achieving the same goal. To eavesdrop on someone saying the safe combination, attackers have to eavesdrop on the conversa-tion AND get safe owners to say the combination. Attackers can't achieve the goal unless both subgoals are satisfied.

That's the basic attack tree. Once you have it completed, you can assign values—I (impossible) and P (possible) in Figure 21.1—to the var-ious leaf nodes. (Again, this is only an illustrative example; do not take the values as an indication of how secure my office safe really is.) Once you assign these values—presumably this assignment will be the result of painstaking research on the safe itself—you can calculate the security of the goal. The value of an OR node is possible if any of its children are possible, and impossible if all of its children are. The value of an AND node is possible only if all children are possible, and impossible otherwise; see Figure 21.2.

The dotted lines in Figure 21.2 show all possible attacks: a hierarchy of possible nodes, from a leaf to the goal. This sample system has two pos-sible attacks: cutting open the safe, or learning the combination by brib-ing the owner of the safe. With this knowledge, you know exactly how to defend this system against attack.

Assigning values like "possible" and "impossible" to the nodes is just one way to look at the tree. Any yes/no value can be assigned to the leaf nodes and then propagated up the tree structure in the same manner: easy versus difficult, expensive versus inexpensive, intrusive versus nonintru-sive, legal versus illegal, special equipment required versus no special equipment. Figure 21.3 shows the same tree with "no special equipment" and "special equipment required" node values.

Assigning "expensive" and "not expensive" to nodes is useful, but it would be better to show exactly how expensive. You can assign numeri-cal values to nodes. Figure 21.4 shows the tree with different costs assigned to the leaf nodes. Like yes/no node values, these can propagate up the tree as well. OR nodes have the value of their cheapest child; AND nodes have the value of the sum of their children. In Figure 21.4, the costs have propagated up the tree, and the cheapest attack has been highlighted.

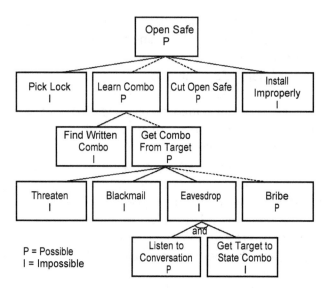

Figure 21.2 Possible attacks.

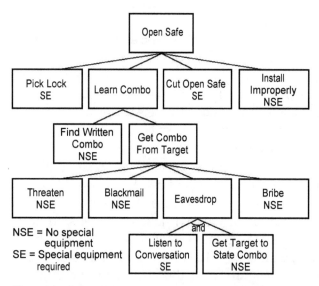

Figure 21.3 Special equipment versus no special equipment attacks.

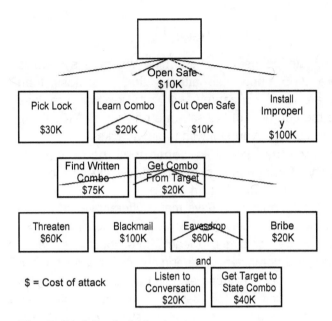

Figure 21.4 Cost of attack.

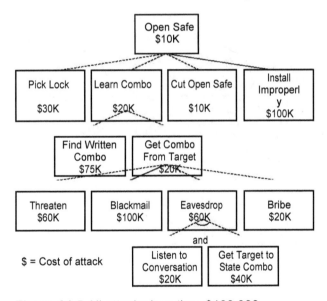

Figure 21.5 All attacks less than $100,000.

Again, this tree can be used to determine where a system is vulnera-ble. Figure 21.5 shows all attacks that cost less than $100,000. If you are only concerned with attacks that are less expensive (maybe the contents of the safe are only worth $100,000), then you should only concern yourself with those attacks.

There are many other possible continuous node values, including probability of success of a given attack, likelihood that an attacker will try a given attack, and so on.

In any real attack tree, nodes will have many different values corresponding to many different variables, both Boolean and continuous. Different node values can be combined to learn more about a system's vulnerabilities. Figure 21.6, for instance, determines the cheapest attack requiring no special equipment. You can also find the cheapest low-risk attack, most likely nonintrusive attack, best low-skill attack, cheapest attack with the highest probability of success, most likely legal attack, and so on. Every time you query the attack tree about a certain characteristic of attack, you learn more about the system's security.

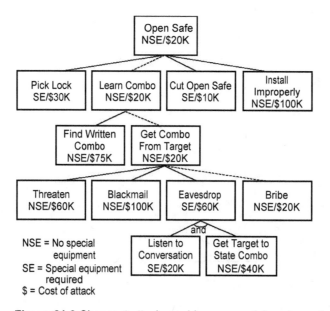

Figure 21.6 Cheapest attack requiring no special equipment.

To make this work, you must marry attack trees with knowledge about attackers. Different attackers have different levels of skill, access, risk aversion, money, and so on. If you're worried about organized crime, you have to worry about expensive attacks and attackers who are willing to go to jail. If you are worried about terrorists, you also have to worry about attackers who are willing to die to achieve their goal. If you're worried about bored graduate students studying the security of your system, you usually don't have to worry about illegal attacks such as bribery and black-mail. The characteristics of your attacker determine which parts of the attack tree you have to worry about.

Attack trees also let you play "what if" games with potential counter-measures. In Figure 21.6, for example, the goal has a cost of $20,000. This is because the cheapest attack requiring no special equipment is bribing the person who knows the combination. What if you implemented a countermeasure—paying that person more so that he or she is less sus-ceptible to bribes? If you assume that the cost to bribe that person is now $80,000 (again, this is an example; in the real world you'd be expected to research exactly how a countermeasure affects the node value), then the cost increases to $60,000 (presumably to hire the thugs to do the threat-ening).

PGP ATTACK TREE

Figure 21.7 is an attack tree for the PGP e-mail security program. Since PGP is a complex program, this is a complex tree, and it's easier to write it in outline form than graphically. PGP has several security features, so this is only one of several attack trees for PGP. This particular attack tree has "read a message encrypted with PGP" as its goal. Other goals might be: "forge someone else's signature on a message," "change the signature on a message," "undetectably modify a PGP-signed or PGP-encrypted message," and so on.

If software can be modified (Trojan horse) or corrupted (virus), it can be used to have PGP generate an insecure public/private key pair (e.g., with a modulus whose factorization is known to the attacker).

What immediately becomes apparent from the attack tree is that breaking the RSA or IDEA encryption algorithms is not the most prof-itable attack against PGP. There are many ways to read someone's PGP-

Figure 21.7 PGP attack tree

Goal: Read a message encrypted with PGP (OR)
1. Read a message encrypted with PGP
  1.1. Decrypt the message itself (OR)
    1.1.1. Break asymmetric encryption (OR)
      1.1.1.1. Brute-force break asymmetric encryption (OR)

It is possible to encrypt all possible keys with the recipient's (known) public key, until a match is found. The effectiveness of this attack is greatly reduced by the random padding introduced in the encryption of the symmetric key.

      1.1.1.2. Mathematically break asymmetric encryption (OR)
        1.1.1.2.1 Break RSA (OR)

It is not currently known whether breaking RSA is equivalent to factoring the modulus.

        1.1.1.2.2 Factor RSA modulus/calculate ElGamal dis-crete log

Either of these would require solving number theoretic problems currently conjectured to be very difficult.

      1.1.1.3. Cryptanalyze asymmetric encryption
        General cryptanalysis of RSA/ElGamal (OR)

No techniques are currently known for general crypt-analysis of RSA or ElGamal. Cryptanalysis of one ciphertext would imply a general method to break RSA/ElGamal.

        1.1.1.3.2. Exploiting weaknesses in RSA/ElGamal
(OR)

There are a few weaknesses known to exist in RSA; however, PGP implementation has mostly eliminated these threats.

continues

Figure 21.7 *(Continued)*

1.1.1.3.3. Timing attacks on RSA/ElGamal

Timing attacks have been reported on RSA; they should also be feasible on ElGamal. Such an attack, however, requires low-level monitoring of the recipient's computer while he is decrypting the message.

1.1.2. Break symmetric-key encryption
1.1.2.1. Brute-force break symmetric-key encryption (OR)

All symmetric-key algorithms supported for use by PGP have key sizes of at least 128 bits. This is currently infeasi-ble for brute-force searching.

Brute-force searching is made somewhat easier by the redundancy included at the beginning of all encrypted mes-sages. See the OpenPGP RFC.

1.1.2.2. Cryptanalysis of symmetric-key encryption

The symmetric-key algorithms supported by PGP 5.x are IDEA, 3-DES, CAST-5, Blowfish, and SAFER-SK128. No efficient methods are currently known for general cryptanalysis of these algorithms.

1.2. Determine symmetric key used to encrypt the message via other means
1.2.1. Fool sender into encrypting message using public key whose private key is known (OR)
1.2.1.1. Convince sender that a fake key (with known pri-vate key) is the key of the intended recipient
1.2.1.2. Convince sender to encrypt using more than one key—the real key of the recipient, one a key whose pri-vate key is known
1.2.1.3. Have the message encrypted with a different public key in the background, unknown to the sender

This could be done by running a program that fools the user into believing that the correct key is being used, while actually encrypting with a different key.

Figure 21.7 *(Continued)*

1.2.2. Have the recipient sign the encrypted symmetric key (OR)

If the recipient blindly signs the encrypted key, he unwittingly reveals the unencrypted key. The key is short enough so that hashing should not be necessary before signing. Or, if a message can be found that hashes to the value of the encrypted key, the recipient can be asked to sign the (hash of the) message.

1.2.3. Monitor sender's computer memory (OR)
1.2.4. Monitor receiver's computer memory (OR)

The (unencrypted) symmetric key must be stored somewhere in memory at some point during the encryption and decryption. If memory can be accessed, this gives a way to capture the key and get at the message.

1.2.5. Determine key from random number generator (OR)
    1.2.5.1. Determine state of the random number generator when message was encrypted (OR)
    1.2.5.2. Implant software (virus) that deterministically alters the state of random number generator (OR)
    1.2.5.3. Implant software that directly affects the choice of symmetric key
1.2.6. Implant virus that exposes the symmetric key
1.3. Get recipient to (help) decrypt message (OR)
    1.3.1. Chosen ciphertext attack on symmetric key (OR)

The cipher feedback mode used by PGP is completely insecure under a chosen ciphertext attack. By sending the (encryption of the) same key to the recipient, along with a modified body of the message, the entire contents of the message can be obtained.

1.3.2. Chosen ciphertext attack on public key (OR)

Since RSA and ElGamal are malleable, known changes can be made to the symmetric key which is encrypted. This modified

continues

Figure 21.7 *(Continued)*

(encrypted) key can then be sent along with the original message. This opens up the possibility of related-key attacks on the sym-metric algorithms. Or, a weak ciphertext can be found whose decryption under the symmetric key algorithm reveals informa-tion about the modified key, which then leads directly to infor-mation about the original key.

1.3.3. Send the original message to the recipient (OR)

If the recipient decrypts and replies to this message automatically, the plaintext message is immediately revealed.

1.3.4. Monitor outgoing mail of recipient (OR)

If the receiver replies to the original message in a nonencrypted manner, information about the original message may be gleaned

1.3.5. Spoof reply to: or from: field of original message (OR)

In this case, the receiver may reply directly to the forged e-mail address, and even if the reply is encrypted, it will be with a key whose private key is known.

1.3.6. Read message after it has been decrypted by recipient
   1.3.6.1. Copy message off user's hard drive or virtual memory (OR)
   1.3.6.2. Copy message off backup tapes (OR)
   1.3.6.3. Monitor network traffic (OR)
   1.3.6.4. Use electromagnetic snooping techniques to read message as it is displayed on the screen (OR)
   1.3.6.5. Recover message from printout
         1.3.6.5.1 Recover message from a paper printout
         1.3.6.5.2 Recover message from the photo-sensitive drum in the printer
         1.3.6.5.3 Eavesdrop on the communications between the computer and the printer
         1.3.6.5.4 Recover message from the printer's memory
1.4. Obtain private key of recipient
   1.4.1. Factor RSA modulus/calculate ElGamal discrete log (OR)

Figure 21.7 *(Continued)*

Either of these would require solving number theoretic prob-lems currently conjectured to be very difficult.

1.4.2. Get private key from recipient's key ring (OR)
    1.4.2.1. Obtain encrypted private key ring (AND)
        Copy it from user's hard drive (OR)
        Copy it from disk backups (OR)
        Monitor network traffic (OR)
        Implant virus/worm to expose copy of the encrypted private key

Given the recent Melissa virus incident, something like this is feasible. Other options include making the file publicly readable, or posting it to the Web.

    1.4.2.2. Decrypt private key
        Break IDEA encryption (OR)
            Brute-force break IDEA (OR)

IDEA uses 128-bit keys. This is currently infeasible for brute-force searching.

        1.4.2.2.1.2. Cryptanalysis of IDEA

No efficient methods are currently known for general cryptanalysis of IDEA.

        Learn passphrase
          Monitor keyboard when user types passphrase (OR)
          Convince user to reveal passphrase
(OR)
          Use keyboard-logging software to record passphrase when typed by user (OR)
        Guess passphrase
1.4.3. Monitor recipient's memory (OR)

The private key must be stored somewhere in memory when the user decrypts any messages sent to him.

continues

Figure 21.7 *(Continued)*

1.4.4. Implant virus to expose private key

Really a more sophisticated version of 1.4.2.1.4. in which the
virus waits for the private key to be decrypted before exposing it.

1.4.5. Generate insecure public/private key pair for recipient.

---

encrypted messages without breaking the cryptography. You can capture the
person's screen when he decrypts and reads the messages (using a Tro-jan
horse like Back Orifice, a TEMPEST receiver, or a secret camera), grab the
person's private key after he enters a passphrase (Back Orifice, or a
dedicated computer virus), recover the person's passphrase (a *keyboard
sniffer* that simply captures user keystrokes, TEMPEST receiver, or Back
Orifice again), or simply try to brute-force the person's passphrase (it will
have much less entropy than the 128-bit IDEA keys that it generates). In the
scheme of things, the choice of algorithm and the key length is prob-ably the
least important thing that affects PGP's overall security. PGP not only has to
be secure, but it has to be used in an environment that lever-ages that
security without creating any new insecurities.

Figure 21.8 is a more general attack tree: reading a specific
message, either in transit or on one of two computers.

Figure 21.8 Attack tree for reading a specific e-mail message.

Goal: Read a specific message that has been sent from
one Win-dows 98 computer to another.

    1. Convince sender to reveal message (OR)
      1.1. Bribe user
      1.2. Blackmail user
      1.3. Threaten user
      1.4. Fool user
    2. Read message when it is being entered into the computer (OR)
      2.1. Monitor electromagnetic emanations from computer
          screen (Countermeasure: use a TEMPEST computer)

Figure 21.8 *(Continued)*

2.2. Visually monitor computer screen

2.3. Monitor video memory

2.4. Monitor video cables

3. Read message when it is being stored on sender's disk (Counter-measure: use SFS to encrypt hard drive) (AND)

    3.1. Get access to hard drive (Countermeasure: Put physical locks on all doors and windows)

    3.2. Read a file protected with SFS

4. Read message when it is being sent from sender to recipient (Coun-termeasure: use PGP) (AND)

    4.1. Intercept message in transit (Countermeasure: Use transport-layer encryption program)

    4.2. Read message encrypted with PGP

5. Convince recipient to reveal message (OR)

    5.1. Bribe user

    5.2. Blackmail user

    5.3. Threaten user

    5.4. Fool user

6. Read message when it is being read (OR)

    6.1. Monitor electromagnetic emanations from computer screen (Countermeasure: use a TEMPEST computer)

    6.2. Visually monitor computer screen

7. Read message when it is being stored on receiver's disk (OR)

    7.1. Get stored message from user's hard drive after decryption (Countermeasure: use SFS to encrypt hard drive) (AND)

        7.1.1. Get access to hard drive. (Countermeasure: Put physical locks on all doors and windows)

        7.1.2. Read a file protected with SFS

    7.2. Get stored message from backup media after decryption

8. Get paper printout of message (Countermeasure: store paper copies in safe) (AND)

    8.1. Get physical access to safe

    8.2. Open the safe

9. Steal sender's computer and try to recover message

10. Steal recipient's computer and try to recover message

CREATING AND USING ATTACK TREES

How do you create an attack tree? First, you identify the possible attack goals. Each goal forms a separate tree, although they might share subtrees and nodes. Then, think of all attacks against each goal. Add them to the tree. Repeat this process down the tree until you are done. Give the tree to someone else, and have him think about the process and add any nodes he thinks of. Repeat as necessary, possibly over the course of several months.

The process still requires creativity, but the structure takes an ad hoc brainstorming process and replaces it with a repeatable methodology. Remember to look for attacks throughout the vulnerability landscape, and at every step of the attack process. Of course there's always the chance that you forgot about an attack, but you'll get better with time. Like any security analysis, creating attack trees requires a certain mindset and takes practice.

Once you have the attack tree, and have researched all the node values (these values will change over time, both as attacks become easier and as you get more exact information on the values), you can use the attack tree to make security decisions. You can look at the values of the root node to see if the system's goal is vulnerable to attack. You can determine if the system is vulnerable to a particular kind of attack; distributed denial-of-service, for instance. You can use the attack tree to delineate the secu-rity assumptions of a system; for example, the security of PGP might assume that no one could successfully bribe the programmers. You can determine the impact of a system modification or a new vulnerability dis-covery; recalculate the nodes based on the new information and see how the goal node is affected. And you can compare and rank attacks: which are cheaper, which are more likely to succeed, and so on.

One of the surprising things that comes out of this kind of analysis is that the areas people think of as vulnerable usually aren't. With PGP, for example, people generally worry about key length. Should they use 1024-bit RSA or 2048-bit RSA? The attack tree shows that the RSA key length doesn't really matter. There are all sorts of other attacks—installing a keyboard sniffer, modifying the program on the victim's hard drive— that are much easier than breaking the public key. Increasing the key length from 1024 bits to 2048 bits doesn't affect any of the overall diffi-culty of the attack tree; it's the computer-security attacks that are much more troublesome. Attack trees give you perspective on the whole sys-tem.

Another thing that makes attack trees valuable is that they capture knowledge in a reusable form. Once you've completed the PGP attack tree, you can use it in any situation that uses PGP. The attack tree against PGP becomes part of a larger attack tree. For example, Figure 21.8 shows an attack tree whose goal is to read a specific message that has been sent from one Windows 98 computer to another. If you look at the leaf nodes of the tree, the entire attack trees for PGP and for opening a safe fit into this attack tree.

This scalability means that you don't have to be an expert in everything. If you're using PGP in a system, you don't have to know the details of the PGP attack tree; all you need to know are the values of the root node. If you're a computer-security expert, you don't have to know the details about how difficult a particular model of safe is to crack; you just need to know the values of the root node. Once you build up a library of attack trees against particular computer programs, door and window locks, network security protocols, or whatever, you can reuse them whenever you need to. For a national security agency concerned about compartmentalizing attack expertise, this kind of system is very useful.

22

Product Testing

and Verification

We've touched on security testing repeatedly in this book. In Chapter 7 we talked about choosing a cryptographic primitive, and how the best way to test cryptography is years of public cryptanalysis. In Chapter 8 we talked about assurance levels for secure computers—the Orange Book, the Common Criteria—and test-ing to verify compliance. Chapter 13 discussed software reliability, and how bugs turn into security vulnerabilities. Testing is where the rubber meets the road: It's one thing to model the threats, design the security policy, and build the countermeasures, but do those countermeasures actually work? Sure, you've got a pretty firewall/antivirus pack-age/VPN/pay-TV antifraud system/biometric authentication sys-tem/smart card–based digital cash system/e-mail encryption product, but is it actually secure? Most security products on the market are not, and the reason is a failure of testing.

Normal security testing fails for several reasons. First, security flaws can appear anywhere. They can be in the trust model, the system design, the algorithms and protocols, the implementation, the source code, the human–computer interface, the procedures, or the underlying computer system (hardware, operating system, or other software). Second, a single flaw can break the security of the entire product. Remember that security is a chain, and only as secure as the weakest link. Real products have a lot of links. Third and most important, these flaws cannot be found through normal beta testing. Security has nothing to do with functionality. A cryptography product can function normally and be completely insecure. Flaws remain undiscovered until someone looks for them explicitly.

Throughout this book I have maintained that security is difficult to get right. It's one thing to design a secure system, another to implement it properly, and quite another to implement it without iatrogenic effects . . . but it's a completely different thing to test and verify that you got it right.

In a previous life I was president of Counterpane Systems, a cryptography and security consulting company. Much of my time was spent eval-uating computer security products. Generally, I was called in at the end of product development to verify that the product was indeed secure. Smarter companies called me in earlier—during the design phase—to make sure that the design was secure; sometimes I evaluated the actual product built to the design I previously analyzed. This chapter is the distillation of that experience.

THE FAILURE OF TESTING

Reread Chapter 13 on software reliability. Recall the phrase "Satan's computer," and how security products need to work in the presence of a malicious adversary. Now think about functional testing.

Functional testing won't find security flaws. Unlike almost all other design criteria, security is independent of functionality. If you're coding a word processor, and you want to test the print functionality, you can hook up a printer and see if it prints. If you're smart, you hook up several kinds of printers and print different kinds of documents. That's easy; if the software functions as specified, then you know it works.

Security is different. Imagine that you are building an encryption function into that same word processor. You test it the same way: You encrypt a series of documents, and you decrypt them again. The decryp-tion recovers the plaintext; the ciphertext looks like gibberish. It all works great. Unfortunately, the test indicates nothing about the security of the encryption.

Functional testing is good at finding random flaws that, when they happen, will cause the computer program to behave weirdly (generally, to crash). Security flaws have much less spectacular effects; unless they fall into the wrong hands, they're usually invisible. Security testing is not about randomly using the software and seeing if it works. Security testing is about deliberately searching out problems that compromise security. Functional testing would never figure out that an attacker can create a Web page that, when viewed with certain versions of Microsoft Internet Explorer 3.0 and 3.0.1, can run an arbitrary program on the viewer's machine. That's just not something a beta tester can look for.

Imagine a vendor shipping a software product without any functional testing at all: no in-house testing, no outside beta testing. All the vendor does is ensure that the program compiles, and then they ship. The odds of this software not having any bugs is zero. Even if it is a simple product, it will have thousands of bugs. It will crash all the time, and fail in unimag-inably bizarre ways. It won't work.

Now imagine the same vendor shipping a software security product without any security testing at all: no in-house security testing, no outside analysis. All the vendor does is go through their normal functional test program, and then they ship. The odds of this software not having any security bugs is zero.

Unfortunately, far too much software, even security software, has exactly this problem.

Even a moderately comprehensive security analysis won't help much. I've already used the figure of 5 to 15 bugs per thousand lines of code. And that's in final products, after all testing. We've all seen the enormous number of bugs in Microsoft operating systems, and that's after hundreds of man-years of testing. Similarly, a few days, weeks, or even months of security analysis will not do any better.

Another problem is that security can only be analyzed by experienced security testers. Remember that the best thing you can say about security products is: "I can't break it, and all these other smart people can't break it either." Only experienced security experts can reliably discover security flaws, so the quality of any security test effort depends on the quality of the testers.

Sometimes security flaws are discovered by accident. A good exam-ple is the password protection flaw in Microsoft Bob: It let you reset the password if you entered the wrong one three times. These are the excep-tions, though. The probability of stumbling on a security flaw randomly is very low, sometimes approaching zero. Explicitly checking for them is much more efficient.

Unfortunately, there is no such thing as a comprehensive security checklist. Those of us who do this kind of thing frequently have devel-oped our own security checklists: lists of attacks and potential vulnerabil-ities that we've either seen in commercial products, read about in academic papers, or thought of on our own. These lists are huge—a cou-ple of years ago I had 759 separate attacks on my list—but they are not comprehensive.

It is easy to test for any given weakness. Some are easier to test for than others. Testing for every weakness on my list is time-consuming, but straightforward. Testing for every known weakness is harder still; it means that I have to keep my list up to date. It takes time, but I can do it. But here's the rub: Testing for all possible weaknesses is impossible.

Note that I didn't say "very hard" or "incredibly difficult." I said "impossible."

Testing for all possible weaknesses means testing for weaknesses that you haven't thought of yet. It means testing for weaknesses that no one has thought of yet: weaknesses that haven't even been invented yet. It's like building a bridge. You might be able to say that the bridge cannot collapse as a result of natural causes. More likely, you will be able list the conditions that cannot be the proximal cause of a collapse. You might even be able to delineate the sorts of terrorist attacks that the bridge can withstand. But you can never say that the bridge will stand in the face of technology that hasn't been invented yet.

Nothing here is meant to imply that this holds true for mass-market software only. This discussion applies equally to security hardware, large proprietary systems, military hardware and software, and everything else. It even applies to security technologies having nothing to do with com-puters. The problems are there regardless.

So what is a system developer to do? Ideally, he has to stop relying on his in-house developers and beta testers. He has to hire security experts to do his security testing. He has to spend a lot of money on this; assume it takes the same level of effort to test the security of a system as it did to design and implement it in the first place.

No one is going to do that, with the exception of the military. And even the military is probably not even going to do that, with the excep-tion of things like nuclear command and control systems.

What companies are going to do is what they've done all along. They're going to release insecure products and fix security problems that are discovered, and published, after the fact. They're going to make outlandish claims and hope nobody calls them on it. They're going to hold cracking contests and other publicity stunts. They'll issue new versions so fast that by the time someone bothers to complete a security analysis, they'll say "but that was three versions ago." But the products will be insecure nonetheless.

DISCOVERING SECURITY FLAWS AFTER THE FACT

Every day, new security flaws are discovered in shipping software products. They're discovered by customers, researchers (academics and hackers), and criminals. How frequently depends on the prominence of the product, the doggedness of the researchers, the complexity of the product, and the quality of the company's own internal security testing. In the case of a popular operating system, it might happen several times per week. In the case of an obscure encryption program that no one's heard of, it might happen once a lifetime.

Anyway, someone finds a security vulnerability. Now what?

There are several things he can do. He can keep quiet and tell no one. He can tell his confidants. He can alert the product vendor. He can just tell his customers, trying to keep the bug obscure so that only his products protect the user. (I've seen companies do this.) Or he can tell the world. (Of course he can always try to commit a crime using the vulnerability, but let's assume that he is an honest bloke.) The practice of telling the world is known as *full disclosure,* and it has become popular over the past several years. And it is the subject of a violent debate.

But first a soupçon of history.

In 1988, after the Morris worm illustrated how susceptible the Inter-net is to attack, the Defense Advanced Research Projects Agency (DARPA) funded a group that was supposed to coordinate security response, increase security awareness, and generally do good things. The group is known as CERT—more formally, the Computer Emergency Response Team—and its response center is in Pittsburgh at Carnegie Mellon University.

Over the years CERT has acted as kind of a clearinghouse for secu-rity vulnerabilities. People are supposed to send vulnerabilities they find to CERT. CERT then verifies that the vulnerability is real, quietly alerts the vendor, and publishes the details (and the fix) once the vendor fixes the vulnerability.

This sounds good in theory, but worked less well in practice. There were three main complaints. First, CERT was slow about confirming vulnerabilities. CERT got a lot of vulnerabilities reported to it, and they had a backlog of vulnerabilities to deal with. Second, the vendors were slow about fixing the vulnerabilities once CERT told them. CERT wouldn't publish until there was a fix, so there was no real urgency to fix anything. And third, CERT was slow about publishing reports even after the fixes were implemented.

The full-disclosure movement was born out of frustration with this process. Internet mailing lists like Bugtraq (begun in 1993) and NT Bug-traq (begun in 1997) became forums for people who believed that quietly alerting the vendor was futile, and the only way to improve security is to publicize bad security. It was a backlash against the academic ivory tower and its secret knowledge. As one hacker wrote: "No more would the details of security problems be limited to closed mailing lists of so-called security experts or detailed in long, overwrought papers from academia. Instead, the information would be made available to the masses to do with as they saw fit."

Today, many researchers publish vulnerabilities they discover on these mailing lists, sometimes accompanied by press releases. The press troll these mailing lists and write about the vulnerabilities, augmented by the usual flurry of factoids, in both the computer and mainstream press. (This is why there have been so many more press stories about computer vulnerabilities over the past few years.) The vendors scramble to patch these vulnerabilities as soon as they are publicized, so they can write their own press releases about how quickly and thoroughly they fixed things. Security is getting better a lot faster because of full disclosure.

At the same time, hackers use these mailing lists to learn about vulnerabilities and write attack programs. Some attacks are complicated, but those that can understand them can write point-and-click programs that allow those who don't to exploit the vulnerability. Those opposing full disclosure argue that publishing vulnerability details does more harm than good by arming the criminal hackers with tools they can use to break into systems. Security is much better served, they counter, by not publishing vulnerabilities in all their gory details.

Full-disclosure proponents retort that this assumes that the researcher who publicizes the vulnerability is always the first one to discover it, which simply isn't true. Sometimes, vulnerabilities have been known by attackers (sometimes passed about quietly in the hacker underground) for months or years before the vendor ever found out. The exploits are didac-tic, they say. The sooner a vulnerability is publicized and fixed, the better it is for everyone.

Muddying the waters is the sobering reality that patching a vulnera-bility does not equal fixing the problem; many system administrators don't implement the patches from the vendors. Companies finesse this, saying things like: "We issued a patch. What else can we do?" In the real world, defective products are often recalled. This never happens in the computer world. So even after the vendor releases the vulnerability fix and the press furor dies down, many systems are still vulnerable.

An example might make this clearer. In April 1999, someone discov-ered a vulnerability in Microsoft Data Access Components that could let an attacker take control of a remote Windows NT system. This vulnera-bility was initially reported on a public mailing list. Although the list mod-erator withheld the details of that risk from the public for more than a week, some hacker reverse engineered the available details to create an exploit based on the vulnerability.

At about the same time, Microsoft issued a patch to prevent attackers from exploiting the vulnerability on users' systems. Microsoft also pub-lished a security bulletin on the topic, as did several other security news outlets.

But Microsoft's patch didn't magically fix the vulnerability. Over Halloween weekend of that same year, hackers used the vulnerability to attack and deface more than 25 NT-based Web sites, all owned by secu-rity administrators who didn't bother (or didn't even know to bother) updating their configurations in the intervening six months.

That's the debate in a nutshell.

Microsoft would never have fixed the vulnerability if the exploit script hadn't existed. In other instances, they have gone so far as to com-pletely ignore the problem, dismiss the vulnerability as "completely theo-retical" and therefore not worth worrying about, or claim the researcher was lying. Microsoft treats security vulnerabilities as public relations prob-lems. When an exploit exists, they do something, but usually not before. So publicizing the vulnerability caused it to be fixed.

Publishing also caused the exploit script to be written, enabling a bunch of criminal hackers to take advantage of the vulnerability (1) dur-ing the window between when the vulnerability was announced and when Microsoft published the patch, and (2) afterward, because many sys-tem administrators didn't implement Microsoft's patch.

Was publishing better, or would it have been better to keep quiet?

Sometimes it depends on the vendor. Most companies react well to attacks against their systems. They acknowledge and fix the problem, post the fix on their Web sites, and everything goes back to normal. Some vendors react less well; the various digital cellular companies responded with all sorts of lies, insults, and misdirection in response to the published breaks of their encryption algorithms. The entertainment industry responded by initiating legal action against the people who exposed the DVD player's lousy security (and the people who subsequently talked about it). Generally, exposed vulnerabilities that can't be fixed easily—it's a lot harder to modify 10 million fielded cellular telephones than it is to post a software fix on the Internet—aggravate companies more.

Sometimes the researcher has no choice. One NSA employee, speak-ing off the record, claimed that his colleagues have discovered several new Internet attacks but have been prohibited from publishing them. Some have been later discovered by other researchers; others remain secret. Sometimes he has a choice, but chooses to remain silent. Steve Bellovin suppressed a paper he wrote on attacks against the DNS system for several years. Bellovin and Cheswick purposely didn't talk about the SYN flood attack in their firewalls book.

Netscape used to offer $1,000 (and a free T-shirt) rewards to anyone who found a security bug in their software. They wrote quite a few checks, except for a 1997 incident when Danish hacker found a security hole and demanded more money. As it turned out, he didn't get his money: His description of the effects of the bug enabled Netscape engi-neers to reproduce and fix it without his help. In 2000, a French researcher figured out how to break the security in the CB (Groupement des Cartes Bancaires) smart card system. Then, depending on whom you believe, he offered his services to Groupement or tried to blackmail them. He was arrested, and eventually received a suspended sentence.

Security is by nature adversarial, even in the ivory towers of academia. Someone proposes a new scheme: an algorithm, a protocol, a technique. Someone else breaks it. A third person repairs it. And so on. It's all part of the fun. But when it comes to fielded systems, it can get a lot trickier. Is the benefit of publicizing an attack worth the increased threat of the enemy learning about it? (In NSA's language, this is known as the *equities issue.*) Why should the company profit from the work of the researcher? Will the company ignore the problem unless the researcher calls the press? Does the researcher even care about the public's reaction? What's the researcher's agenda anyway?

This last question isn't discussed as much as it should be. Publishing a security vulnerability is a publicity attack; the researcher is looking to get his own name in the newspaper by successfully bagging his prey. Some-times the publicizer is a security consultant, or an employee of a company that offers vulnerability assessments or defensive network security prod-ucts. This is especially true if the vulnerability is publicized in a press release; sending something out on PR Newswire or Business Wire is expensive, and no one would do it unless he thought he was getting something in return.

In general, I am in favor of the full-disclosure movement, and think it has done a lot more to increase security than it has to decrease it. The act of writing this book, which can be read by both the good guys and the bad guys, does not cause the insecurities I talk about. Similarly, publiciz-ing a vulnerability doesn't cause it to come into existence. Given that vendors don't bother fixing vulnerabilities that are not published—this is not just a jeremiad against Microsoft, we've seen this from almost every major software company—publicizing is the first step toward closing that vulnerability. Punishing the publicizer feels a lot like shooting the mes-senger; the real blame belongs to the vendor that released software with the vulnerability in the first place.

There are exceptions to this rule.

First, I am opposed to publicity that primarily sows fear. Publishing vulnerabilities for which there's no real evidence is bad. (An example of this is when someone found a variable containing the three letters "NSA" in Microsoft's cryptography API and announced that the National Secu-rity Agency had installed a trap door in Microsoft products, solely on the basis of the variable name.) Publishing security vulnerabilities in critical systems that cannot be easily fixed and whose exploitation will cause seri-ous harm (the air traffic control software, for example) is bad. I believe it is the researchers' responsibility to balance disclosing the vulnerability ver-sus endangering the public.

Second, I believe in giving the vendor advance notice. CERT took this to an extreme, sometimes giving the vendor years to fix the problem. The result is that many vendors didn't take the notifications seriously. But if the researcher tells the vendor that the vulnerability will be published in a month, then the vulnerability announcement can occur at the same time as the patch announcement. This benefits everybody.

And third, I believe that disseminating exploits is often going too far. Writing research papers on vulnerabilities benefits research, and makes us smarter at designing secure systems. Writing demonstration code is often a necessary part of research. Distributing attack tools to the masses, on the other hand, is a bad idea. It serves no good to create attack tools with point-and-click interfaces that any novice hacker can use. They assist criminals. They make networks less secure. They are part of the problem, not part of the solution.

There is a large gray area here between what is good and what is bad. Vulnerability assessment tools can be used both to increase security and to break into systems. Remote administration tools look a lot like Back Ori-fice. If a company like Microsoft lies to the press and denies that a pub-lished vulnerability is real, is it then okay for the researcher to publish an attack script? I try to follow the "be part of the solution, not part of the problem" rule. Full disclosure is part of the solution. Fixing problems and improving network security is part of the solution. I'm willing to live with tools that have both good and bad uses, but I don't like tools that have only bad uses.

There's a quotation etched in stone in the CIA lobby: "And ye shall know the truth, and the truth shall set ye free." (It's from the New Testament: John 8:32.) Those who know the truth are able to use that knowledge to win out over those who do not know it (or who refuse to believe it). Full disclosure gets us closer to the truth than anything else.

OPEN STANDARDS AND OPEN SOURCE SOLUTIONS

In Chapter 7, I talked about the security benefits of public cryptography over proprietary cryptography. Since the only evidence we have that a cryptographic primitive is secure is for many experts to evaluate it over a long period of time, making a cryptographic primitive public is the most cost-effective way of doing that. The exact same reasoning leads any smart security engineer to demand public solutions for anything related to secu-rity, including open source software.

Let's review: Security has nothing to do with functionality. Therefore, no amount of beta testing can ever uncover a security flaw. The only way to have any confidence in the security of a system is over time, through expert evaluation. And the only way to get that expert evaluation is if the details of a system are public.

A good security design has no secrets in its details. In other words, all of the security is in the product itself and its changeable secret: the cryptographic keys, the passwords, the tokens, and so forth. The antithesis is *security by obscurity*: The details of the system are part of the security. If a system is designed with security by obscurity, then that security is delicate. As the designers of the once-proprietary digital cellular security systems, the DVD encryption scheme, and the Firewire interface learned, sooner or later the details will be released. A bad system design is secure as long as the details remain secret, but quickly breaks once they are released. A good system design is secure even if the details are public.

So, given that good security design does not use obscurity, and that so much can be gained by publishing the details of the security system, it makes a lot of sense to do so. And systems that are public are likely to be better scrutinized, and more secure, than systems that are not.

This reasoning applies directly to software. The only way to find security flaws in a piece of code is to evaluate it. This is true for all code, whether it is open source or proprietary. And you can't just have anyone evaluate the code, you need experts in security software evaluating the code. You need them evaluating it multiple times and from different angles, over the course of years. It's possible to hire this kind of expertise, but it is much cheaper and more effective to let the community at large do this. And the best way to facilitate that is to publish the source code.

The counter argument is that publishing source code only gives attackers the information they need to find and exploit vulnerabilities. Keeping the source code secret, they say, denies attackers this intelligence.

Other than croggle at its naïveté, I'm not sure how to respond to this. Making source code public does not increase the number of vulnerabili-ties, only the awareness of them by the general public. Vendors who keep their source code secret are more likely to be sloppy. Vendors who make their source code public are more likely to have their vulnerabilities dis-covered, so they can fix them. Secret software is fragile; it's like steganog-raphy. Publishing source code provides a much more robust security than keeping it secret ever can.

However, open source software does not guarantee security. There are two caveats to keep in mind.

First, simply publishing the code does not automatically mean that people will examine it for security flaws, and it certainly doesn't mean that experts will examine it for security flaws. Researchers found buffer overflows in the MIT code for Kerberos ten years after the code was released. Another open-source package, the Mailman program for managing mail-ing lists, had glaring security problems for over three years . . . until the original author looked at the code again and found them.

Security researchers are fickle and busy people. They do not have the time, nor the inclination, to examine every piece of source code that is published. So while opening up source code is a good thing, it is not a guarantee of security. I could name a dozen open source security libraries that no one has ever heard of, and no one has ever evaluated. On the other hand, the security code in the various open source secure UNIX flavors has been looked at by a lot of crackerjack security engineers.

Second, simply publishing the code does not automatically mean that security problems are fixed promptly when found. There's no reason to believe that a two-year-old piece of open source code has fewer security flaws than a two-year-old piece of proprietary code. If the open source code has been well examined, this is likely to be true. But just because a piece of source code has been open source for several years does not, by itself, mean anything.

I'm a fan of open source, and believe it has the potential to improve security. But software isn't automatically secure because it is open source, just as it isn't automatically insecure because it is proprietary. Others have pointed out that open source code is believed to be more secure, and this unfounded belief causes people to trust open source code more than they should. This is a bad thing.

Also note that this analysis completely sidesteps the relevant question of which process is more likely to produce secure software, by design, in the first place. Open source is a business model first, and a security strat-egy second. Unfortunately, the traditional proprietary software method-ologies are probably more likely to produce high-quality large software. Maybe the best thing for security is to create proprietary software and then, after the fact, turn it into open source (which is what Netscape did with its browser code).

REVERSE ENGINEERING AND THE LAW

In a perverse twist on the full-disclosure and open source movements, some companies have attempted to defend themselves by making it illegal to reverse engineer their software. In the United States, the Digital Millennium Copyright Act (DMCA) criminalizes reverse engineering, and there are similar provisions in the Uniform Computer Information Transactions Act (UCITA)—currently becoming law in several states.

We've already seen some effects of this. The DVD Copy Control Association has loosed a barrage of legal proceedings against those who reverse engineered their DVD security scheme, and against those who wrote public-domain tools that exploit the miserable security. People have been arrested. Mattel successfully sued the hackers who reverse engineered the poor security in CyberPatrol, their surf-blocking software.

This sets a dangerous precedent. The laws don't increase the security of systems, or prevent attackers from finding flaws. What they do is allow product vendors to hide behind lousy security, blaming others for their own ineptitude. It's certainly easier to implement bad security and make it illegal for anyone to notice than it is to implement good security. While these laws have the side effect of helping stem the dissemination of hacked software—both the DVD and Mattel cases are examples—the laws will reduce security in the long run.

CRACKING AND HACKING CONTESTS

You see them all the time: "Company X offers $10,000 to anyone who can break through their firewall/crack their algorithm/make a fraudulent transaction using their protocol/do whatever." These are cracking contests, and they're supposed to show how strong and secure the targets of the contests are. The logic goes something like this: "We offered a prize to break the target, and no one did. This means that the target is secure."

It doesn't.

Contests are a terrible way to demonstrate security. A product (or sys-tem, protocol, or algorithm) that has survived a contest unbroken is not obviously more trustworthy than one that has not been the subject of a contest. Contests generally don't produce useful data. There are four basic reasons why this is so.

One, the contests are generally unfair. Cryptanalysis assumes that the attacker knows everything except the secret. He has access to the algorithms and protocols, the source code, everything. He knows the ciphertext and the plaintext. He may even know something about the key. And a cryptanalytic result can be anything. It can be a complete break: a result that breaks the security in a reasonable amount of time. It can be a theoretical break: a result that doesn't work "operationally," but still shows that the security isn't as good as advertised. It can be anything in between. Most cracking contests have arbitrary rules. They define what the attacker has to work with, and how a successful break looks. Some don't disclose the algorithms.

Computer-security hacking contests are generally no better. They don't disclose how the products are being used, so that you can't tell whether a particular attack is a result of a product failure or an implemen-tation failure. They don't clearly delineate between the various pieces of the system: If the contest is to test a firewall, what about vulnerabilities of the operating system that compromise the firewall?

These tests have arbitrary rules of winning. In 1999, Microsoft set up a Windows 2000 Web server and dared hackers to try and break in. The server soon disappeared from the Internet, only to reappear later with Microsoft claiming a power failure as the reason for the disappearance. (Oddly enough, this power failure only affected the test system, and they seemed to have forgotten to install an uninterruptible power supply.)

Unfair contests aren't new. Back in the mid-1980s, the authors of an encryption algorithm called FEAL issued a contest. They provided a ciphertext file, and offered a prize to the first person to recover the plain-text. Since then, the algorithm has been repeatedly broken by cryptogra-phers. Everyone agrees that the algorithm is fundamentally flawed. Still, no one won the contest.

Two, the analysis is not controlled. Contests are random tests. Do ten people, each working 100 hours to win the contest, count as 1,000 hours of analysis? Or did they all try the same dozen attacks? Are they even competent analysts, or are they just random people who heard about the contest and wanted to try their luck? Just because no one wins a contest doesn't mean the target is secure . . . it just means that no one won.

In 1999, *PC Magazine* set up both a Windows NT and a Linux box, and announced a hacking contest. The Linux box was the first one hacked. Does that mean that Linux is less secure? Of course not; it just means that the people who bothered playing the game broke into the Linux box first.

Three, contest prizes are rarely good incentives. Security analysis is a lot of work. People who are good at it are going to do the work for a vari-ety of reasons—money, prestige, boredom—but trying to win a contest is rarely one of them. Security professionals are much better off analyzing systems where they are being paid for their analysis work, or systems for which they can publish a paper explaining their results.

Just look at the economics. Taken at a conservative $200 an hour for a competent cryptanalyst or computer-security guru, a $10K prize pays for just over a week of work—not enough time to even dig through the code. A $100K prize sounds impressive, but reverse engineering the prod-uct is boring and that still might not be enough time to do a thorough job. A prize of $1 million starts to become interesting, but most companies can't afford to offer that. And the analyst has no guarantee of getting paid: He may not find anything, he may get beaten to the attack and lose out to someone else, or the company might change the rules and not pay. Why should someone donate his time (and good name) to the company's publicity campaign?

And four, contents can never end with a positive security result. If something is broken in a contest, you know that it is insecure. But if something isn't broken in a contest, it doesn't mean that it is secure.

The preceding four reasons are generalizations. There are exceptions, but they are few and far between. The RSA challenges, both their factor-ing challenges and their symmetric brute-force challenges, are fair and good contests. These contests are successful not because the prize money is an incentive to factor numbers or build brute-force cracking machines, but because researchers are already interested in factoring and brute-force cracking. The contests simply provide a spotlight for what was already an interesting endeavor. The AES contest, although more a competition than a cryptanalysis contest, was also fair.

Contests, if implemented correctly, can provide useful information and reward particular areas of research. They can help find flaws and cor-rect them. But they are not useful metrics to judge security. A home-owner can offer $10,000 to the first person who successfully breaks in and steals a book on a certain shelf. If no one does so before the contest ends, that doesn't mean the home is secure. Maybe no one with any burgling ability heard about the contest. Maybe they were too busy doing other things. Maybe they weren't able to break into the home, but they figured out how to forge the real estate title to put the property in their name. Maybe they did break into the home, but took a look around and decided to come back when there was something more valuable than a $10,000 prize at stake. The contest proved nothing.

Cryptanalysis contests are generally nothing more than a publicity tool. Sponsoring a contest, even a fair one, is no guarantee that people will analyze the target. Surviving a contest is no guarantee of no flaws in the target.

EVALUATING AND CHOOSING SECURITY PRODUCTS

It's generally not possible for average people—or the average company, or the average government, for that matter—to create their own security products. Most often they're forced to choose between an array of off-the-shelf solutions and hope for the best. The lessons of this book, that it's practically impossible to design secure products and that most commercial products are insecure, aren't heartening. What can the harried system administrator, charged with securing his embassy's e-mail system or his company's network, do? What about the average citizen, concerned about the security of different electronic commerce systems or the privacy of her personal medical information?

The first question to ask is whether or not it really matters. Or, more exactly, whose security problem is this anyway? I care about my personal privacy. I don't really care about Visa's credit card fraud problems. They limit my liability to $50, and will even waive that if I complain. I do care about the PIN on my ATM card; if someone cleans out my account, it's my problem and not the bank's.

Similarly, some systems matter but are not within my control. I can't control what kind of firewalls and database security measures the IRS uses to protect my tax information, or my medical insurer uses to protect my health records. Maybe I can change insurers, but generally I don't have that kind of freedom. (I suppose that if I were wealthy enough, I could choose banks in better regulatory environments—Switzerland, for exam-ple—but that option is out of reach of most people.) Even if laws demand a certain amount of security—privacy, authentication, anonymity, integrity, whatever—there's no guarantee that those in charge of imple-menting the security measures did a good job. I can't audit my govern-ment's security practices just because I want to make sure they are good. The sad truth is that most security problems are just not under the control of most people.

For the purposes of making this section interesting, let's assume a security system under your control. Moreover, you have a financial liabil-ity for the system's security: You will lose money if the authentication scheme is broken, you will get sued if the privacy protections are breached, and so forth. You have gone through the threat modeling and risk assessment, and have decided that you need a certain type of product. How do you go about choosing one? How do you go about evaluating the options?

The problem with bad security is that it looks exactly the same as good security. I can hold two products up: a pair of VPNs, for example. They have the same capabilities and the same features. They use the same buzzwords: triple-DES, IPsec, and so on. They make the same security claims. One is secure and one is broken. The average user has absolutely no way to tell the difference. A security expert can, but it might take him half a man-year of work to give you a useful opinion. It's just not worth the user's money.

I'm continuously amazed by magazine comparison articles evaluating security products. I saw one on firewalls recently. They tried to compare security: Their labs installed the various firewalls and exposed them to a barrage of 300 attacks. Interesting, yes, but only marginally related to how secure the firewall is, against real-world adversaries, in real-world config-urations. All the article talked about was whether the firewall, as config-ured in the laboratory, could withstand attack X, not whether the firewall increased the security of the network inside. Functional comparisons are easy; security problems are hard. I've seen even scarier reviews, where security products were rated only on the user interface. Presumably the reviewers had to measure *something,* and the user interface was the only thing they could see.

But even if they did rate security, does the rating match to the way you use the product? For example, I don't care how secure you can make a particular operating system. I care how secure it is 90 percent of the time, in real-world situations. I care how secure it is when you buy it, with the default out-of-the-box settings. Or how secure it is after the average sysadmin installs it. That's what matters.

It can be easy to spot products that are obviously bad. Products that make obviously wrong claims—"guaranteed unhackable security," "impossible-to-break encryption"—are almost certainly insecure. Products that make bizarre pseudoscientific claims of amazing new break-throughs in technology (generally you see this applied to encryption technology) are almost certainly snake oil. Other warning signs include appealing to nebulous "security experts," using ludicrous key lengths, bucking conventional wisdom without good reason (in security, a lot of benefit comes from following the crowd), and staging weird security con-tests. In this book I outline a number of good security practices: using known and published cryptography, using public protocols, recognizing the limitations of different technologies. Companies that display igno-rance of these principles in their marketing literature should be immedi-ately suspect. It is possible, of course, that a product that exhibits some of these warning signs is good; it's just not likely. Just remember that there are far fewer geniuses than fools.

But those are the easy ones. Once you've eliminated the products from companies who evidently have no clue what they're doing, it gets a lot harder. All the remaining products are buzzword compliant; they all say the right things. One might be older than the other; does that mean it's more secure? One might have more published vulnerabilities than the other. Does that mean that it is less secure because more vulnerabilities have been found and even more are likely still to be found, or is it more secure because more vulnerabilities have been found and fixed? There's no way to know. (This is why so many security companies use ambu-lance-chasing-like advertising: sowing fear, uncertainty, and doubt.)

Unfortunately, it's not good enough to simply throw up your hands and refuse to make a decision. There are security products out there that claim to protect against threats, and consumers have to choose between them. It makes no sense to not install a firewall because you don't know which is the best. The internal network exists. It has to connect to the outside world. You can either choose a firewall, or not have one at all. There's a saying: "Mediocre security now is better than perfect security never."

While it's true that security testing can only show the presence of flaws and not their absence, it's also true that *nothing* can establish the absence of flaws: not provable security, not formal security models, not detailed attack trees. We're back to where we were when choosing a cryptographic algorithm or protocol: Testing, by many people over the course of time, is how we come to trust a security product.

The only thing left to do is to implement a process that assumes the fallibility of the products, and provides security anyway. I'll return to this point in Chapter 24.

23

The Future of Products

One question to ask is what future technologies are likely to help security products. Surely cryptography is always getting better. Surely we're always building better and better firewalls. Won't that help? The answer is both yes and no. Yes, specific technologies are getting better. But no, the fundamental problems aren't being solved.

Technologies improve. CPUs are much faster than they were ten years ago, making it possible to add cryptography almost everywhere. Digital cell phones, for example, could encrypt everything with strong algorithms without perceptibly reducing performance.

The technologies of computer and network security are getting bet-ter. Today's firewalls are much better than the ones designed ten years ago. Intrusion detection systems are still in their infancy, but they are get-ting better.

And the same is true for almost every technology discussed in Part 2. Tamper-resistance technologies are improving; biometric technologies are improving. We're even getting smarter digital copy protection mech-anisms (the DVD debacle notwithstanding).

What aren't changing are the fundamentals of the technologies and the people using them. Cryptography will always be nothing more than mathematics. Security flaws will always litter software. People will (in general) never be willing to remember passwords longer than a certain length. People will always be vulnerable to social engineering.

It's worse yet. Things are getting more complex, and that complexity more than makes up for improvements in any other area. The future of

353

digital systems is complexity, and complexity is the worst enemy of secu-rity. Security is not getting better; it's getting worse.

SOFTWARE COMPLEXITY AND SECURITY

Digital technology has been an unending series of innovations, unin-tended consequences, and surprises, and there's no reason to believe that will stop anytime soon. But one thing has held constant through it all, and it's that digital systems have gotten more complicated.

We've seen it over the past several years. Microprocessors have got-ten more complex. Operating systems and programs have gotten more complex. (Sometimes for no good reason: There's an entire flight simula-tor hidden in every copy of Microsoft Excel 97.) Computers have gotten more complex. Networks have gotten more complex. There are complex network services, downloadable modules, intelligent agents, and distrib-uted computing. Individual networks have combined, further increasing the complexity. The Internet is probably the most complex machine humanity has ever built. And it's not getting any simpler anytime soon.

The global financial system has gotten more complex. The digital sys-tems in your car, dishwasher, and toaster have gotten more complex. The smart cards in your wallet have gotten more complex, as have the net-works they talk with. The locks on your hotel room doors have gotten more complex, as have your burglar alarms, cell phones, and building environmental control systems. Buckingham Fountain in Chicago is remotely controlled by a computer in Atlanta.

As a consumer, I think this complexity is great. There are more choices, more options, more things I can do. As a security professional, I think it's terrifying. Complexity is the worst enemy of security. This has been true since the beginning of computers, and is likely to be true for the foreseeable future. And as cyberspace continues to get more complex, it will continue to get less secure. There are several reasons why this is true.

The first reason is the number of security bugs. In Chapter 13, I talked about software reliability and how it affects security. Just as the number of performance bugs goes up with complexity, so does the number of secu-rity flaws. This is uniformly true. As the complexity of the software goes up, the number of bugs goes up. And a percentage of these bugs will affect security, and not always in tangible ways.

The second reason is the modularity of complex systems. In Chapter 10, I talked about modular code and the security problems associated with it. Complex systems are necessarily modular; there's no other way to han-dle the complexity than breaking it up into manageable pieces. We could never have made the Internet as complex and interesting as it is today without modularity. But increased modularity means increased security flaws, because security often fails where two modules interact.

The third reason is the interconnectedness of complex systems. Distributed and networked systems are inherently risky. Complexity leads to the coupling of systems, which can lead to butterfly effects (minor prob-lems getting out of hand). We've already seen examples of this as every-thing becomes Internet-aware. For years we knew that Internet applications like sendmail and rlogin had to be secure, but the recent epi-demic of macro viruses shows that Microsoft Word and Excel need to be secure. Java applets not only need to be secure for the uses they are intended for, but they also need to be secure for any other use an attacker might think of. Cross-site scripting exploits subtle interactions among CGI scripts, HTML, frames, Web server software, and cookies. In 2000, a bug in Internet Explorer 5.0 locked up Windows 2000 when it was installed with 128-bit cryptography. Photocopiers, maintenance ports on routers, mass storage units: These can all be made Internet-aware, with the associated security risks. Rogue printer drivers can compromise Win-dows NT; PostScript files can have viruses. Malicious e-mail attachments can tunnel through firewalls. Remember the version of Windows NT that had a C2 security rating, but only if it was unconnected to a network and had no floppy drive? Remember the WebTV virus? How long before someone writes a virus that infects cell phones?

The fourth reason is that the more complex a system is, the more recondite it is. In Chapter 17, I talked about social engineering and the poor interactions between people and security. These problems are exac-erbated by complex systems. The people running the actual system typi-cally do not have a thorough understanding of the system and the security issues involved. And if someone doesn't understand a system, he is more likely to be taken advantage of by someone who does. Complexity not only makes it virtually impossible to create a secure system, it also makes the system extremely hard to manage.

The fifth reason is the difficulty of analysis. In Chapters 18 through 21, I outlined a procedure for designing and analyzing secure systems:

understanding the threat model, defining the protection mechanisms, and designing the security. The more complex a system is, the harder it is to do this kind of analysis. Everything is more tortuous: the specification, the design, the implementation, the use. The attack tree for any complex sys-tem is gargantuan. And, as we've seen again and again in this book, every-thing is relevant to security analysis.

The sixth (and final) reason is the increased testing requirements for complex systems. In Chapter 22, I talked about security and failure test-ing. I argued that the only reasonable way to test the security of a system is to perform security evaluations on it. However, the more complex the system is, the harder a security evaluation becomes. A more complex sys-tem will have more security-related errors in the specification, design, and implementation. And unfortunately, the number of errors and difficulty of the evaluation does not grow in step with the complexity, but in fact grows much faster.

For the sake of simplicity, let's assume the system has ten different set-tings, each with two possible choices. Then, 45 different pairs of choices could interact in unexpected ways, and there are 1,024 different configu-rations altogether. Each possible interaction can lead to a security weak-ness, and should be explicitly tested. Now, assume that the system has 20 different settings. This means 190 different pairs of choices, and about a million different configurations. Thirty different settings means 435 dif-ferent pairs and a billion different configurations. Even slight increases in the complexity of systems means an explosion in the number of different configurations . . . any one of which could hide a security weakness.

The increased number of possible interactions creates more work during the security evaluation. For a system with a moderate number of options, checking all the two-option interactions becomes a huge amount of work. Checking every possible configuration is a Herculean task. Thus, the difficulty of performing security evaluations also grows very rapidly with increasing complexity. The combination of additional (potential) weaknesses and a more difficult security analysis unavoidably results in insecure systems.

In actual systems, the situation is not quite so bad; often options are orthogonal, in that they have no relation to or interaction with each other. (Of course, as systems get more complex you get more couplings.) This occurs, for example, if the options are on different layers in the com-munication system and the layers are separated by a well-defined interface. For this reason, such a separation of a system into relatively indepen-dent modules with clearly defined interfaces is a hallmark of good design. Good modularization can dramatically reduce the effective complexity of a system without the need to eliminate important features. Options within a single module can, of course, still have interactions that need to be analyzed, so the number of options per module should be minimized. Modularization works well when used properly, but most actual systems still include cross-dependencies that allow options in different modules to affect each other.

A more complex system is less secure on all fronts. It contains more weaknesses to start with, its modularity exacerbates those weaknesses, it's harder to test, it's harder to understand, and it's harder to analyze.

It gets worse. This increase in the number of security weaknesses interacts destructively with the weakest-link property of security: The security of the overall system is limited by the security of its weakest link. Any single weakness can destroy the security of the entire system.

Real systems show no signs of becoming less complex. In fact, they are becoming more complex faster and faster. Microsoft Windows is a poster child for this trend to complexity. Windows 3.1, released in 1992, has 3 million lines of code. In 1998, Windows NT 5.0 was estimated to have 20 million lines of code; by the time it was renamed Windows 2000 (in 1999), it had between 35 million and 60 million lines of code, depend-ing on whom you believe. See Table 23.1.

TABLE 23.1 TREND TO COMPLEXITY IN SOURCE CODE

Operating System	Year	Lines of Code
Windows 3.1	1992	3 million
Windows NT	1992	4 million
Windows 95	1995	15 million
Windows NT 4.0	1996	16.5 million
Windows 98	1998	18 million
Windows 2000	2000	35–60 million (estimate)

The size of Windows 2000 is absolutely amazing, and it will have even more security bugs than Windows NT 4.0 and Windows 98 com-bined. In its defense, Microsoft has claimed that it spent 500 people-years to make Windows 2000 reliable. I only reprint this number because it serves to illustrate how inadequate 500 people-years are.

You can also see this complexity increase in the number of system calls an operating system has. The 1971 version of UNIX had 33. By the early 1990s, operating systems had about 150. Windows NT 4.0 SP3 has 3,433. See Table 23.2.

TABLE 23.2 TREND TO COMPLEXITY IN OPERATING SYSTEMS

Operating System	Year	System Calls
UNIX 1ed	1971	33
UNIX 2ed	1979	47
SunOS 4.1	1989	171
4.3 BSD Net 2	1991	136
Sun OS 4.5	1992	219
HP UX 9.05	1994	163
Line 1.2	1996	211
Sun OS 5.6	1997	190
Linux 2.0	1998	229
Windows NT 4.0 SP3	1999	3,433

Early firewalls had to deal with FTP, telnet, SMTP, NNTP, and DNS. That's all. Modern firewalls have to handle hundreds of protocols, and a labyrinthine set of network-access rules. Some neoteric protocols are designed to look like HTTP, in order to "work with" (i.e., avoid) firewalls. And dial-in users didn't used to have to be concerned with firewalls; now home broadband users, on DSL and cable modems, do. Even worse, there's software available that lets home users set themselves up as Web servers. More features, more complexity, more insecurity.

Public-key certificates in X.509 version 1 were specified in 20 lines of ASN.1 notation. X.509 version 3 certificates took about 600 lines. SET certificates: about 3,000 lines.

The entire SET standard is 254 pages long. And that's just the formal protocol specification; there's also a 619-page programmer's guide and a 72-page business description. For various reasons it seems that SET will never see widespread use, but in any case I believe that we are not capable of implementing something this labyrinthine without bugs. The performance bugs will be (for the most part) fixed during beta testing; the security bugs will lie dormant. But they will be there. If the right person finds one, he will announce his findings to the press. If the wrong person finds one, he will use it to attack the online credit card system: maybe to mint money, maybe to create valid-looking but phantom credit card accounts, maybe just to screw with credit card processing and bring the system to its knees.

Complexity is creeping into everything. The 2000 Mercedes 500 has more computing power than a 747-200. My old thermostat had one dial; it was easy to set the temperature. My new thermostat has a digital interface and a programming manual. I guarantee that most people will have no idea how to set it. Thermostats based on Sun Microsystems's "Home Gateway" system come with an Internet connection, so you can conveniently contract with some environmental control company to operate your too-complicated thermostat. Sun is envisioning Internet connections for all your appliances and your door locks. Do you think anyone will have checked the refrigerator software for security bugs? I've talked about modern malicious code, and the interactions among Java, HTML, CGI scripts, and Web browsers. Isn't anyone else worried that the new cell phones, equipped with the Wireless Access Protocol, will be able to download Java applets? It's only a matter of time before we have a cell phone virus.

Computer games used to be simple. Now they're networked. Anyone can go to a Web site and set himself up for multiplayer play. Now anyone else can log in to his machine across the Internet. Presto, he's a server. Mom and Dad might keep some proprietary information on their computer—work secrets, financial information—and suddenly Junior has invited the world to log on. Has anyone checked these games for security bugs? A vulnerability in the automatic update feature in the game Quake3Arena allows an attacker to update *any* file on the user's com-puter. Napster also opens your computer up as a server, and overflow bugs have already been found in the software.

It gets worse. The current generation of video game machines—the Sega Dreamcast, Sony PlayStation 2—comes with features like 56K modems, IP stacks, and Web browsers. Millions of these have been sold. Maybe the browsers and operating systems will be secure; if they are, they'll be the first ever. It'll be big fun; you're playing Sonic over modem with some other kid, and he'll get root on your game machine and win. If it's just a game console: woo hoo! It doesn't matter. But remember that the game companies are going to want you to do all your e-shopping with your game console. There'll be credit card numbers, electronic wallets, who knows what. Welcome to a world where a buffer overflow in Tekken 3 can compromise your financial security.

This kind of function creep happens everywhere: Today's toys are tomorrow's critical applications. Mass-market software is good at adding features and functionality, but much less good at reliability. Despite this, and despite the fact that the software and networks have not been designed for critical applications, they're being used for such anyway. We've become dependent on systems of unknown trustworthiness. Quick-and-dirty "ship the damn thing already" solutions have become part of our critical infrastructure. The Internet is probably the biggest example of this; PC operating systems are another.

Sure, security bugs are found and fixed, but the process is Sisyphean. A software product is released. Over time, security bugs are found and fixed; security is improving. Then the manufacturer comes out with version 2.0—with new code, added features, more complexity—and we're back where we started from. Maybe even worse.

In the military, this is called a "target-rich environment."

The networked systems of the future, necessarily more complex, will be less secure. The technology industry is driven by demand for features, for options, for speed. There are no standards for quality or security, and there is no liability for insecure software. Hence, there is no economic incentive to create high quality. Instead, there is an economic incentive to create the lowest quality the market will bear. And unless customers demand higher quality and better security, this will never change.

I see two alternatives. The first is to slow down, to simplify, and to try to add security. Customers won't demand this—the issues are too com-plex for them to understand—so a consumer advocacy group is required. I can easily imagine an FDA-like organization for the Internet, but in an environment where it can take a decade to approve a new prescription drug, this solution is not economically viable.

The other choice is to recognize that the digital world will be one of ever-expanding features and options, of ever-faster product releases, of ever-increasing complexity, and of ever-decreasing security. If we can accept this reality, we can try to work with it instead of sticking our heads in the sand and denying it.

I repeat: Complexity is the worst enemy of security. Secure systems should be cut to the bone and made as simple as possible. There is no sub-stitute for simplicity. Unfortunately, simplicity goes against everything our digital future stands for.

TECHNOLOGIES TO WATCH

There are technologies on the horizon that may profoundly change secu-rity products, both for good and for bad. Since this isn't supposed to be a book that predicts the future, I will just mention a few of the more inter-esting ones.

> **Cryptographic breakthroughs.** Pretty much no cryptography is based on mathematical proofs; the best that we can say is that we can't break it, and all the other smart people who tried can't break it either. There is always the possibility that someday we will learn new techniques that allow us to break what we can't break today. (There's a saying inside the NSA: "Attacks always get better; they never get worse.") We've seen this in the past, where once-secure algorithms fell to new techniques, and we're likely to see it in the future. Some people even assume that the NSA already knows much of this new mathematics, and is quietly and profitably breaking even our strongest encryption algorithms. I just don't think so; they may have some secret tech-niques, but not many.
>
> **Factoring breakthroughs**. One worry is that all of the different public-key algorithms are fundamentally based on the same two mathematical prob-lems: the problem of factoring large numbers or the discrete logarithm problem. Factoring is getting easier, and it's getting easier faster than anyone ever thought it would. These problems are not mathematically proven to be hard, and it is certainly possible (although mathematicians don't think it likely) that within our lifetime someone will come up with a way to effi-ciently solve these problems. If this happens, we could be in a world where public-key cryptography does not work and parts of this book are a quaint historical oddity. This won't be terrible; authentication infrastructure schemes based on symmetric cryptography can do much of the same job. Even so, I don't think it's likely.
>
> **Quantum computers.** Someday, quantum mechanics may fundamentally change the way computers work. Right now people can barely figure out how to make quantum computers add two 1-bit numbers, but who knows what will happen? Quantum computation techniques will render most pub-lic-key algorithms obsolete (see the preceding item), but will only force us to double the key lengths for symmetric ciphers, hash functions, and MACs.

Tamperproof hardware. A lot of security problems magically get a lot eas-ier if you assume tamperproof hardware and put things inside of it. Break-throughs in tamper-resistance technologies, especially breakthroughs in the cost of different tamper-resistance measures, could make a lot of security problems easier.

Artificial intelligence. Many computer-security countermeasures can be reduced to a simple problem: letting the good stuff in while keeping the bad stuff out. This is the way antivirus software, firewalls, intrusion detection systems, VPNs, credit card antifraud systems, digital cell phone authentica-tion, and a whole lot of other things work. There are two ways to do this. You can be dumb about it—if you see any of these ten thousand bit pat-terns in the file, that means the file has a virus—or smart about it: If the pro-gram starts doing suspicious things to the computer, it's probably a virus and you should investigate further. The latter sounds an awful lot like AI. This kind of thing was tried as an antivirus mechanism, and ended up being less effective than the dumb pattern checkers. Similar ideas are in some intrusion detection products, and it is still unclear whether they do a better job than methodically looking for bit patterns that signify an attack. Still, this could someday be a big deal: If fundamental advances ever occur in the field of AI (a big "if"), it has the potential to revolutionize computer security.

Automatic program checkers. Many security bugs, such as buffer over-flows, are the result of sloppy programming. Good automatic tools that can scan computer code for potential security-related bugs would go a long way to making software more secure. Good language compilers, and good syn-tax checkers, would go a long way to preventing programmers from making security-related mistakes in the first place. We'd have to persuade program-mers to use them, which is probably another matter entirely. (There are a bunch of good tools out there, and almost no one uses them.) And they're never going to catch all problems.

Secure networking infrastructures. The Internet is not secure because security was never designed into the system. People who are working on the Internet-II (and whatever follows that) should be thinking about secu-rity first. These new networks should assume that people will be eavesdrop-ping, that they will attempt to hijack sessions, and that packet headers lie. They should assume mutually distrustful users, and all sorts of business and personal applications. There are a lot of problems that can't be solved with better network protocols, but a lot can.

Traffic analysis. The science of traffic analysis is still in its infancy, and I expect interesting new technologies in the coming decade. Good ways of preventing traffic analysis will go a long way to improving privacy on any public network.

Assurance. Assurance means that a system does what it is supposed to do, and doesn't do anything else. A technology that could somehow provide strong assurance in software would do amazing things for computer security.

Most of these technologies are being worked on today. Practical advances in most of them are far in the future, some of them on the lunatic horizon. I wouldn't discount any of them, though. If there's any-thing the twentieth century has taught us, it's to be parsimonious with the word "impossible."

WILL WE EVER LEARN?

Consider buffer overflow attacks. These were first talked about in the security community as early as the 1960s—time-sharing systems suffered from that problem—and were probably known by the security literati even earlier. Early networked computers in the 1970s had the problem, and it was often used as a point of attack against systems. The Morris worm, in 1988, exploited a buffer overflow in the UNIX fingerd com-mand: a public use of this type of attack. Now, over a decade after Mor-ris and about 35 years after they were first discovered, you'd think the security community would have solved the problem of security vulnera-bilities based on buffer overflows. Think again. In 1998, over two-thirds of all CERT advisories were for vulnerabilities caused by buffer over-flows. During a particularly bad fortnight in 1999, 18 separate security flaws, all caused by buffer overflows, were reported in Windows NT–based applications. During the first-week-of-March stretch I opened this book with, there were three buffer overflows reported. And buffer overflows are just the low-hanging fruit. If we ever manage to eradicate the problem, others—just as bad—will replace them.

Consider encryption algorithms. Proprietary secret algorithms are regularly exposed and then trivially broken. Again and again, the market-place learns that proprietary secret algorithms are a bad idea. But compa-nies and industries continue to choose proprietary algorithms over public, free alternatives.

Or look at fixable problems. One particular security hole in Microsoft's Internet Information Server was used by hackers to steal thou-sands of credit card numbers from a variety of e-commerce sites in early

2000. Microsoft issued a patch that fixed the vulnerability in July 1998, and reissued a warning in July 1999 when it became clear that many users never bothered installing the patch.

Isn't anyone paying attention?

Not really. Or, at least, far fewer people are paying attention than should be. And the enormous need for digital security products necessi-tates experts to design, develop, and implement them. This resultant dearth of experts means that the percentage of people paying attention will get even smaller.

Here is a paradigmatic scenario for the design of most products with security in them. The manager finds some guy who thinks security is cool and designates him as the person in charge of that part of the system. This person might know something about security, or he might not. He might read a book or two on the subject, or he might not. Designing security is fun—cat and mouse, Spy vs. Spy, just like in the movies—so he does. Implementing it is just like implementing anything else in the product: Make it work and meet your deadline. Everything works great—after all, security has nothing to do with functionality—so the manager is happy.

However, due to the general lack of security expertise, the security features are completely ineffective. No one has any reason to believe that this is so, so no one knows.

It's a little better if the product being designed is a security product. It's more likely that the designers will understand security. But they can't do everything. Someone who designed a firewall product once told me about buffer overflows in his code. He said that he did all he could to ensure that there were none—and I believe that he was thorough—but he said that he couldn't control the rest of the programmers on the team. He tried, but he couldn't. Several serious vulnerabilities due to buffer overflows in the code have been discovered, and fixed, over the years. No one believes there aren't more, waiting to be discovered.

I've been constantly amazed by the kinds of things that break security products. I've seen a file encryption product with a user interface that accidentally saves the key in the clear. I've seen VPNs where the tele-phone configuration file accidentally allows untrusted persons to authen-ticate themselves to the server, or where one VPN client can see the files of all other VPN clients. There are a zillion ways to make a product inse-cure, and manufacturers manage to stumble on a lot of those ways again and again.

They don't learn because they don't have to.

Computer security products, like software in general, have an odd product quality model. It's unlike an automobile, a skyscraper, or a box of fried chicken. If you buy a physical product, and get harmed because of a manufacturer's defect, you can sue . . . and you'll win. Car makers can't get away with building cars that explode on impact; lunch counters can't get away with selling strawberry tarts with the odd rat mixed in. It just wouldn't do for building contractors to say things like: "Whoops. There goes another one. But just wait for Skyscraper 1.1; it'll be 100 percent col-lapse-free." These companies are liable for their actions.

Software is different. It is sold without any liability whatsoever. For example, here's the language in the Windows 98 licensing agreement: "In no event shall Manufacturer or its suppliers be liable for any damages whatsoever—arising out of the use or of inability to use this product, even if Manufacturer has been advised of the possibility of such damages."

Your accounts receivable database could crash, taking your company down with it, and you have no claim against the software company. Your word processor could corrupt your entire book manuscript (something I spend way too much time worrying about while writing), wasting years of work, and you have no recourse. Your firewall could turn out to be completely ineffectual, hardly better than having nothing . . . and it's your fault. Microsoft could field Hotmail with a bug that allowed anyone to read the accounts of 40 or so million subscribers, password or no password, and not even bother to apologize.

Software manufacturers don't have to produce a quality product because they face no consequences if they don't. (Actually, product liabil-ity does exist, but it is limited to replacing a physically defective diskette or CD-ROM.) And the effect of this for security products is that manu-facturers don't have to produce products that are actually secure, because no one can sue them if they make a bunch of false claims of security.

The upshot of this is that the marketplace does not reward real secu-rity. Real security is harder, slower, and more expensive to design and implement. The buying public has no way to differentiate real security from bad security. The way to win in this marketplace is to design soft-ware as insecure as you can possibly get away with.

Smart software companies know this, and that reliable software is not cost-effective. According to studies, 90 to 95 percent of all bugs are harm-less; they're never found by users and they don't affect performance. It's much cheaper for a company to release buggy software and fix the 5 to 10 percent of bugs after people complain.

They also know that real security is not cost-effective. They get whacked with a new security vulnerability several times a week. They fix the ones they can, write deceptive press releases about the ones they can't; then they wait for the press furor to die down (which it always does). Then they issue a new version of their software with new features that add all sorts of new insecurities, because users prefer cool features to security.

And users always will. Until companies have some legal incentive to produce secure products, they won't bother.

24

Security Processes

I n 1996, a lab full of researchers cloned a Scottish sheep named Dolly. In the media circus that followed, both *Time* and *Newsweek* opined that since cloning humans is immoral we need laws to prevent it.

They missed the point completely. Someone will attempt to clone humans, somewhere on the planet, law or no law. What we need is to accept this inevitability, and then figure out how to deal with the inevitable.

Computer insecurity is inevitable. Technology can foil most of the casual attackers. Laws can deter, or at least prosecute, most criminals. But attacks will fall through the cracks. Networks will be hacked. Fraud will be committed. Money will be lost. People will die.

Technology alone cannot save us. Products have problems, and they are getting worse. The only thing reasonable to do is to create processes that accept this reality, and allow us to go about our lives the best we can. It's no different from any other aspect of our society. No technological security measures can protect us from terrorist attacks. We use products as best as we can, and implement processes—security checkpoints at bor-ders, intelligence gathering on known terrorist groups, counterterrorist activities, vigilant prosecution—to get as much safety as possible.

PRINCIPLES

Compartmentalize

Smart travelers put some money in their wallet, and the rest of their money in a pouch hidden under their clothing. That way, if they're pick-pocketed, the thief doesn't get everything. Smart espionage or terrorist organizations divide themselves up into small cells; people know others in their own cell, but not those in other cells. That way, if someone is cap-tured or turned in, he can only damage those in his own cell. Compart-mentalization is smart security, because it limits the damage from a successful attack. It's common sense, and there are lots of examples: Users get individual accounts, office doors are locked with different keys, access is based on clearance plus need to know, individual files are encrypted with unique keys. Security is not all-or-nothing; security breaches should not be, either.

A similar precept is the one of *least privilege.* Basically, this means that you should only give someone (or, by extension, some computer processes) the privileges needed to accomplish the task. You see this all the time in everyday life: You have the key to your office, but not every office in the building. Only authorized armored-car delivery people can unlock ATMs and put money inside. Even if you have a particular security clearance, you are only told things that you "need to know."

Computers offer many more examples. Users only have access to the servers they need to do their job. Only the system administrator has the root password to the entire computer; users have individual passwords to their own files. Sometimes group passwords protect shared files; only those who need access to those files know the group password. Certainly it's easier to give everyone the root password, but it's more secure to only give people the privileges they need. The whole UNIX and NT permis-sions system is based on this idea.

Many Internet attacks can be traced to breaking this principle of least privilege. Once an attacker gets access to a user account—by breaking a password or something—he tries a bunch of attacks in order to get root privileges. Many of the attacks against Java try to break out of the Java sandbox—a way of enforcing minimal privileges—and into a mode where the attacker can get privileged status. Attacks against the DVD security system, security systems in some transit farecard systems, and many pay-TV security systems can all be traced to the system having a global secret in each of the consumer devices: a violation of least privilege.

Compartmentalization is also important because a system's security degrades in proportion to its use. The larger, more popular, more integral a computer is, the less secure it is. This is one reason why the Internet—

the most widely used network ever—is so insecure. A computer, powered down, in a locked bomb shelter, and surrounded by guards, is more secure than a Web server is. Compartmentalization moves systems closer to the former.

Secure the Weakest Link

The best place to direct countermeasures is at the weakest link. This is obvious, but again and again I see systems that ignore it. You can't just plant a mile-high pole in front of your castle and hope the enemy runs right into it; you have to look at the whole landscape and build earth-works and a palisade. Similarly, just because you're using an encryption algorithm with a 256-bit key doesn't mean you're secure; the enemy is likely to find some avenue of attack that ignores the encryption algorithm completely.

I'm continually amazed by the number of commercial security sys-tems with gaping holes that the designers never noticed, because they spent all their efforts securing the pieces they understood well. Look at the entire vulnerability landscape, create an attack tree: find the weakest link and secure it. Then worry about the next weakest link. You'll end up with a much more secure system that way.

Use Choke Points

A *choke point* forces users into a narrow channel, one that you can more easily monitor and control. Think of turnstiles at a train station, checkout lanes at a supermarket, and doors to your house. Think of firewalls, routers, login screens, and Web sites that force you go to the homepage first. Think of the single back-end processing system that credit card sys-tems use to detect fraud. Choke points make good security sense.

Choke points only work if there's no way to get around them. One of the common ways to defeat a firewall is to go around it: find an unse-cured dial-up connection into the network, for example. People some-times leave dial-up connections running on their computers. Sometimes routers, large storage devices, and even printers can have unsecured main-tenance dial-up ports. These all allow attackers to bypass choke points.

Networks have more subtle breaches of this type. Sometimes a company has strong network security in place, and for whatever reason links its network to that of another company. That other company may not be as secure. This both violates the choke points, and means that the network has a new weakest link that needs securing.

Provide Defense in Depth

Defense in depth is another universal security principle that applies to com-puters just as it applies to everything else.

A good perimeter defense—door locks and window alarms—is more effective when combined with motion sensors inside the house. Forgery-resistant credit cards work better when combined with online verification and a back-end expert system that looks for suspicious spending patterns. A firewall, combined with an intrusion detection system and strong cryptography protecting the applications, is more secure than a firewall alone.

Throughout this book, I've inculcated you with the principle that security is only as strong as the weakest link, and this seems to go against that philosophy. In reality, it depends on the implementation. Recall the attack trees: a series of OR nodes are only as secure as the weakest, while a series of AND nodes are as strong as their combination. In general, the security of a particular technology depends on the easiest way to break that technology: the weakest link. The security of several security coun-termeasures depends on the easiest way to defeat all those countermea-sures: defense in depth.

For example, a network protected by two firewalls, one each at two different network ingresses, is not defense in depth. This system is only as secure as the weakest link: An attacker can attack either firewall. A net-work protected by two firewalls, one behind the other, is defense in depth: An attacker has to penetrate one firewall and then the other in order to attack the network. (It always amazes me when I see complex networks with different brands of firewalls protecting different access points, or even the same brand of firewall with different configurations. It just makes no sense.)

Fail Securely

Many systems have a property that I call *default to insecure*. This means that if the system fails, then the user reverts to a less-secure backup system. For example, in the United States, VeriFone processes credit card transactions using a live database terminal. When the clerk takes your card and swipes it through the VeriFone terminal, that terminal calls back to a database and confirms that the card is not stolen, that you have available credit, and so forth. Think back to a time when, for whatever reason, the terminal didn't work: it was broken, the phone line was down, whatever. Did the merchant tell you that he wouldn't accept your credit card? Of course not. He pulled out the old system of paper slips and did the transaction manually.

This cavalier approach to security is pervasive, and it's the reason denial-of-service attacks can become invasive attacks. I already talked about attackers tripping burglar alarms until they are turned off. Other attacks are subtler. Few people have the discipline not to communicate if they cannot communicate securely. Even the military, which you think would take this seriously, has screwed this up again and again.

What you want is for systems to *fail securely*; that is, fail in such a way as to be more secure, not less. If an ATM's PIN verification system does not work, it should fail in such a way as to not spit money out the slot. If a firewall crashes, it should crash in such a way as to not let any packets in. If a slot machine fails, it should not send coins pouring into the payout tray.

This same principle is used in safety engineering, and is called *fail-safe*. If a microprocessor in an automobile fails, you don't want it failing by forcing maximum throttle. If a nuclear missile fails, you don't want it fail-ing by launching. Fail-safe is a good design principle.

Leverage Unpredictability

Again and again in this book I rail against *security by obscurity*: proprietary cryptography, closed source code, secret operating systems. Obscurity has its uses: not in products, but in how products are used. I call this *unpre-dictability*.

One of the strengths a defender has against an attacker is knowledge of the terrain. Just as an army doesn't broadcast the location of its tanks, antiaircraft batteries, and battalions to the enemy, there's no reason to broadcast your network topology to everyone that asks. Too many computers respond to any query with their operating system and version number; there's no reason to give out this information. Much better would be a login screen that reads: "Warning: Proprietary Computer. Use of this system constitutes consent to security monitoring. All user activity is logged, including the hostname and IP address." Let attackers wonder if you can trace them.

If you're building a proprietary security system—for an electronic banking application, for example—it's important to use a strong, public, trusted encryption algorithm. Assuming you've chosen one, there's no real benefit in announcing its name.

This is one of the principles behind proxy firewalls; there's no point in broadcasting to the world valid hostnames and usernames. This is also the principle behind bespoke network countermeasures—network bur-glar alarms, honey pots, and similar countermeasures—the network administrator knows how the network works, and what people should be doing. When someone pokes around in a fake dormant account, for example, the administrator should know that it is an attacker. An attacker shouldn't know what types of equipment are running where, what pro-tocols are allowed under what conditions, and what ports are open under what conditions. I am amazed by the number of servers, applications, and protocols that announce themselves to the world: "Hello! I am random-serviceV2.05." Many hacking tools scan for particular versions of software running on particular machines . . . known to have particular vulnerabil-ities. If networks are unpredictable, attackers won't be able to wander around so freely. Without this kind of information, it's much harder to profile a target and determine what attacks to try. It's the difference between walking in a sunny meadow at midday and a briar patch at mid-night.

This unpredictability also extends to response. The Patriot missile actually wasn't that good at knocking incoming Iraqi Scuds out of the sky, but you would never know that from the official Pentagon reports. Just because the United States knew how ineffective its antimissile defenses were, that was no reason to let the enemy know.

Unpredictability is a powerful tool, used by terrorists, authoritarian brainwashers, and those who just want to dominate others. It works well in digital security, too.

Embrace Simplicity

I said this a chapter ago: Complexity is the worst enemy of security. A system is only as secure as the weakest link, so a system with fewer links is easier to secure. Complex systems are less secure than simple ones, guar-anteed. To quote Einstein: "Everything should be as simple as possible, but no simpler."

Folk sayings often disagree, and contrarians could easily reply with: "Don't put all your eggs in one basket." This is true, and the defense in depth principle supports this. But remember that guarding several baskets is harder than guarding one. Where security is concerned, it is smarter to follow Mark Twain's advice in *Pudd'nhead Wilson:* "Put all your eggs in the one basket and—WATCH THAT BASKET."

Enlist the Users

Security is a lot easier if you assume trusted and intelligent users, and a lot harder if you assume malicious and ignorant users. Security measures that aren't understood and agreed to by everyone don't work. Remember that the hardest security problems to solve are the ones that involve people; the easiest are the ones that involve bits. Sure, you have to protect against insider attacks, but for the most part, insiders are your allies. Enlist their support as much as possible and as often as possible.

Assure

What we really need is assurance: assurance that our systems work prop-erly, that they possess the properties we want and only those properties. Most attacks in the real world result in failures of assurance—the products doing something unintended—rather than function: the products failing to do what they were intended to do.

Assurance is hard, something that we don't really know how to provide in complex systems. It involves a structured design process, detailed documentation, and extensive testing. The NSA has detailed assurance projects; similar processes would make our systems more secure as well.

Question

Constantly question security. Question your assumptions. Question your decisions. Question your trust and threat models. Keep looking at your attack trees. Trust no one, especially yourself.

It's amazing what you'll find.

DETECTION AND RESPONSE

Detection is much more important than prevention. As I have said repeatedly in this book, it is fundamentally impossible to prevent attacks. We can do demonstrably better than we are, but everything we know about complex systems tells us that we cannot find and fix every vulnera-bility. There will always be attackers; we just have to catch and punish them.

I'm continuously amazed by how many computer-security vendors are oblivious to this. You never see a door lock with the advertising slogan: "This lock prevents burglaries." But computer-security vendors make those kinds of claims all the time: "Firewalls prevent unauthorized traffic from entering your internal network." "Authentication mechanisms prevent unauthorized people from logging on to your computers." "Encryption prevents unauthorized people from reading files." All of these claims are spurious. Prevention mechanisms are good, but prevention is only one part of a security solution—and the most fragile part. Effective security also includes detection and response.

In the real world, people understand this. Banks don't say: "We have a vault, so we don't need an alarm system." Museums don't fire their night guards because they have door and window locks. In the best of worlds, all prevention buys you is time. In the real world, prevention can often be bypassed completely.

In a few isolated cases, all you can rely on is prevention. Against eavesdropping attacks against a radio circuit, encryption (a prevention countermeasure) has to work perfectly. There's no way to detect the eavesdropping, so no response is possible. Most of the time, though, detection and reaction are possible.

And they provide much more security. Most home-security systems—door locks—can be defeated by a brick through a window. Why are more houses not robbed, then? Why isn't the public clamoring for polycarbonate windows? Because of detection and response.

Detect Attacks

Modern society doesn't prevent crime. It's a myth. If Alice wanted to kill Bob, she could. The police couldn't stop her (unless she were a complete idiot, I suppose). They can't protect every Bob in the world; they don't have the manpower. He's on his own. He can hire a bodyguard if he can afford it, but that doesn't guarantee anything either.

What society does is detect crime after the fact. "Hmm, officer, we just found Bob's bullet-riddled body buried in the end zone at Giants Sta-dium. I think I detect a crime here." We investigate crimes that we have detected, collect evidence that can be used (here's the critical piece) to convince a group of neutral parties that the defendant is guilty, and then punish that person. This punishment process is supposed to act as some kind of back channel into society at large and have a preventive effect on copycat criminals. (Yes, the point of sentencing is to punish the guilty, but the real benefit to society is in preventing more crime.) Even better, the mere threat of the whole process is supposed to have a preventive effect.

And it's a good thing that the whole complicated system works, more or less, because preventing crime is a whole lot harder than detecting crime. In the digital world, the same truth holds. Credit card companies do what they can to prevent criminals from committing fraud, but mostly they rely on detection and, in extreme cases, prosecution. Cell phones can be cloned, but detection mechanisms limit financial losses.

Think of antishoplifting technologies. You can make things hard to steal by bolting them down, attaching cables to them, locking them in glass cases, or putting them behind the counter. This works, but reduces sales because the consumer likes to touch the merchandise. In response, industry has developed many theft detection technologies: tags attached to the merchandise that cause an alarm to sound if they are removed from the building. (There's another interesting antishoplifting technology used for garments: tags attached to the garment that spread colored dye if removed improperly. This is known as *benefit denial*.)

On the Internet, detection can be a lot of work. It's not enough to put up a firewall and be done with it; you need to detect attacks against the network. This means reading, understanding, and interpreting the reams of audit logs that the firewall produces. This means reading, under-standing, and interpreting the reams of audit logs that the routers, servers, and other devices on the networks produce—we have to assume that some attacks will bypass the firewall. These bypass attacks always leave footprints somewhere; detection means finding them.

Good detection means finding intruders in something approaching real time, while they are still engaged in the attack. (Responding after the attack appears in the morning newspapers is often too late.) This necessarily means a real-time monitoring system, whether it is a security-conscious network operations center monitoring your computer network, an AI program looking for anomalous Visa spending patterns or phone calling card usage patterns, or the NORAD ballistic missile track-ing systems. The sooner you detect something, the sooner you can respond.

Analyze Attacks

Simple detection isn't enough; you need to understand the attack and what it means. Traditionally, the military breaks the process down into four generic steps:

> **Detection.** Perceiving that you're under attack. Imagine that three key servers on your network crash at the same time. Is that an attack, or just a problem with your networking software? Or maybe a freak coincidence? If you don't even know you're under attack, it's impossible to respond.
>
> **Localization.** Determining where the attack is. Just because you know that your network is under attack, it doesn't necessarily mean that you know which computers or ports are under attack. You might know that the server crashes are the result of an attack, but have no idea what the attacker has done to cause the crashes, and what other things he is doing.
>
> **Identification.** Determining who the attacker is and where he is working from. Each attacker has different strengths and weaknesses, depending on who he is and where he is working from. An attacker in the United States, for example, can be dealt with differently than an attacker in Moldavia. (This step is more important in a traditional military process than in net-work security.)
>
> **Assessment.** Understanding the attacker, his strategy and tactics, his capabilities, and maybe even his vulnerabilities. This information is critical to determining a suitable response. A script kiddie deserves a very different reaction than an industrial spy. The kiddie is likely to just go away if you respond at all; a more tenacious attacker won't be dissuaded so easily.

Each of these steps is more difficult than the previous one, and each requires more detailed information and expertise of analysis. And often this analysis requires human expertise; a computer alone is going to fail sooner or later (although an automatic program may do a pretty good job most of the time).

Each step also gives you more information about the situation, and the more information you have (and the sooner you have it), the better armed you are. Unfortunately, most network administrators never know they're under attack, or if they do, they don't understand where the attack is coming from. Identification and assessment is particularly hard on the Internet, where it is easy for an attacker to disguise his location.

Speed is of the essence. The faster you can analyze an attack, the faster you can respond.

Respond to Attacks

It's all about response. A burglar alarm that rings and rings, with no one to respond to it, is no better than no burglar alarm at all. It's like a car alarm sounding in a bad neighborhood; no one pays attention. Response is what makes detection valuable.

Sometimes the response is easy: An attacker has stolen someone's phone calling card number, so don't allow that number to be used any-more. Sometimes it's more complicated: "Someone has broken into our electronic commerce server. We can shut the server down, but we'll lose $10 million for every hour we're down. Now what?"

Response is complicated, and often involves intelligent people mak-ing split-second decisions without a lot of time to fully think things through. "He's over the wall and approaching the skylight. What do we do now?" It depends a lot on the situation. You can do nothing. You can shoo him away. You can shoo him away and try to make sure he can never get back. You can shoo him away, try to figure out how he got in, and close the vulnerability.

That's only one half of response: making the problem go away. Equally important is the other half: tracking down and finding the attack-ers. This can be very difficult on some systems; on the Internet an attacker can engage in what is called *connection laundering:* hopping from one com-puter to another to disguise the origin of a connection. The police don't have a lot of investigative time for this, unless lives or a lot of money is involved, and I expect private companies to offer this kind of forensic ser-vice. A company that has a broad view of the entire Internet can even start collecting dossiers on particular attackers.

Prosecution opens a can of worms that is completely foreign to most computer people: the legal system. Identifying an attacker isn't enough;

you also need to be able to prove it in court. There have been cases in England where people have been accused of this or that ATM fraud. The defense attorney requests details about the bank's security mechanisms: the technologies, the audit logs, the procedures . . . everything he can think of. The bank turns to the judge and says: "We can't show them that, it would compromise security." The judge throws out the case. The secu-rity system might be the paragon of detection—it might correctly finger the criminals—but if it can't survive the discovery process, it's not suffi-ciently useful.

When John Walker was put on trial for spying, the NSA carefully weighed the risks of making information about the cryptography devices he compromised public versus keeping the full extent of the damage he caused secret. Good detective security measures need to be able to go through the legal process—including inquisitional cross-examinations with the help of expert witnesses—without losing their effectiveness in the process. And good detection and audit mechanisms should produce audit logs that are admissible in court, and that prove guilt. And it should be possible to make these logs public without revealing any organizational secrets: something called *knowledge partitioning*. A legal discovery process should not result in any security violations.

Be Vigilant

Vigilance means continuous. For detection and response to be effective, it needs to work all the time: 24 hours a day, 365 days a year. Guard services offer 24-hour protection. Security-alarm monitoring companies don't go home for the weekends. It can't be any different in the digital world. You can't put a splash screen on your network connections saying: "Please restrict all hacking attempts to within the hours of nine in the morning and five in the evening, Monday through Friday, excepting holidays." Attackers follow their own schedules.

Attacks often happen at inconvenient times. Criminal hacking follows the academic year. All sorts of commerce fraud—ATMs, credit cards— goes up during the Christmas season as people find themselves in need of money. Smart criminals attack banking systems Friday afternoon, after they've closed for the weekend. In 1973, the Arab countries attacked Israel during Yom Kippur: the holiest Jewish holiday of the year. If some-one were going to launch a serious attack against a system, he would pick an equally inconvenient time.

Vigilance means immediateness. In any aspect of security, timeliness is next to godliness. It's much more useful to detect an attack in progress than a week, or even an hour, after it has happened. It's far better to upgrade your systems in response to a vulnerability now, and not next month. Sometimes reacting late is no better than not reacting at all.

Vigilance also means preparedness. Any detection and response team needs to know what to do when an attack occurs. When Yahoo! got whacked with a denial-of-service attack in 2000, it took them three hours to get back up and running. Partly this was because Yahoo! had never seen this kind of attack before. Whenever processes are automated, and exceptions become rarer, people forget how to react. A monitoring and response service is only useful if it regularly sees attacks, and continuously practices how to respond.

Watch the Watchers

The banking industry has long known that layers of audit provide good security. Managers audit the tellers. Internal auditors audit the managers. Outside auditors reaudit things, but with different methods—effectively auditing the internal auditors. The outside auditors act as a trusted third party does in a protocol; they are paid to audit the system and don't care whether they find problems or not; they get paid regardless. The casino industry likes to call this process "people watching people watching people." Dealers watch the players, floormen watch the dealers, pit bosses watch the floormen, and surveillance watches the pit bosses.

In the banking industry, this process is enhanced by mandatory vaca-tions. The idea is that if someone else is doing your job, then maybe he'll notice evidence of your crimes. One example is Lloyd Benjamin Lewis, an assistant operations office at a large bank. He engaged in large-scale fraud over two years, and during that time never took a single vacation day, sick day, or was late to work. He had to be there, otherwise the fraud might be discovered.

It's not enough to have a good system administration staff who knows all about computer and network security, monitors the systems, and responds to attacks 24 hours a day. Someone has to watch them. It's not just because they might be malicious, although this has happened. (There is a long history of crimes committed by senior bank officials, since they're the ones most likely to get away with it. Someone who was charged with auditing slot machines, making sure they were not rigged by the house, was caught modifying the ROMs so he could force them to produce a jackpot at will.) The real reason is that people are people; they make mis-takes. Even processes have security flaws, and there has to be another process in place to catch and fix them. It's a lesson that has long needed to be applied to cyberspace.

Recover from Attacks

When a French banking smart card was broken in 2000, they had a problem. There was nothing they could do about it except turn the system off or live with the problem. We saw similar problems in the New York City transit farecards, a Canadian cash card, and the DVD encryption scheme. If you spend all your time thinking about preventive countermeasures, you can forget to plan what to do if those countermeasures fail.

Preventive countermeasures fail all the time. Fixing the problem and tracking down the bad guys are part of a good response, but so is recovering from a compromise. This can mean designing systems so that they can be upgraded in the field, and building processes to facilitate that upgrade. This can mean building systems with emergency cryptography, emergency protocols, or emergency procedures. This can mean cutting your losses and returning your system to a secure state.

I've seen too many security systems with the implicit assumption: "If someone breaks the security, we all go home and get new jobs." That just doesn't cut it. Compromise recovery should be a core element of any security system.

COUNTERATTACK

In the war for security, it sometimes looks pretty bleak. Attackers have it easier. They can cheat. They can invent new science and new technology to attack systems already in place. They can use techniques the defenders never considered. They don't have to follow the defender's threat model.

And the odds are in their favor. The defender occupies what Karl von Clausewitz calls "the position of the interior." An attacker needs to find one successful attack: one minor vulnerability that the defender forgot to close. A defender, on the other hand, needs to protect against every possible attack. He needs to think of everything; he can't afford to miss one.

And the defenders are in disarray. They make stupid mistakes. They write buggy code. They don't install security upgrades and patches. They have near theological beliefs about the security of products. They don't understand the real threats against themselves, and they don't protect themselves accordingly.

Time is on the attackers' side. Systems have to go on working, day in and day out. Attackers can sit and wait, looking for a vulnerability, wait-ing for the defenders to drop their guard, changing strategies and tactics to suit the situation.

One solution is to go on the offensive.

We don't fight crime by making our banks 100 percent immune to attack; we fight crime by catching criminals. Luckily, criminals are pretty stupid. And given the kind of salary a good computer security expert can command, computer crime doesn't pay nearly as well.

If the United States was ever the target of a nuclear attack by the USSR, the planned response was to counterattack. Mutual assured destruction is about as surreal as a security defense gets, but it worked.

The Pinkerton Detective Agency was established in 1852. One of their early services was to protect trains from robbers in the American West. Early on, they realized that it was expensive to put a Pinkerton guard on every train. They also realized that robbing a train was a com-plicated operation—you needed an insider who knew the schedule, a dozen or so people, horses, pack animals, and so forth—and that only a few criminals were capable of pulling it off. So they decided to go after the train robbers directly. It didn't matter if the railroad paid for the pur-suit; the Pinkertons did it because catching train robbers made all of their customers more secure.

The Pinkertons were known for not giving up. If you robbed a Pinkerton-protected train, they would hunt you down. And they were serious; there were gun battles against the Hole in the Wall Gang that involved hundreds of Pinkerton men. There's a scene in *Butch Cassidy and the Sundance Kid* where they're being chased after a train robbery by a group who just will not give up. "Who are these guys?" Butch says to Sundance. They were the Pinkertons.

Cyberspace needs a few good counterattacks like this. Today's situation is a kind of Prisoner's Dilemma for hacking: If you don't face consequences for your actions, it's in your best interest to beat the system. Breaking into networks is not a game; it's a crime. Stealing money by hacking a digital payment system is a crime. Distributing copyrighted material on the Internet is a crime. And criminals should be prosecuted. This prosecution does two things. One, the convicted criminal is less likely to do it again. And two, everyone else is less likely to do it in the first place.

This is not meant to be a call for the vigilante-like "justice" we've seen out of the FBI and others over the past decade. In the 1980s, they knew little about computers and networks and computer crimes. Everything was potentially dangerous, and everything was investigated haphaz-ardly. In 1989, when the Macintosh ROM source code was stolen and broadcast on the Internet by the NuPrometheus League, the FBI investi-gated dozens of completely random computer people. In 1990, the Secret Service raided the headquarters of a role-playing game company, Steve Jackson Games, because the company was working on a role-playing game (not even a computer program) that had something to do with "cyberpunks" and hackers, and because they believed an employee, Loyd Blankenship, was a member of the "Legion of Doom" hacker group. In 1999, the DVD Copy Control Association tried to gag 500 Web sites whose only crime was writing about the DVD encryption break. And in 2000, Microsoft tried to force Slashdot to delete postings about its propri-etary extensions to the Kerberos protocol.

This is also not meant to be a call for overreaction, which we saw a lot of in the 1990s. David Smith, the author of the Melissa virus, faces five to ten years in prison. Kevin Mitnick got (and served) almost five years, and was prohibited from using a computer for another three. (All his skills are related to computers, and he has been prohibited from lecturing on the subject. Supposedly, his parole officer suggested he get a job at Arby's.) Kevin Poulson received almost the same sentence. The Chinese government sentenced a hacker to death for hacking a bank computer and stealing $87,000. (To be fair, all bank robbers get the death penalty in China.) I am reminded that in the American West in the 1800s, horse thieving was often punished by hanging. This is because the society wanted to send a clear message that stealing horses was not to be tolerated. Various European governments sent a similar message in the 1970s when they started gunning terrorists down in the streets. The message was a very clear: "We're not playing games anymore." Some of the overreactions we're seeing in hacker prosecution reflect this same sort of moral panic.

This is also not meant as a call to extinguish legitimate researchers or hackers, full disclosure mailing lists, or the right to evaluate security prod-ucts. In the United States, laws have been passed that prohibit reverse engineering of copy protection systems. The entertainment industry lob-bied hard for these draconian laws, using them in an attempt to hide their incompetent security countermeasures. No other industry tries to pro-hibit someone who purchases a product from taking it apart to see how it works. No other industry tries to prevent *Consumer Reports*–style evalua-tions of its products' effectiveness. Shooting the messenger is simply another overreaction to the situation.

What this is a call for is an increase in prosecution of people who engage in criminal activity and for the issuance of fair sentences. There's a pervasive mentality of: "If I just stay still and don't make any noise, no one will bother me." Companies are reluctant to prosecute computer crimi-nals because they fear retaliation. The reality is that until we prosecute the criminals, they will continue to disseminate attack tools and break into computer networks. Once we start prosecuting criminals, hacking into other people's networks will be much less cool. This isn't a perfect solu-tion—hacking tools are likely to go underground—but it will make a dif-ference. There were two positive effects from the terrorist crackdown of the 1970s: The real terrorists trod a lot more carefully, and all the wannabes took off their armbands.

MANAGE RISK

There's no such thing as perfect security, but that's not necessarily a prob-lem. In the United States alone, the credit card industry loses $10 billion to fraud per year; neither Visa nor MasterCard are showing any signs of going out of business. Shoplifting estimates in the United States are cur-rently at $10 to $26 billion per year; but rarely is *shrinkage* (as it is called) the cause when a store closes its doors. Recently, I needed to notarize a document; that is about the lamest security protocol I've seen in a long time. Still, it works fine for what it is.

After you've identified a risk, you can do one of three things with it: You can accept it, you can reduce it, or you can insure yourself against it.

Security does not have to be perfect, but the risks have to be manageable. The credit card industry understands this. They know the losses due to fraud. They also know that losses from phone credit card transactions are about five times the losses from face-to-face transactions (when the card is present), and that losses from Internet transactions are about twice again that amount. (Much of the cost of card-not-present fraud is borne by the merchants, who have little or no recourse when they are stuck with the bill.) They're pushing Internet alternatives like SET precisely because the risks are getting worse.

A closed system like this is an exception. My primary fear about cyberspace is that people don't understand the risks, and they are putting too much faith in technology's ability to obviate them. Compared to the physical world, cyberspace is both exactly the same and very different (see Chapter 2). And products alone cannot solve security problems.

The digital security industry is in desperate need of perceptual shift. Countermeasures are sold as prophylactics: ways to counter threats. Good encryption prevents eavesdropping. A good firewall prevents network attacks. PKI is sold as trust management, so you can avoid mistakenly trusting people you really don't. And so on.

This paradigm is better suited to national security than to the commercial world. Business is about taking risks, which is why in the real world much more focus is put on detection and reaction than on prevention. Web sites don't need unhackable passwords, they just need them strong enough to prevent attacks most of the time. The credit card industry doesn't need foolproof smart cards; they just need them strong enough to limit attacks so that the detection and response mechanisms can kick in. (It's actually worth noting that the credit card industry has built a multi-billion-dollar business based on a very insecure combination of magnetic stripe cards and merchant-run terminals.)

Once you start thinking of security this way, everything else falls into place. If security is about avoiding threats, then it is a cost center. Security has to be justified, and a central IT department approves security budgets. If security is about managing risk, it becomes a way to create revenue. If a company can figure out how to manage the risk of putting their order-ing system online, then they can grab more market share. If a credit card company can figure out how to manage the risk of a certain class of customers, then they can sell more credit cards. All business is risk, and those who are better at managing that risk are more profitable.

Security is old, older than computers. And the old-guard security industry thinks of countermeasures as ways to manage risk. This distinc-tion is enormous. Avoiding threats is black and white: Either you avoid the threat or you don't. Managing risk is continuous: You either accept it, reduce it, or insure against it.

A secure computer is one you've insured.

I believe that insurance is the future of digital security. You can buy insurance against almost any other security risk: theft, vandalism, rogue employees shooting the executive team, or whatever. Why not digital security risks?

It's a good question, and one that the big insurance companies have not ignored. Every one of them is working on insurance for computer-security risks: insurance for corporate intranets, insurance against denial-of-service attacks, insurance against Web site defacement, whatever. This is hard to do correctly, since no one knows what the risks are, but there's so much demand that the insurance companies aren't waiting.

A standard joke in insurance circles goes something like this: A com-pany goes to an insurance company, trying to get some bizarre risk insured. The insurance company asks a series of questions:

> "How big is the potential
> loss?" "We don't know."
> "How likely is a loss to
> occur?" "We don't know."
> "How much is your company
> worth?" "This much."
> "That's the premium; send it in."

Right now, insurance companies are offering antihacking insurance, but I don't believe that they fully understand the risks. Most of the policies are complicated and unwieldy, and contain so many provisions, that I won-der if they'll ever pay off. The point of standardizing security processes is that the risks can be quantified. If a thousand companies use the same security countermeasures, an insurance company can amortize the risks and write policies. This is how ADT Security Services works. Companies don't buy the service because it makes their warehouses more secure; they buy it because they can get a better deal on their insurance.

Eventually there will be two types of network insurance. The first type is the obvious one: Someone breaks into your network and causes damage, and you want the insurance company to compensate you for your loss. But the second type is even more important: Someone breaks into your network and wreaks havoc with your customers, their proprietary information, and their reputations. The third-party liability can be huge. Not only is it a breach of fiduciary responsibility, but the resulting lawsuits could easily exceed the net worth of the attacked company. A warranty-type of insurance to deal with this kind of threat is critical.

Risk management is the future of digital security. Whoever learns how to best manage risk is the one who will win. Insurance is one critical component of this. Technical solutions to mitigate risk to the point where it is insurable is another.

OUTSOURCING SECURITY PROCESSES

Security processes are a way of mitigating the risks. Network security products will have flaws; a process is necessary both to catch attackers exploiting those flaws, and fixing the flaws once they become known. Insider attacks will occur; a process is necessary to detect the attack, repair the damage, and prosecute the attacker. Large systemwide flaws will com-promise entire products and services (think cell phones, think DVD); a process is necessary to recover from the compromise and stay in business. Counterintelligence is the only way to stay abreast of what's really going on. Insurance will handle the residual risk.

None of this is easy, and it all requires experts. And as more and more aspects of our lives move into cyberspace, the demand for cyberspace security (and hence the demand for these experts) increases. The only workable solution is to leverage these experts as much as possible. Out-sourcing is the only way to do this efficiently.

Think about a security-monitoring center for a large network. It takes five trained security analysts to man a single 24x7 seat; a concerted attack can require the attention of half a dozen analysts. A single organization can't afford to hire all those people for the few events they're needed; an outsourced service can deploy those people when needed. An outsourced service can train those analysts, both in the classroom and through experience. An outsourced service can actively test new security countermeasures, analyze new intrusion tools, and stay abreast of hacking techniques and product vulnerabilities. And an outsourced service can see large swaths of the Internet, and not just one organization's network.

In the near term I see the rise of a variety of cyberspace outsourced security services, similar to what we see in the physical world from private security guard companies like Allied Security and alarm service companies like ADT. There's too much specialized knowledge required to secure cyberspace; only a specialized company can provide it. My consulting company, Counterpane Systems, offered outsourced cryptography and security design and analysis. Other companies are offering risk assess-ments, policy development, installation, testing, update management, and so forth.

We're also seeing a more intimate service: Managed Security Moni-toring. Someone has to monitor security products in real time and respond to events as they occur. They (a single person won't be there 24 hours) have to be versed in attackers and their tools. They have to be able to maintain the security products in the face of the ever-changing net-works and ever-changing services running on those networks. Compa-nies just can't do this for themselves. They're in the business of making cars, selling books, or doing whatever, not of securing their networks. Just as they outsourced the management of their networks to an ISP and the hosting of their Web sites to an ASP (Application Service Provider), they will outsource the security of their network to a company that specializes in that. (Of course there will always be specialized networks—banking, cellular telephone, credit card— that require proprietary systems, and there will be security consultants that specialize in that, too.) This is what my new company, Counterpane Internet Security, Inc., does.

This is the normal evolution of security services. No one hires their own guards; they outsource. No one hires their own security auditors; they outsource. Even something as mundane as document shredding is best outsourced to a company that specializes in that sort of thing.

Aside from access to expertise and availability, other benefits of out-sourcing come from the aggregation of security expertise. These out-sourced security companies will be able to engage in active intelligence gathering among hackers to learn about new attacks, and potentially even counterintelligence activities to stop criminals. They can spot patterns across multiple customers. And they will be able to respond to attacks across a variety of customers: They could see an attack in New Delhi and protect their clients in New York.

In the real world, organizations outsource security. No company directly hires its own security guards; everyone uses a guard company. Banks outsource cash transport to armored car companies. Companies hire outside auditors to secure their business practices. Computer and net-work security is no different. It's complex, important, and distasteful. It requires vigilance. In the digital world, outsourced services are the only ones that can supply that vigilance.

25

Conclusion

Mark Loizeaux is president of Controlled Demolitions; he blows up buildings for a living. Complaining about the inep-titude of modern terrorists, he's quoted in the July 1997 *Harper's Magazine* as saying: "We could drop every bridge in the United States in a couple of days. . . . I could drive a truck on the Verrazano Nar-rows Bridge and have a dirt bike on the back, drop that bridge, and I would get away. They would never stop me."

As technology becomes more complicated, society's experts become more specialized. And in almost every area, those with the expertise to build society's infrastructure also have the expertise to destroy it.

Ask any doctor how to poison someone untraceably, and he can tell you. Ask someone who works in aircraft maintenance how to drop a 747 out of the sky without getting caught, and he'll know. Now ask any Internet security professional how to take down the Internet, perma-nently. I've heard about half a dozen different ways, and I know I haven't exhausted the possibilities.

The knowledge is there; the systems are vulnerable. All it takes is someone with just the right combination of skill and morals. Sometimes it doesn't even take that much skill. Timothy McVeigh did quite a num-ber on the Oklahoma City federal building, even though his banausic use of explosives probably disgusted a professional like Loizeaux. Dr. Harold Shipman murdered possibly as many as 150 of his patients, using artless techniques like injecting them with morphine.

At first glance cyberspace is no different from any other piece of our

389

society's infrastructure: fragile and vulnerable. But as I argued in Chapter 2, the nature of the attacks is very different. McVeigh had to acquire the knowledge, go to a private farm and practice, rent the truck, fill it with explosives, drive to the federal building, set the fuse, and get away. Dr. Shipman had to build a medical practice and meet his patients; our hypo-thetical aircraft maintainer had to work on the planes. They all had to get close to their target, put themselves at risk, get in, get away, make mis-takes. And they had to know what they were doing.

Or think of nuclear proliferation. When the knowledge for manufac-turing nuclear bombs became accessible by the public, there was still no large-scale proliferation of nuclear munitions. Why? Because the knowl-edge about how wasn't the critical barrier, it was the vast resources and unwieldy engineering programs that only a handful of countries could assemble.

Cyberspace is different. You can be elsewhere, far away from the site you are attacking. You can have no skill, nothing more than a software package you downloaded from some Web site somewhere. And you don't even have to put yourself at risk. An ethical hacker could describe a vulnerability on the Internet, a criminal hacker with fewer ethics could write an exploit that demonstrates the vulnerability, and then someone with no skill or ethics could use it to break into computers. A Philippine student could write a worm that infects ten million computers, and costs $10 billion in damage, time, and lost productivity. Or maybe there's a Web site in some badly policed Third World country that includes a Java application: "Click here to bring down the Internet." It's not a pretty thought.

In the late nineteenth century, French sociologist Emile Durkheim postulated that anomie led people to become criminals. You can extend his arguments to the hacker psychology we're seeing now: No one is con-nected to anyone else, people feel anonymous behind their handles, and there are no repercussions to actions; this leads some people to do antiso-cial things. The miasma of the Internet virtually guarantees it.

Technology alone cannot prevent this, just as it could not prevent McVeigh or Shipman. Both of them were captured (and others were dis-suaded) by security processes: detection and response. (In the case of Ship-man, the detection and response processes were egregious, and he got away with his massacre for decades.) Forensics techniques figured out what happened, investigative techniques figured out who did it, and laws punished the guilty.

There are no technical solutions for social problems. Laws are vital for security.

If someone invented the unpickable door and window lock or the perfect burglar alarm system, no one would turn around and say: "We don't need police or those obsolete breaking and entry laws." If the his-tory of criminal activity has shown anything, it is the limits of the tech-nology. We need guards to watch the products and police to investigate crimes. We need laws to prosecute people who engage in electronic com-merce fraud, computer trespassing, and theft, or people who write the tools that facilitate these crimes. We can deploy the best technology we can in order to prevent them from doing it in the first place. We can deploy the best technology we can in order to detect their crime after the fact. But we are going to have to rely on guards to catch them and the judicial system to convict them. We can make it as hard as possible for a marketing research firm to illegally collect data on people, but we need laws to prosecute the infractions.

In short, we need to ensure that people put themselves at risk when committing crimes in cyberspace.

We also need to learn from our mistakes.

When a DC-10 falls out of the sky, everyone knows it. There are investigations and reports, and eventually people learn from these acci-dents. You can go to the Air Safety Reporting System and read the detailed reports of tens of thousands of accidents and near-accidents since 1975.

Security debacles are different; there's often no fireball and no imme-diate repercussions. Most successful attacks—against banks, against corpo-rations, against governments—go unmentioned in the media. Some of them even go unnoticed by the victims. We know all about the metal-lurgy of MD-80 jackscrew gimbal nuts, but little about how attackers have been stealing credit card numbers off Web sites. It's like the Soviet Union's Aeroflot; officially there were never any crashes, but everyone knew that occasionally planes would mysteriously never reach their desti-nations.

And those that go public are not rewarded. When Citibank lost $12 million to a Russian hacker in 1995, it announced that the bank had been hacked into and instituted new and more profound security measures to prevent such attacks from occurring in the future. Even so, millions of dollars were withdrawn by people who believed their funds were vulner-able immediately after Citibank's announcement. Ultimately Citibank recovered, but the lesson to Citibank was clear and unambiguous: "Don't publicize."

We need to publicize attacks. We need to publicly understand why systems fail. We need to share information about security breaches: causes, vulnerabilities, effects, methodologies. Secrecy only aids the attackers.

The myopic view of those who seek to ban reverse engineering just makes things worse. Why should people who buy software be prohibited from figuring out how it works, unlike purchasers of, for example, auto-mobiles? Why should software be exempt from *Consumer Reports*–style analysis and testing? Again, secrecy only aids the attackers.

And we need real product liabilities. This one seems obvious: Ven-dors won't produce secure software until it is in their best interest to do so.

The blend of no liabilities/no reverse engineering is particularly dam-aging. If researchers are prohibited from analyzing product security, how does it make sense to shield product vendors from liability? And if ven-dors have no liability for producing lousy products, how can it be illegal to point the flaws out?

Throughout this book I argued that security technologies have their limitations. I do not mean to imply that they're useless. Countermeasures like cryptography, tamper resistance, and intrusion detection make a sys-tem more secure than otherwise. The technologies stop the script kiddies, the ankle biters, the desultory attackers who don't really know what they're doing. But they're like the X-ray machines and metal detectors at airports: They do nothing to stop professionals, but they keep all the ama-teurs from hijacking planes.

The average person cannot tell good security from bad security. It works the same. It costs the same. (Bad security might even look better and cost less; a company that doesn't worry too much about security can devote more engineering resources to nifty features.) The advertising is the same; the product literature is the same. It's not different until you look under the hood: examine the source code, pick apart the hardware. And then only if you're an expert. The average person still won't be able to tell a quality product from snake oil.

The world is filled with specialties that are critical to public safety and security, and yet are beyond the comprehension of the general popula-tion. People can't tell a safe airline from an unsafe airline—that is, until one airline's 737s start plowing into mountainsides—yet 1.6 million peo-ple in the United States fly every day. People can't possibly differentiate between a quality drug and a worthless one, yet the U.S. market for pre-scription drugs is $60 billion per year. People ride roller coasters, trust their money to bizarre financial derivatives, and eat processed meats—all without really worrying if they're safe.

Commerce works the same way. When was the last time you per-sonally checked the accuracy of a gas station's pumps, or a taxicab's meter, or the weight and volume information on packaged foods? When was the last time you went into a building's office and demanded to see the cur-rent elevator inspection certificate? Or examined a pharmacist's license?

We have often relied on the government to step in as a consumer advocate in areas where most people don't have the skill or expertise to properly assess the risk and make intelligent buying decisions. The FAA regulates aircraft safety; the DOT regulates automobile safety. States reg-ulate weights and measures at merchants. You can't expect a family on its way to Walt Disney World to make an intelligent decision about whether their particular aircraft is safe to fly, whether their rental car is safe to drive, or whether their hotel's second floor balcony will drop into the atrium below. You can argue about whether or not the government does a good job at this role—since voters don't understand how to evaluate risks, they don't reward government for good risk evaluation—but it is not unrea-sonable to give them this role.

But while an FDA for Internet security and reliability is worth con-sidering, government regulation's chilling effect would probably take away everything that makes the Internet what it is. Regulation is often misdirected (how much money has been spent making sure that airplane seat cushions float, and how many people have successfully paddled away from a crash as a result?) and slow. It took three and a half years to approve Interleukin-2; that's forever in the world of the Internet. On the other hand, the FDA's slowness has been a good thing at times: It's why the United States didn't have a thalidomide disaster on the scale of Britain's. And why Laetrile was never approved for sale in the U.S. market.

Also possible is an Underwriters Laboratory model for cyberspace security. Underwriters Laboratory is a private lab that tests and certifies electrical equipment. (They also provide ratings for safes.) *Consumer Reports* does a similar service for other products. A private company can do the same for computer and network security, but the costs quickly become exorbitant. And new laws in the United States are moving in the opposite direction, making it illegal for companies and individuals to eval-uate the security of products.

Still another model is licensing, like Medical Doctors and Registered Nurses. Engineers who are certified and have liability insurance can put "PE" after their name. But certifications are local, and the Internet is global. And still there is no guarantee.

All this seems to leave us in a quandary. We need technological solutions, but they're not perfect. We need experts to build, configure, and manage these technological solutions, but there aren't enough experts to go around. We need strong laws to prosecute criminals and a willingness to do so, but most companies who are attacked don't want to go public.

In Chapter 24, I argued that the only way to maintain security in the face of the technological limitations is to build security processes. And that these security processes are not reasonable to build inside an organization, and will most likely be outsourced to cyberspace security professionals. This seems to be the only way out of the previous paragraph's bind as well.

Assuming you can trust the outsourcing organization.

In my first book, *Applied Cryptography,* I wrote: "Encryption is too important to be left solely to the government." I still believe that, but in a more general sense. Security is too important to be left solely to any organization. And it is too personal to be left to an arbitrary organization.

Trust is personal. One person might trust the government completely, while another might not trust the government at all. Different people might trust different governments. Some people might trust dif-ferent corporations, but no governments. It is impossible to design a secu-rity system (product or process) that is devoid of trust; even the person who writes his own security software has to trust his compiler and com-puter.

Unfortunately, most organizations don't realize whom they trust. Some might blindly trust companies for no good reason. (Witness the blind faith some people have in a particular operating system, or firewall manufacturer, or encryption algorithm.) Others might blindly trust their employees. (I've heard it said that the real question is not how much your firewall costs, but how much it costs to buy your sysadmin.)

Given that security is all about limiting risk, organizations need to trust entities that limit their risk. This means entities that come with insur-ance. Trusted entities will also have things like a proven track record, a good reputation, and independent certifications and audits. None of this counts as proof, but all of it counts as evidence.

The decision is not whether to trust an organization, but which organization to trust. A company's own MIS department is probably less trustworthy than an outsourced organization that takes security seriously.

Security is not a product; it's a process. You can't just add it to a sys-tem after the fact. It is vital to understand the real threats to a system, design a security policy commensurate with those threats, and build in appropriate security countermeasures from the beginning. Remember that perfect solutions are not required, but systems that can be completely broken are unacceptable. And good security processes are essential to make products work.

It is prudent to prepare for the worst. Attacks and attackers always get better, and systems fielded today could be in place 20 years from now. The real lesson of Y2K was the amount of ancient computer code out there: code that was updated for Y2K compliance rather than replaced. We're still stuck with mistakes made in analog cellular systems decades ago, and digital cellular systems years ago. We're still stuck with an inse-cure Internet, and insecure password-protected systems.

But by the same token, we're still stuck with insecure door locks, assailable financial systems, and an imperfect legal system. None of this has caused the downfall of civilization yet, and it is unlikely to. And neither will our digital security systems, if we refocus on the processes instead of the technologies.

Afterword

I started writing this book in 1997; it was originally due to the publisher by April 1998. I eventually delivered it in April 2000, two years late. I have never before missed a publication deadline: books, arti-cles, or essays. I pride myself on timeliness: A piece of writing is finished when it's due, not when it's done.

This book was different. I got two-thirds of the way through the book without giving the reader any hope at all. And it was about then I realized that I didn't have the hope to give. I had reached the limitations of what I thought security technology could do. I had to hide the manuscript away for over a year; it was too depressing to work on.

During the early months of 1999, I also became disillusioned by my consulting practice. Counterpane Systems had been providing cryptogra-phy and computer-security consulting for several years, and business was booming. Most of our work was design and analysis. A company would come to us with a security problem, and we would design a system that was secure given the threats. Or a company would come to us with an already designed system that purported to be secure against a list of threats, and we would poke holes in the solution and then fix them. We could invoice as many hours as we could stay awake. The only problem was that our beautiful designs were being broken in the real world. Beautiful cryptography was regularly compromised through bad implementations. Carefully tested implementations were being broken through human errors. We would do all this work, and systems were still insecure.

I came to security from cryptography, and thought of the problem in a military-like fashion. Most writings about security come from this perspective, and it can be summed up pretty easily: Security threats are to be avoided using preventive countermeasures.

This is how encryption works. The threat is eavesdropping, and encryption provides the prophylactic. This could all be explained with block diagrams. Alice is communicating with Bob; both are identified by boxes, and there is a line between them signifying the communication. Eve is the eavesdropper; she also is a box and has a dotted line attached to the communications line. She is able to intercept the communication. The *only* way to prevent Eve from learning what Alice and Bob are talking about is through a preventive countermeasure: encryption. There's no detection. There's no response. There's no risk management; you have to avoid the threat.

For decades we have used this approach to computer security. We draw boxes around the different players and lines between them. We define different attackers—eavesdroppers, impersonators, thieves— and their capabilities. We use preventive countermeasures like encryption and access control to avoid different threats. If we can avoid the threats, we've won. If we can't, we've lost.

Imagine my surprise when I learned that the world doesn't work this way. I had my epiphany in April 1999: that security was about risk management, that the process of security was paramount, that detection and response was the real way to improve security, and that outsourcing was the only way to make this happen effectively. It suddenly all made sense. So I rewrote this book and reformed my company. Counterpane Systems is now Counterpane Internet Security, Inc. We provide Managed Security Monitoring services—detection and response—for networks.

In the world of Alice and Bob and Eve, that answer made no sense. When the model was invented, communication was over radio or long wires. Detection isn't possible. Response isn't possible. But in today's electronic world, it's a lot more complicated. An attacker doesn't passively monitor a communication. He breaks into a firewall. He tries to steal money using a forged smart card. He manipulates a digital network. Today's world is much more like the physical world, with all its potential for rich interaction.

And it's not all or nothing. If Eve could eavesdrop, she could eavesdrop on everything. If she could not eavesdrop, she could not eavesdrop on anything. Today's electronic world is more complicated. Someone could steal some money, but not a lot. A particular counterfeiter might want to make a few copies of a DVD, but not ten thousand. An attacker might break into a network and poke around for ten minutes, then be discovered and shut out. Just like in the real world.

And in the real world, security threats are everywhere. They're not things to be avoided, they're opportunities to make money. The prize doesn't go to the company that best avoids the threats, it goes to the company that best manages the risks. (Just look at the credit card industry.)

At Counterpane Internet Security, we believe that computers alone cannot defend against a human attacker, so our service is centered around trained security analysts. Probes on customer networks collect information from a variety of devices—security and networking—and sift through them looking for footprints of attacks. Then we forward anything suspicious to trained analysts. These analysts know about attacks, can separate real attacks from false positives, and know how to respond.

I've realized that the fundamental problems in security are no longer about technology; they're about how to use the technology. There's no way to turn what we do into a product. At Counterpane, we've built a human–computer cyborg. People are critical in every other aspect of security; we believe they're a critical component of computer security as well.

So, if this book seems a little self-serving, that's why. Both the book and the new company grew from the same epiphany, that expert human detection and response provides the best possible security. The book tracks my thinking in reforming my company, and explains the service that we offer.

You can learn more about us at www.counterpane.com. Thanks for reading.

Resources

The ideas in this book have been heavily influenced by the ideas and writings of others. I deliberately did not disrupt the flow of text with footnotes or citations. What follows is a list of some of my more useful sources.

All URLs are guaranteed accurate as of 1 July 2000. Some Internet pundits have decried the Web as useless for scholarly archives, claiming that URLs move or disappear regularly. Consider this list to be an ongo-ing experiment to prove or disprove that thesis.

Ross Anderson's writing are always interesting and worth reading. His Web site is www.cl.cam.ac.uk/users/rja14/. Look for his new book, coming out next year: *Security Engineering: A Comprehensive Guide to Building Dependable Distributed Systems* (John Wiley & Sons, 2001).

Dorothy Denning has written about cryptography, computer and database security, and (more recently) information warfare. I used her most recent book, *Information Warfare and Security* (Addison-Wesley, 1999), as well has her classic *Cryptography and Data Security* (Addison-Wes-ley, 1982).

Whit Diffie's writings and speeches have affected my thinking. I recommend the book he co-wrote with Susan Landau: *Privacy on the Line* (MIT Press, 1998).

Carl Ellison has continued to write common-sense essays and papers on public-key infrastructure. Much of his writing can be found on his Web site, world.std.com/~cme/.

Ed Felton has spoken on the insecurities inherent in software modu-larity, and on Java security. I always learn something when I hear him. I first saw the figures on page 160 in one of his talks.

Dan Geer's speeches have been similarly educational.

Dieter Gollmann's excellent text, *Computer Security* (John Wiley & Sons, 1999), was a very useful resource.

David Kahn's classic book *The Codebreakers* provided invaluable historic background on the subject of cryptography.

Stuart McClure, Joel Scrambray, and George Kurtz wrote *Hacking Exposed* (Osborne/McGraw-Hill, 1999), which I strongly recommend. I wrote the Foreword to the second edition, which should be available by the time this book is published.

Gary McGraw has written extensively about secure software engineering, as well as the pros and cons of open source software. I used his book, *Securing Java* (John Wiley & Sons, 1999), written with Ed Felton.

Peter Neumann's observations on computer security are so profound and obvious that I often forget that I didn't always believe him. His back-page column, "Inside Risks," running for the past ten years in *Communi-cations of the ACM*, is always interesting. I strongly recommend his book *Computer-Related Risks* (Addison-Wesley, 1995) and the Internet RISKS Forum mailing list he moderates.

Marcus Ranum's essays, speeches, and dinnertime banter have long been a source of inspiration and common sense. I strongly recom-mend reading everything he's written. His Web site is at http://pubweb.nfr.net/~mjr/.

Avi Ruvin, Dan Geer, and Marcus Ranum co-wrote the *Web Secu-rity Sourcebook* (John Wiley & Sons, 1997), which I recommend highly.

Winn Schwartau's *Time Based Security* (Interpact Press, 1999), con-tains ideas very similar to my own on the importance of detection and response in computer security.

Diomidis Spinellis provided the data on complexity of operating sys-tems and programming languages on pages 357 and 358 in his article "Software Reliability: Modern Challenges" (in G. I. Schuëller and P. Kafka, editors, *Proceedings ESREL '99—The Tenth European Conference on Safety and Reliability,* pages 589–592, Munich-Garching, Germany, Sep-tember 1999).

Richard Thieme's musings on hacking and the epistemology of the Internet have long been a source of inspiration. The comment about the dead Marine and Mogadishu was from one of his stories. You can find his writings at www.thiemeworks.com.

Hundreds of essays, articles, and papers are published each year on computer security. I feel as if I've read them all, and undoubtedly thoughts, ideas, ruminations, nuances, and clever one-liners from my readings have crept into this book. I apologize for not giving everyone the credit they deserve.

Acknowledgments

Oodles of people read this book in various stages of completion. I would like to thank Steve Bass, Susan Greenspan, Chris Hall, John Kelsey, and Mudge, who read an early draft of this book. Their comments helped me shape its final tone and scope. I would also like to thank Beth Friedman, who helped with a major edit about halfway through the completion of this book and minor edits throughout the process, and helped keep both the copyeditor and proofreader in line; Karen Cooper, who helped proofread the book; and Raphael Carter, who helped with a major edit toward the end of the process. And I would like to thank Michael Angelo, Ken Ayer, Steve Bass, David Dyer-Bennet, Ed Bennett, Russell Brand, Karen Cooper, David Cowan, Walt Curtis, Dorothy Denning, Carl Ellison, Andrew Fernandez, Gordon Force, Amy Forsyth, Dean Gahlon, Drew Gross, Gregory Guerin, Peter Gutmann, Mark Hardy, Dave Ihnat, Chris Johnston, James Jorasch, Arjen Lenstra, Stuart McClure, Gary McGraw, Doug Merrill, Jeff Moss, Simona Nass, Artimage Nelson, Peter Neumann, Andrew Odlyzko, Doug Price, James Riordan, Bernard Roussely, Tom Rowley, Avi Rubin, Ryan Russell, Adam Shostack, Simon Singh, Jim Wallner, and Elizabeth Zwicky, who read and commented on all or part of the book in its almost-final form. These people did a lot to make the book complete, accurate, and interesting. Any remaining omissions, lingering errors, or residual prolixity are solely my own fault. Open source pundit Eric Raymond has said: "Given enough eyeballs, all bugs are shallow." We'll see if this holds true for books, too.

Index